THE GLADSTONIAN TURN OF MIND
ESSAYS PRESENTED TO J.B. CONACHER

Edited by Bruce L. Kinzer

Two remarkable men inspired this collection: William Ewart Gladstone, the Victorian statesman who is its subject, and historian James B. Conacher, whose colleagues and former students have written these ten essays in his honour.

In different ways, the essays in the volume illuminate the paradoxical elements that made an individual regarded by many of his contemporaries as highly unconventional into a distinctively representative figure of his age. They reflect a variety of perspectives – religious, political, social, and historiographical – on the man and his era. Some of the essays deal with specific aspects of Gladstone's career and span the decades from the publication of his first book in 1838 to his proposal for a campaign against the House of Lords in 1894. Others place him in a wider context: one examines the policy implications of Gladstone's attitudes to the nations of Europe, another the treatment given him by historians after his death.

Together these essays constitute an impressive body of scholarship, a lucid and engaging study of an important Victorian, and a fitting tribute to a distinguished historian.

James Blennerhasset Conacher
Photo by Robert Lansdale

EDITED BY BRUCE L. KINZER

The Gladstonian Turn of Mind: Essays Presented to J.B. Conacher

UNIVERSITY OF TORONTO PRESS
Toronto Buffalo London

© University of Toronto Press 1985
Toronto Buffalo London
Printed in Canada

ISBN 0-8020-5667-9

Canadian Cataloguing in Publication Data

Main entry under title:

The Gladstonian turn of mind

Includes index.
ISBN 0-8020-5667-9

1. Gladstone, W.E. (William Ewart), 1809-1898 –
Addresses, essays, lectures. 2. Great Britain –
Politics and government – 1837-1901 – Addresses,
essays, lectures. 3. Conacher, J.B. – Addresses,
essays, lectures. I. Conacher, J.B. II. Kinzer,
Bruce Lawrence, 1948
DA563.5.G53 1985   941.08'092'4   c85-098419-x

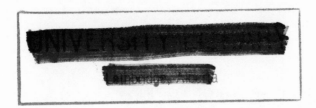

Contents

vi Contents

Preface

Readers of this volume will need no introduction to the work of J.B. Conacher and the character of his contribution to our understanding of the early- and mid-Victorian political system. The common element that draws together the following essays derives appropriately from Professor Conacher's abiding interest in the personality and career of W.E. Gladstone, that extraordinary man who stamped so massive an imprint on the political culture of the Victorian age. Indeed, Professor Conacher's writings on the high politics of the 1846-59 period have done much to establish the context of Gladstone's crucial journey from the Conservative party to the Liberal party.

Students of Victorian political history have no cause to regret that their preoccupations have become less fashionable than formerly in the wake of the central position assumed by social themes in Victorian studies over the last two decades. Political studies have benefited enormously from the richer understanding of Victorian society that has evolved from the work of social historians. The essays presented here show that a volume whose main focus is Gladstone need not be exclusively political in nature. For their part, few social historians would wish to deny that a community's self-definition is expressed in the politics it pursues. However, the meaning a society gives to its political experience, though important in itself, may not correspond closely with the actual mechanics and substance of high politics as conducted by the politicians.

In certain fundamental respects the world of the politicians is less a strand in a large, complex, and unified web than an autonomous web that links up at certain critical points with the network of webs that constitutes society. In this, perhaps, lies the endless fascination it has held for many of the most able students of Victorian England, among whom J.B. Conacher must be included. Gratitude for and admiration of his scholarly and personal life, and a shared conviction that the craft of political history is a worthy avocation, have brought together students, colleagues, and friends of Professor Conacher in a tribute to one of its most outstanding practitioners.

ACKNOWLEDGMENTS

Various people have given much of themselves to this enterprise. Trevor Lloyd and R.J. Helmstadter participated from its inception (I am ashamed to say how long ago that was) and the former has been especially instrumental in furthering the volume along through its various stages of development. J.M. Robson (Victoria College, University of Toronto) most generously provided access to the J.S. Mill Project word processor, which Rea Wilmshurst commanded with her usual mastery. N. Merrill Distad took it upon himself, with the editor's strong endorsement, to compile the Conacher bibliography. From the time the collection was submitted to the University of Toronto Press, I have been the beneficiary of the editorial experience and judgment of R.I.K. Davidson. Finishing touches were applied by Rosemary Shipton who, as copy-editor, managed to put right what I had put wrong without injuring my feelings. To each of these individuals, and to the contributors themselves, I want to offer my thanks.

This book has been published with the help of a grant from the Social Science Federation of Canada, using funds provided by the Social Sciences and Humanities Research Council of Canada, and a grant from the Andrew W. Mellon Foundation to the University of Toronto Press.

J.M.S. CARELESS

J.B. Conacher: A Personal Appreciation

James Blennerhasset Conacher, Jim to his friends, belongs to the world of university scholarship almost by prescriptive right, in background and family as well as career. Born in Kingston, Ontario, in 1916, he grew up in this university centre, where his father was a professor of French at Queen's University. Jim took his own BA at Queen's in 1938, his MA there in 1939, before proceeding on to Harvard for doctoral work in history. Ultimately he and his younger brother Desmond were both to become professors, both located at the University of Toronto; the former in history, the latter in classics. Whether heredity, environment, or personal capacity was the most influential in Jim's particular case might be left to social scientists to solve – perhaps. The fact remains that his life and prime interests have been shaped in a university setting, in which throughout he has been devoted teacher, productive scholar, and vigorous academic statesman.

In his graduate studies at Harvard, Jim worked especially with David Edward Owen, who became his doctoral supervisor, a talented nineteenth-century British historian and one of the great teachers at that institution. The young Canadian's training, however, was soon affected, as was that of so many of his contemporaries, by the impact of world war. He returned to Canada after a year, went on the staff of the Privy Council Office in Ottawa, then joined the Canadian army in 1941. He went overseas as a lieutenant in the Signal Corps, was attached to the Army Historical Section, and served in wartime London at Canadian military headquarters, preparing draft materials for the projected Canadian military history of the Second World War. This major work came out in the early postwar years, written by Colonel C.P. Stacey, the head of the section, a distinguished Canadian historian who was also to be Jim's colleague later at the University of Toronto. But the apprentice-historian's contributions, particularly on the Canadian campaign in Sicily, would enter into the final composed record; and he gained considerably as well through 'learning by doing,' from on-the-job training in handling primary documentation, even if it was hardly yet of much antiquity.

Jim Conacher gained still more from his time of military service: he married Muriel in 1943. A Canadian army nursing officer, she had nursed him in military hospital during a serious illness. Thus he returned to civilian life a husband as well as a captain; and at his discharge in 1946, faced a task again so common to his contemporaries – that of picking up a scarcely started career, or, more simply, of turning up some family-supporting job. He found it in the Department of History at Toronto, then expanding with the postwar need for educating large contingents of returning veterans, although it was nothing like the subsequent expansion when their offspring began to crowd into university gates. Entering the Toronto department as lecturer in 1946, he rose to assistant professor in 1952. It was a well deserved promotion, after six hectic postwar years of teaching on a history staff that was still small by later standards, and hard put to cope with veteran-enlarged numbers. During this strenuous phase, moreover, he had successfully managed to complete his PH D requirements for Harvard, earning his degree in 1949 for a thesis essentially built on his military researches into the Sicilian campaign.

To bring in the personal note, I well recall him at this time: tall, keen, warm-hearted, amiably resolute; in fact, he has hardly changed at all. I had joined the Toronto department just before him. We came together there as the first two postwar 'juniors' amid a coterie of long-established elders, who were thoroughly friendly but augustly different in our eyes. I specially remember a trip the two of us made down to Harvard (to discuss the progress of our respective theses) in an old car Jim had borrowed; a trip that involved a loose wheel in the heights of the Berkshires, a conflagration that blocked us in Troy, New York, all-night trucks that shook our cheap main-street hotel in Gananoque – and a great deal of fun besides. Still further, the Conachers' cordial hospitality, from their first days in a small Toronto apartment, stays always in my mind, as does a friendship now running back close on forty years.

As most juniors did in those days (in Canada at least), we taught as generally needed, and had to take time to develop our own special historical fields of interest. Jim did publish an early article in the *Canadian Historical Review* of 1949 on the Battle of Agira in 1943; yet he did not stay with military history, for British history drew him increasingly. Here he made a foray into Tudor times, then the nineteenth century, and eventually a research concentration on its mid-century years became his basic choice. Before that determination developed clearly, however, he showed his scholarly and editorial abilities in quite a different area, seventeenth-century New France. In 1951-2 he admirably edited and introduced two volumes in the Champlain Society Series of the *Historia Canadensis* originally published by François Du Creux in 1664, and translated into English by P.J. Robinson.

Jim's link with the Champlain Society did not end in 1952. He held the post of editor for the series from 1950 to 1962, assuming overall editorial responsibility for a number of other volumes in this valuable scholarly set of primary Canadian documents. He also went further into the realm of Canadian historical scholarship by serving as a joint editor of the *Canadian Historical Review* between 1949 and 1956. He became one of a tripartite directing team with Gerald Craig (another recent Toronto junior appointment) and myself; and the 'three Cs' of the early fifties were only too conscious of our place as whippersnappers among our learned betters, telling them what could or could not go in the long-reputed journal, and daring to tamper with their punctuation. I came to know and respect the clear, conscientious Conacher judgment still more from our editorial conclaves – and, in them, we acquired our own readily agreed standards and even terminology. Thus, after we had published a conceivably marginal article on polar bears in the Middle Ages, we classed other uncertain ones with our own rating, as one, two, or 'three polar-bear' ventures.

But British history, to repeat, was Jim's growing concern, arising out of his student background, his time with Owen at Harvard, and his increased teaching in the field at Toronto, where, after Frank Underhill's departure in the mid-fifties, he had the leading responsibility for work in the modern British area. Meanwhile, he also produced major collective reviews of recent works in British history for the CHR between 1953 and 1956. In 1956-7 a sabbatical and a Nuffield grant took him to England to research the Peelites, while in 1962-3 a leave and a Canada Council award similarly carried him to study the Aberdeen Coalition. His inquiries were further supported by the Humanities Research Council in 1967-8, the Canada Council in 1969-70; all vital, when the sources lay at such a distance. His researches came out in scholarly conference papers; for example, in 'Peel and the Peelites' at the Anglo-American Historical Conference of 1957, in 'Politics in the Age of Palmerston' at the Mid-West Conference on British Studies in 1958, and in 'Mr. Gladstone Seeks a

Seat,' published in the Canadian Historical Association *Report* for 1962. They led on to other published articles or chapters in collaborative works; but, most important, over the next decade, to scholarly volumes of his own that made him a recognized authority on British politics of the mid-nineteenth century.

He had been appointed an associate professor at Toronto in 1958, professor in 1963. By the later sixties his position as a mature, established nineteenth-century British historian in North America was being widely realized, indicated by his visiting professorship at Notre Dame in 1965-6 and his presidency of the Mid-West Conference on British Studies in 1968-9 – not to mention his arduous but highly effective administrative work on the American Historical Association's convention in Toronto in 1967 as its chairman for local arrangements. Then in 1968 there appeared *The Aberdeen Coalition, 1852-1855*, by J.B. Conacher, glowingly described by its reviewer, R.K. Webb of Columbia, in the CHR as 'Epic in proportion and form ... with a compelling, precise, delicate and witty style.' Beyond that, said Webb, the book 'demonstrates the essence and consequences of the flux of party, as could be done in no other way, and shows us, in the coalition, the crucible from which the parliamentary forms of Victorian Liberalism came.'

This masterly study was followed in 1970 by an edited and introduced collection of readings, *The Emergence of British Parliamentary Democracy in the Nineteenth Century*; and in 1972 by *The Peelites and the Party System, 1846-1852*, which took his thoroughly informed analysis back before the Aberdeen Coalition. Two more volumes were intended to complete this authoritative series on the Peelites (that on the Crimean War years now at completion, and its successor, from 1856 to 1859, already under way). But first came a more extensive and general work, published in 1975, *From Waterloo to the Common Market* (Volume Five in *The Borzoi History of England*), which proved that Jim Conacher could work broadly as well as deeply in lucidly presenting the course of modern British history from the early nineteenth century to the mid-twentieth. Along with these major items of scholarship went still more papers, reviews, and minor pieces. Jim's industry and dedication as a scholar did not flag, though he had now made his lasting mark and had other compelling interests as well.

Strong among these was teaching. He not only did full service in undergraduate work, and took it seriously, but also increasingly attracted graduate students – who saw that here they had found a worthy mentor and a helpful, stimulating guide. His standards stayed firm, and he went on seeking the best from his students; but kindness and understanding were there as well as integrity and drive; and so were good humour and a genial pleasure in anecdote. Jim's former graduate or undergraduate students could individually testify to his high value as a teacher, some by their participation in this very book. But speaking generally, it is evident that through them, and their own researches and books, Professor J.B. Conacher powerfully forwarded the redevelopment of British studies in Canada; and there is no reason to confine that statement to this country alone. As teacher, he has transmitted more than his learning to novitiates since the 1940s: his zest for learning, besides.

Strong also in Jim was his concern for, and participation in, university affairs at Toronto. He took them no less seriously. He had always been a diligent member of a succession of faculty committees, and no less diligent in carrying out departmental duties; but the swelling growth of the university through the 1960s and onward, and the complex problems that this raised at Toronto, as at other institutions, gained his particular attention. He dealt with these problems, for example, on faculty councils, on the University Senate in the late sixties and early seventies, and on the Governing (unicameral) Council that later succeeded it. He played prominent roles on key committees to restructure university functions and relationships in response to the sheer academic explosion; and in those roles largely followed his favourite Peelites in middle-road liberal-conservatism – although radicals would inevitably deem this stance a tory reaction, and last-ditchers one altogether too liberal. In Jim's case, the centre did not yield. He stuck boldly to his guns (and did not go in for a Charge of the Light Brigade, to twist a Crimean metaphor rather badly), thus surviving many a contest undeterred.

The various university posts and duties he assumed are too numerous to detail here. To give a few instances, he was chairman of the Department of History at Toronto from 1972 to 1977, and saw it through the trying transition from open-horizon expansion to harder days of slowdown. He was on the university's Research Board from 1972 to 1975, the Graduate Council in the same period, the Committee on Academic Standards, 1973-7. He chaired the Budget Advisory Committee, 1978-81, and the Governing Council Committee on Academic Affairs in 1979-80. These constitute an almost random selection of his appointments or elections; but they do suggest how broad and continual his service to the Toronto university community has been. More than that, he was also actively engaged in building staff organization. As well as holding council membership, he was president of the Toronto Faculty Association in 1971-2, and was earlier involved in the thrust that produced the Canadian

Association of University Teachers. Still further, he has functioned on
other Canada-wide academic bodies, including the Social Science Research Council and the Canadian Historical Association, of which he was
president in 1974-5. All in all, Jim's contributions to his university and his
profession have been quite as marked as those he has made to historical
scholarship and to the teaching of its rising practitioners.

Now, at the point of his retirement, what else is there to say about his
very active career – as if this has not been enough to show its extent? A
good deal more; though one must keep in mind limits of space. I could go
on with a further assessment of the man in his later years, more personal
reminiscences, and some suggestion of his other interests which still have
not been included. Let me take up the first topic briefly. Jim is inherently
earnest; he cares about people, ideas, causes; he works with them and for
them with force and determination. Belief in principle and firm moral
and religious convictions play an essential part in his conduct, whether
private or public. He could be termed old-fashioned, but in the best,
approving sense: and would we had more like him in universities still, if it
be old-fashioned to strive to maintain academic leadership and look for
excellence. In any case, he is stalwart, not stiff-necked, and quite aware of
the necessary art of the practical. In upholding positive stands, he equally
shows an openness to argument and negotiation, a constructive approach,
and concern for a moderated balance – as a latter-day Peelite should do,
in fact.

Beyond all this, there is his sociable, companionable nature. The
thought of his hospitality at once recalls many evenings spent at the
Conachers, from small affairs with Jim, Muriel, their children Pat and
Desmond, and a few friends, to large gatherings to entertain some visiting
worthy, along with numerous colleagues. Muriel's role (and first-rate
cooking) was no less evident than her husband's on these occasions. They
seemed to have a regular stream of perambulating Britons, Australians,
or Americans arriving, often friends made during times they had passed
in Britain. Certainly, these visitors were on to a good thing; but so were my
wife and I, and many of Jim's other Canadian and Toronto associates. We
all knew that a Conacher party was one not to be missed. And former
students would similarly know and happily remember the cordiality extended at the family home on Welland Avenue.

Sojourns and work in a much-loved London, British and continental
European trips, lectures and conferences in England, Canada, and the
United States: these, too, may fairly be numbered among Jim's enduring
interests and activities. There should assuredly be added the months he

has enjoyed since his early years at the family summer place on Garden Island opposite Kingston, once an island-depot in the historic lumber trade, where Lake Ontario and the St Lawrence come together. Through Garden Island stays he has annually renewed his ties with Kingston and its neighbourhood, and has written, relaxed, and renewed himself as well; though when he returns to Toronto each fall, tanned and refreshed, his tales of trials on the way back seldom get much commiseration. In Toronto, moreover, Jim has also entered into church and social work, another side of a manifestly full life that has, in simple essence, engaged him in performing a host of services throughout its length. An academician foremost, no doubt; but he has widely exercised his talents, not begrudged them.

From my personal experience, again, I see him in departmental or faculty meetings, making his case with decision and good spirit, getting to the core of problems, offering well-deliberated answers. I see him similarly at founding meetings of the Canadian Association of University Teachers, committed and responsible; energetically organizing historical meetings like the CHA of 1955, the AHA of 1967; reading and editing varied manuscripts, never stinting his generously given efforts. Others would have to speak of his classes, seminars, and theses direction, his own writing and research procedures. Being myself a parochial Canadian historian, I do not know the critical mysteries of the modern British craft. But this I do know. As an influential leading scholar and academic figure, as a perceptive, enlivening individual, and a tried, considerate friend, Jim Conacher deserves every tribute – including that which is offered in the following pages by a group of his past and present co-workers. It comes as well with much gratitude and affection, for the man whose career it both appreciates and celebrates.

THE GLADSTONIAN TURN OF MIND

RICHARD J. HELMSTADTER

Conscience and Politics: Gladstone's First Book

On 7 August 1838 Gladstone sent in the last portion of his substantial manuscript on *The State in Its Relations with the Church* to John Murray the publisher. He had worked at feverish pace on his first book from some time late in June, and, with the help of James Hope, had managed to complete and revise the entire work within a remarkably short time. It was an impressive show of energy. But one should not be misled into thinking that the book was a matter of impulse, something hastily produced and less than carefully conceived. Morley suggests that Gladstone wrote the book in polemical response to Thomas Chalmers' *Lectures on Religious Establishments*, delivered in London in April 1838.[1] It is certainly true that Gladstone disapproved strongly of some of Chalmers' leading arguments, and it may be that Chalmers' lectures encouraged him to publish his own views as soon as possible. It is also abundantly clear that Gladstone had been reading and thinking about the relation of church and state for nearly ten years before he heard Chalmers' lectures.

He began reading Burke as a schoolboy at Eton, and in the summer of 1829, at home for the long vacation after his first year at Oxford, he began systematic study of that fundamental Anglican treatise on church and state, Richard Hooker's *Laws of Ecclesiastical Polity*. Over the next ten years, as his journal demonstrates, he read widely on the interpenetration of politics and religion, from ancient classics to modern pamphlets and sermons, from Aristotle and Augustine to Arnold and Wardlaw. As member of Parliament for Newark after the general election of 1832 he took as his special area of concern the political interests of the church. And from late 1832 he began to write on the relations of church and state, a little for newspapers, far more in the form of memoranda to help him organize his own thinking.

Some time before 12 March 1837 he started to write his book; his journal entry for that day reads: 'rewrote some of my (supposed) Introduction, enlarging withal.'[2] He wrote a good deal of the work in the spring of 1837, and by 1 March 1838 he was considering as a title 'The duties of the state towards the church.' He continued to enter frequently in his journal the familiar words, 'wrote on church and state.' Much of the book must have been completed by the time Chalmers delivered his lectures. The major arguments must have been thought through. The major literary sources that had so much to do with shaping the book had, as the journals make clear, already been read. Gladstone worked very hard to pull the book together and to revise it in the early summer of 1838, but it would be seriously misleading to suppose that it was a rapidly composed reaction to Chalmers' lectures. Written over the course of at least sixteen months, based on a programme of systematic reading carried on for nearly a decade, informed by six years of practical experience in Parliament, and carefully revised under the watchful eye of James Hope, *State and Church* must stand as the embodiment of Gladstone's considered judgment on the place of the church in the constitution, a subject of lively interest and critical importance to many at that time. Two unrevised editions were subsequently published in 1839, and a fourth edition, much expanded to explain and reinforce the original, appeared in 1841.[3]

State and Church was not enthusiastically received. *The Times* (9 and 21 January 1839) complained justly of the book's murky style and involuted language – Gladstone always preferred the impenetrable deep to the clear surface – and went on, outrageously, to accuse the author of being a covert enemy of the church. Peel, Gladstone's political chief, was dismayed by the book, and is said to have called it 'trash.'[4] Sir James Graham told Teignmouth that 'he could not understand it.'[5] John Keble, in a long and thoughtful notice in the *British Critic* (October 1839), suggested, presciently, that Gladstone wrote too much as a politician, too little as a churchman. In Keble's view, which he shared with Newman, Gladstone placed too high a value on the connection of church and state and might be prepared to compromise church discipline in the face of political imperatives. By far the most influential review of Gladstone's book was Macaulay's brilliantly written essay in the *Edinburgh Review* (April 1839), an essay that long outlived its subject. Gladstone's abhorrence of oversimplification and his clumsiness as a stylist engaged Macaulay's passion for elegant language, for simply expressed ideas, and for sound, practical common sense. Macaulay urged what became the dominant line in criticism of Gladstone's book, a line almost precisely opposite to Keble's. Macaulay's Gladstone, 'the rising hope of those stern and unbending Tories,' was hopelessly idealistic and abstract, out of touch with the realities of practical possibility. His high moral vision of the state Macaulay dismissed as a delusion, of no real interest to practical men of affairs. Gladstone's elaborately complex theory of church and state was reduced by Macaulay to a simplistic formula from which bigotry, intolerance, and persecution were the logical results. Gladstone's theory of church and state, Macaulay wrote, had about it an aura of orthodoxy because it was 'conveyed in language which has a certain obscure dignity and sanctity.' In reality, however, the theory, if it had any chance of practical implementation, would be deeply dangerous. 'All the general reasonings on which this theory rests evidently lead to sanguinary persecution ... Why not roast dissenters at slow fires?'[6]

Historians have not treated Gladstone's first book much more sympathetically than did his contemporaries.[7] To some degree this is a matter of Macaulay's continuing influence. His review is more accessible than Gladstone's book, and *State and Church* is not much read, even by Gladstone's biographers. Philip Magnus dismisses the 'unfortunate book' in a paragraph marred by such obvious errors that it is clear he did not give the work serious attention. John Morley, still the best biographer, recognized how important the book was to Gladstone, and he gives a balanced account of its reception. But, anxious to move on to political action and the years of political power, Morley makes no effort to describe the book itself or to make its arguments clear. E.J. Feuchtwanger takes up the plausible argument that Gladstone's book, which Feuchtwanger characterizes as abstract and uncompromising, was an academic treatise, a product of the cloister, written by a young man with almost no experience of power, a man whose spirit had not yet migrated from Oxford to Westminster.[8] Gladstone himself lends credence to this view: 'The dominant tendencies of mind,' he wrote of this early period, 'were those of a recluse, and I might, in most respects with ease, have accommodated myself to the cloister.'[9] More interested in why Gladstone abandoned the position established in *State and Church* than he is with the position itself, Feuchtwanger argues that as he gained experience in government and moved towards maturity as a man of affairs, Gladstone left behind the abstract, systematic theorizing of his younger days. Hence his progress towards liberal practicality and away from rigid orthodoxy and conservatism.

While he was warden of St Deiniol's Library, Alec Vidler wrote the only substantial modern study of *State and Church*. Vidler uses Gladstone's book as a springboard from which to leap into a wide-ranging and general discussion of church and state in the modern world. He makes no effort to place Gladstone's work in historical context, and he deliberately passes over those portions of the book that he feels have lost their relevance in the twentieth century. As far as it goes, Vidler's treatment of Gladstone's book is helpful and sympathetic. He dwells more on the substantial merit of Gladstone's early version of religiously informed politics than does any other commentator, and he strongly claims that Gladstone's retreat in the 1840s from his earlier theory of church and state has been exaggerated.[10]

Within the past few years Colin Matthew and Deryck Schreuder have each taken up the problem of how *State and Church* bears on Gladstone's subsequent liberalization. Matthew, in the introduction to the third volume of *The Gladstone Diaries* (1974), has written an excellent synoptic comment on Gladstone's first book, and he, like Vidler, stresses that there are lines of continuity running from that work through the more liberal views Gladstone developed in the 1840s and beyond. In harmony with the main stream of Gladstone scholarship, however, Matthew accepts the traditional view that Gladstone did in fact abandon in the 1840s the theoretical core of *State and Church*. The crisis, 'on what was for Gladstone the central point of principle,' came with Peel's proposal in 1844 to enlarge and make permanent the annual parliamentary grant to Maynooth College, a seminary in Ireland preparing men for the Roman Catholic priesthood. In great anguish Gladstone resigned from Peel's cabinet when it became clear that the government was determined to press ahead with the Maynooth grant. 'Maynooth he saw as the battleground for "National Religion," and it was in that "Serbonian bog" that Gladstone's model for state and church sank to its axels.'[11] When the Maynooth proposal came before Parliament in the spring of 1845, Gladstone supported it, and Matthew dates Gladstone's abandonment of the synthetic vision of religion and politics proclaimed in his first book from this act. 'Intellectually and ecclesiastically the author of *The State in Its Relations with the Church* (1838) witnessed the collapse of his political and ecclesiastical empire and built anew on the basis of free trade, a colonial empire, and, however reluctantly, a secular state.'[12]

Deryck Schreuder sees *State and Church* as the first major attempt of the young, inexperienced, and idealistic Gladstone, deeply impressed by the great social and constitutional changes taking place in early Victorian England, to develop a systematic view of politics that would reflect his intense personal commitment to Anglicanism.[13] According to Schreuder, Gladstone's book presented a variant of the classic Anglican vision of establishment contained in Richard Hooker's late Elizabethan treatise, *Of the Laws of Ecclesiastical Polity*. Hooker saw the church and the state as two aspects of a single society. Gladstone saw the church and the state as two great moral agencies, in close symbiotic relation, with the church serving as the conscience of the state. In company with most of those who have written on the subject, Schreuder dismisses Gladstone's book as romantically abstract, irrelevant to the practical political and economic problems of its time.[14] He recognizes, however, that throughout his career Gladstone remained a devotee of conscience, always ready to find a moral base for political action. Where was that moral base located? Not in the church, after the mid-forties, at least not in the church as presented in *State and Church*. Schreuder argues that Gladstone discarded the central theories of his book in the face of practical political pressures at the time of the crisis over Maynooth. After Maynooth, Schreuder maintains, Gladstone discovered a new location for the conscience of the state. Avoiding the abstract rigidities of the book, which had become politically embarrassing, the mature Gladstone sought the conscience of the nation in the people, in the electorate, a flexible sort of conscience that would effectively support his growing appreciation of political pragmatism.

The most recent and by far the most substantial work on Gladstone's religious development and the relation between his politics and his religion is Perry Butler, *Gladstone: Church, State, and Tractarianism*. Butler's excellent book, which draws heavily on the published *Diaries* as well as on a wide array of unpublished letters and papers, provides a clear and convincing account of Gladstone's transition from evangelicalism to high churchmanship in the 1830s. The importance of his undergraduate education, in which Aristotle loomed large, as a formative force in Gladstone's early political thinking is stressed by Butler. And Butler documents in some detail the development of Gladstone's relationships with the men of the Tractarian movement. The brief chapter on Gladstone's first book is a good guide to the major arguments of that work.[15] Butler sees *State and Church* as a work of abstract theory inspired by youthful idealism. He argues that Gladstone, as he gained practical experience as a member of Peel's government in the early 1840s, gradually lost confidence in his theory of church and state. The crisis over the Maynooth grant was the occasion for his conscious rejection of the theory as impractical.

Apart from Vidler and Butler, scholars have not discussed Gladstone's theory of church and state in any detail. A systematic, critical analysis of the theory itself has seemed unnecessary to those who have been more interested in Gladstone's change of direction in 1845, more interested in the Liberal politician than in the young tory champion of the church. *State and Church*, however, is worthy of more detailed attention. The book presents within a single theoretical framework the young Gladstone's ideas about the nature of the state, the role of government, the place of the Church of England in English society, and the constitutional connection between church and state. Even if Gladstone had thrown all these ideas overboard in 1845, they remain interesting for what they reveal of the young politician.

But Gladstone did not repudiate his book on church and state in 1845, or even in 1868 when he wrote *A Chapter of Autobiography* to explain his support for the disestablishment and disendowment of the Church of Ireland. Indeed, he never rejected the central, theoretical arguments of his early work. Those who claim that he dismissed his theory, or at least began to dismiss it, at the time of Maynooth, claim too much. Gladstone did change his mind, as time passed, about how the theory of church and state could practically be applied. He certainly did abandon some of the positions he had taken up in 1838 and 1841 as applications of his theory. His support for the Maynooth grant is a central instance. Other examples include his support in 1847 for a measure that would permit Jews to sit in Parliament; his leading role in the disestablishment of the Irish church; his successful effort to abolish compulsory church rates in 1868; his support in the early 1880s for the right of Charles Bradlaugh, a notorious unbeliever, to take his seat in Parliament; and, especially after 1859, his increasingly warm sympathy with nonconformity. What looks like a steady drift, after 1845, to increased liberalism should, however, not be misinterpreted. Gladstone did not give up the principles of *State and Church*. As he grew more familiar with political power, Gladstone grew more skilful as a politician, and more flexible, more pragmatic, more astutely unpredictable in manoeuvre. Yet he retained at the centre the emphasis on conscience he had announced in 1838, and he retained, at least as an ideal, the theory of church and state and unified society that he had developed in his first book.

In dedicating his book on state and church to 'The University of Oxford; tried and not found wanting,' Gladstone wrote of his 'hope that the temper of these pages may be found not alien from her own.' This was a modest hope. His book was very Oxonian indeed. It owed little to Gladstone's nearly six years of experience in politics. It owed a great deal to the profound impact of Oxford upon Gladstone's mind and spirit. The dominant tone of the book, a tone at once speculative and dogmatic, suggests more Christ Church and the Bodleian than the Colonial Office and the House of Commons. More importantly, Gladstone's specific idea of the church and his basic conception of the state were both shaped by influences closely associated with Oxford.

The idea of the state that Gladstone propounds and works with in *State and Church* is essentially Aristotelian. Oxford, when Gladstone was there as an undergraduate, was the centre of Aristotelian influence in Britain. Aristotle pervaded the classics curriculum, and with the movement away from mere 'scholarship,' or technical skill with language, to an emphasis on content, the study of Aristotle gained in importance. Writing of this change away from grammar and translation towards history and philosophy, a change fully under way while Gladstone was at Oxford, Mark Pattison tells us that 'Aristotle soon riveted attention in a peculiar way; and from this time a history of Aristotle in the University is a history of University improvement.'[16] Under the supervision of Robert Biscoe, a noted Aristotelian, Gladstone at Oxford systematically studied Aristotle's *Rhetoric* and the *Nicomachean Ethics*, and with these works he began the long continued practice of making analytical summaries of the books that he considered most important.[17] In *State and Church* Gladstone draws heavily on Aristotle's *Politics*, a work to which he gave a great deal of time in the summer of 1834 and the autumn of 1835.[18] Gladstone's idea of the state is a Christian version of the idea of the state that Aristotle develops in the *Politics*.

For Aristotle, the state is the essential condition of the good life, the form of social organization that makes possible civilized morality and human fulfilment. The state, he wrote, is something that exists in nature, and 'man is by nature a political animal; it is his nature to live in a state.'[19] Outside the state, 'divorced from law and morals,' man is the worst of all the animals, savage, unrighteous, gluttonous, sunk in sexual licence.[20] 'Justice is something essential in a state; for *right* is the basis of the political association and right is the criterion for deciding what is just.'[21] The establishment of ethical behaviour is thus a central function of Aristotle's state, a function exercised through custom and through law, a form of encapsulated custom.

The ethical concerns of the state as described in the *Politics* run beyond the mere enforcement of law. The state is more than 'a mutual guarantee of rights'; its rulers should 'make it their business to have an eye to the goodness or badness of the citizens.'[22] Virtue as well as lawfulness is the concern of the state, and the state should actively encourage its citizens to be good and just. These virtues, moreover, underpin the comprehensive goal of the state, the good life: 'The state is intended to enable all, in their households and their kinships, to live *well*, meaning by that a full and satisfying life.'[23]

Aristotle takes up the proposition that the state exists only to protect life and property so that he might reject this view as much too narrow. Maintaining the conditions within which economic life can flourish is recognized in the *Politics* as an important aspect of statecraft. But Aristotle warns those who direct the affairs of state not to make this their entire policy.[24] A regulated economy, he argues, cannot be the essence of a state. Commercial treaties among communities do not constitute a state, and, similarly, commercial arrangements among ten thousand individuals, no matter how comprehensive or strictly enforced, would not create a state. 'A state is something more than an investment; its purpose is not merely to provide a living but to make a life that is worthwhile.'[25]

A central theme running through the *Politics* is the isolation and insufficiency of individuals outside the state. Aristotle saw the state as the highest form of human social organization, as something whole, perfect, self-sufficient, and independent. Individuals and all organizations other than the state he saw as partial, imperfect, and interdependent. Men and women require each other for reproduction. Strong men need intelligent men to direct their labours. A diversity of skills among individuals can create an harmonious common life within a community. Therefore man first created the household, in order to live, and the village helped him to live more safely and prosperously.[26] The state, the final and supreme form of association, is composed of several villages. The state, then, had its foundation in the most elementary and compelling need of individuals to associate with others; 'while it started as a means of securing life itself, it is now in a position to secure the good life.'[27]

Gladstone transmuted Aristotle's treatment of individuals and association into Christian terms. In the beginning all was unity, peace, and harmony. But 'one act disorganized the earth and all its moral destinies.'[28] After the fall, man found his law of conduct in himself rather than in God, and self-worship remains in the world as the great engine of evil. God designed the redemption of mankind by His Son to be accomplished in the fulness of time, and He also designed a set of secondary disciplines to combat the progress of selfishness. These secondary disciplines all have a similar principle; they are all versions of association, community, the common life.[29] The principle of mutual association works to diminish in men their self-regarding appetites and to dampen their proud individual wills. The common life also encourages the opposite of selfishness –

kindness and justice, and ideas of right and reciprocal duty. 'He who has to care for his family or his country, and who has learned to identify himself with their interests in thought and deed, feels that the weight upon him is greater than that of any merely individual concern, and exerts himself with more of general vigour, than if he stood an isolated savage in the forest.'[30] The common life, then, in any form, has inherent powers of good.

Gladstone identifies the two highest forms of the common life, apart from the church, as the state and the family.[31] He grants high importance to the state for essentially the same reasons as does Aristotle. The state establishes the fundamental condition of order within which a variety of specialized activities and diverse human talents can operate in concert. The state, in contrast to most other forms of association, has general, indeed, unlimited, purposes, and it is essentially concerned with the growth and formation of the character of its citizens so that they might lead a civilized life. The state, he writes, gives 'scope and space to the highest energies of the human understanding: it is also directly the parent, and the object, of some of the noblest feelings which belong to our nature ... It is also that comprehensive and overreaching form of the natural human life which includes and harmonises all its other forms, under which they must fall, and to which they must adapt themselves.'[32]

Unlike Aristotle, Gladstone assigns a high and general moral purpose to the family as well as to the state. His sentimental and romantic view of the family as a school of love includes no mention of the economic activities that loom large in Aristotle's treatment of the household and the family. Nowhere in *State and Church*, in fact, did Gladstone introduce a sustained discussion of material matters. So intent was he on the ethical element in life that he tended to see institutions exclusively in terms of their moral implication. This constitutes an imbalance in his book, a weakness recognized by Gladstone when his energies were engaged at the Board of Trade in the early 1840s. When he wrote his first book, however, he believed that it was his duty 'to plead earnestly for those great ethical laws under which we are socially constituted, and which economical speculation and material interests have threatened altogether to subvert.'[33]

Acknowledging his debt to the *Politics*, Gladstone contrasts his Aristotelian vision of the overarching state, bound to promote generally the good of man, with the Lockean theory of the state presented by Bishop Warburton in *The Alliance between Church and State* (London, 1736).[34] Warburton, following Locke, had argued that the purpose of the state was merely to protect life and property and to maintain civil order. Gladstone was scornful of this narrow, low, property-oriented view of the state, a view that had powerful defenders at the time he wrote his book. There is no evidence that Gladstone in the 1830s tried to come to grips with utilitarian materialism. He did not read Bentham, James Mill, John Stuart Mill, or the political economists. He makes fleeting reference to Poulett Scrope's *Principles of Political Economy* in *State and Church* in order to dismiss political economy generally as concerned with 'undigested materials of a future science,' and as rooted in materialism.[35] Gladstone's impressively ambitious programme of reading was oriented towards theology ancient and modern, and towards history and humane letters. He spent large blocks of time not with Adam Smith or David Ricardo but with Aristotle and Plato; with Augustine, Dante, Machiavelli, and Hooker; with Bishop Butler, Burke, Coleridge, Maurice, Arnold, and Newman. Bacon's *Novum Organum* was one of the works he studied carefully in the autumn of 1834, and he followed it in December 1834 with Locke's *Essay Concerning Human Understanding* and his *Two Treatises of Government*. This represents his most serious engagement with what one might call progressive materialism. The great majority of the books he worked with reflect the general bias of the Oxford reading list in *Literae Humaniores*. And his theory of the state reflects the bias of his reading.

In his famous essay on Gladstone's book, Macaulay pressed a vigorous, manly, and blunt attack on Gladstone's conception of the state.[36] His own view of the ends of civil government is easily stated: 'That it is to protect our persons and our property, that it is designed to compel us to satisfy our wants, not by rapine, but by industry; that it is designed to decide our differences, not by the strong hand, but by arbitration; that it is designed to direct our whole force, as that of one man, against any other society which may offer us injury; these are propositions which will hardly be disputed.'[37] There is a suggestion here that the state might be something more than an ordered collection of individuals, a suggestion of nationalism, a hint at organic community, but the emphasis in the passage is on the other side. For Macaulay, the state had a limited range of duties, and those duties had chiefly to do with the protection of life and property. 'Without a division of labour the world could not go on.'[38] Because the state has material welfare as its province, however, does not mean that spiritual or moral welfare is less important. But the two areas are quite separate. 'No two objects,' Macaulay wrote, 'more entirely distinct can well be imagined. The former belongs wholly to the visible and tangible world in which we live; the latter belongs to that higher world which is beyond the reach of our senses. The former belongs to this life; the latter to that which is to come.'[39] He retreats a little from the implications of this position when he introduces the idea of secondary ends. The state, like all organizations, should be constructed with a view towards its primary, main end. If it can promote other good works without sacrificing its primary purpose, so much the better. Therefore a national gallery, a national library, support for voyages of discovery or scientific works are all, in Macaulay's view, legitimate collateral ends.[40]

Gladstone, of course, placed moral welfare, an intangible quality, among the ultimate ends of the state. Macaulay recognized that this view of the state lay at the heart of Gladstone's book, and he mounted an assault upon it by appealing to a general prejudice he assumed his readers would hold against state intervention. If one accepts, he wrote, that the duties of government are paternal, if one accepts Gladstone's contention that 'Government occupies in moral the place of το παν in physical science,' then how does one limit the ambitions of rulers? 'Why should they not take away the child from the mother, select the nurse, regulate the school, overlook the playground, fix the hours of labour and of recreation, prescribe what ballads shall be sung, what tunes shall be played, what books shall be read, what physic shall be swallowed? Why should they not choose our wives, limit our expenses, and stint us to a certain number of dishes of meat, or glasses of wine, and of cups of tea?'[41] All these activities were recommended for the state by Plato, 'whose hardihood in speculation was perhaps more wonderful than any other peculiarity of his extraordinary mind.'[42] Gladstone, warned Macaulay, took his inspiration from Plato, but he lacked the courage to follow his idea of the paternalistic state to its logical conclusions.

Macaulay considered that Gladstone's principal philosophical reference was to Plato.[43] This view has modern support from the current editor of *The Gladstone Diaries*.[44] Matthew argues that the powerful strain of idealism in Gladstone's *State and Church* was essentially Platonic and immediately derived from Coleridge's *On the Constitution of Church and State According to the Idea of Each* (1830). Matthew, moreover, contends that Gladstone's book suffered from a deep-seated internal contradiction, a contradiction hinted at by Macaulay. The strongly idealistic premise of the organic state, a premise for which Gladstone drew heavily on Coleridge, was not carried forward in detail to its logical conclusions. 'Indeed, when he came to consider the rights of individuals and the historic position of the rights of dissenters to exist without persecution, Gladstone was forced back on that utilitarian tradition which he had earlier in the book so vehemently condemned ... Thus at the heart of the book lay a profound contradiction, the result of the attempt to use two quite separate philosophical traditions to justify first an Ideal of society, then anomalies to that Ideal which already existed.'[45] Macaulay and Matthew, however, overemphasize the influence of Plato and Coleridge on Gladstone, and this leads them to mistake the character of Gladstone's idea of the state and to misunderstand how Gladstone justified toleration and anomalies in that state.

Gladstone, to be sure, read Plato. The *Phaedo* was one of his set books at Oxford. He studied the *Republic* in August and September 1832.[46] Five years later, when his own work on *State and Church* was well under way, he read *Timaeus* and *Critias* and the *Laws*. There are probably more references to Plato in *State and Church* than to Aristotle, but it is a mistake to conclude that Gladstone's view of politics and the state were seriously influenced by Plato. Committed though he was to the idea that the state embodied a comprehensive form of common life, Gladstone was repelled by the communism of the *Republic*. The Gladstonian conscience was particularly offended by the 'monstrous' proposition that the citizens of the *Republic* should share in common their women and children.[47] As evidence bearing on the extent of Plato's influence on Gladstone's thinking, however, the basic method, form, and structure of *State and Church* are more important than his reaction to specific ideas in Plato's work.

The method of *State and Church* is at once analytical and historical. Gladstone begins with man's nature after the fall, and with the state as it is found in nature. From his analytical examination of the nature of the state he proceeds, by deduction, towards 'its purposes and conditions of action so far as they respect religion.'[48] This style of argument he calls 'ethical,' a style of argument that he thought 'lies in a region of abstraction to which the temper of the age, and the prevailing pursuits of this country, are averse.'[49] His object is to make clear those principles (*axiomata summa*) upon which the relations of state and church are based. In the fullest development of the book, that is, the fourth edition, this mode of abstract reasoning dominates the first five chapters, or roughly one-half the work; chapters six through ten are historical, or as Gladstone had it, 'experimental' in method. For Gladstone aimed not only at establishing a theory. He was equally interested in showing how that theory applied to the political life of his own time. Therefore he considered it necessary to exhibit, as he put it, 'the actual course of the principle of national religion, since it has approached to its critical periods, in our own country, to pave that way which ought to join the region of theory with the arena of practical life.'[50]

Gladstone conceived his book as a contribution to political science, a science that included theory and practice, and a science that had not yet reached the stage of perfect development. History must supplement general principles, not only in order to lead practice towards right theory, but also because the general principles were not yet powerful enough to take full account of historical reality. He approved Bacon's opinion that of all the sciences, politics was the 'most immersed in matter, and hardliest reduced to axiom,' and Algernon Sidney's observation that 'the political science ... of all others is the most abstruse and variable, according to accidents and circumstances.'[51] Political science, for Gladstone, was an inseparable combination of the analytical and the historical, and this was the method of *State and Church*.

Why does Gladstone call his method 'ethical'? Without doubt he intends a reference, and a reference his contemporary readers would have recognized immediately, to Aristotle's *Ethics*.[52] The method of *State and Church*, then, is Aristotelian, a method of approach to political subjects that was strongly and indelibly impressed on Gladstone's mind at Oxford. In his undergraduate studies the *Ethics* was the central work, the focus, of his reading for the *Literae Humaniores* portion of his degree. In addition to his work on mathematics, he spent his early terms at Oxford concentrating on history and scholarship (ie, technical facility with Greek and Latin), reading such writers as Thucydides, Polybius, Aeschylus, Sophocles, Virgil, Terence, and Pindar. With his basic reading in history completed, and his facility with the ancient languages well developed, he began intensive study of the *Ethics* in the spring of 1831 and continued to work with that subject until his final examinations in November 1831. His brilliant performance on that portion of the examination dealing with the *Ethics* was the highlight of his success in the schools, the crowning achievement in his solid double first.[53]

It is interesting to notice that Gladstone's concentrated work on the *Ethics* coincided with his first involvement in practical politics. While reading the *Ethics* in May 1831 he organized a petition against the Reform Bill and wrote a long pamphlet attacking the bill. He read a portion of the *Ethics* on the very day of his famous anti-reform speech in the Union.[54] The impression Aristotle made on Gladstone may have been deepened by the concurrence of his encounter with the *Ethics* and his first exciting taste of political action.

In calling his book on state and church a work of 'political science,'

Gladstone implicitly acknowledged his debt to Aristotle. The philosopher himself refers to the *Ethics* as a work in political science.[55] More significantly, when Gladstone was at Oxford 'political science' or simply 'science' commonly referred to Aristotle's *Ethics*.[56] For Aristotle, the *Ethics* was a contribution to political science because its central concern was with the good, and 'while it is desirable to secure what is good in the case of an individual, to do so in the case of a people or state is something finer and more sublime.'[57] Gladstone could not have said it better.

The method of the *Ethics* is to analyze certain general terms – the good, happiness, the nature of man, virtue, and justice – and then to work out practical rules for good conduct. Aristotle presents the *Ethics* as a practical treatise, aimed at making men good. But the situations encountered in life are so complicated and various that it is impossible to reduce them all to axioms. Therefore neither the general principles of ethics nor the application of those principles can be a matter of rigid precision. 'Any account of conduct must be stated in outline and not in precise detail.'[58] Specific application of general principles thus becomes more a matter of history than science. The *Politics*, in a sense a sequel to the *Ethics*, follows the ethical method. Aristotle analyzes the nature of the state and proceeds to show how the general principles of politics relate to specific states and specific historical situations. This two-part method is fully discussed by Aristotle in Book VI of the *Ethics*, where the philosopher distinguishes between types of knowledge.[59] Scientific knowledge is knowledge of certainties. It consists of deductions from first principles. The first principles are established by intuition; that is, they are apprehended directly as self-evident truths. Another type of knowledge is prudence, or practical wisdom, a region of variables and particular facts, of judgment and experience rather than deduction and demonstration. Ethics and politics belong in the region of prudence rather than science; 'prudence is not concerned with universals only; it must also take cognizance of particulars, because it is concerned with conduct, and conduct has its sphere in particular circumstances.'[60]

Gladstone clearly recognized and appreciated the dualism inherent in Aristotle's ethical method. His recognition is implicit in *State and Church*, where he follows the method himself, and explicit in an essay on Bishop Butler that he wrote a few years later.[61] The dualism Colin Matthew finds in *State and Church*, which he sees as contradictory philosophical traditions stemming from the idealistic Coleridge and the utilitarian Locke, can also be viewed as a reflection of a controlled and systematic duality within the political science of Aristotle.

The approach to conduct generally, and to politics, which Aristotle advocated, made a deep impression on Gladstone in his years at Oxford, a time when he was most open to impression, years to which he looked back with 'a warm glow of reverence, gratitude, and attachment.'[62] During his long career in politics Gladstone developed his own peculiar blend of idealism and pragmatism. Aristotle and Oxford provided a model, and perhaps the inspiration as well, for Gladstone's distinctive version of the politics of conscience.

It is clear that Gladstone, from his undergraduate days until the end of his life, retained a warm admiration for Aristotle and a deep sense of indebtedness to him. When young William Henry Gladstone went up to Oxford in 1859, his father urged upon him the importance of Aristotle: 'the fruits of his mental efforts will remain unrivalled in their class until time shall be no more.'[63] A year later Gladstone pressed upon his son the high value of three works of philosophy: Aristotle's *Ethics* and *Politics* and Bishop Butler's *Analogy of Religion*.[64] Aristotle's *Politics*, he told him, was superior to Plato's *Republic*. Plato's philosophy he characterized as 'quasi spiritual and highly imaginative,' while Aristotle's 'deals in a most sharp, searching and faithful analysis of the facts of human life and human nature.'[65] Morley has noted that in 1880 Gladstone told Sir Francis Doyle that he was influenced little by living teachers, but very greatly by Aristotle, Augustine, Dante, and Butler in addition to the four Gospels.[66] And a year before he died he referred to Aristotle's *Ethics* as one of those great books that are best read directly, without the interference of criticism and commentary.[67] The influence of Aristotle on Gladstone's political life has never been discussed. Does Aristotle's doctrine of the mean – in Victorian terms the *via media* – help shape Gladstone's liberalism? Does the Aristotelianism of liberals such as T.H. Green who argued for a morally active state suggest a philosophical continuity between Gladstone and the new liberalism? These, of course, are questions beyond the scope of this essay. It is sufficient here to note that Gladstone never abandoned the Aristotle he had learned to honour and respect at Oxford.

State and Church reflects a broad range of Gladstone's reading, and it would be a mistake to exaggerate the Aristotelianism of the book. Gladstone draws on a number of modern writers. He makes frequent reference to Burke and Coleridge, for example, to help him explain his view of the state as a partnership having as its end the promotion of the good life. He cites Burke's memorable description of the state, 'a partnership in all art; a partnership in every virtue, and in all perfection.'[68]

He calls on Coleridge's vision of the 'unity of the people,' and the Coleridgean emphasis on 'whatever is beneficent and harmonising in the aims, tendencies and proper objects of the State.'[69] Gladstone admired the spirit of Burke and Coleridge, although he found Burke wanting in method and detail and thought Coleridge's discussion of church and state incomplete and too abstact.[70] Burke and Coleridge, moreover, along with F.D. Maurice and Wordsworth, and the Tractarians at Oxford, seemed to Gladstone signs of the times, grounds for hope that the true idea of the state as a living fellowship in the good life might make practical progress against the low, atomistic, mechanical, and materialistic idea of the utilitarians.

When Gladstone moved his attention from the nature of the state to the relations between church and state he stopped following Aristotle and turned to Christian guides. Gladstone's argument for why the state must establish and support a religion is as follows. The state, he maintained, is, in some ways, a person. It has a vital personality. Therefore, like a person, the state must have a conscience. In common with the popular Judeo-Christian view, Gladstone believed that morality at its highest level was inseparable from religion, that, indeed, true religion was the best teacher and only sure anchor of true morality. His position is at one with that of Richard Hooker, the first comprehensive theorist of the Anglican establishment, who wrote: 'Let Polity acknowledge itself indebted to Religion; godliness being the chiefest, top and wellspring of all true virtues, even as God is of all good things.'[71] The conscience of the state, therefore, must be the church.

It would be inaccurate to suggest that Hooker was not one of Gladstone's Christian guides.[72] His initial encounter with Hooker in the summer of 1829 may well mark the beginning of his drift away from evangelicalism.[73] Late in life Gladstone claimed that Hooker convinced him of the truth of the doctrine of baptismal regeneration, 'and the way was thus opened for further changes.' As late as 1880, about to meet Parliament for the first time after the general election of that year, Gladstone recalled a remark of Hooker's, 'that even ministers of good things are like torches, a light to others, waste and destruction to themselves.'[74] And he made clear his admiration for the first five books of the *Laws*.[75] The direct influence of Hooker on *State and Church* is, nevertheless, limited. This is principally because Gladstone vigorously rejected the central theme of Book VIII of Hooker's *Laws*, the idea that the church and the commmonwealth need not be, and were not in England, two separate corporations. In England, Hooker contended, and Gladstone noted that the contention was contrary to fact even in Hooker's day, 'there is not any man of the Church of England but the same man is also a member of the commonweath; nor any man a member of the common-wealth which is not also of the Church of England.'[76] Consequently, 'the church and the commonwealth therefore are in this case personally one society.'[77] Hooker pursued this theme in order to establish the legitimacy of the royal supremacy. While Gladstone had no quarrel with the royal supremacy he was strongly committed to the view that the Church of England retained a sacred identity and status entirely separate from and independent of the state. Furthermore, in the nineteenth century it was no longer possible to ignore the religious pluralism of English society. Hooker, Gladstone concluded, could therefore not contribute in a major way to a modern theory of the establishment.[78]

Gladstone does, however, credit Hooker with understanding the idea of the personality of the state, a key idea in Gladstone's own theory. 'And thus much at least is clear,' Gladstone wrote of the eighth book of the *Laws*, 'there can be no doubt that it teaches, or rather involves, as a basic and pre-condition of all its particular arguments, the great doctrine that the state is a person, having a conscience, cognisant of matters of religion, and bound by all constitutional and natural means to advance it.'[79] On this question of personality, Gladstone may have read more into Hooker than he had warrant for. Hooker is intent on defending the national identity and integrity of the English state, a commonwealth under God and no mere subdivision of Latin Christendom. But Hooker does not use language that suggests 'the great doctrine that the state is a person.'

That doctrine, more properly that metaphor, has a long history in European political philosophy. Plato, in the *Republic*, presented the city-state as 'the individual writ large.' Mediaeval writers on political theory pressed the analogy to detailed extremes. Nicholas of Cusa likened the emperor to the head, the subjects to the flesh, the laws to the nerves, and the offices of state to the limbs.[80] Thomas Hobbes introduced the analogy towards the beginning of *Leviathan*, where he calls the state an 'artificial man,' and describes its anatomy in mechanistic terms.[81] For Hobbes, the unity and personality of the state are entirely the products of human artifice; they are created by the contract through which men create the state.[82] In the late seventeenth century and in the eighteenth, the contractualist theory of the state, and the analogy between man and the state, were commonplace in English political thought. Locke subscribed to this view, as did his disciple Bishop Warburton, who refers to 'the artificial man, society,' in *The Alliance between Church and State*.[83]

Following in the contractualist tradition, Edmund Burke accepted the position that the state is 'wholly artificial, and made, like other legal fictions, by common agreement.'[84] As he put it in the *Reflections on the Revolution in France*, the state is 'a contrivance of human wisdom to provide for human wants.'[85] For Burke, however, the state took on a genuine life of its own and developed, through time, many attributes of personality. The state, in his eyes, had an almost mystical reality that he approached with reverence and awe, a reality that was the product of age, tradition, and shared experience. 'Alas,' he wrote of the revolutionaries in France, 'they little know how many a weary step is to be taken before they can form themselves into a mass which has a true politic personality.'[86] It was important to Burke's vision of its moral role that the state be seen as having an existence separate from the existence of individuals living within it. Society requires that the passions of individuals be controlled. 'This can only be done *by a power out of themselves.*'[87]

Coleridge, like Burke, saw the state as 'a moral unit, an organic whole,' not merely a convenient legal arrangement for the maintenance of order.[88] He considered, moreover, that there is such a close correspondence between the body politic and the body natural that there exists in the language hardly another metaphor 'so commensurate, so pregnant, or suggesting so many points of elucidation.'[89] Unlike Burke, Coleridge did not push the metaphor beyond a figure of speech, and he reminded his readers that 'no simile runs on all four legs.'[90] Gladstone was disappointed in Coleridge's treatment of the state because 'it does not specifically include the element of its living personality and consciousness,' an element that Gladstone considered critically important.[91]

Gladstone's conception of the state's corporate personality is similar in several ways to Burke's and probably draws more heavily from Burke than from Coleridge or any other writer. Gladstone knew Burke's books and speeches very well. He had read a great deal of Burke while he was at Eton.[92] During the highly charged spring of 1831, up at Oxford protesting against the Reform Bill, he read the *Reflections* and reread *An Appeal from the New to the Old Whigs*.[93] In his language, in his reverential approach to politics and the state, in his deep respect for tradition, and his commitment to a state consecrated by religion, Gladstone reflects the influence of Burke. This influence Gladstone never fully acknowledged. He considered Burke an unsystematic writer, unlike Aristotle, and he took from Burke no organized system of ideas. Perhaps he was unaware of the degree to which he shared portions of Burke's political vision.

For Gladstone, as for Burke, the personality of the state was a living reality with a capacity for action and reflection.[94] There is an element of confusion in Burke's treatment of the state as both an artificial product of contract and a living personality created by time. Gladstone avoids this confusion by rejecting the ideas of contract and artificiality. In Gladstone's view the state, like the family, is a natural form of human association.[95] Like the family, the state is universal; like the family its purpose is essentially moral; and like the family it is a creation of God. The state is 'independent of the will of man alike in the origin and in the exercise of its power; it both precedes and survives the individual; and it perpetually presents to him the images and associations of duty, of permanency, of power, of something greater and better than himself. It claims to represent to us, in that relative sense which alone the conditions of our earthly sojourning will admit, the principles of the Divine nature, inclusively of the power to assert them.'[96] The state is created in God's image. Like man, the state is but a shadow of God's glory, but it is 'a shadow truly projected from the substance.'[97] The personality of the state, then, 'is not any mere metaphysical or theological abstraction, nor a phrase invented for the purpose of discussion, but a reality.'[98] This enthusiastic celebration of the state is as far removed from the tradition of the contractualists as it is from the utilitarianism of Adam Smith or Jeremy Bentham.

Gladstone pays surprisingly little heed to the possibility of tyranny or oppression in the state. He writes, of course, with England in mind, and he assumes English liberties and the English form of government. That the English state might go too far in its moral role as the enemy of individual selfishness is a consideration that does not occur to Gladstone. He does recognize, however, that the state, inherently moral though it might be as a divinely ordained form of the common life, is capable of evil as well as good.[99] Therefore some means must be found to ensure the morality of the state. 'This remedy has been recognized by the common, the almost universal sense of mankind, as being found in collective religion.'[100]

While he emulates the language of the *Reflections* when he writes of the need for an established church that can consecrate the state, Gladstone's intention is quite different from Burke's. Burke, for all the misty reverence of his rhetoric, shared a long-held traditional idea of religious establishment that is open to cynical interpretation. From Plato and Aristotle through Machiavelli and his heirs runs the argument that an established religion props up the state by stimulating in the people a respect for order and stability. This is what Burke means by the consecration of the state by the church.[101] It is an historical irony that during the whole of Gladstone's political career, defence of the church establishment in Ireland, and to some extent in England, contributed more to political turmoil than to stability. Beginning with the storm over Maynooth in 1845, Gladstone opted consistently for stability rather than defence when it seemed to him that political pressure against the privileges of the established church could not remain unanswered. In the end, faced with the choice, as he saw it, between disorder and disestablishment in Ireland, he chose disestablishment. He did not wrestle much with the question of social order in *State and Church*. Political stability is not entirely neglected as an issue in his book, but it is certainly not given much emphasis. Gladstone, at that time more high-minded and less experienced than the Burke of the *Reflections* and the *Appeal*, considered politics a subdivision of ethics. He took political stability for granted as a precondition of civilized life, and he assigned to the established church an exclusively moral and religious role. For him the object of the church establishment was 'the greatest holiness of the greatest number.'[102]

The established church, in Gladstone's words, was the conscience of the state. To understand what Gladstone meant by 'conscience,' one must turn to the works of Joseph Butler, to both *The Analogy of Religion* and the *Sermons*. Bishop Butler was one of Gladstone's favourite writers. He described Butler, along with Aristotle, Augustine, and Dante, as one of his four 'doctors.'[103] Over the years he wrote a number of laudatory essays on Butler, which he published in 1896 as *Studies Subsidiary to the Works of Bishop Butler*. He spent his last few years of active life preparing for the press a copiously annotated edition of *The Works of Joseph Butler* (London, 1897). 'It is Butler,' wrote Gladstone, with a characteristic touch of extravagance, 'who, more than any other writer, opens to us the one pervading scheme, upon which He deals with His creatures.'[104] Gladstone began his study of Butler while he was at Oxford.[105] Butler was then the only modern writer on the *Literae Humaniores* reading list, a Christian complement to Aristotle in ethics and political science, and this alone must have given him prestige among the undergraduates. Gladstone certainly was impressed by Butler, perhaps as much as he was by Aristotle. Aristotle, in his view, had laid the foundations of political science. Butler had developed a method, in his work on probability, that could serve as a practical guide to statesmen.[106] There are few references to Butler in *State and Church*, but it is probable that Butler's influence on the book is second only to that of Aristotle. Butler provided Gladstone with the method by which he justified a specifically Anglican establishment, with a Christian imprimatur for Aristotle's discussion of prudence, and with a model of moral anatomy and a definition of conscience.[107]

Butler, who was himself deeply influenced by Aristotle, developed in the mid-eighteenth century a system of ethics and psychology, a system designed to counteract the growing influence of the sensationalist utilitarians. Within Butler's system, which he presented in his *Fifteen Sermons*, particularly in the preface and in sermons I, II, and III, a man's behaviour is determined by three levels of motivation.[108] On the lowest level, a man is motivated by his passions, instincts, or appetites. Men, on this level, are not distinguished from other animals. The middle level is occupied by the affections, by enlightened self-love – Butler calls it 'cool self love,' as distinct from the hot self-love of the passions – and by benevolence. This level of motivation draws on man's reason and on the experience of individual men. Butler's discussion of ethical action on this plane parallels Aristotle's *Ethics*; cool self-love is Aristotle's prudence.[109] At the top of Butler's hierarchy is the conscience, which he defines as a 'principle of reflection,' or 'faculty,' which all men have by nature, and which 'tends to restrain men from doing mischief to each other, and leads them to do good.'[110] The three levels constitute a hierarchy of moral authority, not necessarily a hierarchy of power. The conscience is thus 'a faculty in kind and in nature supreme over all others, and which bears its own authority of being so.'[111] But the conscience is not innately stronger than man's other motivations. Man's will is free, but his nature is best fulfilled when he submits to the superintendency of his conscience.[112]

Lord Acton observed that if the conscience was as Butler described it, a natural moral faculty common to all men, there would be no need for laws or churches.[113] Butler, however, had dealt with this objection. The conscience and the affections incline man towards good behaviour, but those faculties do not adequately define or apprehend what is good. True religion does not demand affections or a conscience different from those natural to all men. But true religion defines the good with particularity. 'Let the man of ambition go on still to consider disgrace as the greatest evil; honour as his chief good. But disgrace in whose estimation? Honour in whose judgement? This is the only question.'[114] The unerring judgment and infinite wisdom of God are revealed through religion. The church, then, is the schoolmaster of the conscience, and the true church is the best teacher. Butler thus establishes both the relevance of Greek ethical thought to the Christian world, and the relevance of Christianity to the conscience and the natural affections.[115]

Gladstone described the constitution of the state in terms very similar to those Butler applied to the constitution of man. The established church was the conscience of the state, and the church had among its duties the guidance of the lawgiver whose natural principle of action was prudence. The church, along with the lawgiver, also acted to promote social order by diminishing among the people the lustful selfishness of unbridled individualism, the analogue in Gladstone's state to Butler's appetites and passions. In his moral anatomy of the state, moreover, Gladstone saw the relation between the church and the civil government as being naturally harmonious, a precise parallel with the analogous faculties in Butler's moral anatomy of man. While 'there are partial exceptions,' Gladstone wrote, 'the same acts which are favourable to politic designs are the acts that general morality approves.'[116] (Ireland, he was to discover, seemed to abound in exceptions.) For Butler's man, 'duty and interest are perfectly coincident; for the most part in this world, but entirely and in every instance if we take in the future, and the whole.'[117] Prudence is concerned with the practical affairs of men whereas conscience reaches out towards God, but in this harmonious world both lead to the same end. Moral truth is one.

Deeply impressed by the identity of truth, Gladstone put forth with keen insistence the position that the state should establish the true church, at least the church combining the least error with the most truth. Gladstone heaped scorn on Bishop Warburton's utilitarian argument that the state should establish the church of the majority in order to achieve, through it, the greatest political influence. 'The state in this view has no conscience.'[118] While he agreed with Thomas Chalmers that the state is not competent to judge among the details of theological discussion, Gladstone disagreed sharply with Chalmers' comfortable opinion that the state should establish some (any) form of Protestantism because any reasonable and educated man could perceive the errors of popery.[119] It was critically important, in Gladstone's view, that the state establish the particular church that most fully taught the truth. He had no affection for the undiscriminating Protestantism that saw roughly equal merit in the various reformed denominations. He had no sympathy for those broad churchmen who, like Thomas Arnold, put national unity ahead of doctrinal purity. The established church must be what Gladstone called 'determinate'; it must have a well-defined body of doctrine; it must be a church with creeds and formularies.

How was the state to determine which church was the true church? There could be no certainty, in this world, that any one particular church was the true church of Christ, and yet Gladstone considered it essential that the state choose to establish and support one church and one only. The state, as a single person and capable of moral choice, must recognize that the truth is one. If the state, cynically and with an eye to immediate political effects, should adopt the policy of ancient Rome, that mistress of statecraft, and support any number of churches and cults, then 'we are travelling back again from the region to which the Gospel brought us, towards that in which it found us.'[120] If the state does not commit itself to the unity of truth, if the state supports a variety of religious persuasions that 'are fundamentally or substantially at variance,' then the national life must be curtailed of its inner fullness; 'a discordant action is established in the leading faculty of its being.'[121] How can the state determine which theological doctrines, which ecclesiastical systems, are fundamentally at variance? Gladstone argued that it was beyond the competence of the state to discriminate among theological doctrines. Legislators, he maintained, are, by and large, not qualified to deal in detail with matters of theology.[122] Furthermore, no criteria exist, outside the church itself, which might enable legislators to distinguish truth and error, or essentials and non-essentials, in religious matters. Therefore, Gladstone concluded, the only prudent course of action for the state was establishment of the one true church, and none other. But how were legislators to know which church to establish?

Gladstone recognized that, to a considerable degree, subjective judgment would determine the decision of legislators. Men would be guided by personal faith. Muslim rulers would establish Islam; one could not expect them logically to do otherwise.[123] But Gladstone was not very much interested in Islamic countries. His concern was strongly focused on England, with Scotland and Ireland towards the periphery, and with some small attention given to English possessions overseas. For England, he offered two methods of reaching the conclusion that the Anglican church should be the sole recipient of state support.

In England, according to the first method, the will of God working through history had made it possible for legislators to have direct access to religious truth through revelation. In England the preponderance of the population, the greater portion of the social forces, and consequently nearly all the legislators belonged to the Anglican church, or as Gladstone called it variously, the catholic church, the church of Christ, or simply 'the' church. The Anglican church, that is to say, the catholic church in England, Gladstone saw as the authentic church of Christ with an unbroken history from the time of Christ and the apostles. In his identification of the Church of England with the catholic church of Christ

Gladstone was encouraged and influenced by the religious atmosphere at Oxford during his undergraduate days, and by the early writings of the Tractarians. For Gladstone, as for the Tractarians, the historical continuity of the Church of England was an essential mark of its identity with the true church of Christ. Historical continuity was embodied in the doctrine of apostolic succession, a doctrine to which Gladstone gave considerable attention in 1837.[124] Gladstone had been raised in an evangelical household, but by the mid-thirties he was a High Churchman with a strong commitment to catholic doctrine. His persuasion, in the summer of 1828, of the truth and importance of the doctrine of baptismal regeneration is the key moment in his adoption of a catholic view of the sacraments. His commitment to the doctrine of apostolic succession is the most important step towards his catholic view of the church.[125]

The doctrine of apostolic succession, for Gladstone, distinguished the historically authentic church from upstart, parvenu dissenting denominations, and also implied the divine origin of the visible church. In no sense was the church a creation of the state. 'Her foundations,' Gladstone wrote, 'are on the holy hills. Her charter is legibly divine.'[126] In England, then, where by happy accident most men and almost all men of power were personally members of the true church, legislators had personal access to true catholic doctrine through revelation and the authentic traditions of the church. Taught the truth by their church, these men knew which church the state should support; 'they will not be perplexed by being left to determine this great question upon calculations of expedience, or by the results of an analytical inquiry into the composition of different religions.'[127] There is a curiously naïve element in this argument of Gladstone's. It might seem a proclamation of *cuius regio, eius religio*. But Gladstone was certainly not a relativist, at least he did not intend relativism. He was a true believer, an enthusiast, so convinced that the Church of England was the true church that he was willing to accept her own claims without independent verification. In the nature of the case, of course, clear-cut, objective verification of revelation and the teachings of the church could not be achieved. Gladstone implicitly acknowledged that this was so in the second major argument he offered to justify the state's exclusive support of the Church of England.

This second argument was derived from Butler's *Analogy of Religion to the Constitution and Course of Nature*.[128] In his *Analogy*, Butler, proceeding from the settled assumption that the truth is one and the universe is in harmony, argued that men could rationally approach the supernatural world through analogy with the natural. The same rules and principles governed both. Argument from analogy, Butler freely admitted, could not reach absolutely certain conclusions. Reasoning by analogy from the known to the unknown produced conclusions whose validity was a matter of probability. Absolute certainty, however, was in all things beyond the grasp of men, who are beings of limited capacity. Certainty was for the Infinite Intelligence. 'But to us, probability is the very guide of life.'[129] Butler's insistence that men conducted their lives on the basis of probable evidence carries powerful echoes of Aristotle's *Ethics*, and perhaps this is one of the reasons Gladstone was so receptive to Butler's dictum that probability is the guide of life.[130] For Butler, probable evidence in the moral sphere carried with it an absolute obligation to act: 'a greater presumption on one side, though in the lowest degree greater, determines the question, even in matters of speculation; and in matters of practice, will lay us under an absolute and formal obligation, in point of prudence and of interest, to act upon that presumption or low probability.'[131]

In adopting Butler's method to justify the establishment of the Church of England, Gladstone, like Butler, assumed that the truth is one and that the universe is harmonious. He believed, as he put it, in 'the essential oneness of the Divine will; the manifest convergency of the Divine Dispensations; the stamp of concord on all practices or institutions whose origin is from heaven.'[132] Truth in politics could no more be antagonistic to religious truth than the natural world could be antagonistic to the supernatural. Therefore, Gladstone reasoned, statesmen might fairly judge ecclesiastical organizations through analogy with the state and its various departments.[133] Public men understood the value of permanency and stability in the laws and institutions of the state. English statesmen, Gladstone assumed, shared that attachment to custom and unbroken tradition that he himself found so attractive in Aristotle and Burke. The Anglican church, judged by analogy on the criteria of excellence that Burke developed for the state, could have no serious rival in England. Through apostolic succession the Church of England traced her institutional history, in a sense unbroken, back to the time of Christ. And the organization, traditions, creeds, and laws of the church suggested the probability of stability in the future. Men of public power in England, consequently, should recognize the value of establishing the Church of England quite apart from its highest or transcendental character.[134]

In Gladstone's opinion the various denominations of Protestant dissenters were not suitable candidates for state support because they had no record of historical continuity and no powerful principles of institutional authority. No statesman, taking a long view, could see any guarantee of stability in a denomination that had been founded within the past one hundred or one hundred and fifty years. These newly invented sects, moreover, took their definitions, their reasons for being, from the unsupported opinions of mere men. Dissenters, on their own authority, decided what to accept and what to reject in revelation and in the historic Christian heritage. But no genuine principle of authority guided their selections. Mere human opinion, underpinned by human pride, lay at the core of dissent. Therefore, 'the hazards of ruinous disorganisation' should be apparent to the statesman when he considered dissent.[135]

Gladstone recognized that liberty of opinion had become a Protestant shibboleth, and he claimed that he himself placed high value on that liberty. He deplored the strong tendency of the Roman Catholic church to discourage freedom of thought among her members, 'to bar, in the greatest possible degree, all active exercise of their intellectual faculties upon religion.'[136] He saw little merit in the 'inert acquiescence' favoured in the Romish system.[137] His own preference was for the *via media* between the tyranny of Rome and the proud self-will of Protestant dissent. The *via media*, the Church of England, included acceptance of the full Christian heritage along with liberty of opinion. Believing as he did that the truth was one, and that the principle of the Anglican church was unity, where did Gladstone see room in the church for freedom? Anglican liberty, for him, was the liberty of each churchman to study freely, and as deeply as possible, revelation and the teachings of the church in order that he might actively accept the truth. 'Freedom is opposed to force, not to certainty, nor to unity.'[138] There need be no more tension between freedom and authority within the church than in a mathematics classroom where pupils give free assent to the propositions of Euclid as soon as they understand them.

His commitment, at once intellectual and temperamental, to an active, manly approach to religious truth is one of the reasons Roman Catholicism had little appeal for Gladstone. His distaste for what he considered the intellectual tyranny of Romanism, moreover, was reinforced by his enthusiasm for the works of Bishop Butler. He found Butler's intemperate anti-Catholicism embarrassing, but Butler's deeply Aristotelian proposition that probability is the law of life seemed to Gladstone a profound criticism of the Roman pretensions to infallibility.[139] Gladstone shared a wide range of the anti-Catholic views common to many Englishmen of his day, but in *State and Church* he grounded his case against Romanism principally on what he considered Rome's arrogant disregard for the principle of national sovereignty. The English Reformation he saw as a national rebellion against foreign domination in matters of religion, not a movement away from catholic tradition.[140] 'For as religion,' he wrote, 'has ever been the determining principle in the national life of England, so the national life could not but exercise the most powerful influence upon discussions and measures critically affecting religion.'[141] The Reformation was the point at which English legislators chose to reject Rome and to establish catholicism in the form of the Church of England.

In the light of his elaborate argument that the state, for its moral well-being, should establish the one true church, and mindful of his loyal conviction that the Church of England embodied catholic truth, it is a little surprising that Gladstone also argued vigorously in favour of toleration. Macaulay, as we have seen, thought that the thrust of State and Church was towards intolerance. Insofar as intolerance means overt suppression of religious opinion by the state, however, Macaulay was mistaken. Gladstone had absolutely no inclination whatsoever towards any form of force as a method for advancing truth or suppressing error in religion. On the contrary, raised as he was in a Canningite household, Gladstone had a very strong temperamental preference for toleration. His record on toleration, from Catholic emancipation in 1829, through papal aggression at mid-century, to the Bradlaugh case in the 1880s, is almost consistently liberal, especially after 1845. It is possible that his emotional commitment to toleration was more powerful than his intellectual conviction, for his treatment of toleration in State and Church, forcefully unequivocal though it is, seems justification of a position already arrived at rather than an argument that genuinely advances a case.

The difficulties Gladstone faced in attempting to find a theoretical basis for toleration were considerable. His dogmatic faith in the validity of catholic doctrine prevented his accepting any theory that supported genuine liberty of opinion. He could not accept Locke's proposition that religious truth was so uncertain a matter that the state was not warranted in using force to suppress or advance religious opinions. Nor could he accept the utilitarian argument that civil rights were more important than religious doctrines.[142] And he rejected the idea that liberty of thought was a 'sacred and indefeasible right,' an essential condition of individuality.[143] He admitted the legitimacy of the state's using force, strictly for political reasons, against 'religious opinions which have specific consequences hostile to the social order.'[144] Nevertheless, Gladstone strongly inclined towards disallowing coercion in religious matters, and he maintained that his general theory of establishment included as an essential element full toleration to those who separated from the established church.[145] His theory of toleration, however, does not flow from Aristotle, Hooker, Butler, or Burke. And it seems, in itself, unreasonable, dogmatic, and arbitrary.

Gladstone grounded his theory of toleration on the argument that the authority to use coercion in religious matters 'has not been expressly given to man, and that it is an authority which, except by explicit commission from God, he cannot have.'[146] There was some force, Gladstone recognized, in some utilitarian arguments for toleration. He agreed that coercion was not generally an effective teaching device, and he maintained that, in practice, coercion in religion tended to corrupt the coercers.[147] The basis of his theory, however, what he called 'the determinate and conclusive reason against persecution,' is that God has not given man, either in the state or in the church, the authority to use force in religion.[148] As a reasonable man, Gladstone acknowledged that there were many things lawful for which divine authority was not expressly given. As a dogmatist, and displaying his life-long tendency to find a principle to support his preference, he arbitrarily decided that God had outlawed intolerance. 'It is quite enough,' he wrote, 'to occupy the purely negative ground that the prerogative of persecution has not been given us and therefore is not ours.'[149]

Gladstone treated exclusion from public office as something entirely different from persecution. In the ideal state, he argued, all governors should be members of the national church. In England, for historical reasons, dissenters and Roman Catholics were permitted to hold most offices, although the state had the theoretical right to exclude them. Gladstone maintained that the test most widely in operation in 1838, an oath sworn on the faith of a Christian, was the very minimum that should be accepted. Therefore he opposed the admission of Jews to Parliament until 1847, when he supported their admission on the ground that their small numbers could have no general impact on the legislature.[150]

There remains for discussion one portion of Gladstone's general theory that is interesting in itself, and of great importance for its application to Ireland. Throughout his book, Gladstone takes as his model for the ideal state a highly integrated, cohesive, generally homogenous community. He admired the common life to which the small city states of ancient Greece aspired, and he believed that some modern states, including England, were unified communities having well-defined corporate personalities.[151] For societies that approached the ideal of unity,

Gladstone used the terms nation, society, community, and state interchangeably. He did, however, sometimes use the term state to mean the governing body, distinguished from the nation or the people.[152] In all cases he laid it down as the duty of the state, narrowly conceived as the governing body, to choose and support the national religion. 'In the state, as the natural organ of the nation, are evidently concentrated and represented both its intellectual and its moral life.'[153] While Gladstone tended to glorify the state, he also recognized that ultimately the real power of the state was limited by its ability to gain the assent of the nation. The state should lead the nation, but it could not for any length of time dictate against the will of the people. 'The physical force, which existing law has at its command, cannot permanently maintain that which is opposed to the profound, pervading, and permanent convictions of a nation.'[154]

In the case of England, Gladstone recognized no serious tension between state and people over the establishment of the Church of England. Such was not the case in some other parts of the empire. In Scotland the will of the people, enshrined in law by the Act of Union, determined the establishment of a Presbyterian church. Gladstone's position was that the legal compact with the Scottish nation, a compact reflecting social reality, must be respected.[155] In India, where England governed an immense population professing various forms of heathenism, the ability of the state to advance Christianity was severely restricted. 'We rule by opinion and consent; I trust not by force, and that consent and good will are the actual, as they are the rightful, title of our empire.'[156] In India it was the duty of the state, regarding religion, only to support 'the proffer of Christianity so far as the people are willing to receive it.'[157] Scotland and India were, for Gladstone, cases in which the proper course of the state with respect to religion was clear. The Irish problem was cloudy.

In Ireland the state and the nation were not unified, and there were obvious reasons to doubt that the Irish people freely assented to English government. The state had established the Church of Ireland, the local manifestation of the true church of Christ, and it maintained apostolic succession and taught catholic doctrine. This made the Irish situation very different from that in areas of the empire, such as Scotland or India, where no apostolic church was established. Unhappily, the Irish church had made little progress in converting the Irish people from the perversions of Romanism. In such cases, where the religion of the state and the religion of the nation were not in harmony, Gladstone saw three possible outcomes. One body, over a period of time, might gradually win the other over to its way of worship. Or the issue might reach the crisis of civil war, and the victorious body might impose its creed on the vanquished. Or, by common consent, the issue of exclusive establishment might be abandoned altogether, and the sovereign element in the moral life of the nation would be lost. If moral persuasion did not succeed, Gladstone concluded, 'we must anticipate one of two disastrous alternatives – either disorder and disruption of the social life, or its declension and moral torpor.'[158] Although the Church of Ireland had a record of nearly three centuries of failure, Gladstone argued in his book that its exclusive establishment should be maintained. He firmly believed in the ultimate victory of the truth, and he hoped that the Church of Ireland, suitably reformed, might in time achieve visible success.[159]

Because he judged that the Church of Ireland might succeed in converting the Irish nation, and because he did not yet realize how serious was the threat of civil unrest in Ireland, Gladstone vigorously opposed both partial disendowment of the Church of Ireland and concurrent endowment of Roman Catholicism. Because he did not yet appreciate that the Irish social order was in jeopardy, Gladstone, in *State and Church*, treated the question of the established church in Ireland as a matter of spiritual truth. The opportunity to defend the Irish church he welcomed as a high and glorious duty. He disdained what he considered the opportunistic moves of short-sighted politicians who sought Irish support through concessions in religious matters. He was convinced that the great majority of the Irish people were in a condition of spiritual error. 'We believe, accordingly, that that which we place before them is, whether they know it or not, calculated to be beneficial to them; and that if they know it not now, they will know it when it is presented to them fairly. Shall we, then, purchase their applause at the expense of their substantial, nay, their spiritual interests?'[160]

Specifically, in *State and Church*, Gladstone deplored the annual parliamentary grant to the college at Maynooth that trained candidates for the Roman priesthood.[161] He saw this grant as a form of concurrent endowment, and a violation of the principle of exclusive establishment. While he found it an annual embarrassment, he was willing to see the grant continued on the ground that Parliament was obligated to carry it on by the spirit of the Act of Union. When he learned, in early 1844, that Peel's government, of which he was a member, planned to increase the grant to Maynooth and make it permanent, he was appalled.[162] He eventually resigned from the government, and considered retiring from politics altogether. But he manfully resisted the temptation to sacrifice his promising career, and, to the surprise of many, he actually supported the improved Maynooth grant in the House of Commons.[163] In his speech he threw overboard 'the rigid theory of exclusive support to the Church.'[164] One week later, in an emotional letter to John Henry Newman, he wrote: 'The state cannot be said now to have a conscience, at least not by me.'[165] Gladstone himself certainly seems to provide supporting evidence for those who conclude that in 1845 he rejected the elaborate theory of church and state developed in his first book. 'Scarcely had my work issued from the press,' he wrote in a now famous passage in *A Chapter of Autobiography*, 'when I became aware that there was no party, no section of a party, no individual person probably in the House of Commons, who was prepared to act upon it. I found myself the last man on the sinking ship.'[166]

A close look at the book, however, and the Maynooth speech as well, suggests that the conclusion is too simple. John Keble, in his perceptive review of *State and Church* for the *British Critic*, noticed in the book 'an unconscious tinge, we will not say of Erastianism, but of State as distinct from Church policy.'[167] He saw in Gladstone's language 'a certain utilitarian tone.'[168] And he feared that Gladstone might too readily accept concession and compromise in church affairs.[169] Keble had good grounds for his concern, and events in 1845 and after proved his prophecy. In matters of religious doctrine Gladstone tended, in *State and Church*, and throughout his life, towards rigid dogmatism. In matters of politics and statecraft, however, he was at base, throughout his life and in his book as well, flexible and pragmatic.

The state, Aristotle had argued in the *Politics*, had as its ultimate end promotion of the good life; its primary end, however, was the maintenance of civil order, the protection of life itself. As Gladstone put it in *State and Church*: 'The state has for primary ends, to be sought at once by direct means, those conditions of external order and security which the church is rather ordained to reach indirectly by a spiritual process mainly contemplating higher matters. These lower ends of the state are first in time and necessity; and without their attainment in some tolerable measure, it cannot so much as itself exist to contemplate the higher, because civil society is virtually dissolved.'[170] When social order was at risk, Gladstone saw the first duty of statesmen to be restoration of stability through appropriate political means. Questions of the good life and religious truth would have to be temporarily demoted in importance.

Gladstone reversed his position on the Maynooth grant in 1845 because he had become persuaded that social order in Ireland was in grave danger. In his speech supporting the increased grant, he emphasized the extreme poverty and large numbers of the Irish Roman Catholics. The grant, he argued, would be a gesture of conciliation that might reduce the Irish sense of injustice. If, he asked, religion demands that 'immoveable considerations of abstract duty are to be urged against all concessions, how is society to subsist in peace, and what is to be the fate of our common country?'[171] Compromise and conciliation were the keynotes of the speech; emphasis on first principles, a narrow vision of religious truth, and an abstract, scholastic theory of establishment characterized the earlier book. The political philosophy presented in the book, however, explicitly condoned compromise. Aristotle, Butler, and Burke, the three writers who most profoundly influenced Gladstone's *State and Church*, all insisted that rigid formulae could not be strictly applied to ethical or political activity. And Gladstone made it clear in 1845 that his support for the Maynooth grant did not involve rejection of the principles and theories elaborated in his book.

The social crisis in Ireland demanded compromise in the relation of church and state in that portion of the kingdom. This was unfortunate, but, he cautioned, it should be understood that the ideal relation of church and state could never be achieved in political reality. Compromise would continue to mark the relation of church and state in England as well as Ireland, but in England, a basically unified country, the established church was not in serious danger.[172] Towards the end of his Maynooth speech, Gladstone summed up his thinking about the relation of compromise and principle, and by implication the relation of the Maynooth grant to his book, with a strikingly apt quotation from a speech by Burke: 'It is a very great mistake to imagine that mankind follow up practically any speculative principle, either of government or of freedom, as far as it will go in argument and logical illation. We Englishmen stop very short of the principles upon which we support any given part of our constitution, or even the whole of it together ... Man acts from adequate motives relative to his interests, and not on metaphysical speculations. Aristotle, the great master of reasoning, cautions us, and with great weight and propriety, against this species of delusive geometrical accuracy in moral arguments, as the most fallacious of all sophistry.'[173] The political philosophy of *State and Church*, that is to say, could accommodate Peel's Maynooth grant.

For Gladstone the Maynooth crisis did not centre so much on the principles of his book, or his idealism, or his reputation for political consistency, as it did on the Church of Ireland. The anguish and sense of personal crisis he experienced in 1844 and 1845 arose principally from his deep grief for the Church of Ireland. He had a strong aversion to supporting Romanism, but he suffered more from his conviction that the policy implied by the Maynooth grant, necessary though it was, would severely damage the Church of Ireland and probably lead to her disestablishment. 'The Irish Church question is on me like a nightmare,' he noted in his journal on 25 April 1845. A month later he wrote of Maynooth, 'I cannot yet overcome my dread of the subject. It is a Trojan horse, full of armed men. But I have acted deliberately with an unhesitating judgement.'[174] His vision of the future, gloomy and foreboding, was accurate. Twenty-three years later he himself played a major role in the disestablishment of the Church of Ireland.

Gladstone wrote no sustained work of political philosophy after *State and Church*. As time went by, the Westminster of his manhood dominated the Oxford of his youth. Gladstone became more the man of power, less the schoolman. He became more engaged with circumstance and practical politics, less concerned with abstract theory. He retained his admiration for the philosophical guides of his youth, particularly Aristotle and Bishop Butler. He retained his dogmatic churchmanship, his vision of the high moral role of the state, and his conviction that politics should be guided by conscience. When he wrote *State and Church* he believed that catholic conscience and practical politics must coincide and he probably continued to hope that in the long run this would be the case. Maynooth, however, helped to impress upon him the imperfections of the world. The tinge of 'state as distinct from church policy' that Keble had noticed in his book grew larger. His politics became more pragmatic, and he used the rhetoric of conscience more flexibly than might seem warranted by the strict formulations of the book. He grew more comfortable and more effective in the world of practical politics, and that world seemed clearly to be moving away from the ideal of establishment defined in *State and Church*. Gladstone, nevertheless, at no time disavowed his continuing attachment to the ideals he published in his first book.

NOTES

1 John Morley, *The Life of William Ewart Gladstone* (3 vols., London, 1903), I, 169-72.

2 *The Gladstone Diaries*, ed. M.R.D. Foot, Vols. I-II (Oxford, 1968), II, 284.

3 The first edition was published in December 1838. In this essay all references are to the fourth edition, and the short form *State and Church* will be used.

4 *Diaries*, ed. Foot, ii, 580n.

5 Ibid.

6 'Church and State,' *Edinburgh Review*, 69 (April 1839), 248. It should be noted that Gladstone had his revenge when he reviewed G.O. Trevelyan's *Life of Macaulay* for the *Quarterly Review* in 1876. In that long review, which set the tone of Macaulay criticism for nearly a century, Gladstone praises Macaulay's style but criticizes his inclination to write history on a superficial level with little attention to profound problems of human nature and society.

7 This essay was substantially written before the appearance of Perry Butler, *Gladstone: Church, State, and Tractarianism* (Oxford, 1982). A brief comment on Butler appears above, 7.

8 E.J. Feuchtwanger, *Gladstone* (London, 1975), chap. 1.

9 Philip Magnus, *Gladstone* (London, 1954), 42.

10 Alec Vidler, *The Orb and the Cross* (London, 1945).

11 *The Gladstone Diaries*, ed. M.R.D. Foot and H.C.G. Matthew, Vols. iii-iv (Oxford, 1974), iii, xxxi.

12 Ibid., xxiv.

13 Deryck Schreuder, 'Gladstone and the Conscience of the State,' in *The Conscience of the Victorian State*, ed. P.T. Marsh (Syracuse, 1979), 73-134.

14 Ibid., 77.

15 Butler, *Gladstone*, chap. 3.

16 Mark Pattison, 'Oxford Studies,' in *Essays by the Late Mark Pattison*, ed. Henry Nettleship (2 vols., London, 1889), i, 463.

17 *Diaries*, ed. Foot, i, 10 November 1829 to 27 February 1830 for *Rhetoric*; and January 1830 to 10 May 1830 and May to November 1831 for *Ethics*.

18 Ibid., ii, 15 August to 6 September 1834; 27 October to 19 December 1835. Gladstone first opened the *Politics* 6 February 1834, when he noted in his journal: 'how full of matter.' He finished reading the work 20 November 1835, and commented: 'a book of immense value for all governors and public men.' Between 24 November 1835 and 19 December 1835 he indicates that on twelve days he 'wrote on *Politics*.' There is no evidence that Gladstone gave as much attention to any other book he read in the decade after leaving Oxford.

19 Aristotle, *The Politics*, trans. T.A. Sinclair (London, 1962), 28 (i, ii).

20 Ibid., 29.

21 Ibid.

22 Ibid., 119 (III, ix).
23 Ibid., 120.
24 Ibid. (I, xi).
25 Ibid., 119 (III, ix).
26 Ibid., 26-7 (I, ii).
27 Ibid., 28.
28 *State and Church*, I, 48.
29 Ibid., 50.
30 Ibid., 55.
31 Ibid., 72-6.
32 Ibid., 84.
33 Ibid., viii.
34 Ibid., 19. For a direct attack on Locke's ideas about the duties of the
    state, see ibid., 171. Locke was a favourite target for Gladstone's dis-
    approbation of utilitarianism.
35 Ibid., 1-2.
36 Macaulay's review was reprinted in the Albany edition of his *Works*
    (London, 1898), IX, 111-85.
37 Ibid., 118.
38 Ibid.
39 Ibid., 120.
40 Ibid., 174-6.
41 Ibid., 120.
42 Ibid.
43 Ibid., 175.
44 *Diaries*, ed. Foot and Matthew, III, xxvi-xxvii.
45 Ibid., xxvii.
46 *Diaries*, ed. Foot, I, 568ff.
47 Ibid., 588.
48 *State and Church*, I, 36-7.
49 Ibid., 45.
50 Ibid., II, 1.
51 Ibid., I, xi-xii.
52 In several places in the *Diaries* Gladstone uses 'ethical' in a way that un-
    mistakably refers to the *Ethics* of Aristotle: see *Diaries*, ed. Foot, I, 358,
    382. Alec Vidler, *The Orb and the Cross*, 84-5, notes that F.D. Maurice
    and John Keble both commented on the Aristotelian character of *State and
    Church*.
53 *Diaries*, ed. Foot, I, 392.
54 Morley, *Gladstone*, I, 74; *Diaries*, ed. Foot, I, 359.

55 *The Ethics of Aristotle*, trans. J.A.K. Thomson (London, 1976), 65 (I, iii).
56 *Diaries*, ed. Foot, I, 392: Gladstone notes that he was examined by 'Hampden in science.' This usage continued for some time, and gradually became less specific. Gertrude Himmelfarb, in 'The American Revolution in the Political Theory of Lord Acton,' *Journal of Modern History* (December 1949), 301, points out that Lord Acton used interchangeably the terms 'political science,' 'ethics,' and 'liberty.'
57 *Ethics*, 64 (I, ii).
58 Ibid., 93 (II, ii).
59 Ibid., 203-25 (VI).
60 Ibid., 213 (VI, vii).
61 *Gleanings of Past Years* (7 vols., London, 1879), VII, 168-9, in which Aristotle's method is systematically described and identified with the Kantian distinction between *vernunft* and *verstand* and the Coleridgean distinction between reason and understanding.
62 *Gleanings*, vii, 16.
63 *Correspondence on Church and Religion of William Ewart Gladstone*, ed. D.C. Lathbury (2 vols., London, 1910), II, 162.
64 Ibid., 163.
65 Ibid., 164.
66 Morley, *Gladstone*, I, 207.
67 *The Works of Joseph Butler*, ed. W.E. Gladstone (2 vols., London, 1897), I, xi.
68 *State and Church*, I, 23.
69 Ibid., 78, 115.
70 Ibid., 10.
71 *The Works of That Learned and Judicious Divine, Mr. Richard Hooker*, ed. John Keble (3 vols., Oxford, 1845), I, 427.
72 As an undergraduate Gladstone read Hooker's *Laws of Ecclesiastical Polity*; he dipped into Hooker again in 1833, and in the summer of 1838 while he was writing *State and Church* (*Diaries*, ed. Foot, I, 250 ff; II, 56 ff, 383).
73 Morley, *Gladstone*, I, 160-1.
74 Ibid., III, 2.
75 *State and Church*, I, 11.
76 *Hooker's Works*, II, 485.
77 Ibid., 488.
78 *State and Church*, I, 14-16.
79 Ibid., 14.
80 Otto Gierke, *Political Theories of the Middle Ages* (London, 1900), iv.

81 Thomas Hobbes, *Leviathan* (London, 1904), xviii, xix: 'For by art is created the great Leviathan, called a Commonwealth, or State (in Latin Civitas) which is but an Artificial Man.'
82 Ibid., 112-14.
83 William Warburton, *The Works of William Warburton* (12 vols., London, 1811), VII, 26.
84 *Appeal from the New to the Old Whigs*, in *The Writings and Speeches of Edmund Burke* (London, 1901), IV, 170.
85 *Reflections*, in *Writings and Speeches*, V, 123.
86 *Appeal*, IV, 170.
87 *Reflections*, V, 123. Burke's italics.
88 S.T. Coleridge, *On the Constitution of the Church and State*, in *The Collected Works of Samuel Taylor Coleridge* (Princeton, 1976), X, 107.
89 Ibid., 85.
90 Ibid., 86.
91 *State and Church*, I, 10.
92 *Diaries*, ed. Foot, I, 61, 75-80.
93 Ibid., 360, 362.
94 *State and Church*, I, 65-8.
95 Ibid., 72.
96 Ibid., 85.
97 Ibid.
98 Ibid., 63-4.
99 Ibid., 60-3.
100 Ibid., 63.
101 *Reflections*, V, 183.
102 *State and Church*, I, 258.
103 Morley, *Gladstone*, I, 207.
104 *Studies Subsidiary to the Works of Bishop Butler* (London, 1896), 12.
105 *Diaries*, ed. Foot, I, 303, 387, 389.
106 *Studies Subsidiary*, 67.
107 While Gladstone's fondness for the works of Butler is well known, Butler's influence on *State and Church* has hardly been noticed.
108 *Sermons by Bishop Butler*, in *Works*, ed. Gladstone.
109 See William A. Goligher, 'Butler's Indebtedness to Aristotle,' *Hermathena*, 12 (1902).
110 Sermon I, in *Works*, II, 36-7.
111 Sermon II, ibid., II, 51.
112 Ibid., 54-6.

113 *Selections from the Correspondence of the First Lord Acton*, ed. J.N. Figgis and R.V. Laurence (London, 1917), 279.

114 Sermon XIII, in *Works*, II, 202.

115 See *State and Church*, I, 49-55.

116 Ibid., 87.

117 Sermon III, in *Works*, II, 65.

118 *State and Church*, I, 18.

119 Ibid., 30.

120 Ibid., 125.

121 Ibid., 126.

122 Ibid., 119.

123 Ibid., 296-7.

124 *Diaries*, ed. Foot, II, 274.

125 William Palmer's *A Treatise on the Church of Christ* (London, 1838), came into Gladstone's hands as he was writing hard in the summer of 1838. Palmer's views of the church accorded well with Gladstone's, and probably helped Gladstone put his own ideas into more systematic order. But Gladstone did not have a chance to read Palmer carefully until after the text of *State and Church* was completed. See the entries in the *Diaries*, ed. Foot, II, from 28 July through August 1838.

126 *State and Church*, I, 4.

127 Ibid., 118.

128 Gladstone does not acknowledge his debt to Butler in *State and Church*, but he does so fully in *Studies Subsidiary to the Works of Bishop Butler*, 11. There he claims that the method developed by Butler in the *Analogy* is of great practical value to statesmen, and he offers as a specific example the usefulness of the method to statesmen faced with the claims of conflicting religious professions.

129 Joseph Butler, *The Analogy of Religion*, in *Works*, ed. Gladstone, I, 5.

130 For Gladstone's affection for this dictum, see *Studies Subsidiary*, 10-12.

131 *Analogy*, I, 6. See *State and Church*, I, 298, on probable evidence and religious truth.

132 *State and Church*, I, 250-1.

133 Ibid., 182ff. Affirming that 'truth and public utility coincide,' Bishop Warburton developed a similar argument in *The Alliance between Church and State*, in *Works*, VII, 90ff.

134 *State and Church*, I, 184.

135 Ibid., 180.

136 Ibid., II, 56.

137 Ibid., 61.
138 Ibid., 138.
139 *Studies Subsidiary*, 12.
140 *State and Church*, II, 96.
141 Ibid., 151-2.
142 Ibid., I, 320.
143 Ibid., 311.
144 Ibid., 306.
145 Ibid., II, 283.
146 Ibid., I, 317.
147 Ibid., 314-15.
148 Ibid., 317.
149 Ibid., 320.
150 Ibid., 321ff.
151 Gladstone assumed that England was a much more homogeneous society than was the case, and this encouraged him to underestimate radically the size and political significance of Protestant dissent. See his *Chapter of Autobiography* (1868), in *Gleanings*, VII, 144.
152 *State and Church*, I, 274.
153 Ibid., 277.
154 Ibid., 280.
155 Ibid., II, 284ff.
156 Ibid., I, 303.
157 Ibid.
158 Ibid., 278-9.
159 Ibid., II, 13-14.
160 Ibid., 14.
161 Ibid., 300ff.
162 *Diaries*, ed. Foot and Matthew, III, 354ff.
163 *Hansard*, 79: 522ff (11 April 1845).
164 Ibid., 79: 540 (11 April 1845).
165 *Correspondence*, ed. Lathbury, I, 72.
166 *Gleanings*, VII, 115.
167 *British Critic*, October 1838, 369.
168 Ibid.
169 Ibid., 386.
170 *State and Church*, I, 116.
171 *Hansard*, 79: 551 (11 April 1845).
172 Ibid., 79: 537 (11 April 1845). This remained Gladstone's view through-

out his life, even after he came to appreciate the strength of Protestant non-conformity in England. See 'Is the Church of England Worth Preserving?' (1875) in *Gleanings*, VI, 143-89.

173 *Hansard*, 79: 552 (11 April 1845).
174 *Diaries*, ed. Foot and Matthew, III, 455-6.

JOHN KENYON

Gladstone and the Anglican High Churchmen, 1845-52

On Sunday evening, 15 April 1835, two years after he was first elected to the House of Commons, Gladstone wrote to his friend Henry Manning: 'Politics would become an utter blank to me were I to make the discovery that we were mistaken in maintaing their association with religion.'[1] He was in fact expressing a fear that would never be realized. Throughout his long career, he always remained convinced that there was a vital connection between his religious opinions and his political actions. At the same time, because of the changing character of the age in which he lived, it was impossible for him to maintain intact the principles that he had held as a young man during the 1830s. The years between 1845 and 1852, described by Gladstone himself as 'an age of religious warmth and excitement,'[2] were to prove a crucial stage in his reappraisal of these principles. The sensitive issue for him was the establishment of the Church of England. In Gladstone's first book, *The State in Its Relations with the Church*, written in 1838, he had argued that the established church was the conscience of the state and therefore it was the duty of the state to give full and exclusive support to that church. After 1845 his speeches in the House of Commons made widely known the changing character of his ideas about the proper relation between church and state.[3] It is the purpose of this paper to consider the ways in which this process of change affected his relations with one group in the church, the High Churchmen.

While they were always a minority group within the Church of England, High Churchmen nevertheless exercised a powerful influence in its affairs. Their leading personalities were men of exceptional distinction: Pusey and Keble, William Palmer and Samuel Wilberforce, Church and Mozley among the clergymen, Sidney Herbert, Roundell Palmer, and Gladstone himself among the politicians. They firmly believed that, whatever its imperfections, the Church of England had always been and still remained a living branch of the universal Christian church. Although it could no longer claim visible union with the rest of Catholic Christendom, its bishops and ministers were able to trace their line of succession from the apostles; they continued to administer the major sacraments of the baptism and the Eucharist; they acknowledged the same scriptures and creed as had the whole church in the days of perfect union. High Churchmen believed therefore that the Church of England exercised a unique role in English religious life. Such a 'high' conception of the church was significantly different from that held by the other major party in the Church of England, the Evangelicals, who laid far greater stress on individual as compared to corporate religion. As a result, they had far less concern for the outward framework of any visible church, even the Church of England.

Although High Churchmen shared the same understanding of the nature of the Church of England, they were sharply divided over the question of its establishment. On the one side were the Protestant High Churchmen who maintained the traditional belief in the principles of 'the Constitution in Church and State'; on the other were the Anglo-Catholics whose experience of whig government during the 1830s convinced them of the danger to the spiritual nature of the church from its too close connection with an unsympathetic state.

Protestant High Church doctrine was most clearly formulated by William Palmer, Fellow of Worcester College, Oxford, not to be confused with his namesake of Magdalen, the brother of Roundell Palmer. Palmer of Worcester is perhaps the least remembered of the leaders of the Oxford movement, but between 1830 and 1850, despite his forbidding personality, he enjoyed a great reputation both in the church and at Oxford. The son of an Irish army officer, his early religious training had been not in the evangelicalism characteristic of this class, but in the sacramental principles of the High Anglican tradition. His graduate study at Oxford confirmed for him his belief that the Church of England represented the primitive Christianity of the apostolic age that had been so distorted elsewhere by the later developments of Roman Catholicism, 'the mother of superstition and error.'[4] Palmer's hostility towards the Roman Catholic church was further strengthened by the more secular consideration that its control over the majority of the Irish people provided a major threat to the privileged position of his class in that country.

Palmer supported the established church in Ireland, therefore, as a bulwark against an aggressive and corrupt Roman Catholicism. He was convinced that the Church of England played the same role. His reading of seventeenth-century history persuaded him that Roman Catholicism, with its spiritual intolerance and its divided allegiance between papal and national authority, had proved as great a danger to the security of the state as it had to the church. The British people had, indeed, suffered their worst humiliations in the period when Charles ii, secretly, and James ii, openly, had attempted to restore Romish absolutism. In sharp contrast, the special relationship created between the Church of England and the state as a result of the Glorious Revolution of 1688, which guaranteed that Britain would remain a Protestant nation, had brought about a period of unrivalled greatness and prosperity. Church establishment and the Protestant ascendancy became, therefore, two major axioms in Palmer's thought.

As a result, Palmer could not ignore the challenge to these principles implicit in the whig government's Irish church policy, with its proposed reconstruction of the established church in that country. In June 1833 he attended the famous conference at Hadleigh with H.J. Rose, Arthur Perceval, and Richard Hurrell Froude, which was to mark the opening of the Oxford movement. It soon became apparent, however, that he differed radically even at this time from Froude over the policy that should be adopted to meet this threat to the church, most obviously with regard to the question of its establishment.

Palmer was well aware that the constitutional changes that had taken place between 1828 and 1832 had done much to destroy the conditions that had previously justified the special relationship between the Church of England and the state. In spite of this, he had little sympathy for the growing demand for its disestablishment that was now being urged, by Froude especially, as the only safeguard for its integrity. Palmer believed that such an action would certainly be premature and might prove disastrous. It would entail the sacrifice of its endowments on which was based the Anglican parochial system, and which made possible the dissemination of the religious truth which that church possessed. The collapse of the system would allow the triumph of Roman Catholicism with all the consequences that would entail.

Developments after the death of Froude in 1836 made the division between Palmer and the Anglo-Catholics even wider. He disliked especially the ideas expressed in *Tract 90*, although he bitterly resented what he considered the persecution of Newman after its publication. For his part, Newman found it equally difficult to appreciate Palmer's churchmanship: 'He was the only really learned man among us ... But he was deficient in depth ... Nor had he any insight into the forces of personal influence and congeniality of thought in carrying out a religious theory ... Mr. Palmer had a certain connection, as it may be called, in the Establishment, consisting of High Church dignitaries, arch-deacons, London rectors and the like, who belonged to what was commonly called the high-and-dry school ... Of course their *beau ideal* in ecclesiastical action was a board of safe, sound, sensible men. Mr. Palmer was their organ and representative: and he wished for a committee, an association with rules and meetings to protect the interests of the Church in its existing peril.'[5]

Among the Anglo-Catholics it was John Keble who exercised the same kind of influence as Palmer did among the Protestant High Churchmen. Like Palmer, he had been brought up in the 'high-and-dry' tradition of churchmanship and he opposed Catholic emancipation in 1829 on the ground that 'the settlement of the Catholic question in the way now proposed involved a great and certain danger to the Church Establishment.'[6] The fundamental changes in church-state relations between 1828 and 1832 made it necessary, however, for Keble to reconsider his position. As a result he now believed that it was possible 'to form an exaggerated opinion of the necessity and sacredness of the alliance of Church and State; to sacrifice more or less of the very being of the Church ... in order to secure its well being.'[7] In order to avoid the creation of 'a mere Parliamentary Church' in England it might be necessary to sacrifice the material benefits of establishment in order to recover for the church her independence and apostolic character.

Keble was also much more ready than Palmer to accept the possibility of disestablishment because he did not ever share the fear of the Roman Catholic church that so dominated the minds of the Protestant High Churchmen. Indeed, during the 1830s he appeared to contemporaries to share the growing doubts of Froude and Newman about the claim of the Church of England to be part of the universal church. Together with Newman, he was responsible for the posthumous publication of Froude's *Remains*, which was to cause great offence to Protestant opinion by its attack on the character and motives of the English reformers of the sixteenth century. It was widely assumed in 1845 that he would soon follow Newman into the Church of Rome.

Keble was certainly conscious of his anomalous position at this time. When he explained his reasons for remaining in the Church of England, it was natural that he wrote especially with those people in mind who, like himself, were haunted by the thought: 'What if the exclusive claim of the

Roman Catholic Church be true? What if it should prove that as yet I have been living without the pale of Christ's Kingdom?'[8] He was indeed to stay within the church until his death in 1866, but he did so not because he was able to resolve these doubts, but rather on the grounds of what one contemporary described as 'the legitimate influence of the hereditary Church.'[9] For Keble this was always to remain man's first loyalty: 'Wherever he has been called, there let him abide with God ... in whatsoever state you are, therewith be content until you discern an unequivocal manifestation of God's will calling you out of it.'[10] He was, therefore, most sensitive to the essential need to maintain the Catholic character of the Church of England, even if this meant its disestablishment, so that those who thought as he did could remain within it without compromising their fundamental beliefs.

Gladstone grew up in a very different religious tradition from that of Palmer and Keble. As he wrote, 'My environment in my childhood was strictly evangelical.'[11] After he graduated from Oxford in 1832, however, he made a grand tour through Europe. On 31 March, in entering St Peter's at Rome, he experienced his 'first conception of unity in the Church.'[12] It was this experience that began a major change in his religious opinions. As he wrote later: 'From this time I began to feel my way by degrees into or towards a true notion of the Church.'[13] During the 1830s he found himself more and more in sympathy with High Church rather than evangelical principles. But these were the principles not of the Anglo-Catholics, but of the Protestant High Churchmen. Gladstone's judgment of the influence on himself of the Anglo-Catholic *Tracts for the Times* was unequivocal: 'They had little to do with my conversion: nothing with it at all, I should be inclined to say, except insofar as it was partly, and very considerably, due to them that Catholicism, so to speak, was in the air, and was exercising an influence on the religious frame of men without their knowing.'[14] At the same time, he maintained that it was Palmer's *Treatise on the Church of Christ*, written to justify the claims of the Church of England to be a true part of the universal church, that had given him 'the clear, definite and strong conception of the Church which, through all the storm and strain of a most critical period, proved entirely adequate to every emergency and saved me from vacillation.'[15] On the major issue of the establishment of the Church of England, Gladstone made clear his orthodox High Church opinions by his publication of his book *The State in Its Relations with the Church*.

This last matter became of crucial importance when, at the start of 1845, the prime minister, Sir Robert Peel, moved to increase the grant paid to the Roman Catholic training college at Maynooth, and also make it permanent, whereas it had previously depended on an annual parliamentary vote. Such government assistance to an institution that was not merely non-Anglican but also non-Protestant appeared to many a further threat to the exclusive relationship hitherto claimed between the state and the established church. As a result of the introduction of this motion, Gladstone resigned from the government and, on 4 February, explained in the House of Commons his reasons for doing so. His decision, he declared, was motivated in part by his conviction that he could not honestly judge these new proposals if his freedom of action was limited by a prior commitment. He went out of his way to emphasize that he still believed his views on church-state relations, as he had previously expressed them, were 'the most salutary and the best in every condition of the public sentiment that will bear their application.'[16] All that he seemed to promise the government was not to promote 'a religious war' over the matter. In the light of Gladstone's reputation, it was not surprising that Sir Robert Inglis, a leading representative of the Protestant High Churchmen in Parliament, should now invite him to lead the opposition to the measure.

Inglis, a man of formidable personality, was the very model of those 'stern and unbending Tories' who, according to Macaulay, had so welcomed the arguments put forward by Gladstone in justification of church establishment in 1838. Even after sixteen years, he remained convinced that the granting of Catholic emancipation had been a betrayal of the Church of England. Gladstone has given an account of a revealing conversation he had with Inglis during the crisis over Maynooth: 'In the course of this conversation, he went back to the fatal character and consequences of the Act of 1829, and wished that his advice had been taken, which was that the Duke of Cumberland should be sent as Lord Lieutenant of Ireland with thirty-thousand men. As that good and very kind man spoke the words, my blood ran cold.'[17] During the debate on the Maynooth grant, Inglis made clear his determination to oppose the motion: 'The Protestant colours were still at the mast head: and so long as a single shred of the old flag lasted, he for one would endeavour to nail it to the mast, and he would fight as unflinching for it and under it as when in brighter days it waved entire and untorn over an Empire.'[18]

Inglis must have heard with dismay, therefore, Gladstone's announcement on 11 April that he would vote in support of the motion. Gladstone's speech justifying his action appeared less than convincing to many of his audience. George Smythe, a member of the Young England group, 'that curious translation of the Oxford Movment by Cambridge from religion to politics,'[19] and who was in fact to vote in the same lobby as Gladstone, maintained: 'In all that cloud of variegated phraseology in which as usual the other night he wrapped and shrouded his mysterious divinity, there was only one phrase which was intelligible to vulgar minds like mine. He said that, notwithstanding his cherished convictions, he would vote in favour of the bill.'[20] Outside the House of Commons, Charles Wordsworth, most orthodox of High Churchmen and whose appointment as first warden of Glenalmond College Gladstone had helped to secure, was even more severe: 'For many years I looked upon Gladstone ... as the *man* to save the country, or rather the nation: it was almost (if I may speak so strongly) his mission from God to do so to save it in the way in which I believe it is to be saved (under providence) – viz. *upon the principles of the constitution in Church and State*: but in an evil hour, as I think, his faith failed him; fascinated by the practical abilities and power of Sir Robert Peel, he lost sight of his own position, and at last fell from the high ground he fancied untenable, but was not more so than the high ground has often been in faithless times.'[21]

By his apparently unjustified reversal of policy over the Maynooth question, Gladstone certainly left himself open to the charge of political deviousness. Nevertheless, Wordsworth's condemnation might have been modified if he had realized just how much Gladstone had changed his opinions about church establishment in the years before 1845. Gladstone himself was well aware of this development. Even as early as 1839 he had been seriously disturbed by a comment made by Keble in his review of *The State in Its Relations with the Church*. Keble had asked whether 'however fearful the view which may be taken of a world anti-Christianized by the downfall of Establishments, might not a sadder picture be drawn, and one at least as like to be realized, of a Church turned anti-Christian by corrupt Establishments?'[22] Gladstone told his friend, J.R. Hope, that in making this point Keble was expressing a fear that he himself had felt, even if he had not considered it in his book.

By 1845, therefore, Gladstone was aware that some High Churchmen were questioning the principle of establishment. His own growing doubts were the result of his understanding of the nature of the state in which he lived. He once described this to Newman as the transition stage between the mediaeval conception of the state as a family and the modern conception of it as a club. If the state was considered as a family, with its government having the status and duties of parents, then it was reasonable to think of its having a conscience embodied in the established church. If, however, it had become an impersonal club, with the government merely the organ of those influences which predominated within it, then this was no longer possible. Gladstone maintained that in England 'the state is neither a family nor a club, but it is on the path of transition from the former to the latter. It is less like a club than America or France: it is less like a family (I mean, as to duties, not their fulfillment) than Austria or Russia.'[23] When the transformation was completed, it would be impossible to apply the theories previously expounded by Gladstone to the relations between the Church of England and the state.

Gladstone's support for the increased Maynooth grant in 1845 was, therefore, another stage in his advance to a belief in a religiously neutral state. At the same time, he was well aware how much of a shock this would be for those who had previously supported him. In two lengthy letters written to Henry Manning during April 1846 he discussed thoroughly his future prospects. The arguments for ending his political career at this time and fulfilling his early ambition of becoming a clergyman were certainly very strong ones. Gladstone accepted that it would still be necessary to defend the interests of the established church in Parliament, though the growing secularization of the state made it impossible to restore its former special position within the community. He wondered, however, whether he was now the right man to act as a spokesman for the church in the House of Commons, or whether he might do more harm than good by his efforts on her behalf. He was especially concerned that his growing doubts about the validity of the established church in Ireland might 'be fatal to my capacity for doing any good in political life ... because of its sinister alliance with that suspicion of leaning towards the Church of Rome, and therefore of treachery, which now and for many years to come must attach, not without presumption of justice, to those whose names have ever been associated with the Oxford Constellation.'[24] Gladstone was convinced that the best hope for restoring the church's popularity in the country lay not in an aggressive defence of its prerogatives, but in a readiness to sacrifice some of her surviving privileges. Any attempt 'by a knot of men proposing and claiming everything, engaged in constant resistance and protest (like Montalembert in France where there is acute hostility between Church and State) will not suit English conditions.'[25] Gladstone was prepared, therefore, to apply to himself the advice he would give any young man: 'If you want to serve the Church, do it in the Sanctuary, and not in Parliament.'[26] He told Manning that, if he did decide to remain in public life for a time, it would be for secular, not religious, reasons: in order to support the Queen and defend the Constitution during the period of revolution he believed to be imminent.

Political fever was, however, too strong in Gladstone's blood for him to abandon his parliamentary career. Nevertheless, by the time of the general election in 1847 he was facing a major crisis in this career, caused by his difficulty in securing re-election to Parliament.[27] Gladstone had first entered the House of Commons in 1833 as member for Newark, a constituency which, despite the 1832 Reform Act, was still under the control of the Duke of Newcastle. The duke, a fervent Protestant Churchman, bitterly resented Gladstone's decision to vote in favour of the increased grant to Maynooth. When Gladstone rejoined Peel's government as colonial secretary in December 1845 and, as was customary, had to seek re-election, the duke was no longer prepared to give him his patronage at Newark. Despite being a member of the cabinet, Gladstone found it impossible to find another parliamentary seat during the six months the government survived in office.

In May 1847, however, Bucknell Estcourt, one of the sitting members for Oxford University, announced his retirement. Gladstone was immediately suggested as a possibility to succeed him, though more than a few doubted his suitability for the position. Charles Wordsworth expressed the sentiments of the Protestant High Churchmen in describing Gladstone, after his vote for the Maynooth grant, as 'a Janus in politics: an authority of one school and a statesman of another ... He will be the most dangerous representative Oxford ever had.'[28] Anglo-Catholics, for their part, feared that Gladstone was 'too strong from a party point of view for success.'[29] Even Gladstone had his doubts. He wrote to Manning that the question was 'whether I am stiff enough in State and Church politics to be justified in assuming the position.'[30] Only when he was assured of the support of the Anglo-Catholics among the resident voters did he agree to stand.

Even so, Gladstone appeared to have little chance of success. His campaign was dismissed as 'a sort of Tractarian puerility.'[31] His supporters were 'barefaced Puseyites, whom nobody in Oxford, but themselves will join.'[32] The Protestant High Churchmen made it clear they would support Gladstone's opponent, C.G. Round. Gladstone himself was determined not to be elected under false pretences by disguising his changed opinions concerning church-state relations. He told Robert Phillimore, 'a High Churchman of the old type,' that it was now impossible to regulate the connection between church and state according to the abstract principles which he had previously maintained. That, in the end,

Gladstone enjoyed an unexpectedly comfortable margin of victory over Round was the result of his success in securing the support of the Liberal resident voters at the university, who included men such as Jowett and A.P. Stanley.

Although Gladstone was to retain his seat at Oxford until 1865, his hold on it was always tenuous. From the start, the Protestant High Churchmen made clear their lack of confidence in him. The disillusionment of these churchmen was expressed directly to Gladstone by Christopher Wordsworth after the former's success at Oxford in 1847. Wordsworth emphasized how different Gladstone's political behaviour had been from that of his fellow representative at the university:

Sir Robert Inglis has fought the battle of the Church in the House of Commons almost single handed for many years past ... He has not fought it perhaps ... just in the manner I myself should have chosen, but he fought it on principle – the principle which alone, as I think, is safe and right for us to fight on – *The Principle of the Constitution in Church and State*. This he has done in every vote in respect to Ireland, in respect to the Dissenters, in respect to education ... Now, in two out of three of these most important fields of political activity you and he have not acted alike. *You* have acted and spoken as if you considered that the end at which you are both aiming – viz. the well-being and efficiency of the Church - was more likely to be gained by following a different course which, without offence, I may call one of accommodation and compromise rather than of principle.[33]

In the light of such considerations, these churchmen were to make a determined opposition against Gladstone at each successive election at Oxford until they helped to bring about his defeat in 1865.

With no possibility of winning the support of these churchmen, it was essential for Gladstone to establish an effective relationship with the Anglo-Catholics. In spite of the support they had given him in the 1847 election, Gladstone was faced by one major obstacle to achieving this goal. There was little in common between the Anglo-Catholics and Gladstone's closest political colleagues, the so-called Peelites, those Conservatives who had remained loyal to Sir Robert Peel after the repeal of the Corn Laws in 1846. The Anglo-Catholics had, indeed, a long-standing feud with Peel himself, which dated back to 1840 when he had made a more than usually pompous electioneering speech about the necessity to develop a system of national education. Newman had then attacked his arguments in a series of sarcastic letters to *The Times* under the thinly disguised anonymity of 'Catholicus.'[34] In them he accused Peel of adopting the Liberal heresy that education was a good thing in itself. He went on to charge that Peel, as in the case of Catholic emancipation, was prepared to steal from the whigs whatever might give him some political advantage. Always highly sensitive to this kind of attack, Peel, when again in office, made it clear that Newman and the Tractarians could expect no preferment in the church from his government.

Apart from this clash of personalities, there was little common ground between the religious principles held by Peel and the Anglo-Catholics. After Peel's death in July 1850 their mouthpiece, the *Christian Remembrancer*, wrote: 'many excellent individuals who participate in our theological views ... [think] it a serious moral offence against Sir Robert Peel that, considering the amount of power which he wielded and the time during which he was in office, he should have done little for the Church and done that little in so unsatisfactory a manner.' Peel had always remained, the *Remembrancer* continued, 'a most respectable Establishment Christian of the school which had existed when he was a young man.' The chief duty of churchmen, Peel believed, was to set a moral example, especially by going 'to church once every Sunday, unless the weather was too bad or business too pressing.' Finally, the *Remembrancer* condemned Peel as an example of 'the inconceivable ignorance and darkness which over-spread the judgement of such public men whenever they stepped aside from tariffs and treaties and the budget to legislate for the rights of God and the good of soul.'[35] Although not in such harsh terms, Gladstone was to make a similar estimate of Peel's churchmanship. He was 'wholly anti-church and unclerical and undogmatic ... By habit and education, he was quite incapable of comprehending [the anti-Erastian] movement in the church, the strength it would reach and the exigencies it would entail.'[36]

Anglo-Catholics felt the same distrust of Sir James Graham, who had been home secretary in Peel's government. They disliked Graham's capacity for combining a whiggish love of religious toleration, even for Roman Catholics, with a reverence for the traditional principles of 'the Constitution in Church and State' that would have delighted even Sir Robert Inglis. Graham argued that 'those genuine Whig principles, which, as I understood them on my first entrance into public life ... were not incompatible with the firm maintenance of the Established Protestant religion, that religion of perfect freedom, which the Revolution of 1688 bore triumphant over Popery and regal tyranny.'[37] More importantly, Graham possessed an extremely low view of the functions of bishops in the church. In a speech made to the House of Commons in July 1847 he argued that their main duties were in charitable work, in the exercise of church patronage, in the social leadership of the clergy, and in infrequent visitations of their dioceses for the purpose of confirmation or ordination.[38] This brought an immediate and indignant rejoinder from Gladstone, and Graham was never to be forgiven by the Anglo-Catholics. In May 1852 the *Guardian* refused to consider him as a future leader of the Peelites because of 'his most degraded conception of the function of the Bishops,' and hoped that he would soon rejoin the whigs.[39]

The third senior member of the Peelites, Lord Aberdeen, the future prime minister, confused his contemporaries about his attitude to church establishment. According to Gladstone, he was 'altogether enlightened in regard to it and had cast it off, so he obtained from some the soubriquet (during his ministry) of the Presbyterian Puseyite.'[40] In contrast, A.J. Beresford Hope, writing his commentary on the religious issues of the day for the Peelite *Morning Chronicle*, emphasized how much Aberdeen had continued to maintain his belief in the established church as a bulwark against the anarchical conditions he had seen in Europe during the revolutionary wars.[41] It was certainly true that the part he played during the disruption of the Church of Scotland in 1843 did much to identify him as the champion of the temporal power over the spiritual, which did him no good in the eyes of the Anglo-Catholics.

Among the younger Peelites there existed a wide diversity of opinion on religious matters. Edward Cardwell, for example, hoped that in any Peelite ministry the exercise of church patronage would remain 'in hands, like those of Lord Aberdeen himself, free from that bias which Gladstone obeys, and from which my feelings and convictions unite to keep me free.'[42] Conversely, Lord Lincoln, the son of the Duke of Newcastle, who had become Gladstone's close friend while they were undergraduates at Oxford, had been one of those who had fallen under the influence of Newman and Pusey at the university. He had strongly supported the increased grant to Maynooth, which brought him into serious conflict with his father, and the two men were not to be reconciled until the latter's death bed in 1851. At the same time, Lincoln denied being 'what is foolishly called a Puseyite.'[43] In the same way Sidney Herbert, the nearest to Gladstone in his religious thinking, was prepared to dismiss with scorn what he described as 'Puseyite tomfooleries,' and maintained as early as 1850 that 'Tractarianism has had its day.'[44]

It was not possible for Gladstone, therefore, to rely on the support of the Anglo-Catholics on the basis of his political affiliations. That they continued to vote for him in the Oxford University elections between

1847 and 1865 must be explained in terms of his personal appeal for them. His relationship with Stafford Northcote provides a vivid illustration of this appeal.

Northcote, a member of a Devon county family, had been brought up as an evangelical, but the religious controversies of the 1830s gave him a more profound appreciation of High Church principles than he had possessed before. He became convinced that the great problem of the day was the proper relationship between church and state. Indeed, he was prepared at one time to accept Thomas Arnold's contention that the only solution was to restore in whatever way possible the complete identity between the two. As a result, he believed that the great variety of religious opinion in the country, 'Pusey and Evangelicalism, Popery and Dissent,' must be a major source of discord. He was especially concerned about the inability of Sir Robert Peel to counter the ill-effect of this by acting on 'fixed church principles.'[45] At the same time, he had nothing but admiration for Gladstone, whose private secretary at the Board of Trade Northcote became in June 1842: 'he is the one whom I respect beyond measure; he stands almost alone as the representative of principles with which I cordially agree; and as a man of business, and one who humanly speaking, is sure to rise, he is preeminent.'[46] Northcote hoped that Gladstone would become the centre of a new political combination: 'I look upon him as the representative of the party, scarcely developed as yet though secretly forming and strengthening, which will stand by all that is clear and sacred in my estimation in the struggle which I believe will come *ere very long* between good and evil, order and disorder, the Church and the World, and I see a very small band collecting around him and ready to fight manfully under his leading.'[47] In spite of the mystification caused by Gladstone's apparent *volte-face* over Maynooth, Northcote was prepared to play a leading part in his campaign at Oxford in 1847. After Gladstone's success, he wrote to congratulate him: 'It has brought together the younger men without distinction of party, and has supplied the elements of a very noble party which will look to you as their leader: I think men of all kinds are prepared to trust you, and though each feels that he will probably differ from you in some particulars, each seems disposed to waive objections for the general good he expects.'[48]

Northcote's expectation that Gladstone would find it difficult to satisfy his highly critical constituency on all questions was to be quickly confirmed. In December 1847 Lord John Russell introduced into the House of Commons a resolution for enabling Jews elected to Parliament to take the necessary oath without the declaration 'on the true faith of a

Christian.' Gladstone confounded his supporters by making clear his approval of this resolution. He justified his decision by two arguments. First, he believed that 'the most profound and powerful and uniform tendencies of the age' were towards the greater toleration of minorities. The church must at all costs avoid identifying herself with a reactionary opposition to this development: 'As citizens and members of the Church we should contend manfully for her own principles and constitution, and should ask and press without fear for whatever tends to her own healthy development ... but we should deal amicably and liberally with questions either solely or mainly affecting the civil rights of other parties in the country.'[49] Second, Gladstone denied the charge that the admission of Jews would destroy the Christian character of Parliament. It would in fact have no worse effect than that caused by allowing Unitarians to sit as members. The guarantee that Parliament would remain essentially Christian lay no longer in giving orthodox believers a monopoly over its membership, but derived 'from the general preponderance of Christians in its composition, from their generally representing Christian constituencies, from the admitted principles of the constitution under which they are to act, and from the high and earnest love prevalent amongst them.'[50]

Gladstone's vote for Jewish emancipation caused the same shock and dismay among the Anglo-Catholics as had his vote for the Maynooth grant, two years previously, among the Protestant High Churchmen. Indeed, Pusey wrote to him expressing sentiments as bitter as those of Charles Wordsworth: 'I voted for you out of personal affection and regard for you, and the confidence I had in you as a religious man. Had I known that you would have joined in what I account an anti-Christian measure, I could not have helped to put you into a position which would have led you to such a result. I would for your own soul's sake that you had been out of Parliament ... It seems one more hint to Churchmen to have nothing to do with politics. Your election seemed the one thing which could still interest me in them.'[51] But, whereas Wordsworth maintained his implacable opposition to Gladstone, Pusey continued to vote for him while he remained the member for Oxford University. Although he disapproved of many of Gladstone's acts, Pusey never again lost confidence in his 'conscientious motives, high principled sagacity and righteousness.'[52] In the same way, his close friend among the elder generation of Anglo-Catholics, John Keble, could describe Gladstone as 'Pusey in a blue coat; and what can be said more for any layman? ... I am so sure of him that I don't at all mind here and there a speech or a vote which I can't explain.'[53]

If both generations of Anglo-Catholics shared the same admiration for Gladstone's moral character, the younger had their special reason for being attracted to him. This was their understanding of the way his views on the question of church-state relations were becoming more and more liberal. They gave in particular a most enthusiastic response to the major speech he made during the debate on the Ecclesiastical Titles Bill in 1851.

The bill was the result of the establishment by papal brief the previous year of a Roman Catholic hierarchy with territorial titles in Britain for the first time since the Reformation. Lord John Russell, the prime minister, claimed that the bill's purpose was to protect the Protestant religion, and especially the Church of England, from an aggressive papacy, but no doubt the whig government also hoped to take advantage through it of the widespread spirit of 'No-Popery' in the country.

For Gladstone, the major question was whether the restoration of the Catholic hierarchy was a matter affecting the temporal or spiritual function of that church. If the latter, as he himself believed, then the bill, if not challenged, would set a very dangerous precedent for state interference in the spiritual affairs of the Church of England itself. The surest defence of the church would rather be to trust in the principle of religious liberty, not only for itself, but for all religious bodies: 'to cite and appeal to the principle of religious freedom is not merely a cant phrase, but it is a stern reality ... I ask you again, will you go backward or forward in the career of religious freedom? Have you no faith in your free institutions?'[54] Gladstone's arguments were warmly welcomed by Beresford Hope. In particular, he agreed with 'that only true, consistent and rational religious liberty which allows to all denominations liberty of self-development within the bounds of order and morality – to Dissenters, and not only to Dissenters, but also to the Church of England.'[55]

The following year, 1852, Gladstone made his arguments more widely known outside Parliament with the publication of an open letter to the Reverend William Skinner, bishop of Aberdeen and primus of the Scottish Episcopal church. In this letter Gladstone emphasizes the necessity of recognizing how fundamentally the nature of the state had changed in the previous decades. It had been possible previously to believe that the state had a religious character, and that this must be preserved even if it meant sacrificing 'the lesser good of full liberty of conscience.' Recent developments, especially the extension of religious toleration, had completely altered the situation, with the result that 'while the tone and amount of personal religion have been rising in general society, the religious character of the State has progressively declined.' Any such character now claimed by the state would, therefore, be 'a bastard and deceptive one' and, if persisted in, would prove harmful to the Christian nature of the country. Moreover, it was now true that 'religion can live without the aid of Parliament.' The future of the Church of England would no longer depend on its connection with the state, but on its ability to construct a system of self-government that would allow it to exploit 'the strong sentiment of personal duty and responsibility amongst its members.'[56]

Gladstone was in fact now prepared to accept the possibility of the disestablishment of the Church of England if this was the only way to protect its spiritual nature. He had come a long way from the time when, as 'the rising hope of the stern, unbending Tories,' he had believed the church to be the conscience of the state. Now, as the representative figure of 'a High Church Liberalism [which] bids fair to be the order of the day,'[57] he was prepared to support the principle of 'a free Church in a free State.'

The reactions of High Churchmen to Gladstone's arguments were varied. Charles Wordsworth, predictably, was outraged. He was convinced that Gladstone's conversion to the principle of 'religious liberty' was the result not of conviction, but of political expediency. His failure to create and lead a party devoted to the defence of the interests of the church during the Maynooth controversy in 1845 had left Gladstone in an isolated political position, an isolation accentuated by the death of Peel. Wordsworth interpreted Gladstone's 'conversion' in the light of this development. Gladstone's future career now seemed to depend on his winning the support of the electorally powerful dissenting interests in the country. It was not surprising, so Wordsworth argued, that Gladstone was now adopting opinions which, in the end, must inevitably force him to accept 'pure Voluntaryism, or, in other words, the separation of Church and State.'[58]

Even Anglo-Catholics had reservations about some of Gladstone's arguments. Pusey, in particular, was concerned about the implication of the greater role claimed for laymen in the government of the church, which he believed essentially contradictory to the practice of the apostolic church. The *Guardian*, the mouthpiece of the younger generation, took this opportunity to reiterate its reservations about some of Gladstone's recent political activity, especially his support of Jewish emancipation, which, it considered, had been given without due thought for its effect on the church. At the same time, it gave an enthusiastic welcome to the idea of 'religious liberty' for all religious bodies in the community, including the established church.[59]

From now on the younger Anglo-Catholics proved ready to keep, more or less, in step with Gladstone in his intellectual advance towards liberalism. Their attitude was described to Gladstone by Stafford Northcote in January 1853, after another bitterly fought contest at Oxford University: 'they feel that you are after all a thoroughly Oxford man, one whose faults (if there be any) are the faults of Oxford, whose views and principles and models of thinking are essentially their own; that if an Oxford man was challenged to show what his own system could produce, you would be of all others to whom he would point and with pride. Then they feel that you have been exposed to the struggle of real political life, have borne your full share of it; and they see by the effect it has had upon you what are the corrections and modifications the raw Oxford animal requires to make him a statesman ... And every step you take in advance forces them to look into themselves and their principles again and again.'[60]

As the member for Oxford University, Gladstone was able to maintain the political support of these Anglo-Catholics who were to play a large part in the affairs of the university during the 1850s. He had less success with the next generation of Oxford Anglo-Catholics. They were dismayed in particular by Gladstone's decision in 1859 to join Palmerston's government, as the prime minister was clearly influenced in church matters by his evangelical son-in-law, Lord Shaftesbury. In the 1865 election at Oxford, they therefore voted for Gathorne-Hardy, a leading Conservative politician, thus ensuring Gladstone's defeat. After eighteen years the alliance established by Gladstone between liberals and Anglo-Catholics at the university had broken, making possible the triumph of 'the Tory High and Dry section of the Oxford electorate ... the most fanatically retrograde party in the whole country.'[61] For his part, after his defeat, Gladstone accepted an invitation to stand for South Lancashire. He made clear in his first speech to his new constituents that his policy would now be to build a bridge between the England of the past, which Oxford represented, and the England of the future, which he saw foreshadowed in the Lancashire community with 'its development of industry, growth of enterprise, progress of social philanthropy, prevalence of toleration, and ardent desire for freedom.'[62]

NOTES

This paper was written before the publication of Perry Butler's *Gladstone: Church, State, and Tractarianism* (Oxford, 1982), which discusses Gladstone's changing relations with the Anglican High Churchmen over a longer period than covered here. Butler has made the same distinction as I do between the Protestant High Churchmen and the Anglo-Catholics, emphasizing the importance of William Palmer amongst the former. He has a valuable discussion of Gladstone's relationship to the Oxford movement between 1833 and 1851.

1 *Correspondence on Church and Religion of William Ewart Gladstone*, ed. D.C. Lathbury (2 vols., London, 1910), I, 23. Cf. *The Gladstone Diaries*, ed. M.R.D. Foot and H.C.G. Matthew, Vols. III-IV (Oxford, 1974), 16 August 1840, III, 53.
2 3 *Hansard* 95: 1302 (16 December 1847).
3 The most succinct account of Gladstone's religious development is Deryck Schreuder's 'Gladstone and the Conscience of the State,' in *The Conscience of the Victorian State*, ed. P.T. Marsh (Syracuse, 1979), 73-134.
4 W. Palmer, *A Narrative of Events connected with the Publication of the Tracts for the Times* (London, 1888), 4.
5 J.H. Newman, *Apologia pro Vita Sua* (London, 1864; rpt 1962), 125.
6 G. Battiscombe, *John Keble* (London, 1963), 125.
7 J. Keble, 'Preface,' in R.H. Froude's *Remains: Second Part* (Derby, 1839), I, v.
8 J. Keble, *Sermons, Academical and Occasional* (Oxford, 1847), 128.
9 *Guardian*, 4 February 1852, 77.
10 Keble, *Sermons*, xviii.
11 John Morley, *The Life of William Ewart Gladstone* (2 vols., London, 1908), I, 118.
12 Ibid., 64. Cf. *The Gladstone Diaries*, ed. M.R.D. Foot, Vols. I-II (Oxford, 1968), 31 March 1832, I, 462.
13 *The Gladstone Diaries*, ed. Foot, 8 October 1838, II, 43.
14 D.C. Lathbury, *Mr. Gladstone* (London, 1905), 226-7.
15 Ibid., 11.
16 3 *Hansard* 77: 77-82 (4 February 1845). Gladstone had explained his decision to retire to his cabinet colleagues on 2 and 4 March 1844 (*Diaries*, ed. Foot and Matthew, III, 354-9).
17 Reminiscences written in 1897, Gladstone Papers, British Library, Add. MS 44700, f. 59 (printed in *The Prime Ministers' Papers: W.E. Gladstone*, I: *Autobiographica*, ed. John Brooke and Mary Sorensen [London, 1971], 50).
18 3 *Hansard* 79: 52 (3 April 1845).
19 R. Blake, 'The Rise of Disraeli,' in *Essays in British History Presented to Sir Keith Feiling*, ed. H.R. Trevor-Roper (London, 1964), 235.
20 3 *Hansard* 79: 837 (16 April 1845).
21 C. Wordsworth, *Annals of My Life, 1847-1856* (London, 1893), 29.

22 *Correspondence*, ed. Lathbury, I, 17.

23 Ibid., 71-3.

24 Gladstone to Manning, 3 April 1846, Gladstone Papers, Add. MS 44247, f. 302.

25 Gladstone to Manning, 19 April 1846, ibid., f. 309.

26 Gladstone to Manning, 3 April 1846, ibid., f. 301.

27 See J.B. Conacher, 'Mr. Gladstone Seeks a Seat,' Canadian Historical Association, *Report*, 1962, 55-67.

28 Wordsworth, *Annals*, 36.

29 *Letters of the Rev. J.B. Mozley*, ed. A. Mozley (London, 1885), 183.

30 Gladstone to Manning, 14 May 1847, Gladstone Papers, Add. MS 44247, f. 336.

31 *Letters*, ed. Mozley, 183.

32 Ibid., 182.

33 Wordsworth, *Annals*, 37-8.

34 J.H. Newman, 'Tamworth Reading Room,' in *Newman: Prose and Poetry*, ed. G. Tillotson (London, 1957), 75-112.

35 *Christian Remembrancer*, ns 20 (1850), 394-7.

36 Reminiscences written in 1897, Gladstone Papers, Add. MS 44791, f. 77 (printed in *Gladstone, I: Autobiographica*, ed. Brooke and Sorensen, 57-8).

37 C.S. Parker, *Life and Letters of Sir James Graham, Second Baronet of Netherby, 1797-1861* (2 vols., London, 1907), I, 195-6.

38 3 *Hansard* 94: 642-3 (21 July 1847).

39 *Guardian*, 19 May 1852, 329.

40 Reminiscences written in 1897, Gladstone Papers, Add. MS 44791, ff. 77-8 (printed in *Gladstone, I: Autobiographica*, ed. Brooke and Sorensen, 58).

41 [A.J. Beresford Hope,] *Letters on Church Matters by D.C.L.* (2 vols., London, 1851-4), II, 156.

42 Earl of Selborne, *Memorials, Part I: Family and Personal, 1766-1865* (2 vols., London, 1896), II, 306.

43 J. Martineau, *Life of Henry Pelham, Fifth Duke of Newcastle, 1811-1864* (London, 1908), 330.

44 Lord Stanmore, *Sidney Herbert, Lord Herbert of Lea* (2 vols., London, 1906), I, 132-5.

45 A. Lang, *Life, Letters and Diaries of Sir Stafford Northcote, First Earl of Iddesleigh* (2 vols., London, 1890), I, 52.

46 Ibid., 57.

47 Ibid., 65.

48 Northcote to Gladstone, 2 August 1847, Gladstone Papers, Add. MS 44216, f. 103.

49 W.E. Gladstone, *Substance of a Speech on the Motion ... with a View to the Removal of the Remaining Jewish Disabilities* (London, 1848).

50 Ibid., 8. Cf. *Gladstone Diaries*, ed. Foot and Matthew, 16 December 1847, III, 676.

51 Pusey to Gladstone, 13 December 1847, Pusey Papers, Pusey House MSS, Correspondence with Gladstone (Transcripts), I, ff. 279-81.

52 *Guardian*, 3 May 1865, 436.

53 W.R. Ward, *Victorian Oxford* (London, 1965), 145.

54 3 *Hansard* 115: 593 (25 March 1851).

55 [Beresford Hope,] *Letters on Church Matters*, I, 149.

56 W.E. Gladstone, *On the Functions of Laymen in the Church* (London, 1852), 8-18.

57 *Letters*, ed. Mozley, 87.

58 Wordsworth, *Annals*, 115.

59 *Guardian*, 19 May 1852, 328.

60 Northcote to Gladstone, 13 June 1853, Gladstone Papers, Add. MS 44216, ff. 199-200.

61 *Saturday Review*, 20 (1865), 34.

62 *Guardian*, 26 July 1865, 766.

ANN P. ROBSON

A Birds' Eye View of Gladstone

17 October 1881

The Editor of the *Echo*

Sir, will you allow me space in your columns, while thanking you for your kind expressions respecting myself, to disclaim ever having called Mr. Gladstone 'a hoary-headed old humbug.' He may be one; but I do not like alliteration. I did not even call him a dastardly recreant: but I did call him a dastard and a recreant and believe that half England would echo these words if polled.

I remain, Sir, your obedient serv't

Helen Taylor[1]

It is a truth universally acknowledged that Gladstone's great liberal reputation has not been enhanced by the references to him in histories of the women's movement. By the 1890s Taylor's sentiments would have been widely echoed among those actively seeking women's suffrage and the reverberations can still be heard in the opinion of Gladstone expressed in modern discussions of the nineteenth-century failure of women to gain (or be given) the parliamentary suffrage. But this birds' eye view of Gladstone does him less than justice.

The terms dastard and recreant are unfair. Gladstone never consciously acted in bad faith or changed his mind; he never committed himself to votes in national elections for women. Every time he was pressured into speaking on the issue – and remarkably seldom that was: 12 May 1870, 2 May 1871, and 10 June 1884 – he declared it a very significant matter upon which he was not fully determined and for which the time was neither sufficient nor right for the House to declare itself. He never considered himself to have given the supporters of the cause reason to believe him committed, certainly not committed in their favour. And a careful examination of his words shows that he never did. They may have convinced themselves, and indeed they did, that he must by his own logic be led to approve their demands, but his logic was not theirs and it in fact led him always to express hesitancy and reservations.

That is as far as my argument goes: on the evidence of his own words Gladstone was neither a recreant nor a dastard. My focus, therefore, is narrow, concentrating on Gladstone's public pronouncements, for the most part those in the Commons debates on the parliamentary suffrage for women. My thesis is that dismay at the failure of their parliamentary strategy and incomprehension of Gladstone's continued opposition distorted the birds' eye view of Gladstone. Since most of the women and their supporters were Liberals, they naturally looked to that party and to its leader, the greatest Liberal of them all, for the fulfilment of their hopes. When these hopes were dashed they did not abandon their strategy or their Liberalism but their leader, convincing themselves that it was Gladstone, not the party, who had prevented the passage of women's suffrage. This view was written into the early histories of the movement and has remained largely unquestioned in more recent accounts. But although Gladstone may have been the most prominent obstruction, one block does not make a dam. Their chances of winning a real majority were at best slim and more often nil. Gladstone did not improve them but that is as far as his villainy went. Yet it is the implication of betrayal and single-handed thwarting of the wishes of the women and of the House which still lingers around the references to Gladstone in recent accounts of the early women's movement.

Gladstone's present reputation with regard to the Divorce and Matrimonial Causes Bill of 1857 will serve to illustrate the influence of the suffragists' view (especially that of the *Women's Suffrage Journal*) on modern writers and to introduce the larger issue of the vote. Millicent Fawcett, no unqualified champion of his, showed Gladstone in a favourable light: 'In 1857 the movement among women for political recognition was stimulated in quite a different way. In that year the Divorce Act was passed, and, as is well known, set up by law a different moral standard for men and women. Under this Act, which is still in force (1911), a man can obtain dissolution of his marriage if he can prove one act of infidelity on the part of his wife; but a woman cannot get her marriage dissolved unless she can prove that her husband has been guilty both of infidelity and cruelty. Mr. Gladstone vehemently opposed the Bill. It is said that "in a ten hours' debate on a single clause he made not less than twenty-nine speeches, some of them of considerable length." '[2]

Fawcett has a footnote to a passage in Morley's *Life*, where it actually says: 'An unfriendly but not wholly unveracious chronicler says of this ten hours' sitting (August 14 [*sic*]) on a single clause: "Including questions, explanations, and interlocutory suggestions, Mr. Gladstone made nine and twenty speeches, some of considerable length." '[3] Morley gives no indication of the clause or its content. Philip Magnus, writing in 1954, gives an impression of Gladstone's role different from that of Fawcett: 'In July, 1857, Gladstone hurried from Hawarden to Westminster to oppose a Divorce Bill which the Government had introduced ... Gladstone used every method, including obstruction, in a vain attempt to defeat the Bill. He argued with passion, that marriage was indissoluble ... The Bill, despite his efforts, became law.'[4] Marian Ramelson, reflecting, as Magnus probably was, Gladstone's twentieth-century reputation back onto 1857, extrapolates freely: 'Caroline [Norton] also conducted a campaign by pen and conversation to amend the Marriage and Divorce Law Bill which was being advanced by Lord Cranworth. These amendments, aimed at improving the lot of women, found their bitterest opponents in the whole Bench of Bishops and in Gladstone with his followers: however the opponents failed to gain the day and the Bill, as amended, became the 1857 Marriage and Divorce Act.'[5]

Duncan Crow in his discussion of Barbara Leigh Smith's early attempt to gain a married women's property act, which was undermined by the introduction of the Divorce Bill, also singles out Gladstone: 'This proposal [Lord Cranworth's Divorce Bill] was even more iconoclastic than the suggestion that women should have property rights. The opposers of this second Bill had no doubt that it threatened the sanctity of the home. They were violent and interminable in their opposition to it. Gladstone, for example, made twenty-nine speeches against a single clause in the Bill, many of them of substantial length.'[6] To link opposition to married women's property rights and opposition to divorce is historically misleading, and to implicate without qualification Gladstone in both is historically inaccurate. The acquisition by married women of the rights of property was one of the social reforms the elderly Gladstone listed with approval.[7]

Thus has Gladstone's shining armour become tarnished over the years for lack of first-hand attention.[8] With this example as cautionary justification, I shall give Gladstone's own views in some detail, because to understand the strategy of the suffragists and their later assumptions and subsequent bitterness, it is first necessary to hear him as they heard him.

1855 AND 1857: DECEASED WIFE'S SISTER AND
MATRIMONIAL CAUSES BILLS

And hear him they did, at great length it is true but with considerable pleasure, first in 1855 on marrying one's deceased wife's sister and two years later on the subject of marrying at all and especially more than once. On the Deceased Wife's Sister Bill, Gladstone objected to the proposed change primarily because of the Biblical injunction, but secondarily because the relationships considered in the bill were not the same for both sexes; the principle underlying his objections was equality: 'Is this a small change? When was woman first elevated to an equality with her stronger companion? Never, till the Gospel came into the world. It was the slow but certain, and, I thank God, hitherto unshaken result of Christianity, not considered as a system of dogmas, but as one of social influence, to establish a perfect equality between man and woman as far as the marriage tie is concerned.'[9]

Gladstone's main ground for his persistent opposition two years later to the Divorce and Matrimonial Causes Bill was the same – equality. His later reputation as a devious enemy of women's causes has led to the assumption that his opposition to the bill was on anti-feminist grounds; had it been, the suffragists would have been less sanguine in their assumption of support for their cause. It is true that many advanced thinkers and indeed many of the mid-Victorian political public favoured divorce being recognized in the English legal system, but the bill had many critics like Millicent Fawcett who approved Gladstone's opposition to a different moral standard for men and women being written into law. They would not have agreed with Gladstone's opening brief admission that he opposed divorce on principle; they might or might not have believed him when he said that he had 'no desire that the legislation on this subject should be adapted to my views of Christian doctrine.'[10] But they would have agreed with his persistent opposition to the clause pertaining to the grounds for divorce, because Gladstone was supporting amendments to lessen the difference between the grounds for men and those for women.

[A]long with the principle of divorce *a vinculo* you introduce by this Bill another principle of the utmost danger – the principle that the rights of men and women, in regard to the highest relations of the marriage contract, are not equal, but unequal ... I believe that the evil of introducing this principle of inequality between men and women is far greater than the evil which would arise from additional cases of divorce *a vinculo* [if women had the same grounds for divorce as men]; and I take my stand in the first place on this, that if it be assumed that the indissolubility of marriage has been the result of the operation of the Christian religion on earth, still more emphatically I believe it may be assumed that the principle of the equality of the sexes has been the consequence of that religion ... it is the special and peculiar doctrines of the Gospel respecting the personal relation in which every Christian, whether man or woman, is placed to the person of our Lord that form the firm, the broad, the indestructible basis of the equality of the sexes under the Christian law. And I am amazed at the facility with which this question is dealt with by those who think that the act of adultery of itself dissolves the marriage tie ... But if adultery really constitutes in the sight of God that right to release from the marriage tie, and absolutely abolishes the marriage ... where do you find your title to withhold from women the remedy which you give to men? Is it to be found in considerations of social expediency? ... I must confess that it appears to me that a measure so framed is not so much designed in the spirit of preventing a particular sin as by way of the assertion – I must add, the ungenerous assertion – of the superiority of our position in creation.[11]

This speech is surely a remarkable one for 1857, confirming in the minds of his opponents the dire and long-lasting effects of Keble on an Oxford undergraduate. To state that adultery was no greater a sin for a woman than for a man and to claim that the law should recognize this principle was courageous. To imply, indeed to state, that a wife should be forgiven for an adulterous act,[12] and to attribute a contrary attitude to 'the exclusive possession of power and ... the habits of mind connected therewith,'[13] was more advanced thinking than was often to be found outside Parliament, much less in it. His attitude must be seen against the indifference of a mundane mind (unhappily paraphrasing Burke): 'Women are not, and we trust never will be again, looked on and treated as mere marketable goods, to be bought and sold like beasts of burthen; or, if such unholy traffic is carried on, it is, at least, veiled beneath decorous forms, and, losing its grossness, loses at once half its iniquity.'[14] Or Sir Denham Norreys, speaking in the same debate as Gladstone: 'A husband might commit a rape, and yet the wife need not necessarily be entitled to a divorce; but not so in the case of bigamy. And for this reason – a man might commit rape without any vicious intention. He meant to say circumstances might occur in which a man was induced to commit rape without any premeditation, whereas bigamy was always premeditated. There was no parallel at all between the two cases.'[15] In 1878 an archdeacon could still maintain publicly: 'But you know it is absurd to suppose that the seventh commandment is binding on men as it is on women.'[16]

Although there were reasons why many women were anxious for the bill to pass – it would not only bring divorce within the legal system of England but also make possible the protection of a separated wife's earnings – there were also reasons why they would highly approve the grounds of Gladstone's opposition. No knight in shining armour could have professed higher principles.

With hindsight one can see that there were dangers ahead for the women's movement in the very loftiness of these principles, which sprang from Gladstone's deep faith that Christianity was synonymous with the progress of civilization – the underlying basis of his liberalism. It was not the equality of men and women in the earthly city that was Gladstone's concern; it was their spiritual equality. To introduce moral inequality into the statutes of the realm where it had not existed before was to degrade both sexes, women perhaps more than men. But the women sizing up the past of their Liberal leader would hear the stress on equality and might well fail to appreciate the particularity of its application.

Gladstone's occasional use of the singular 'woman' as a collective noun might also have signalled doubts about his position on civic equality. This form became anathema to the movement[17] and by the seventies can serve as a rule of thumb to distinguish those for and those against women's suffrage, although in the fifties it was no more than a straw in the wind. The illustration that flowed from Gladstone's lips to refute one of the attorney-general's arguments was more ominous: 'For the House of Commons, though led by the Attorney General, to instruct the women of England on their duties as mothers and wives, which they have not sufficiently considered, or to teach them their maternal obligations, which they have so incompetently fulfilled, appears to me to be about as conformable to prudence and good sense as if the women of England were to send messages to us when we were engaged in discussing bills of exchange or a tax on bankers' checks, to tell us that we had not sufficiently estimated the circumstances of the case on which we were about to legislate, and to point out to us the mode in which our duties ought to be performed.'[18] However elevated and equal woman was by the Christian ethic, earthly spheres remained separate for men and women.

1867: JOHN STUART MILL'S AMENDMENT TO SUBSTITUTE 'PERSON' FOR 'MAN' IN THE SECOND REFORM BILL

When women's suffrage became a serious political issue with John Stuart

Mill's introduction of an amendment to the second Reform Bill in 1867, Gladstone was leader of the Liberal party in the Commons and heir presumptive in the country. Although Disraeli had twice committed himself in favour of votes for women, the leaders of the women's parliamentary suffrage movement were radicals or liberals who assumed that most of their support would come from the party now led by the unmuzzled member for South Lancashire. They expected a long struggle, however, and were encouraged by the more than eighty supporters Mill's motion found.[19] They did not expect the Liberal leader to be among them and they were right. Nor did he speak with Mill; in fact he did not speak at all, unless 'No, no' counts (one of those interjections which, as Mill would have it, are hard to refute).

The remark which called forth the 'No, no' was made by Sir George Bowyer in support of Mill: he defined Gladstone's position on the suffrage as based on 'a principle that every body was entitled, in the absence of some special disqualification, to exercise the franchise.'[20] When Mill himself had said earlier: 'As was most truly said by my right hon. Friend the Member for South Lancashire, in the most misunder- stood and misrepresented speech[21] I ever remember; to lay a ground for refusing the suffrage to any one, it is necessary to allege either personal unfitness or public danger,'[22] Gladstone had said nothing. The implica- tions of the two versions are significantly different and Mill's was the much more accurate understanding. Gladstone's concern was not with the principle of inclusion but with that of exclusion; Gladstone did not consider universal suffrage practicable and he was anxious to determine the necessary grounds for denying any group the vote. If Gladstone felt that women en masse were unfit to exercise the vote or that there was public danger in their getting the vote, or both, then he would feel justified in excluding them from a franchise bill. This was the principle Gladstone had adopted for determining the refusal of the franchise. (Mill had met him on his own grounds and very nearly convinced him.) It is important to note that Gladstone's principle is in the negative. It does not specify who should exercise the franchise; it specifies the grounds for refusing. This principle, therefore, has nothing necessarily to do with equality; in fact, it has nothing whatever to do with it.

1870: JACOB BRIGHT'S BILL TO REMOVE WOMEN'S DISABILITIES

Gladstone's first speech in the House of Commons on women's suffrage was on 12 May 1870; he rose in response to pressure from Jacob Bright for some indication of the government's position after Bright's bill had received a majority of thirty-three on its second reading in the previous week. (The implications of the majority were not clear since the vote had been in a relatively small House, only 219 taking part.) Gladstone spoke briefly and mainly to explain why he did not wish to speak at all. His position was stated clearly (a relative term with reference to Gladstone); there are two considerations: 'the importance of a measure is not the only criterion of the question whether it is the duty of a Government as such upon all occasions to take part in the debate. Whenever the Government in its official capacity takes part in a debate, it is supposed and understood to invade the liberties of the independent Members of this House, and that is a consideration which often makes it desirable to leave even questions of very considerable importance outside the direct action of the Government, which direct action again has a tendency to draw them within the sphere of political party – a result not always to be desired.'[23]

Gladstone never minimized the importance of the question, consistently saying that the matter demanded full and free discussion untainted by party politics. But having been compelled to rise and speak for the government, he outlined his government's position succinctly: 'We do not attempt to limit the freedom of anyone either in the official body or elsewhere; but, undoubtedly, there is a prevailing opinion, which I, for one, strongly entertain in common with all those who are sitting near me, that it would be a very great mistake to proceed with this Bill.'[24] Gladstone, speaking as prime minister, made it clear both that 'the Government are convinced that the matter is one on which the House is perfectly competent to act for itself,' and that they were 'both surprised and disappointed at the result of the debate on Wednesday last.'

Then Gladstone, speaking simply as the member for Greenwich, gave them his personal reasons for 'cheerfully' casting his vote with the opponents of the bill. He had not been convinced by the arguments. The effects of the proposed ballot, mentioned by supporters of the bill, could not be anticipated; he was not willing to assume that when the Ballot Bill became law, the character of elections would be transformed. Gladstone did not say, he did not even imply, that if in fact the elections were transformed, one objection to women voting would be removed. He simply said that the beneficial effect of the ballot was only an assumption; as an argument in favour of women voting, therefore, it is faulty. Gladstone did not himself put forward any connection between the ballot, the turbulence of elections, and voting women. The next argument brought forward by Bright's supporters that he discussed was the need of property held by women to be represented. He objected to the illogicality of this particular bill: if qualified widows and spinsters voted, then surely married women should too – perhaps through the proxy of a male relative as in Italy. The 'if's with which he prefaced his arguments were, however, not actual conditionals but a debater's tool. 'If that be so,' 'if it be true,' then such and such should logically follow. His listeners should have realized that they were hearing Gladstone's rebuttals, not his convictions, when his argument led to seeming advocacy of the vote for married women; Gladstone supporting the vote for married women in 1870 was as likely as Gladstone accepting women's advice on a tax on bankers' cheques in 1855.

Having addressed the particular points made in the debate by those in favour of the bill, Gladstone then gave his personal reasons for not supporting 'this measure,' an ambiguous term which his listeners might understand to refer either to female suffrage in principle or to Bright's bill in particular. This ambiguity, coupled with Gladstone's debating technique, led to the suffragists misinterpreting the speech and quoting sentences as setting out conditions which, if met, would bring Gladstone's support. But in the context of the debate, it is clear, Gladstone was opposing women's suffrage unconditionally because there was insufficient need or demand to 'justify such an unsettling not to say uprooting, of the old landmarks of society.'[25] He based his opposition not on unfitness but on public danger. In conclusion, Gladstone declined to go into the general arguments, saying it was nearly two o'clock in the morning, and 'the practical matters that we have in hand are amply sufficient for our energies and our best attention.'[26] Although to many deeply concerned over women's rights such a conclusion might sound like a dismissal, to Gladstone it was no more than a statement of fact; there was not sufficient time to allow for the full discussion of such a significant question and the full exploration of the possible consequences. Gladstone a few minutes later entered the lobby with the majority and the bill was defeated 222 to 96.

Lydia Becker began her editorial in the *Women's Suffrage Journal* following the division with a calm assessment of the parliamentary campaign. She pointed out that 'those who contemplated the possibility of the Bill passing unopposed, did not for one moment imagine that if serious opposition were raised the question could be settled in a single session.'[27] Gladstone's position, however, raised her wrath. Either she did not listen, or she did not believe, when Gladstone said in debate that the government 'do not attempt to limit the freedom of anyone either in the official body or elsewhere.' Her reaction was one of outrage:

For some reason, best known to itself, so soon as the government learned that the House had accepted the principle of the Bill, it changed its attitude of neutrality to one of deadly hostility to the measure ... Instead of permitting freedom of action to his colleagues, Mr. Gladstone forbade all of them who were in favour of the Bill to vote with Mr. Bright, while not only were those members of government who opposed it allowed to vote, but every man within reach of the treasury whip received an urgent summons to attend and vote us down. This course was taken by the first minister of the crown ... Under these circumstances, a House assembled at one o'clock in the morning, not to hear reason, but to vote according to the word of command, rejected the Bill ...

We cannot accept the vote of the Friday morning as a reversal of the verdict of the previous week ... So long as the scales of judgment were weighted with reason and argument alone, the balance was declared in our favour. Then the weight of executive power was thrown into the scale against us, and like the sword of the barbarian king it overpowered everything else by arbitrary force.[28]

Whether or not Gladstone was responsible for the size of the opposition vote, Bright's tactics in rousing him to speak were poor ones, illustrating the radicals' faulty interpretation of Gladstone's beliefs on women's suffrage. Nonetheless, Bright repeated them the following year.

1871: JACOB BRIGHT'S SECOND BILL TO REMOVE WOMEN'S DISABILITIES

When Gladstone rose almost exactly twelve months later (3 May), he again made it clear that he was rising only in response to the demand of both the mover (Jacob Bright) of the second reading of the Women's Disabilities Bill and the mover (E.P. Bouverie) of the amendment (to leave out the word 'now' and to add the words 'upon this day six months') to know the position of the government. He prefaced his remarks with a disclaimer which may indicate an awareness that his abrupt conclusion the previous year had been misunderstood and caused irritation: the government was not abstaining 'from taking any part whatever in this discussion ... upon the ground that their mind and time are overcharged with public business.' He then explained in the same terms as the previous year his reluctance to express an opinion: 'we wish in this country that our legislation should be founded on mature and on free consideration of subjects by the public, and we believe that the consideration would be prejudiced by a too early announcement of the views and intentions of the Government on public questions; for a deliberate judgment would be much prejudiced by considerations of party which it is hardly possible to keep out of subjects of this sort after a deliberate expression of its opinion by the Executive Government.'[29] It was therefore right, he concluded, that members of the Liberal party should be free to vote in accordance with their own views and members of the executive free to express their own views. Of some significance, in light of Lydia Becker's denunciation of his attitude in the last debate, was his giving no indication that he was aware of having failed to permit freedom of expression to his colleagues the previous year or of having been thought to have so failed. Indeed, Jacob Bright had received a 'Hear, hear' from Gladstone when he said he hoped it would be a free vote.[30]

Gladstone then stated unequivocally his own position: he was not prepared to vote with Jacob Bright. His main reason was that although he did not think 'our present law perfect I am unwilling to adopt, by the second reading of the Bill, the principle of a measure for its [the present law's] amendment until I have some better prospect than I have at the present moment as to the satisfactory nature of the particular Amendment proposed.'[31] The 'nature of the particular Amendment' means women's suffrage. In the following years parts of this speech were frequently quoted as showing that Gladstone was not opposed to the principle of women's suffrage, but to this particular bill; that is, the 'particular Amendment' is taken to mean Bright's bill, and suffragists saw the arguments which followed his initial statement as implying that if certain objectionable features of Bright's bill were removed then Gladstone would lend his support to the principle of women's suffrage. But these arguments were not conditions; they were, as in the earlier debate, a debater's answer to his opponents' points, following the statement of his personal position – normal debating technique. Gladstone, first – to his own satisfaction – made it quite clear that he did not support the principle underlying Bright's proposed amendment of the present imperfect law. He stated strongly 'his opposition to these revolutionary measures,' and concluded this outline of his own personal position with praise for John Stuart Mill in general but with dissent in particular: 'For the character of Mr. Mill I have a profound respect, and to his authority I should always be inclined to attach much weight; but from his reasoning on this subject I am compelled altogether and fundamentally to dissent.'[32] He then moved on to his opponents' arguments and gave his specific objections to Bright's bill. The first great objection concerned the bill's necessitating 'the personal attendance of women to give their votes ... which would consequently involve them in the general proceedings of contested elections.'[33] Gladstone then quite naturally went on to discuss the possible effect of the ballot on the nature of the proceedings, since that point had been raised by proponents of the bill. He admitted that in other countries secret voting had made elections comparatively tranquil. He hoped the results would be similar in England. At the same time he expressed some nostalgia for the elections of his youth and little love for those of the present. 'But while we have got rid of all that was attractive, we retain much that is dangerous and demoralizing.' Gladstone concluded this point in the argument by coming back to the more specific matter of women's attending elections, tranquil or no. 'I am inclined to say [which surely means he is saying] that the personal attendance and intervention of women in election proceedings ... would be a practical evil not only of the gravest, but even of an intolerable character.'[34] Attendance and intervention would be intolerable; he could not make his opposition much clearer.

After briefly making the point, elaborated upon the previous year, that no bill could be satisfactory that discriminated against married women, Gladstone took up his opponents' argument that women were already voting in municipal elections and, by his own government's act, voting and running in school-board elections. He considered it right that it should be so but they were asked to go further and extend the same principle to national elections. Gladstone would 'go so far as to admit that my hon. Friend [Bright] has a presumptive case for advocating some change in the law; although for my part, I will go no further until I know more of the nature of the change to be effected.'[35] Gladstone was caution itself. A 'presumptive case for advocating some change in the law' was not agreement, and refusal to go any further was disagreement; 'some change in the law' was not a synonym for women's suffrage. 'Without giving any positive opinion on that subject,' he mentioned again as worthy of discussion the possibility broached the previous year of a male proxy for female property owners, but as a substitute for women's voting, not as an argument in its favour.

There was no case, he continued, even a presumptive one, to be entertained 'so far as grievance is concerned ... with regard to the higher circles, to those who are familiarly called the "upper ten thousand." '[36] But he recognized that farther down the social scale there were of necessity many independent single women who had to assume the burdens that belonged to men in providing for their own subsistence. And he recognized that 'they approach the task under greater difficulties than attach to their more powerful competitors in the battle of life.' There was here again no indication of support for the vote. Nor was there when he expressed his disquietude that 'for some reason or other ... women obtain much less than justice under the social arrangements of our life.' He disliked seeing men doing women's jobs particularly because he rarely saw women in 'an employment that ought more naturally to be in the hands of a man.'[37] In concluding this part of his speech Gladstone made another statement that was later picked out to show he was persuaded of the rightness of the suffragists' case: 'I may be told that there is no direct connection between this and the Parliamentary franchise – and I admit it; but, at the same time, I am by no means sure that these inequalities may not have an indirect connection with a state of law in which the balance is generally cast too much against women and too much in favour of men.'[38] Gladstone was again precise in what he said: the 'state of law' did not have a direct connection with the parliamentary franchise. There was therefore not the slightest implication that female suffrage was the solution to the legal imbalance.

He went on to elaborate on the inequalities. The disadvantage voteless women suffered in competing for land tenancy with voting men struck him forcibly. Where the 'irregular relations' between men and women were involved, such as in the Divorce Act ('I have never yet been able to satisfy my mind as to the reasons why, in framing and passing that Act, we chose to introduce into our legislation a new and gross inequality against women and in favour of men'), and in the Contagious Diseases Acts, 'the English law does women much less than justice, and great mischief, misery, and scandal result from that state of things.'[39] At these words all the supporters of the Women's Disabilities Bill must have shifted to the edge of their seats. Gladstone continued:

I may be told that it is not to be supposed that women would in any circumstances, even if in a majority, exercise any preponderating influence on public affairs. They will not and they cannot. It seems to me a self-evident proposition [Bright's opponents leaned forward and his supporters sadly leaned back], and does not weigh with me in reference to the course I should take with regard to this Bill. [Both sides held their breath.] But the question whether it is possible to devise a method of enabling women to exercise a sensible influence without undertaking personal functions and without exposing themselves to personal obligations [the Bright hopes faded] inconsistent with the fundamental principles of their condition as women, is a question which, in my opinion, is very worthy of consideration.[40]

Any flicker of hope raised by the last phrase died as Gladstone repeated that he could not vote for the bill 'with respect to which there is no promise of modification.' But it was just possible to infer from those last words and from Gladstone's concluding statement that the principle of the bill was not wholly unacceptable. '[Y]et I am not sorry to think that some activity of thought in these busy days of ours is directing itself to the subject of the relations which actually exist between men and women in this country; and if it should hereafter be found possible to arrive at a safe and well-adjusted alteration of the law as to political power, the man who shall attain that object, and who shall see his purpose carried onward to its legitimate consequences in a more just arrangement of the provisions of other laws bearing upon the condition and welfare of women, will, in my opinion, be a real benefactor to his country.'[41] This summation in fact misled several listeners, but it seems clear on examination that Gladstone still did not have the vote in mind. A 'safe and well-adjusted alteration of the law as to political power' was hardly another way of saying 'the franchise' in a debate on the franchise. What Gladstone wanted was a way, without directly involving women in political activity, of persuading men to initiate alterations in the law to make more just those provisions bearing on women. Proponents of the suffrage, interpreting the debate, were further misled by Gladstone's abstention on the division,[42] in which the bill was defeated by 69 votes.

It would appear that participants on both sides in the debate were genuinely not sure even at the time which side of the fence Gladstone had landed on, or indeed whether he had jumped at all. Lord John Manners followed Gladstone in debate; he was surely not merely scoring a point or whistling in the dark when he said: 'He could not tell from the speech of the right hon. Gentleman at the head of the Government whether he was in favour or against the measure. He thought, however, he might venture to say that, whatever might be the opinions of the right hon. Gentleman now, he would, before long, be numbered among the supporters of the measure.'[43] Gladstone did not interject. Nor did he respond when Beresford Hope, speaking against the bill, remarked: 'The right hon. Gentleman, indeed, stated that he would not vote for the Bill of the hon. Member for Manchester; but his sibylline tones left the impression that there was such doubt lurking in his mind that in another Session he would be found in the ranks of those who were in favour of women's suffrage.'[44] Dr Lyon Playfair pronounced Gladstone's speech a great encouragement to the promoters of the bill;[45] Mr James in his *tour de force chauviniste* accused Gladstone of seeking popularity by arguing for the bill and concluding against it.[46] Most men would have clarified their position in view of the obvious uncertainty, but perhaps Gladstone felt his silence was necessary to allow full and free discussion. Such a course, if that is a right interpretation, was in the long run misleading and seen by some as close to dishonourable.

Wishful thinking as well as a sensible determination to keep up the spirits of the movement was discernible in Lydia Becker's interpretation in her editorial on this debate:

Except that he [Gladstone] declared that he was not prepared to vote for the Bill, the speech was distinctly in favour of its principle. His objection was to the personal attendance of women at elections. He threw out a suggestion for providing for the actual exercise of the franchise by women without personal intervention at the polls. In laws regulating the relations between men and women, women had less than justice. The man who should arrange a well-adjusted alteration of the law as to political power, and see this carried on to its consequences in a more just arrangement of other laws regarding women, would be a benefactor to his country.

Having thus stated, 'in terms of great moderation,' the reasons why he could not vote for Mr. Bright's Bill, the Prime Minister on this occasion left the right honourable gentleman the member for Kilmarnock in the lurch, and declined to follow him again into the lobby [as he had in 1870].[47]

Becker then addressed the one argument that she said Gladstone had advanced against the bill – the evils of personal attendance at elections – by citing the granting of the municipal vote in 1869. Optimism pervaded her account. His abstention she referred to as his 'surrender,' possibly 'hastened by the knowledge that Mr. Disraeli and his friends had come to support the Bill, and that he would otherwise be placed in the position of refusing his assent to the principle of a great measure of enfranchisement which had been accepted in its integrity by his political opponents.'[48] The editorial, after counting parliamentary friends and foes, closed on a very positive note: 'The following brief notes of comparison will show the progress made. The number of votes against the Bill is the same as last year. The number of votes in favour has increased from 94 to 151. The hostile majority has decreased from 126 to 69 ... This year Mr. Gladstone spoke in favour of the principle of the Bill, and did not vote against it ... A measure which is introduced by one bearing the honoured name of Bright, which Mr. Gladstone has ceased to oppose, for which Mr. Disraeli votes ... may be said to have established a claim for attention which cannot long be delayed.'[49]

Such an interpretation of the situation was based on a disastrously mistaken reading of Gladstone's views. Not trained in debate, Becker could not (or would not) allow for the debater's form: state your position on the resolution, answer your opponents' arguments, restate your own position. She quoted parts of his rebuttal to illustrate his beliefs. She ignored his opening declaration of unwillingness to adopt the principle of the measure, his entire agreement with Bouverie's opposition to these revolutionary measures, and his opinion that women will not and cannot exercise any preponderating influence on public affairs. She thus misled the suffragists into concentrating on the wrong man and on the wrong arguments. And in the future this interpretation was to cast a cloud over Gladstone's reputation for fair dealing with the fair sex.

1872-83: COMMENTS AND INTERPRETATIONS

The next year, when the Women's Disabilities Bill was reintroduced, the *Women's Suffrage Journal* came close to claiming Gladstone as a champion: 'The attitude of the Government has changed from that of hostility to one of friendly neutrality; and it does not need so great a change in the sentiments of Mr. Gladstone as that which is shown in the difference between two speeches on the Bill in 1870 and in 1871, to convert him in 1872 into a positive supporter of the measure. No one has ever accused Mr. Gladstone of going forwards and backwards on any question, and we have no reason to apprehend that ours will be an exception to the rule which governs his course in other subjects.'[50] Becker repeated her response to what she held to be Gladstone's main objection: the course pursued by the administration in refusing women the parliamentary franchise on the grounds of its necessitating personal attendance at the polls seemed 'capricious and exceptional in the extreme' when it had already granted them local franchises and the right to sit on school boards. She concluded: 'Perhaps it was a perception of the hopelessness, after what had been allowed, of finding a logically tenable position for resistance to the present claim that induced the surrender by Mr. Gladstone of the principle contended for in the Bill.'[51] Gladstone did not speak on the 1872 bill or on subsequent bills, none of which came close to acceptance. Indeed, he did not speak again on the question in the House until 1884.[52] So Lydia Becker reiterated her interpretation during the next twelve years and the suffragists followed her official line: Gladstone would support their claim if his conditions were met. 'Woman's suffrage under the condition of Mr. Jacob Bright's Bill would be an arm powerful to obtain justice, powerless to inflict injustice. It exactly fulfils Mr.

Gladstone's desire for a "safe and well adjusted alteration of the law as to political power," which those who are promoting [sic] confidently hope will be carried forward to its consequence in a more just arrangement of the provisions of other laws affecting women.'[53] This context for Gladstone's extrapolated words left little room for any but a favourable interpretation.

It was in this spirit that the women read (or heard) Gladstone's appeal to the women of Scotland during his Midlothian campaign of 1879: 'I therefore think in appealing to you ungrudgingly to open your own feelings and play your own part in this political crisis we are making no inappropriate demand, but are beseeching you to fulfil the duties which belong to you, which, so far from involving any departure from your character as women, are associated with the fulfilment of that character and the performance of that duty ... and the accomplishment of which would ... warrant you in hoping that each in your own place and sphere has raised your voice for justice.'[54] As the movement hitched up its skirts and girded its loins for another great struggle with the anticipated introduction of a Third Reform Bill, many speakers at public meetings referred to Gladstone's Midlothian appeal. He had asked the women to play their part, to fulfil their duty in the political crisis. It seemed logical then that when he brought in another franchise bill he would support the women's claim to a direct part in political decisions, critical or not. But there was nothing in the appeal that referred to suffrage or should have been taken, however obliquely, as a favourable reference to women obtaining the vote. His request was quite specific that they raise their voices 'each in your own place and sphere,' and in Gladstone's mind, consistently since 1855, that place and sphere were not in the public political arena – whatever his listeners might think and feel. To emphasize his position, if it needed emphasis, on 6 July 1883 he voted against a resolution in favour of women's suffrage.

1884: MR WOODALL'S AMENDMENT TO THE THIRD REFORM BILL

The speeches at suffragist rallies in the weeks after the introduction of the 1884 Reform Bill had a common theme. Although Gladstone had never given his support, and therefore there were no unequivocal phrases to extract from his speeches expressing acceptance of women's suffrage, he was quoted and summarized to show the audience and, it would seem, Gladstone himself that logically he could not fail this time to support votes for women householders. Lydia Becker epitomized the tone:

Mr. Gladstone has been in the habit of stating that he adhered to the opinions he had expressed on the subject. The most authoritative expression of his opinions is to be found in his speech in the House of Commons on the Women's Suffrage Bill in 1871.

In the course of that speech Mr. Gladstone said he would set aside altogether the question whether the adoption of the measure would be likely to act in any given sense on the fortunes of one party or another. It would be a sin against first principles to permit ourselves to be influenced by feelings on that point. The hon. member who opposed the Bill based his objection in a great measure on its demanding the personal attendance of women at the polls. That appeared to him an objection of the greatest force. It might be that when they adopted the principle of secret voting they might ensure tranquility at elections. He referred to the grievance of women farmers who were dispossessed because they had no vote, and he said he believed that in the competition for that particular employment women suffered in a very definite manner in consequence of their want of a qualification to vote. He admitted that there was more presumption for a change in the law than the opponents of the measure were prepared to own. Although he was unable to vote for the Bill as it stood, he was not sorry to think some activity was directing itself to the subject of the relations which prevail between men and women, and if it would be possible to arrange a safe and well-adjusted alteration of the law as to political power, the man who should attain that object, and who should see his purpose carried forward, and its consequences, in a more just arrangement of the provisions of other laws bearing on the condition and welfare of women, would in his opinion be a real benefactor to his country.[55]

This summary is not far off the gist of Gladstone's speech in 1871; the import, however, is quite altered by omissions and substitutions. The opinions he adhered to had always in the past led him to oppose the parliamentary franchise for women. Gladstone's introduction of the Reform Bill had, it is true, given the proponents of women's suffrage a number of new points. The most powerful was his claim that the bill was to give the vote to all householders of which, as the suffragists were quick to point out, 600,000 were women. He also acknowledged imperfections in the bill – there were several questions it did not touch – and he referred to women's suffrage as one of these.

Firm in their belief that since 1870 Gladstone had been perceptibly moving in their direction, a belief confirmed by the Midlothian appeal, most supporters of Mr Woodall's proposed amendment to include women felt that Gladstone, and therefore the government, would at the very least be neutral. In that case, by their count, they would have a substantial majority in the House of Commons and sufficient support in the House of Lords (sufficient, at least, to prevent a challenge to the Commons on the issue). Gladstone, being an honourable but shrewd politician, did not comment before the crucial day, apparently seeing no reason to go out of his way to exacerbate possible divisions within his party and to antagonize a part of the public, that, if voteless, was very vocal and exercised (as he would have said) a sensible influence. He kept his views to himself and allowed parliamentary procedure to follow its course without his public intervention. (He had, however, written privately to Woodall, a Liberal, the night before he was due to present his amendment asking him to refrain.) When on the next day, 10 June, Woodall was challenged on a point of order, Gladstone rose to his defence. And yet as soon as Woodall had finished his speech, during which he had animadverted on Gladstone's speech in 1871 without receiving any contradiction or interjection from Gladstone, the latter rose to his feet and in a few minutes brought down the hopes that had risen to fever pitch over the previous months.

This speech, Gladstone's last on the subject of women's suffrage, was a summation of his basic views and typical of his tactics. The grounds on which he rejected the amendment are quite explicit:

There are two questions ... whether women should be enfranchised ... [and] whether that enfranchisement should be effected by a clause introduced in Committee on the present Bill. Now, on the first of these questions I have no opinion to give on the present occasion ... My hon. Friend has referred to a speech of mine. I have not recently referred to it; but so far as my memory serves me, I am not aware of having departed from the general sentiments it embraced; and my own opinions on this subject, if I am to describe them in a very rude outline, are that this is a question of immense difficulty; that it is a question upon which nothing hasty should be done – a question which requires to be absolutely sifted to the bottom; a question which ought to be dissociated from every notion of Party, and every element of political consideration, and upon which the House can only by strict adherence to its Rules arrive at any satisfactory conclusion.[56]

At this time, on the principle, there was no need to commit himself and it would have been politically foolish to do so. Gladstone then addressed himself to the second question, the introduction of this amendment to this bill: 'Not holding myself the most extreme views as to the first [question], I certainly entertain myself, and I have to declare on the part of my Colleagues, the strongest conviction that it is not fit, but unfitting in every sense of the word, to attempt to effect this enfranchisement by the introduction of a clause in Committee on the present Bill.'[57] There seems little reason to doubt Gladstone's sincerity on the second point. He had said many times in debate that he did not want to overload his bill; he was well aware that its success was not assured either in the Commons or the Lords. The cabinet was divided as was the party on the question of women's suffrage, and it was an issue which aroused passion and defied compromise. On the principle of female franchise, one could not be a little bit pregnant; either one was or one was not in favour of the principle of Woodall's amendment. Gladstone himself preferred not to discuss the principle, and with good reason. He undoubtedly wanted a full non-party discussion – the fact that such was impossible did not prevent his wanting it. This is not to fall into the trap of psychohistory but to take Gladstone at his word:

No measure of this importance [the Reform Bill] ever had one-tenth part of the difficulties and dangers to apprehend which this measure has had to apprehend from its indirect and even unavowed friends. It has been our duty to take into consideration all these propositions; and we have determined in our own mind ... to reduce our proposal to a form of strict simplicity, intelligible to the country, not mixed up with a multitude of detailed proposals ... We will disclaim all responsibility for the measure if my hon. Friend [Woodall] carries the Motion he has in view ... But this is no passionate conclusion ... There are among us those who are positively friendly to the proposal of my hon. Friend in wishing it well – going, perhaps, as far as my hon. Friend in wishing it well; but it is strictly a judgment of prudence; and we have felt that if we were to maintain our ground, and to put this great proposal singly in such a way as to give it a fair chance of the judgment of Parliament, it was impossible for us to enter upon the multitude of questions which might fairly be raised in connection with the franchise, and, most certainly, it is impossible to make the proposal of my hon. Friend an exception to that.[58]

Gladstone went on to point out that it would enfranchise at least another 500,000 voters and such numbers would strengthen the position of those who wanted redistribution to accompany the extended franchise, an issue that was threatening to defeat the bill.

Since members felt so strongly on both sides of the question, they were entitled to expect 'a full and dispassionate discussion and investigation' and that was 'not now practicable.' 'This is one of those questions to which, in my mind, a sort of sacredness attaches. This is also one of those questions which it would be intolerable to mix up with purely political and Party debates. If there be a subject in the whole compass of human life and experience that is sacred, beyond all other subjects, it is the character and position of women.'[59] Women have fulfilled their local duties 'without derogating from the high prerogatives of their sex' but 'it is another question how far it is desirable that they should be invited to come upon the same footing with men on the stormy sea of politics. I do not attempt to rule the question; but I say it is the largest social question you can possibly have raised.'[60] It is not desirable that such important questions should be settled now 'because of the bearing which, at this moment, they cannot fail to have upon political and Party issues.'[61]

Gladstone ended with a lengthy repetition of his belief that it was an important question worthy of consideration and of a free vote in Parliament. He did not wish to bind any one of his colleagues or his followers, 'provided only that [they] take the subject from the vortex of political contention,' for it should be dealt with 'carefully' and 'solemnly.' However, 'I am,' he declared, 'bound to say, while thus free and open on the subject myself, that with regard to the proposal to introduce it into this Bill, I offer it the strongest opposition in my power, and I must disclaim and renounce all responsibility for the measure should my hon. Friend succeed in inducing the Committee to adopt his Amendment.'[62] On this note Gladstone sat down. On 12 June the amendment was easily defeated (271 to 135), 104 'known friends' of women's suffrage voting with Gladstone at the whip's behest.

The *Women's Suffrage Journal*'s immediate reaction was a triumph of positive thinking: 'an examination of the division list, taken together with the extraordinary circumstances under which the vote was taken ... justify us in the assumption that the seeming defeat is a virtual victory.'[63] Becker, a staunch Liberal, recognized the necessity of taking 'into account the intense hostility to the enfranchisement of women which is known to be entertained by some members of the Cabinet, and the difficulty thereby placed in the way of the Government allowing the Liberal party to vote according to its convictions.' She realized that friends of the movement would be very hesitant about endangering the Reform Bill for the women's sakes. After the 'strongest pressure' had been put on members, there could be no hope when Gladstone 'in the most emphatic and impassioned manner declared that the Government would decline all further responsibility for the Franchise Bill if the clause were adopted.'[64] She claimed somewhat bitterly that Gladstone, by refusing a free vote, had made it a party question (Gladstone felt that Woodall had done that). The editorial pages concluded with a straightforward summary, without comment, of the speeches, including Gladstone's.

The stiff-upper-lip response of the *Women's Suffrage Journal* was echoed in the speeches at the rallies held throughout the summer. There was still hope: the House of Lords might be persuaded to adopt the women's cause. Even after the Lords dimmed that hope by delaying the Franchise Bill until the autumn, the possibility of a supplementary franchise bill for 1885 (the Reform Bill would not come into effect until the end of that year) was optimistically contemplated.[65]

As long as there remained the chance that Gladstone would eventually allow a free vote, he was for the most part treated respectfully by the *Women's Suffrage Journal* – with one notable exception. On 26 September, journeying from Scotland, he was presented with an address by the local Liberal Association as his train stopped in Preston station. Part of his reply, which brought a mild reproof from the *Women's Suffrage Journal*, read: 'Well, I have shown that the Franchise Bill was a very simple measure, but everything was done by the Tories whenever they could to make it complicated. Why, what did they do? They tried to bring in a woman's franchise. What was the object of that? Do you suppose they were fond of the woman's franchise? (Laughter.) If they were so fond of a Woman's Franchise Bill why did they not bring one in when they were in office for six years? No, gentlemen, their object was to weight the Franchise Bill, and make, as I have said, the ship carry such a cargo as to swamp it.'[66] However, Gladstone's explanation of this slip of the tongue was reported in the next issue of the *Women's Suffrage Journal* with malicious glee.

The remarkable speech of Mr. Gladstone, at Preston station, on which we commented in our last issue, was the subject, on two successive days, of questions in the House of Commons from Mr. Tomlinson. The hon. member for Preston did not succeed in eliciting from the Prime Minister any very clear exposition of the meaning of the expressions he used on that occasion. Mr. Gladstone admitted that the report of the speech, as quoted by Mr. Tomlinson, was perfectly correct, and consequently that he had asserted that the Tories had tried to bring in a woman's franchise in order to weight the Franchise Bill, and to make the ship carry such a cargo as to swamp it. On being pressed by Mr. Tomlinson to state whether he referred to the amendment moved by the hon. member for Stoke, and, if not, to what amendment he did refer, Mr. Gladstone said he did not refer to the amendment moved by the hon. member for Stoke [the Liberal, Woodall], who had evinced the sincerity of his convictions by taking a course which he had a perfect right to do, and which with his views he was bound to do. On being further pressed next day by Mr. Tomlinson to explain to what amendment he did refer,

Mr. Gladstone said that when he made the speech Preston station was in a state of perfect chaos, so that his reference to the matter was not attended with the explanations which, under other circumstances, he should have been disposed to give. He, of course, referred to the debate on women's suffrage, and to no other amendment in the Bill.[67]

There are several possible explanations of Gladstone's remarkable error. He himself in his explanation seemed to imply that his reference was to the large number of Conservatives who had supported Woodall's motion without conviction but with the malicious intention of swamping the Reform Bill. The *Women's Suffrage Journal* thought that the '"perfect chaos" ... had permeated the brain of the right honourable gentleman.'[68]

In 1892 Gladstone made his last public statement on women's suffrage, and it admitted of only one interpretation. The suffragists who had put their eggs into the Gladstonian basket, believing that, if he were not quite convinced, he yet viewed their cause with favour, awaiting only the right moment for a full discussion and a free vote, and really approving of women's participation in activities outside the home – an impression quite reasonable from his comments on local elections and school boards, from his review of *Locksley Hall*, and from the positions held by his wife and daughters[69] – those suffragists would have been dismayed and outraged when Samuel Smith published Gladstone's answer to Smith's letter about the Suffrage Bill then before Parliament. 'In reply to your letter, I cannot but express the hope that the House of Commons will not consent to the second reading of the Bill for Extending the Parliamentary Suffrage to Women.'[70] But there is no reason to believe that Gladstone's convictions had altered over the years; the grounds of his opposition had not. In the letter to Smith he gave greater emphasis and detail to his fears that the nature of womanhood would be irreparably harshened should women be dragged into the public sphere by the granting of female suffrage. The main difference, however, was the greater clarity of his position now that he had no need to debate the arguments in favour of women's suffrage. There was here none of the judicious consideration of the opposing point of view that had raised false hopes among those working for the removal of women's political disabilities.

THE ORIGINS OF THE BIRDS' EYE VIEW OF BETRAYAL

After Gladstone's letter to Smith, there could be no pretence that he was going to lend his support to a women's franchise proposal. He was now eighty-three years old and no amount of positive thinking could lead to a conclusion that he was a possible convert. The consequence was the birth of the myth that he had, in some way, reversed his stand and let the women down. The myth is woven of several strands, spun from the various stages of the parliamentary campaign from 1867 to 1884.

One of the main strands was the belief that Gladstone had, especially in 1871, not been opposed to the principle of women's suffrage but had, on the contrary, laid down certain conditions that at the time prevented his supporting the bill. Up until 1884, it was the suffragist line that if the conditions were met, or if Gladstone's arguments against were answered, he would acquiesce. After 1884, as long as there was a parliamentary campaign being conducted by the suffragists, they continued to maintain that the greatest Liberal of them all had not been opposed on principle to the vote for women. They continued to interpret his words and to extrapolate from them to show that he favoured the representation of women in Parliament, even though he had had reasons – for example, the inopportune timing of their introduction – for opposing the particular bills upon which he was commenting. Lydia Becker's Manchester school in particular held always that Gladstone's arguments put him, whether or not he admitted it, on their side. This belief had as a necessary corollary the stab-in-the-back interpretation of his role in 1884.

To sustain this interpretation, it was necessary to see Gladstone not only as a rock but as a one-man dam in the triumphantly flowing suffragist river. This view was developed by Lydia Becker in the pages of the *Women's Suffrage Journal*. It was Becker who claimed in 1870 that Gladstone had called out the party whip to defeat a bill that had received a majority of thirty-three in the House on its Second Reading. This claim remains true to the facts only by omission. The division took place unexpectedly late at night in a thin House; there was in 1870 far from an overall majority of MPs in favour of women's suffrage. There are also grounds for questioning her assertion that Gladstone called out the whip. Gladstone had no need of the whip and his reference to a free vote would surely have received comment in the House had he then attempted to enforce party discipline. The defeat of the bill could have been the effect of Gladstone's personal influence or the natural response of members who realized that a bill of which the disapproved had received pre-liminary approval in their absence. The last explanation would tally with Mill's account to Charles Dilke:

It seems to me that the position of the Women's Suffrage question is immensely improved by what has taken place in Parliament. You yourself a few weeks ago could not count as many as 100 members of parliament who were known to be in our favour, & there are now, including pairs and absentees, 184, considerably above a fourth part of the House; of whom 29 voted in the second who had not voted in the first division. The amount even of Tory support was most promising, including some of the most prominent members of the party below Cabinet rank, and among others both the whips. We knew that we had not a majority in the House, and that when the thing looked serious, our enemies were sure to rally and outvote us unless the Government took up the cause, which the time had certainly not come for expecting. The rally is the first proof we have had that the thing is felt to be serious. I am in great spirits about our prospects, and think we are almost within as many years of victory as I formerly thought decades.[71]

The figures for the division would support Mill's position;[72] there was no chance that a private member's bill for women's suffrage could, in 1870, have passed through all its stages.

In 1871 Gladstone was again portrayed by Becker as leading the opposition to Bright's bill, and to him was attributed its defeat. But far from leading the opposition Gladstone had not wanted to speak to this bill, no more than to the one the year before. And there was no need, except for Bright's insistence, because (as the women knew in their hearts) there was still nothing like a majority in favour of removing women's political disabilities. The onus for that defeat should not realistically have been put on Gladstone's shoulders, however square they may have been. Even had he spoken in favour the result would most likely have been the same, the failure of the bill – but with a more damaging split in the Liberal party.[73]

The speculation, quite often the assumption, that if Gladstone had adopted the measure it would have become law in 1884 as a matter of course, seems questionable in spite of Mill's earlier optimism. An un-biased examination of the parliamentary situation does not substantiate the view that the inclusion of women's suffrage in the Reform Bill would have meant its adoption. The Reform Bill even unencumbered was not assured of passage. But at the time Lydia Becker was by no means alone in feeling a sense of unfair treatment verging on duplicity. It was she, however, who provided the apparently factual interpretation of the parliamentary situation which has been taken to provide substantiation of Gladstone's villainy. She calculated that Gladstone had compelled 104 'known friends' to vote against Woodall's amendment, thus turning assured success into failure. Positive thinking reached its zenith and

Gladstone's reputation its nadir: 'The true significance of the division may be estimated by an examination of the number of known friends of women's suffrage who voted on this occasion in the Government majority. The number is no less than 104. If these 104 members had voted according to their previous wont and avowed convictions, they would have been deducted from the 271 who voted against the clause – leaving 167 opponents – and, added to the 135 supporters, would have raised the vote in favour of the clause to 239. We may therefore assume that had the question been an open one, and had the 406 members who took part in the division been free to vote according to their convictions, the clause would have been carried by a majority of seventy-two.'[74]

But were the 98 tories who formed part of the women's support in the division voting according to their convictions? Even if the 104 had all voted for the amendment, the tories would still have made up 41% of the ayes, far more than their usual proportion. (In the previous year, in a House it is true only half the size, 19 Conservatives had supported the women.) There is no mention in the *Women's Suffrage Journal*'s account of the tories whose object Gladstone had claimed at Preston 'was to weight the Franchise Bill, and make ... the ship carry such a cargo as to swamp it.' Yet there is no doubt that of the 98 tories who voted for the amendment a large number were spurious supporters. There would not have been a majority of 72 if all had voted in keeping with their genuine feelings on the issue. Sylvia Pankhurst's estimate of 13 is undoubtedly closer to the mark[75] and even that may be generous. Such a slim majority (even accepting Pankhurst's estimate) might well have been small enough either to scuttle in the Commons a bill already running into trouble over redistribution or to encourage obstruction, quite possibly successful, in the Lords. In the mythology, however, Gladstone not only personally betrayed[76] the women but deprived them of a 72-vote majority which would have ensured their inclusion in the Third Reform Act.

THE BIRDS' EYE VIEW BECOMES HISTORY

Helen Blackburn wrote the Manchester myth into history. After Becker's death Blackburn, who had joined Becker on the *Women's Suffrage Journal* in 1874, wrote a commemorative volume which combined an appreciation of Becker and a history of the movement that, according to Blackburn, had been led by Lydia Becker. Blackburn's *Women's Suffrage*, published in 1902, is the most commonly used source on the nineteenth-century suffrage movement, and Blackburn's source for parliamentary developments was the *Women's Suffrage Journal*, not *Hansard*, as a comparison of the two shows.

Both Becker and Blackburn, when reporting the debate of 4 May 1870, summarize the speech made on behalf of the government by the home secretary, H.A. Bruce; both accounts record in exactly the same words that, after explaining that there were occasions when a member of the government felt with regret that he could not give an independent vote,[77] Bruce asked the House to delay its vote until the government had had time to consider the question. But in the *Hansard* version Bruce expressed no such regret. He expressed regret for his remissness in not having consulted his colleagues and asked for a delay in order to ascertain their opinion. He concluded by saying, 'he wished to have it clearly understood that neither personally, nor as a Member of the Government, did he give any expression of opinion upon the matter.'[78] Blackburn ended the description of the defeat of this bill by quoting from the *Women's Suffrage Journal* the account of Gladstone's forbidding his colleagues to vote in favour of the bill and using the whip to call out the anti-vote.[79] Left out in Blackburn's account is the more moderate assessment of the situation (referred to earlier) with which Becker began her account: 'It would have been little short of a miracle if women could have risen from a condition of political non-existence, in one year to the acquisition of the Municipal, and in the next to that of the Parliamentary vote ... Such celerity would have savoured of the magical, and would have been totally at variance with the manner in which grave questions have been hitherto discussed and made their way in this country. No one need feel in the least discouraged because this rapid consummation has not been attained.'[80]

Blackburn's account of 1871 is very brief, again based on selections from the *Women's Suffrage Journal*: although there were the same number of opponents as in the previous year, there were more adherents; moreover, 'Mr. Gladstone's tone of decided opposition had greatly modified; he had spoken apparently in favour of the principle.'[81] The account concludes by quoting Becker's very positive assurances that success cannot now be long delayed. The brevity and extrapolations strengthen the impression which Blackburn and Becker shared that Gladstone, once opposed, had modified his opposition, that his Midlothian speech had shown the progress of his conversion, and that therefore by 1884 he had given them reason to believe that he favoured their cause. The assumption is also strong that the women had a substantial majority in their favour in the House. In her history Blackburn quotes without question, without qualification, Becker's appraisal, already quoted, of the effect of Gladstone's unwarranted and unexpected threat to abandon the Reform Bill if Woodall's amendment were carried.[82] In the context of Blackburn's account, Gladstone's villainy was clear for all to see.

In her history of the movement, written about 1911, Millicent Fawcett's account of 1870 and 1871 modified only slightly the Manchester line: 'It is somewhat difficult to deduce from [his] ... statement the condition of the mind from which it proceeded; but it was generally thought to mean that Mr. Gladstone believed that women had suffered practical grievances owing to their exclusion from representation, and that it would be for their benefit and for the welfare of the country if a moderate measure of women's suffrage could be passed into law.'[83] But she shared in full Manchester's bitterness about 1884. Immediately after the defeat she used the phrase 'throwing the women overboard' in her speeches, and later she headed the chapter on the Third Reform Bill in her history with the same phrase. With acerbity she wrote: 'The Prime Minister's line was that the Government had introduced into the Bill "as much as it could safely carry." The unfortunate nautical metaphor was repeated again and again: "Women's suffrage would overweight the ship." "The cargo which the vessel carries is, in our opinion, a cargo as large as she can safely carry." He accordingly threw the women overboard. So different are the traditions of the politician from the heroic traditions of the seaman who, by duty and instinct alike, is always prompted in moments of danger to save the women first.'[84] In fact, Gladstone did not throw the women overboard. He left them where he had always left them, high and dry, standing on the shore to cheer, but never to steer, the valiant ship of state.

Fawcett's biographer, Ray Strachey, strengthened the picture of villainy by using the word 'betrayal' several times: 'Many of [the suffragists] ... had lost their faith in the Liberal party altogether: Gladstone had betrayed them, their friends had broken their promises, and there was no more hope from that quarter.'[85] She also attributed to Gladstone the initiating of a pattern: 'The action of Mr. Gladstone and his followers in 1884 was but the first of a long series of similar betrayals, and made a rent in the prestige of the Party system from which, in the eyes of those who cared for the suffrage, it never entirely recovered.'[86]

Sympathy for the later suffragettes' policies undoubtedly influenced Strachey's interpretation of Gladstone's role as it did the Pankhurst family version. Despite Sylvia Pankhurst's more realistic estimate of the possible majority in 1884, their accounts only increased the blackness of Gladstone's character. They attributed to Gladstone the deliberate, behind-the-scenes thwarting of Richard Pankhurst's political career because of his advocacy of women's rights.[87] And, Emmeline Pankhurst claimed, 'One of the shrewdest acts of Mr. Gladstone's career was the disruption of the suffrage organisation in England ... by substituting something just as good, that something being Women's Liberal Associations ... The promise of the Federation was that by allying themselves with men in party politics, women would soon earn the right to vote.'[88]

These early accounts of the nineteenth-century struggle for women's suffrage are based on suffragist tradition, a tradition enshrined in the pages of the *Women's Suffrage Journal* by Lydia Becker. Most modern histories, concentrating on the twentieth-century suffragette movement and relying on these sources for their summaries of the nineteenth, naturally echo this interpretation. Marian Ramelson, after having set the tone by her account of Gladstone and the Divorce Bill, points out that the suffragists 'had little doubt that in Gladstone and the Liberals they had good friends'[89] (one would wonder why), and makes it quite clear that their failure to realize that he was 'an inveterate opponent'[90] was caused by the disparity between his speeches and his actions. The reader of Rose Tremain's *The Fight for Freedom for Women* is left in no doubt at all: 'Gladstone himself emphasized this duality of thought by speaking in favour of the measure and then voting against it.'[91] 'The dogged opposition of the leadership of both political parties (in particular that of Mr. Gladstone)'[92] might suggest to the unwary reader of Bauer and Ritt that Gladstone had made many more than three speeches in seventeen years – two reluctantly and only one in a Parliament where there was any real hope of a favourable majority. (Gladstone, however, fares less ill by implication than Disraeli, who had both spoken and voted for women's suffrage.) Nor can Gladstone fairly be described in David Morgan's words as having 'led the opposition to the bill' in the 1870s, except in the obvious sense that he, being the prime minister, was the most conspicuous member; and unfortunately for the success of the women's parliamentary tactics and Gladstone's reputation, the last thing his speeches of the 1870s can be described as doing is 'revealing for all to see the gulf that existed between himself and Suffragists who were, in fact, predominantly Liberals'[93] – although about the gulf Morgan is right. Midge Mackenzie mentions the majority of 33 in 1870 and quotes Emmeline Pankhurst: 'it [the Bill] was killed in committee by Mr. Gladstone's peremptory orders.'[94] Andrew Rosen does little to brighten the picture, describing how 'Jacob Bright's Bill of 1870 passed a second Reading by thirty-three votes, but was subsequently rejected in Committee after Gladstone opposed it,' and then referring to the 104 'known friends' who voted against Woodall's amendment 'to avoid displeasing Gladstone,'[95] without mentioning the tories who had voted for it for the opposite reason.

In all these accounts Gladstone stands virtually alone or else in the forefront, rallying the anti-feminists against the grass-roots sympathizers. Patricia Hollis' picture, although more neutral, also singles out Gladstone: 'On the Liberal side, however, while many backbenchers supported women's suffrage, Liberal Leaders, headed by Gladstone, made their opposition known.' Thus she too implies that the women's failure was due to Gladstone rather than to the lack of sufficient back-bench support.[96] Finally, even in the most detailed account, the strongest impression left with the reader is of Gladstone's duplicity, betrayal, and arbitrary opposition. Constance Rover, in *Women's Suffrage and Party Politics in Britain*, summarizes Gladstone's behaviour by repeating four lines of doggerel:

Perhaps the most appropriate comment on Gladstone's attitude was made in the House on the occasion of the 1884 debate by Baron Henry de Worms (Con. Greenwich), when he quoted:

> When first I attempted your pity to move
> You turned a deaf ear to my prayers;
> 'Twas all very well to dissemble your love
> But why did you kick me downstairs?'[97]

Lydia Becker's *Women's Suffrage Journal* has had a lasting success.

NOTES

1 Draft in Mill-Taylor Collection, London School of Economics, XVIII, 19. Helen Taylor was the daughter of Harriet Taylor Mill.
2 Millicent Garrett Fawcett, *Women's Suffrage* (London, nd), 15.
3 John Morley, *The Life of William Ewart Gladstone* (3 vols., London, 1903), I, 571. My count of speeches and interjections also came to twenty-nine.
4 Philip Magnus, *Gladstone* (London, 1954), 130-1.
5 Marian Ramelson, *The Petticoat Rebellion* (London, 1967), 51.
6 Duncan Crow, *The Victorian Woman* (London, 1971), 157.
7 In his review of '"Locksley Hall" and the Jubilee,' *Nineteenth Century*, 21 (January 1887), 11.
8 Except by Patricia Hollis, who would seem to have read the debate; her opinion is close to Fawcett's: 'only Gladstone consistently argued that women might want to enjoy the privileges of men' (*Women in Public: The Women's Movement, 1850-1900* [London, 1979], 168).

9 3 *Hansard* 138: 278 (3 May 1855).
10 Ibid. 147: 386 (24 July 1857).
11 Ibid. 147: 1272-4 (7 August 1857).
12 Ibid. 147: 854 (31 July 1857).
13 Ibid. 147: 1274 (7 August 1857).
14 Anonymous, *A Woman's View of Woman's Rights* (London, 1867), 9.
15 3 *Hansard* 147: 1574 (13 August 1857).
16 Glen Petrie, *A Singular Iniquity* (London, 1971), 140.
17 'This morning has come from Chapman a proposal for reprinting the article Enfranchisement of Women or as he vulgarly calls it the article on Woman' (J.S. Mill to Harriet Taylor Mill, 6 March 1854, in *The Later Letters, 1849-1873*, ed. Francis E. Mineka and Dwight N. Lindley, Vols. XIV-XVII of *Collected Works of John Stuart Mill* [Toronto, 1972], XIV, 177).
18 3 *Hansard* 138: 276 (9 May 1855).
19 In his *Autobiography* Mill says: 'and when, after a debate in which the speakers on the contrary side were conspicuous by their feebleness, the votes recorded in favour of the motion amounted to 73 – made up by pairs and tellers to above 80 – the surprise was general and the encouragement great' (*Autobiography and Literary Essays*, ed. J.M. Robson and Jack Stillinger, *Collected Works* [Toronto, 1981], I, 285).
20 3 *Hansard* 187: 840 (20 May 1867).
21 Ibid. 175: 324 (11 May 1864).
22 Ibid. 187: 818 (20 May 1867).
23 Ibid. 201: 618 (12 May 1870).
24 Ibid. 201: 619 (12 May 1870).
25 Ibid. 201: 620 (12 May 1870).
26 Ibid.
27 *Women's Suffrage Journal*, 1 June 1870, 29.
28 Ibid., 30.
29 3 *Hansard* 206: 88-9 (3 May 1871).
30 Ibid. 206: 74 (3 May 1871).
31 Ibid. 206: 89 (3 May 1871).
32 Ibid. 206: 90 (3 May 1871).
33 Ibid.
34 Ibid. 206: 91 (3 May 1871).
35 Ibid. 206: 92 (3 May 1871).
36 Ibid.
37 Ibid. 206: 93 (3 May 1871).
38 Ibid. 206: 94 (3 May 1871).
39 Ibid.
40 Ibid. 206: 94-5 (3 May 1871).

41 Ibid. 206: 95 (3 May 1871).

42 Gladstone's abstention does not seem to be explicable. I am indebted to H.C.G. Matthew for the information that Gladstone recorded in his diary for 3 May 1871: speaking in the debate, dining at Grillions, and afterwards attending Lady O. Fitzgerald's. Given the significance attributed to his abstention, his subsequent failure to comment on it verges on duplicity.

43 3 *Hansard* 206: 96 (3 May 1871).

44 Ibid. 206: 99 (3 May 1871).

45 Ibid. 206: 102 (3 May 1871).

46 Ibid. 206: 109 (3 May 1871).

47 *Women's Suffrage Journal*, 1 June 1871, 51-2.

48 Ibid., 52.

49 Ibid., 53.

50 Ibid., 1 April 1872, 41.

51 Ibid., 42.

52 The margins by which the bills were defeated in those years were 1872, 79; 1873, 67; 1875, 35; 1876, 87; 1878, 80; 1879, 114; 1883, 16 (Brian Harrison, *Separate Spheres* [London, 1978], 28-9).

53 *Women's Suffrage Journal*, 1 November 1873, 155.

54 *Midlothian Speeches 1879*, ed. M.R.D. Foot (Leicester, 1971), 94. Delivered Wednesday, 25 November 1879, in the Corn Exchange, Dalkeith.

55 *Women's Suffrage Journal*, 2 June 1884, 122.

56 3 *Hansard* 288: 1957-8 (10 June 1884).

57 Ibid. 288: 1958 (10 June 1884).

58 Ibid. 288: 1959-60 (10 June 1884).

59 Ibid. 288: 1962 (10 June 1884).

60 Ibid.

61 Ibid. 288: 1963 (10 June 1884).

62 Ibid. 288: 1963-4 (10 June 1884).

63 *Women's Suffrage Journal*, 1 July 1884, 139.

64 Ibid.

65 Woodall's speech at the annual meeting of the Central Committee of the National Society for Women's Suffrage reported in ibid., 1 August 1884, 192.

66 Ibid., 1 October 1884, 226. The editorial comment was: 'If Mr. Gladstone has been correctly reported, he appears to have overlooked the fact that the effort to bring in the women's franchise emanated from the Liberal ranks.'

67 Ibid., 1 November 1884, 239. Cf. 3 *Hansard* 293: 159 (24 October 1884).

68 *Women's Suffrage Journal*, 1 November 1884, 239.

69 His wife was president of the Women's Liberal Federation; one daughter was vice-principal of Newnham College; and another daughter acted as his social secretary.

70 *Female Suffrage: A Letter from the Rt. Hon. W.E. Gladstone, M.P., to Samuel Smith, M.P.* (London, 1892).

71 Mill to Dilke, 28 May 1870, *Later Letters*, xvii, 1727-8. Dilke had doubted 'our carrying this bill for a great time – now that we have once been well beaten – because there is no force at the back of the movement except that of justice.'

72 Harrison, *Separate Spheres*, 28-9. Harrison is realistic in his assessment of Gladstone's role.

73 'Liberal Antis were powerful, however, and in the relatively uncontaminated woman suffrage divisions of 1867, 1871, 1872, 1873 and 1892 predominated over Liberal suffragists: in only six of the 24 woman suffrage divisions before 1914 did the Liberals and Radicals contribute less than a third of the anti-suffrage vote' (ibid., 39-40).

74 *Women's Suffrage Journal*, 1 July 1884, 140.

75 E. Sylvia Pankhurst, *The Suffragette Movement* (London, 1931), 69.

76 It may be unnecessary to stress that the accusation of betrayal is based on an *ignoratio elenchi*: in order for there to have been a betrayal, there had to have been previously expressed support.

77 Helen Blackburn, *Women's Suffrage* (London, 1902), 106, and *Women's Suffrage Journal*, 1 June 1870, 29.

78 3 *Hansard* 201: 237-9 (4 May 1870).

79 Blackburn, *Women's Suffrage*, 107.

80 *Women's Suffrage Journal*, 1 June 1870, 29.

81 Blackburn, *Women's Suffrage*, 117-18.

82 Ibid., 164-5.

83 Fawcett, *Women's Suffrage*, 27.

84 Ibid., 28.

85 Ray Strachey, *Millicent Garrett Fawcett* (London, 1931), 121.

86 Ray Strachey, *The Cause* (London, 1928), 278.

87 Christabel Pankhurst, *Unshackled* (London, 1959), 19.

88 Emmeline Pankhurst, *My Own Story* (London, 1914), 14-15; quoted in Midge Mackenzie, *Shoulder to Shoulder* (London, 1975), 8.

89 Ramelson, *Petticoat Rebellion*, 77.

90 Ibid., 84.

91 Rose Tremain, *The Fight for Freedom for Women* (New York, 1973), 43.

92 *Free and Ennobled*, ed. Carol Bauer and Lawrence Ritt (New York, 1979), 208.

93 David Morgan, *Suffragists and Liberals* (Oxford, 1975), 13.

94 Mackenzie, *Shoulder to Shoulder*, 6.

95 Andrew Rosen, *Rise Up Women!* (London, 1974), 10-11.

96 Hollis, *Women in Public: The Women's Movement, 1850-1900*, 282.

97 Constance Rover, *Women's Suffrage and Party Politics in Britain, 1866-1914* (London, 1967), 120.

PATRICIA JALLAND

Mr Gladstone's Daughters: The Domestic Price of Victorian Politics

[Mary Drew is] just as much Mr. Gladstone's daughter and as little the Rev. H. Drew's wife as ever, to my mind, and I think it may remain so to the end perhaps.

[A Newnham student's view of Helen Gladstone:] one could not be ten minutes in her company without knowing that he *was* her father. Indeed I think one of the things that kept her such a very 'unmarried' person was her ingrained attitude of daughter.[1]

The proverb that there is a woman behind every successful man is well illustrated in the case of William Ewart Gladstone, who had the immense advantage of three women contributing substantially to his domestic life. Gladstone's political success was in part a family enterprise, with costs and benefits shared by all its members. Catherine Gladstone was a mixed blessing as a party leader's wife, but an invaluable personal companion for her husband. Two of Mr Gladstone's daughters, Mary and Helen, had to look after their mother as well as their father in the years after 1880. Mary accepted the full-time responsibility of caring for the 'Grand Old People' until her marriage in 1886, at the mature age of thirty-nine. Helen ultimately had to sacrifice her career as vice-principal of Newnham College, Cambridge, after Mary's marriage. Yet neither daughter regarded the domestic price as too high. They believed they were working for a greater cause. Gladstone inspired an almost religious reverence in his daughters, so that commitment to his political crusade involved a high degree of willing sublimation.

The Gladstone family necessarily revolved around the towering figure of Mr Gladstone, with little thought for the individual sacrifices imposed on his children. As Mary Drew remarked in 1898, 'so few people have ever lived their whole life ... with their father in the centre of history.'[2] Six of the seven surviving Gladstone children found it almost impossible to leave the parental home at Hawarden. In 1891, the third daughter, Agnes, who married at the age of thirty-one, made the revealing comment that 'I am the only one of the seven with a separate home and life apart.'[3] Helen remained a spinster, and Mary married late. William married at thirty-five, Henry at thirty-eight, Stephen at forty-one, and Herbert at the ripe old age of forty-seven – the last three during their parents' old age or after their death. Even in a society where upper-class males frequently postponed marriage, these figures were unusual. Stephen remained at Hawarden as rector from 1872, and William managed the family estate. This self-contained Victorian family was bound to make greater domestic demands upon the daughters than the sons, but the whole family was confined within the world that Mr Gladstone's political life created at home.

This essay will focus on Mr Gladstone's daughters, especially Mary and Helen. Catherine has already received ample attention as Gladstone's wife,[4] but the two younger daughters, Mary and Helen, have not been given their proper share of the credit for the family's political enterprise and domestic stability. Both women inherited something of their father's intellectual ability and political skills, though Mary's portion was greater. Mary is the more unusual and interesting of the two daughters because she shared her father's political world more enthusiastically and intimately, and yet abandoned it all for marriage to a minor country clergyman in 1886. Moreover, far more primary evidence exists for Mary's personal feelings and experiences, as her detailed daily diaries and vast correspondence have largely been preserved. Mr Gladstone's daughters are also revealing as a case study in the peculiar situation of the Victorian spinster, constrained by social assumptions which greatly restricted the options of upper middle- as well as lower-class women. The conventions of Gladstone's family life were founded on the dominant Victorian social values of the primacy of social duty and parental authority, however benevolently exercised.

Mary and Helen Gladstone illustrate the important social role played by many spinster daughters in middle- and upper-class Victorian families.[5] The number of women who remained spinsters was sufficiently large to cause contemporary concern. In the years 1851 to 1911, between 29 and 35 per cent of all women aged twenty-five to thirty-five were unmarried; and between fifteen and nineteen per cent of women aged thirty-five to forty-five were unmarried.[6] This problem of surplus females was largely created by a natural demographic imbalance between the sexes, caused by higher male mortality rates and aided by male emigration. Among the upper classes the problem was augmented by the number of men serving abroad in the colonial service, and by the convention of postponing marriage until the man's income allowed him to support a family at the appropriate social level. Women without husbands were anomalies in a social system where marriage and motherhood were considered the appropriate female vocations. The dominant image in Victorian literary fiction portrayed the spinster as a victim and social failure, condemned to a lonely life of futility, ridicule, or humiliation. Recent historical research on the middle-class spinster in Victorian society has concentrated on the minority who became governesses, emigrant gentlewomen, or writers. Historians have neglected the majority of middle- and upper-class spinsters who performed a vital social role within the Victorian family. Outside employment was generally socially unacceptable and these women were usually dependent on family charity. But they frequently repaid any financial debt in kind, and the extent of the family's obligation to single women merits further analysis. Thousands of spinsters cared for elderly parents until their deaths; they became resident maiden aunts, nurses, and unpaid housekeepers.

William Gladstone's views on women have an obvious bearing on the development of his daughters. S.G. Checkland commented on the young Gladstone that 'Women, for William, were saints on the model of his sister Anne, utterly pure, unhardened by the kind of struggles with the world that formed a man. Those who intruded into the male intellectual supremacy repelled him.' The sources for Gladstone's assumption of female inferiority were biblical and social. His early models of the perfect feminine type were his pious, hypochondriac mother and his capable sister Anne, who was indispensable to her sickly family until her own slow death from tuberculosis. The younger sister, Helen, always felt inadequate by comparison with the idealized dead sister, and ultimately defied and alienated her family by her conversion to Roman Catholicism and her addiction to opium. Gladstone treated Helen harshly, showing no understanding of the boredom and frustration suffered by his clever, uneducated spinster sister, who had no worthwhile outlet for her emotional problems or her abilities. 'William had absolutely no idea of the need for career fulfilment felt by women who, like Helen, had no husband or children.'[7] This idealized and restrictive view of women's roles explains Gladstone's opposition to votes for women, as in 1892 when he expressed the fear lest 'we should invite her unwittingly to trespass upon the delicacy, the purity, the refinement, the elevation of her own nature, which are the present sources of its power.' He readily accepted the Victorian concept of 'separate spheres' based on the 'permanent and vast difference of type' between the two sexes.[8]

It is remarkable that Gladstone achieved a relatively healthy, realistic, and balanced relationship with his own wife and daughters, given his assumptions and early experience. This adjustment can be largely attributed to his marriage with Catherine Glynne, which relaxed and mellowed him. The vivacious, extroverted wife humanized the repressed, earnest, ascetic husband. Many years of social contact with the Glynne sisters and the Lyttelton women ended his idealization of the passive, martyred, invalid female. Gladstone may have grown to regret his insensitive treatment of his sister as he matured, and he was certainly more tolerant and understanding in his attitude towards his daughters. But his fundamental view of women as domestic companions and helpmates remained unchanged, and was never directly challenged by his wife and daughters. They were allowed at times to engage in intellectual and political pursuits, rare for Victorian women, but only because of their relation to himself and his cause.

Catherine Gladstone ably fulfilled the supportive role of loving wife and mother without any evident sense of sacrifice, and also revelled in the political limelight. Mary commented that her mother 'loves being inside the mainspring of history, and all the stir and stress and throb of the machine is life and breath to her.'[9] Election campaigns stimulated her, she had an amazing constitution, and she hated being separated from her beloved William. Mary noted in 1883 how bored Catherine became away from Downing Street: 'She is curiously dependent on excitement, it acts just like a tonic on her – when she is without it, she rather slips down the hill.'[10] Catherine supported her extraordinary husband with a blind devotion. She rarely tried to influence Gladstone on specific political issues, but her ambition for her husband caused her to interfere to keep him in office. In 1874 she tried to persuade him not to retire, and in the 1890s she pressed him unwisely into prolonging his term of office. The rest of the family was sometimes neglected because of Catherine's anxiety to protect William's health and spirits at all costs. Her support, vitality, and extraordinary charm more than compensated for her deficiencies as a politician's wife. She was chaotic, lacking organizational skills and a disciplined mind, but confident that her daughters and servants would cover up for her. The exasperated Mary complained in 1882: 'Mama has *really* very little to do, as she scarcely ever answers any business letters herself and never reads anything but the newspapers. She still has 12 writing tables and spends endless time and strength in walking from one to the other, and hunting for papers or cheques which she has put down on one of them.'[11] Yet in many respects Catherine appeared to be the ideal wife for Gladstone, providing a loving and stable home base.

The lives of Mary and Helen Gladstone were largely shaped by their family's expectations and by their reverence for their famous father. Mary stated in her will in 1886: 'I would leave him everything I have if it were to show in everyway what I owe him.' After the 1880 election victory Mary believed that 'Heaven has called him back to this post, and I like to think of the whole world recognizing what he is.'[12] She believed her father held a glorious position in the hearts of the people, and continually marvelled at the brilliance of his intellect and the 'floods of oratorical wonders.' Helen did not share Mary's intense enthusiasm for politics, but her devotion to her father shone through her letters: 'I am sure you do not know what a spur and strength you are to your sons and daughters – though indeed I know I don't live up to what your example and teaching should lead me to.'[13] It was a small step from filial duty to personal sacrifice in this rarefied atmosphere.

The personal cost of being Mr Gladstone's daughter was quite considerable for Mary until she was thirty. Born in 1847, she had a sheltered childhood in an extended, happy family that included the twelve Lyttelton cousins as well as the seven Gladstone children. Like most Victorian girls of her class, Mary and her sisters had no formal education, except for a series of governesses and visiting tutors. Mary wrote in old age in 1919 that 'a lifelong depreciation started in my childhood when old Mrs. Talbot gave me the impression that I was "wanting," i.e. half-witted. My governess, from 10 to 17 years, continued to treat me as half-witted, so I grew up as a nonentity.' The governess gave no encouragement and her effectiveness may be judged from Mary's comment that it was Mary Herbert 'who really taught me how to read.'[14] If Mary Gladstone's adult letters and diaries suggest to the modern reader that she was not obviously ill-educated, Mary's own efforts at self-education were responsible. Her brothers occasionally helped her in their school holidays, while her voracious adult reading was guided by her friend, Lord Acton. Though this abysmal education for girls was entirely typical of upper- and middle-class Victorian society, it is revealing that Mr Gladstone thought it satisfactory for his own daughters. His sons were sent to Eton and their academic progress was a cause of much family concern. Yet, despite Gladstone's own formidable intellect and the obvious ability of his three daughters, he saw no reason to develop their potential in any structured or comprehensive manner, except for daily scripture lessons. Gladstone's attitude to his daughters' education was based entirely on the assumption that they would marry early and well, and bear children soon after. Agnes was the only one of the three daughters who justified this assumption, having five children. But even Agnes did not marry Edward Wickham until the age of thirty-one, after submitting two years earlier to her mother's veto on her proposal to start training as a nurse.

Mary was over-protected and given little independence until her late twenties. Although she officially 'came out' at seventeen, she was far more interested in music, religion, and her father's career than in the few balls she attended. It was not until the age of twenty-three that Mary first attempted to assert her independence, on the issue of a clothes allowance. Catherine gave her little encouragement to dress well and little money was spent on clothes, as the Gladstone children were 'taught to give away nearly all that was not necessary for boots and gloves.'[15] Mary admired beautiful women like her mother and the three Talbot sisters, though they clearly contributed to her own sense of inadequacy. Mary would have made a greater social impact and suffered less had she inherited more from her mother and less from her father. During a visit to Ashridge in 1870 she was tormented by comparisons with the Talbot sisters, and her own assumption that 'the gentlemen here think me a very staid young woman only perhaps rather dull.' The Talbot sisters evidently sympathized and prompted a written request to Catherine that Mary should begin to buy all her own clothes: 'I think I ought to know how to manage my money – fancy at 23 not buying your clothes – you see everybody does when they come out.' Catherine's ill-considered response provoked rebellion from her daughter: 'I don't mean to be uncivil, but I really think you rather look upon Helen and me as babies ... you may trust me to buy my clothes.'[16]

Mary Gladstone's emotional development was retarded by her family life, leaving her immature and naïve in her attitudes to sexual relationships. Her hero-worship of her father probably further limited her ability to develop close relationships with other men for many years. In their different ways both brilliant parents unintentionally made her feel inadequate. Throughout her early years Mary suffered quietly from an inferiority complex and a 'terrific feeling of shyness.' She threw herself into the social activities of the extended family and was intensely involved in religion and music, but increasingly felt the lack of a sense of purpose in her later twenties. Her social life included country-house visiting, where the men were out all day shooting, leaving 'a large proportion of petticoats' within. Mary began to judge this an overrated pastime and certainly 'a delusion for daughters': 'dining in company with 20 or 30 palls after a bit ... in fact I am beginning to feel horribly useless and idle.'[17]

Two personal landmarks in the 1870s helped Mary Gladstone towards maturity. The first was her struggle to come to terms with her unrequited love for A.J. Balfour – the first and perhaps the greatest love of her life – at the age of twenty-four. She had few suitors after 'coming out,' in part because her formidable father was a deterrent to most young men. A.J. Balfour was one of the few men who could equal her father in Mary's eyes, and he spent considerable time with the Gladstone and Lyttelton girls from 1870 to 1874. Mary felt deeply hurt because it was her beloved cousin, May Lyttelton, who captivated Balfour, while she herself had 'not the shadow of grounds for hope.' Mary confided sadly to her mother in 1871 that she had failed to prevent her love for Balfour developing, though she was learning to hide it better: 'I never allow myself to think of the future unless to try and face the reality of his not caring ... for *anybody* to know is like taking the bandages off a wound.' But she reassured Catherine that she would not indulge in self pity and depression, 'because I believe I have plenty of good sense to keep up my cheerfulness and nobody has mercifully greater enjoyment of life, simply as life.' Even in 1885 the love and hurt remained: 'how shall I be able to help loving him always but I can think *now* quite calmly of all that is past, and see that it must have been good for me.'[18] This experience helps to explain the fourteen-year gap between 1871 and 1885 before Mary fell in love again.

The second trauma that affected Mary very deeply in the 1870s was the death in 1875 of her closest friend, May Lyttelton. May's death seems to have marked the real turning point in Mary's growth to maturity. She was stunned and became more dissatisfied with the superficial and inadequate aspects of her own life. A year afterwards Mary told her mother: 'I cannot say there is much that is satisfactory to look back upon.' At the age of thirty-two, in 1879, she considered life 'a great failure on the whole in spite of there being very jolly things in it occasionally.'[19] She was unmarried and had no significant role in life. As her female friends married, she felt increasingly lonely and afraid of the state of spinsterhood.

Mary's life was dramatically transformed after 1879. This remarkable change was almost entirely due to her increasing involvement in her father's political career, which gave her a vital new sense of value and purpose. She had no other options, and May's death had highlighted the futility of her earlier existence. Mary inherited her father's instinctive love of politics, and her total absorption in political life from 1880 to 1885 probably also involved a degree of emotional sublimation after her experience with A.J. Balfour. She was exceptionally fortunate in that her father became prime minister at just the right time to provide a satisfying role for her when it was most needed. There was no social or domestic taboo on an informal career as her father's secretary, unlike the veto on the unlucky Agnes' nursing career. Mary was permitted to play a supportive role within the family setting, and because her father was prime minister, those limits allowed considerable scope for her talents and interests.

Mary's diary after 1878 reveals a growing fascination with politics, amounting almost to an obsession from 1880 to 1885. She shared Lord Acton's view of politics: 'Politics came nearer religion with me, a party is more like a Church, error more like heresy, prejudice more like sin.' The issues that appealed to Mary's imagination most powerfully were the traditional Gladstonian Liberal questions, especially justice for Ireland and opposition to tyranny abroad.[20] Mary's enthusiasm was fully aroused by the great Midlothian campaign of 1879-80, in which she participated: 'it was more than a royal progress ... the whole population was mad with excitement.' She also took an extremely active part in her brother Herbert's unsuccessful contest in Middlesex in 1880. Mary provided much needed moral support, as at Finchley, 'where it was horrid, great row and series of fights. Pepper and snuff freely scattered, we all sneezed and coughed.'[21] During her father's second ministry Mary spent countless hours in the ladies' gallery and filled her diary with well-informed commentary on the debates, enlivened by touches of humour and human interest. During the debate on the 1881 Irish Land Bill, for instance, she noticed that Lord Alington 'in fine rage with Ld Salisbury came and swore at him' while 'the Ld Chancellor was sick on the Wool Sack.' Her comments were generally partisan. She noted in her diary that Disraeli's death in 1881 promoted a 'rush of highest flown praise. First rate nonsense rampaged for a week.'[22]

From 1880 to 1885 Mary had the opportunity to indulge her passion for politics at the centre of Gladstonian Liberalism in 10 Downing Street. During her father's second ministry she acted as his unpaid private secretary. Mary described her numerous functions to her brother Henry in April 1882: 'all I have to do is – the clerical correspondence which Herbert used to have charge of – the daily orders for the H. of Commons – the petitions to H. of C. – all paper relating to Queen Anne's Bounty,

Charter House, Trinity Ho. nominations ... Then I enter all the calling cards on an alphabetical list, and surreptitiously return them – also keep the engagement books and answer invitations.'[23] Mary acted as her father's scribe and general factotum, as she noted in her diary in September 1881: 'Copied out a large important letter to Ld. Hartington. We have to do a good deal of copying and decyphering these days, such anxious Transvaal news, the Volksraad fighting over the Convention, wretched Irish things going on besides many Continental clouds.' The incessant calls on her time and attention sometimes became irritating: 'my head swims with the no. of things to answer and dovetail. 16 notes per diem and everything pulling at me at once, and all the time Mama thinking I have nought to do.'[24]

In 1882 Mary was also given special responsibility as secretary for ecclesiastical patronage. This was a function inherited from her brother Herbert, though neither of them would appear to have been suitably qualified for the position. Gladstone felt a deep responsibility for making good church appointments, and was therefore delegating important work to his daughter. Mary delighted in the clerical responsibility, 'because of the definiteness supplying some little backbone to one's life,' particularly after her aimless existence in the 1870s. Mary's correspondence with her father from 1882 to 1885 frequently dealt with the election of churchmen, providing information on particular livings and the attributes of likely candidates. She had to deliver 'snubs to poor clerical applicants' and seek informed opinions on church patronage. Mary often discussed clerical appointments with her cousin, Lavinia Talbot, wife of the warden of Keble College, Oxford – as in her search for the perfect incumbent for the Westminster deanery: 'My private plan is the Bishop of Oxford, then Church to Oxford, and Liddon to St. Pauls. But I fear the Bishop wouldn't, also I expect the P.M. may have other ideas.'[25]

Mary Gladstone's work at Downing Street included an important role as social organizer and hostess, often taking over the tasks her mother might have been expected to perform. Catherine had a disorderly mind and a supreme disregard for the niceties of social etiquette. She was a careless household organizer and indifferent hostess, with little interest in the etiquette of returning social calls and giving dinner parties. Since her husband was even more likely to give unintended social offence, it was left to Mary to compensate for her parents' deficiencies. Catherine had for many years been fairly dependent on Mary's practical management skills and had relied on her daughter to manage the household, the servants, and the accounts during her own absences from Hawarden. After this experience Mary readily took over the role of social organizer in Downing Street, working hard to ensure that the right people were entertained at the appropriate times, and that a successful social balance was maintained at dinner parties. She often had to arrange dinner parties for over forty people, sometimes at very short notice. Many hours each week were spent 'at the visiting book, dividing and selecting and plucking for the 4 parties.' A typical day was recorded in her diary in 1884: 'Horrid morning doing flowers and interviews till I was nearly dead. Drove the P.M. twice round the park and arranged dinner table and drawing room and precedence and leading in. Mama recovered from her ailment but bad headache all day, so could not appear.' Occasionally her social responsibilities at Downing Street were rather more philanthropic in nature, as when '40 Wapping girls came to tea' on 31 July 1884.[26] Mary enjoyed organizing and participating in most of these social functions. She was an excellent conversationalist with a wide knowledge of topics ranging through politics, theology, music, contemporary literature, and even cricket.

Mary used her positions as political hostess and private secretary to exercise considerable influence over her father. She had already earned her reputation as the family domestic manager, and more perceptive observers recognized that her powers could readily extend into the political sphere. Lord Rosebery was convinced that Mary's presence in Scotland would aid her father's campaign in 1880: '[the Roseberys] talk as if the whole election depended on my coming or not. They have got a ridiculous notion that I am the wirepuller about everything in my family.' This 'notion' may well have persuaded Mary to intervene more directly after the victorious Midlothian campaign. Since her father's resignation in 1875, Lords Granville and Hartington had been jointly leading the party. In 1880 Gladstone was determined to be prime minister again, yet he obstinately insisted that Hartington must make the first move. Mary and Catherine Gladstone tried to open lines of communication between the two families in April 1880 by writing letters to Lucy Cavendish, which were probably intended for the eyes of her brother-in-law, Lord Hartington. Mary's letter gave heavy-handed hints that 'the giant's hand is needed,' and that 'it would be glorious, Papa forced by England to become Prime Minister' if only Lord Hartington would 'behave with splendid humbleness.'[27] Hartington might well have been irritated rather than influenced if Lucy ever showed him this letter. But political circumstances rather than feminine persuasion made Hartington decide that Gladstone must take office since he appeared to be the people's choice. Mary's intervention in this instance was clumsy and ineffective, though not entirely unjustified; her political judgment improved with experience during the next five years.

Mary recognized the significance of her role as Gladstone's confidante within a few months of the 1880 election: 'It is rather appaling [sic] finding myself this time so much in the position of "a political intriguer." I mean people like Mr. MacColl, Ld. Rosebery, Ld. Reay and Ld. Acton write me heaps of letters, suggestions, questions, things to mention if possible to "the Dictator" as Ld. R. calls him, papers, general opinions, etc. etc.' Lord Acton assured Mary that she had a vital social role in political inner circles and Mary noted that her father 'has left the Airlies, Lowes, and Trevelyans specially in my hands to soothe.'[28] Mary helped to smooth the ruffled feelings and comfort the hurt pride of those aspirants for cabinet office who had been overlooked or treated with some insensitivity. She became her father's confidante because she was naturally more interested in politics than her mother, and had a more informed and critical political judgment. Their discussions tended to take place at the tête-à-tête breakfasts that Mary valued highly. In November 1881, for example, they had a long talk on the perennial question of Gladstone's retirement. Mary diplomatically urged her case by citing Lord Acton's views: 'how it would be a serious flaw in his political career, to damage and perhaps ruin the Lib. party by retiring from the leadership while enjoying health and strength.' If nothing else, Mary reinforced her father's reluctance to resign. Gladstone generally seems to have encouraged his daughter's involvement, whereas Mrs Gladstone seems rather to have resented and belittled it. On one occasion when Mary suggested she retire to another table at breakfast, Gladstone rejected the idea on the grounds that Rosebery would be disappointed. Mrs Gladstone commented: 'Oh no, he only uses her as a "pis-aller" when he can't get our ear.'[29]

Perhaps Mary's most important political function was to act as mediator between Gladstone and his colleagues, best illustrated by the case of Lord Rosebery. Despite mutual friendship and admiration, the relationship between Gladstone and Rosebery was strained and ambivalent. As Feuchtwanger notes, 'Gladstone was too self-centred a man to be able to meet with sympathy the hypersensitivity and inner weaknesses of Rosebery.'[30] Rosebery irritated the prime minister intensely as he vacillated about accepting office from 1880 to 1886, while Gladstone in turn alienated the younger man by his lack of generosity and understanding. Mary Gladstone tried hard to minimize the damage caused by her father's cavalier and insensitive treatment of the brilliant young aristocrat, which might easily have caused Rosebery to leave the party altogether.

Mary was very friendly with Rosebery and corresponded with him frequently after 1880. In May 1880 Mary asked Rosebery always to write 'anything you hear, which you think might be good to reach my Father.' In return she confided in him several 'Dead Secrets' upon which she requested his opinion. After failing to persuade Rosebery to take office in 1880, Mary reassured him that, at thirty-three, this was a brief postponement of a brilliant career as 'a David to Saul.'[31] But from 1881 to 1883 Gladstone unwisely gave Rosebery undersecretaryships, instead of a cabinet seat combined with responsibility for Scottish affairs, which Rosebery keenly desired. Not surprisingly, Rosebery was dissatisfied and Mary wrote numerous letters attempting to justify and explain one man to the other. Some of the advice she gave Rosebery was particularly revealing, showing how far she understood her father's limitations. In May 1881 Mary urged Rosebery to see her father to try to avoid misunderstanding: 'I am sure the more openly you speak to him the better as he is not exactly quick at understanding people's insides.' This was strong criticism indeed from an adoring daughter, emanating from her personal experience of her father's unfortunate tendency to alienate talented colleagues like Rosebery and Chamberlain. Nearly two years later, the Gladstone-Rosebery relationship deteriorated still further and Mary tried once again to reconcile Rosebery: 'My heart bleeds for you in this miserable misunderstanding ... nobody is to blame. His character is so extraordinarily simple. I don't think he knows how to understand these ins and outs ... To him in a way, political life is very simple: "follow the man you trust and wait till that man sees the proper moment to rearrange" ... I see the huge sacrifice you make in now wishing to resign. There is one greater still to which you are called and that is not to resign ... Even if it is you who has most to forgive, then to you falls the higher part in forgiving.'[32] On several occasions Mary requested that Rosebery should not tell her mother she had been 'bothering' him. This again hints at jealousy on Catherine's part at having her own role partially usurped by her daughter. It also suggests that Mary recognized that her mother often unconsciously reinforced her father's insensitivity towards Rosebery. As late as 1892 Mary was still acting as intermediary when relations between Gladstone and Rosebery were very strained. She helped to persuade an exceedingly reluctant Rosebery to join the Grand Old Man in 'this last and greatest battle ... it is in your hands to make it a lighter or a heavier burden.'[33]

Occasionally Mary Gladstone used her own position and family contacts to lobby for pet causes. In 1885 she became involved in W.T. Stead's campaign against child prostitution, despite the discouragement of many of her friends. In June 1885 she asked her Talbot cousins to impress on her father the need to take a strong line: 'Oh don't leave any stone unturned ... I feel sometimes we do not any of us work hard enough on this awful subject.' A few months later, Mary ordered fifteen copies of Josephine Butler's *Rebecca Jarrett* and tried to induce her family and friends to read and act upon it. The long-suffering Lavinia Talbot was delegated to persuade Lady Salisbury to read Butler's book. Four years later, Mary was afraid of losing her temper and 'breaking down' because of her brothers' harsh criticism of Stead's 'battle for morality': 'That cause for which he is risking everything, touches me so deeply, I cannot trust myself to speak of it.'[34] Stead's campaign appealed to Mary precisely because she saw it as a great moral cause. She did not take up other working-class social questions because she accepted so completely the ideological framework of Gladstonian Liberalism. Her awareness of the reality of widespread poverty and suffering was later more fully awakened by her experience as a clergyman's wife. Even then she continued to place the emphasis on the need to reform the individual sinner rather than transform society.

Mary fully appreciated the social and intellectual advantages she enjoyed because of her privileged position at 10 Downing Street and she employed them to great effect. She had some misgivings in April 1880: 'Isn't it dreadful to think of beginning all over again, cards and parties and things.' But the tedious chores were soon largely forgotten in the sheer exhilaration of her role, and she never resented the lack of official remuneration for her many duties. Mary thrived on life at the centre of the political world, where cabinets were continued over luncheon and the prime minister discussed affairs of state with her over breakfast. She delighted in regular visits to the theatre, concerts, and art galleries, maintaining an intelligent criticism of the arts and literature in her correspondence and diaries. Frequent visits to Oxford and Cambridge gave her access to the recognized intellectual world and she made the most of stimulating discussions with eminent academics. She found her political life 'interesting, absorbing and exciting. How often it has happened to me lately to find reality so far outdo expectations in enjoyment of life.'[35]

Mary Gladstone's political involvement caused a dramatic change in her personal and social life after 1879. A circle of eminent and talented male friends replaced the diminishing group of unmarried female friends of her youth. The glittering new group included Lord Rosebery, Sir Arthur Gordon, Professor James Stuart, George Russell, Edward Burne-Jones, and Henry Holland. The close friendship and esteem of Lord Acton, in particular, worked wonders for Mary's self-confidence. During a successful visit to Walmer Castle in 1881, she noted: 'altogether it was a very different thing to the snubbed Mary Gladstone of 1870.' Her inferiority complex disappeared as she found herself the centre of a dazzling group of eminent men closer to her parents' age and of comparable stature. She commented in 1885 that 'there are about six who each think I am specially dedicated to them in a sort of sacramental friendship.'[36]

Mary's self-esteem benefited further from a number of proposals of marriage from younger admirers. Clearly she blossomed in her early thirties. She rather regretfully turned down Edward Ottley, the curate of Hawarden and a man of 'great personal beauty' in 1879: 'just one or two differences and it might have been perfect. As it is I have had no kind of repentance though I do love him really in a way – but not the real way.' Hallam Tennyson also suffered a broken heart on Mary's account from 1879 to 1883, though the association was gradually restored to a comfortable friendship. One evening in 1883, when Hallam was feeling especially depressed, he told Mary that she must marry some time, only to receive the reply, 'I thought very likely not.'[37] By this time Mary was far more happily resigned to the likely prospect of spinsterhood, because she was finding considerable fulfilment in her political life.

To the surprise of her family and friends, Mary Gladstone did eventually achieve the goals of marriage and motherhood that her father clearly saw as the feminine ideal. When Mary fell in love with Harry Drew at the advanced age of thirty-nine, it came as a shock, not least because he was a poor curate at Hawarden and nine years her junior. Mr Drew's appeal lay partly in his intelligence, sensitivity, and 'great personal beauty.' The fact that he was a clergyman living in a world so far removed from politics no doubt also contributed. There was no question of competition with Mary's formidable father, as in the case of political suitors. A clergyman had the additional advantage of a vocation that assured Gladstone's supreme respect. Mary was able to gain personal happiness through marriage by retreating entirely from her father's political world. She explained the situation in a farewell letter to Lord Rosebery from Hawarden on 29 December 1885:

The person I am going to marry is a curate here, and it means a complete change of life to me. I do not shrink from this and I think I have realised in my soul all it means – But he is the first who has loved me who I have loved, and so though he has none of the things which would recommend him to the world, and is most shy and humble and quiet and penniless, everything else must go to the winds. As he is here, you see I shall still be more or less with my parents, so that I keep the very best of the old life. I don't expect my friends to understand it. They will think it giving up *the* most interesting and unique kind of life in the world, for one which is quite the ordinary lot of ordinary mortals – But so we are made, and in spite of everything, the one most precious gift of Heaven, is the fact of two beings becoming one.[38]

Many of Mary's friends and relatives were delighted for her, including A.J. Balfour's sister, who suffered far more than Mary from the restrictions of Victorian spinsterhood. Alice Balfour made the interesting remark that it was such a comfort to have one's duty in life clearly laid out: 'It is one of the drawbacks of remaining unmarried that one has not those plain duties put before us.'[39]

The Gladstone and Lyttelton families, however, tended to emphasize the loss to the 'Grand Old People' rather than the gain for Mary. Mary had made herself indispensable at home and her marriage would automatically disrupt her parents' self-centred routine. She was made all too painfully aware that she must view her engagement through the critical eyes of 'brothers and sisters and mothers and fathers and cousins and aunts.' The emphasis on the inconvenience her marriage would cause the prime minister was inevitably a factor in her family's response. Her sister Agnes thought it pathetic to think of their mother so late in life 'without her front tooth.'[40] Catherine Gladstone's stunned response reflected a rather selfish and possessive attitude to the spinster daughter she had so long taken for granted. Catherine expressed her misgivings to her niece, Lucy Cavendish, in her usual careless, erratic style: 'I try and put away all selfish feelings – we have had our darling Mary close with us for many years ... the difference of age is a bore but then she is so very young for her age ... I have been *immensely taken by surprise* – another drawback is poverty. It does make a difference that there cannot be more than 2 or 3 children ... as to London, I dare not think of that – and the gap.'[41] Mrs Gladstone invariably placed her husband's comfort before her children's interests, and in this case the family's overwhelming sympathy at her loss tended to encourage a rather ungenerous attitude to her daughter's marriage. However, the relatives all stressed the consolation to the 'Great People' in having the Drews living with them at Hawarden: 'It is very nice for you to have a real substantial reason for keeping dear Mary with you.'[42]

For Mary herself there was an identity crisis to confront. She was fully aware of the major break in her life that this marriage involved, and more than a little afraid that she would lose her hard-won sense of self-identity. Alice Balfour tried to reassure her: 'I don't see why your new life should be so absolute a goodbye to the me-in-the-world parts of the old. Don't go and resolve beforehand that the break will be complete.'[43] During December 1885 Mary suffered 'the great crisis of my life,' as she fought the doubts and fears that marriage would mean a 'White Burial' of 'awful overwhelming change.' By January 1886 the 'nightmare of uncertainty' was over and the wedding day brought complete relief: 'still the great wonder was to feel it all so natural, to feel I was I when I thought I was going to be somebody else.'[44] These fears were understandable after Mary's years of insecurity and inadequacy in a family dominated by her brilliant parents. Once established as a capable and popular woman in her own right, she was terrified that her own identity would again be lost, in marriage.

Mary Gladstone's fears were never realized because she had chosen her husband and future life wisely. She exchanged her father's full and satisfying world of politics for the equally demanding and all-embracing life of a clergyman's wife. Politics and religion had always been her two great passions and she was able to satisfy them both at different stages of her life. She would have been bored as the leisured society wife of an upper-class politician. The adjustment to her new life was sometimes difficult in the first months, and she missed being at the centre of the political stage, particularly during the 1886 Home Rule crisis. But gradually she settled calmly into rural married life. Her previous enthusiasm for the excitement of the metropolis and national politics was overtaken by a mature contentment in domestic routine. Mary's life was soon dominated by teas for 'district mothers,' Sunday school classes, and choir practice, while Harry prepared sermons and visited parishioners. She found fulfilment in sharing the burden 'of a young clergyman's life, the perpetual contact with sickness and suffering, Sin and Death and every form of sorrow and poverty.'[45] Six weeks after the wedding Mary confessed that she never missed 'the old life and excitement one bit' and increasingly appreciated 'the wonderful snugness and serenity, quietness and assurance of married life.' Fifteen years later, her friend Maggie

Cowell-Stepney remarked on the happiness of Mary's life: 'Perfect peace, but strenuous life and *no* dullness.'[46]

Mary's responsibility for her parents did not cease with marriage and for this reason, too, her choice of husband was particularly important. A year after the wedding she assured her mother that Harry was the ideal husband: 'He is a most wonderful person for fitting in to all my nooks and crannies, and yet at the same time keeping his own individuality, letting me propose and plan and initiate, and yet like a firm rock for me to lean upon.'[47] Harry Drew was also the right man to deal with her father. For twelve years the Drews lived with the elder Gladstones at Hawarden Castle, a difficult arrangement made practicable by Harry's busy, independent life and quiet strength of character, combined with William Gladstone's respect for clergymen. During these years Mary had two miscarriages, but was overjoyed at the birth of a daughter in 1890. In their extreme old age her parents' demands on Mary's time, care, and attention increased. She continually had to arrange for other members of the family to entertain and care for her parents, if the needs of her own little family were not to be neglected. She wrote a typical note to her mother in 1896: 'You may imagine how divided I feel, always one string pulling me towards you and the other towards Harry, but as you will have Gerty and Will as well as Lucy, I feel how well off you are next week.'[48] The conflict between filial and wifely duty was all the greater up to 1894 because Catherine so often implied that her husband's national importance must give him precedence over everybody else.

Life with the 'Great People' sometimes even tried Harry Drew's patience. In 1893 he resigned the Hawarden curacy, feeling the need for greater independence and wider experience after spending all his pastoral life at Hawarden. William Gladstone sought to arrange matters so that Harry Drew might replace Stephen Gladstone as rector of Hawarden. Mary tried to explain Harry's hurt pride to her father: 'I hope you will not think me ungrateful, but it gave him the feeling that it was mostly for my sake, and because he was my husband – and no man of strong individuality can like this.' Harry resisted the family pressure and went off for a term of duty at a church in South Africa, leaving Mary behind to look after the old couple. Fortunately for all, a vacancy arose at the nearby parish of Buckley in 1897, providing scope for Harry Drew, 'and dear Mrs. Gladstone will not feel she is losing Mary, when she is within a short drive of her.'[49] Even so, Mary thought her mother found their move even harder to bear than the emptiness caused by William's death in 1898: 'the chief revolution has been our move to Buckley after half a century of life with her. She had always dreaded the moment when we should leave the house, and it did seem specially hard that the moment should have been identical with *his* leaving it ... The parish here, with its masses of poverty and ignorance and sin was at first a fearful effort. I hated it, but have blessed it since, and I do bless it. It is a thirsty land and we can have the joy of watering and refreshing it a little.'[50]

Mary Gladstone was more fortunate than her sister Helen in her circumstances, temperament, and her love of politics. Mary largely escaped 'home duties' at the age of thirty-nine through marriage, and on balance the advantages of being the prime minister's daughter outweighed the drawbacks for her. But, with Mary's marriage, Helen inherited primary responsibility for their parents, and this involved far greater sacrifice for her. The two sisters were fundamentally similar in character. Helen's Newnham students subsequently recalled her earnestness, sincerity and simplicity, and her 'wealth of human sympathy.' She was a woman of 'compelling personality' and intense individuality, whose habitual self-control was the result of disciplining her naturally impulsive temperament.[51] Like her sister and father, she was deeply religious, and her Christianity was the mainspring of a life devoted to service to others. Helen was perhaps the stronger of the two sisters and the more single-minded. Whereas the extrovert element in Mary's character delighted in a variety of people, places, and interests, Helen was more self-contained and reserved. Consequently, up to the age of twenty-eight, Helen seems to have been even more overwhelmed by her parents than the younger Mary.

Early in 1877 Mary conceived 'my Grand Plan of Helen going to Cambridge for a year or so to Newnham Hall, a sort of College where she can learn and go to lectures.' Mary and Helen had to work hard to convince their parents and brothers of the value of the 'startling plan,' to ensure that it did not meet the same fate as Agnes' nursing scheme in 1871. Their arguments reveal the limitations of Helen's life until then. Helen told her family that her time had been largely wasted and she would benefit from disciplined courses in reading and thinking: 'whatever my life is to be, home duties, or parish, these things ought to be useful to me.' She explained her 'great need of stirring up ... practically it is impossible to do much at home, even if I had the needful energy and perseverance.' Once safely at Newnham, Helen argued that her fellow students had a distinct purpose in life, which was 'a refreshing change from the aimlessness of most girls' lives.' Mary reported to the family that Helen was transformed by Cambridge. Previously she never had a real friend, whereas 'now she loves and is beloved by many girls ... her intellectual life is stimulated, her moral life strengthened and encouraged.' The persistent sister argued that Helen's life was 'so much fuller and richer, so useful, so much influence. You see the change in her at once and I really think it has stimulated her interest in everything.'[52]

Whatever the advantages to Helen might be, the parents had to be convinced that higher education would not be dangerous and unsuitable for their daughter. Helen assured the family that Newnham provided 'a most judicious combination of freedom, instruction, and chaperonage, so that while the greatest advantages to the minds of young women are given, anything strong-minded and unfeminine is strongly discouraged.' Mary arranged for their mother to visit Newnham, which successfully modified 'Mama's feeling of aversion ... she was astonished at the refinement and grace of the place and people.' Helen particularly promised to 'take care about getting masculine – I hate that sort of thing especially.' She also reiterated in several letters that 'if Mary was to marry or I was in any special way needed at home, I would give it up *at once*.' She added that a desultory home life was 'the distinct duty' of many women, but the Newnham training should teach them how to make their home lives 'less desultory.' Another rather effective argument was that she could help to break down prejudice against higher education for women: 'the fact of a daughter of Papa (independent quite of my own character) being sent here ought to have a good influence both as to manners and religion.'[53]

The plan was so successful that in 1880 Helen became secretary and assistant to Eleanor Sidgwick, vice-principal of Newnham, and two years later succeeded her in that position. Her duties involved the organization of lectures and teaching, as well as college housekeeping and the personal and moral supervision of the students, 'insensibly helping to mould the habits and customs of this entirely new community.' Cambridge provided personal fulfilment for Helen, but there was always a conflict with her view of her family responsibilities. She often worried in her early terms at Newnham 'whether I ought to stay so much away from home another year still.' But her parents made few demands in term time up to 1885. Helen wrote supportive letters to her father on political questions, and was generally relieved when Cambridge commitments released her from the doubtful pleasures of the London season. She was nervous when she occasionally took Mary's place at Downing Street: 'I've enjoyed having the charge of the P.M. but have had the cares a good deal of whether I was seeing to him properly.'[54]

Helen Gladstone's major crisis occurred in 1886, when Mary married and Helen was offered significant promotion shortly afterwards. The Gladstone family assumed that Helen would simply take over Mary's domestic duties, as one relative commented to Mrs Gladstone: 'I hope Helen will now try to take [Mary's] place and make home her first duty. You certainly should have one of them to help you.'[55] Helen tried to respond unselfishly to Mary's marriage, but found the prospect of her own new family responsibilities 'rather grim.' 'Home duties' were 'so pressing' that she made arrangements with Newnham 'for being a great deal at home,' with the possibility of retiring altogether if necessary at short notice. The conflict of interests was intensified a few months later when Helen was invited to become the first principal of the newly established Royal Holloway College, London. Helen agonized over the dilemma of career versus domestic responsibilities, circulating a memorandum to her closest friends and relatives giving both sides of the case and requesting their views. However, Helen herself loaded the evidence on the domestic side. She argued that if she went to Royal Holloway, she would be starting with a morally wrong action from the 'home duties' perspective. Even if such a decision was justified in an ordinary case, 'is it the same thing when the parents are people (both great in their different ways)' who had given up their lives for others?[56]

Nora Sidgwick, Helen's predecessor and mentor at Newnham, was the only person to question Helen's assumption that a woman's primary obligation was to her parents: 'Most people think it would be absurd under ordinary circumstances to remain unmarried for the sake of parents, though there are careers where it is right to do so. I cannot myself see that marriage is from this point of view so entirely different from other callings in life as many people assume.' Helen's parents wisely allowed Helen to make the decision herself, but given the views of other members of the family, and Helen's own sense of duty, the outcome was a foregone conclusion. Mary recognized that Royal Holloway was 'a Serious Call,' and 'one can scarcely exaggerate the importance and seriousness of the work.' But even she concluded that, if Helen accepted, 'it would be simply impossible for her to be much at home ... she would be far more tied and bound than by most marriages.'[57] So Helen refused the Royal Holloway offer, and temporarily stayed on at Newnham with time off for 'home duties.'

Helen Gladstone felt obliged to make the personal sacrifice, even though she was so much more effective and fulfilled at Newnham than in her filial capacity at Hawarden and Downing Street. As soon as she replaced Mary in 1886 she felt inadequate: 'Mary is Mary, and I can't expect to replace her in anything like a full measure.' During the Royal Holloway crisis in July 1886, Helen did not estimate the value of her assistance to her parents very highly: 'I am not of much use to my Father while he is in office, excepting by chance in times like this fortnight – but out of office if he has no secretary it may be different. I am not of any immense use to my Mother at any time, but at least I am available (even while at Newnham) for helping in all special society things, in all times when she is not well, and in all times when her duties take her elsewhere and she wants someone to be with my Father.'[58] Helen had always been bored by society functions, she found domestic duties onerous and tedious, and she lacked Mary's organizing abilities on the home front. As a domestic household manager she was surprisingly ill-at-ease and inefficient, preferring 'to put one's shoulder to the wheel and help at home in any crisis or trouble than continuously in the everyday home life.'[59] Helen tried to be a dutiful daughter, but she was temperamentally unable to transfer to her 'home duties' the independence, happiness, and assurance she enjoyed in her chosen environment at Newnham.

Helen Gladstone found the political responsibilities less of a strain than the domestic duties, though she lacked Mary's natural flair and enthusiasm for politics. She took over Mary's work as personal secretary in 1886, and was 'a perfect tower of strength' in helping her parents through the 1886 Home Rule crisis and the elections of 1886 and 1892. But the years after 1886 were politically more frustrating and less rewarding for the Gladstone family, and Helen shared the family depression. She found the 1892 campaign 'ghastlily [sic] horrible,' since it was so clear the Liberal majority would be tiny and the ministry faced a terrible struggle, with small prospect of passing Home Rule. There was 'a feeling of such crushing finality about it, and a pathos simply beyond words and almost beyond thought with regard to Father ... And all the while we had to go about, driving endless miles, he making speeches, all of us grinning and waving and nodding.'[60] Occasionally Helen was used as an intermediary by hopeful supplicants seeking her father's favour, and she was sometimes prepared to preside at political meetings, though not to speak. During the 1890s she was president of the Women's Liberal Association in Cambridge, and on the executive of the Women's Liberal Federation at a national level. But her political role was almost entirely supportive and rarely gave her the fulfilment she found at Newnham.

The final sacrifice was required of Helen in the 1890s when her father became prime minister for the last time, and when she subsequently had to care for both parents through their final illnesses. Mary and Helen arranged to live alternately with their octogenarian parents in Downing Street during the 1893 session: 'Helen's having practically refused the Headship of Newnham privately before it was offered her, was done entirely to enable her to be of use to parents.' Mary added a significant comment on the trials of looking after their mother: 'You know how it takes a life time to learn how to live with her, and is really impossible for daughters in law unless they utterly give up their own wills.'[61] Helen left Newnham for ever in November 1896, 'to take my share regularly of home duties.' She even allowed her father to glimpse the pain it caused her to sever her last links with Newnham: 'You will not think I have done this lightly or easily.' One of Helen's students subsequently remarked: 'that her life at Newnham brought her great happiness no one can doubt or that she missed it sorely.'[62]

Unfortunately for Helen, her resignation coincided with the Drews' move to Buckley rectory. Helen wrote a letter of utter depression to Mary, apologizing for being a 'selfish brute' in not sharing their happiness: 'but the prospect of Hawarden with only me, is one to me so almost hopeless (seldom able to satisfy Mama and with no time to do any work for Father – except the letters – almost always inefficient in my own eyes and everybody else's), that the only way is to sort of set one's teeth and go on from day to day.' She took the usual Victorian spinster's role in caring for her father up to his death in 1898, and her mother until her death in 1900. From Cannes in 1897, Helen sent Mary long, detailed accounts of the bad health of both parents, which clearly depressed her intensely: '[Father] does mind so dreadfully when he has a bad day, one cannot help being depressed too.'[63] Her mother's mental condition deteriorated in her last years, when she required constant attention. Helen's sense of filial obligation did not end even with their deaths, for then she felt tied to Hawarden Castle to help John Morley with her father's biography. However, in 1901 she became warden of the Women's University Settlement in Southwark, which she considered 'an adequate reason' for leaving Hawarden: 'If I thought it made any real difference to the Biography, it would be a sufficient obligation.'[64] Helen enjoyed five useful years at the settlement before retiring in 1906 to Hawarden, where Mary joined her on Harry Drew's death in 1911.

Judged by the standards of later twentieth-century feminists, Mary and Helen Gladstone were unfortunate in their society, and unduly deferential in their family life. The two sisters inherited many of their parents' talents, but the application of those abilities was severely restricted by their male-dominated environment and by Victorian conventions regarding the role and obligations of unmarried daughters. Both women suffered from a deplorable early education and a sheltered upbringing, enduring lives of aimless futility and frustration until Helen was twenty-eight and Mary over thirty. In many respects their emotional and social development was retarded because of their over-protective and self-contained family life, and the discouraging impact of their formidable father on potential suitors. Given the circumstances, it was sheer luck for Mary that she finally married a suitable clergyman for love at the relatively advanced age of thirty-nine. Though Mary was in her element as private secretary to the prime minister, she would have been increasingly frustrated as an aging spinster, caring for her difficult parents and lacking other outlets for her talents. In later life Helen had to make the greater sacrifice, as she remained unmarried and lacked Mary's instinctive enjoyment of her parents' political life. The conflict between Helen's career and 'home duties' began as soon as Mary married, and the outcome was inevitable given Victorian assumptions regarding the female role and Helen's high sense of family duty.

Judged by the standards of their own time, however, both women were extremely fortunate. Their father's position provided them with unique social, political, and intellectual opportunities, which their own characters and ability enabled them to use very effectively. Mary was a complex woman with passionate interests in politics, religion, and family life. Since her father was Liberal leader, and she married a clergyman, she was able to satisfy different aspects of her personality at various stages in her life. Helen was not quite so fortunate, but still had more opportunities than most other Victorian spinsters. Mary's persistence ensured that Helen gained a higher education at Cambridge, while Helen's own enthusiasm and ability ensured success at Cambridge beyond all her expectations. She was also lucky in that Mary married late, so that the conflict between her career and 'home duties' only started when she was thirty-seven and had already enjoyed ten years of Newnham life.

The major beneficiaries of the Gladstone family enterprise were the two principals, William and Catherine. Their personal investment in Mary and Helen was repaid at a high, sometimes a sacrificial, rate of interest. Yet because of their parents, and despite their parents, Mr Gladstone's daughters enjoyed many more years of satisfying life than most Victorian women. Lucy Masterman's remark that Mary Gladstone 'was bigger than the life she was called upon to live'[65] could be applied to many other Victorian spinsters who were less privileged and less fulfilled than Mr Gladstone's daughters.

NOTES

I wish to thank Dee Cook for her excellent work as research assistant, Colin Matthew, Trevor Lloyd, and John Hooper for their valuable suggestions, Christopher Williams and A.G. Veysey for their kind assistance at the Clwyd Record Office, and the Australian Research Grants Committee for financial support.

Abbreviations

G/G   Glynne-Gladstone MSS, St Deiniol's Library, Hawarden

MGD MSS   Mary Gladstone Drew MSS, British Library Add. MSS

Masterman, *Diaries   Mary Gladstone: Her Diaries and Letters*, ed. Lucy Masterman (London, 1930)

MGD   Mary Gladstone Drew

CG   Catherine Gladstone

HG   Helen Gladstone

WEG   W.E. Gladstone

1 Frances Horner to D.D. Lyttelton, [1892] Chandos MS 5/10, Churchill College, Cambridge; *Newnham Letter*, Jan. 1926, 'Helen Gladstone: In Memoriam,' 72, G/G, 135/124.

2 MGD to D.D. Lyttelton, 5 December 1898, Chandos MSS II, 3/28.

3 Agnes Wickham to CG, 29 September 1891, G/G 30/10. Agnes omitted the long spells her brother Henry had spent in India.

4 See, eg, Georgina Battiscombe, *Mrs. Gladstone: The Portrait of a Marriage* (London, 1956); Mary Drew, *Catherine Gladstone* (London, 1919).

5 The role of the Victorian spinster will be analyzed further, in the comparative context of about fifty political families, in the final chapter of my book on 'Women in British Political Families, 1870-1914,' to be published by Oxford University Press in 1985.

6 *Census of England and Wales, 1911*, General Report, Table XXXI, 90.

7 S.G. Checkland, *The Gladstones: A Family Biography, 1764-1851* (Cambridge, 1971), 395 et passim.

8 Gladstone to Mr Samuel Smith, 11 April 1892, in *Women in Public: The Women's Movement, 1850-1900*, ed. P. Hollis (London, 1979), 320.

9 Masterman, *Diaries*, 424.

10 MGD to Henry Gladstone, 2 February 1883, G/G 43/2.

11 MGD to Henry Gladstone, 28 April 1882, G/G 43/2.

12 Mary Drew's will, 1886, MGD MS 46268, f. 3; MGD to Lavinia Talbot, 24 April 1880, MGD MS 46236, f. 63.

13 HG to WEG, 2 September 1881, G/G 23/11.
14 Masterman, *Diaries*, 2, 26. 'Old Mrs. Talbot' was Mrs John Chetwynd-Talbot.
15 Ibid., 24.
16 MGD to CG, nd, [24] and 28 November 1870, MGD MS 46222, ff. 145-7, 152. The Talbot sisters were Lady Brownlow, Lady Pembroke, and Lady Lothian.
17 MGD to Henry Gladstone, 15 November 1877, G/G 43/2.
18 MGD to CG, nd [October 1871], MGD MS 46222, ff. 158-9; MGD to L. Talbot, nd [December 1885], MGD MS 46236, f. 268.
19 MGD to CG, 23 November 1876, MGD MS 46222, f. 312; Masterman, *Diaries*, 144 [January 1879].
20 MGD to D.D. Lyttelton, nd, Chandos MSS II, 3/28; MGD to L. Talbot [December 1879], Masterman, *Diaries*, 184.
21 MGD to Henry Gladstone, 11 December 1879, G/G 43/2; MGD diary, 22-4 March 1880, MGD MS 46259, f. 55.
22 MGD diary, MGD MS 46259, f. 109; Masterman, *Diaries*, 224-5.
23 MGD to Henry Gladstone, 28 April 1882, G/G 43/2.
24 Masterman, *Diaries*, 233, 202.
25 MGD to L. Talbot, 29 July 1881, MGD MS 46236, f. 105.
26 Masterman, *Diaries*, 246, 270, 303; MGD diary, MGD MS 46261, f. 54.
27 Battiscombe, *Mrs. Gladstone*, 177-9.
28 MGD to L. Talbot, 14 March and 26 May 1880, MGD MS 46236, ff. 59, 74.
29 MGD diary, 15 November 1881, MGD MS 46259, f. 115; MGD to L. Talbot, 26 May 1880, MGD MS 46236, f. 74.
30 E.J. Feuchtwanger, *Gladstone* (London, 1975), 265.
31 MGD to Rosebery, 22 July 1880, 20 April 1881, Rosebery Papers, National Library of Scotland, MS 10015, ff. 17, 33-4.
32 MGD to Rosebery, 11 May 1881 and December 1882, Rosebery MS 10015, ff. 37, 80-1.
33 MGD to Rosebery, 11 May 1881 and 6 August 1892, Rosebery MS 10015, ff. 37, 104-5.
34 MGD to L. Talbot, 30 June 1885, Masterman, *Diaries*, 357-9; MGD to Henry Gladstone, 1 October 1889, G/G 43/3.
35 MGD to L. Talbot, 24 April 1880, MGD MS 46236, f. 65; MGD diary, 24-31 August 1880, Masterman, *Diaries*, 208.
36 MGD diary, 5-6 September 1881, Masterman, *Diaries*, 232; MGD to L. Talbot, nd [Christmas 1885], ibid., 374.
37 MGD to M. Cowell-Stepney, nd [19-20 August 1879] and September 1883, MGD MS 46249, ff. 23, 25, 133-5.
38 MGD to Rosebery, 29 December 1885, Rosebery MS 10015, ff. 97-8.
39 Alice Balfour to MGD, 31 December 1885, MGD MS 46238, f. 89.

40 MGD to A.J. Balfour, 4 October 1888, Balfour Papers, British Library, Add. MS 49794, ff. 185-6; Agnes Gladstone to Henry Gladstone, 4 February 1886, G/G 42/5.

41 CG to Lucy Cavendish, 26 December 1885, G/G 35/6.

42 Janet Wortley to CG, 29 December 1885, G/G 54/8.

43 Alice Balfour to MGD, 31 December 1885, MGD MS 46238, ff. 90-1.

44 MGD to CG, 11 December 1885, MGD MS 46223, ff. 228-9; MGD diary, 2 February 1886, MGD MS 46262, f. 7.

45 MGD to CG, 21 May 1887, G/G 30/12.

46 MGD to L. Talbot, 22 March 1886, MGD MS 46236, f. 271; *Margaret Cowell-Stepney: Her Letters, 1875-1921*, ed. B. Eliott Lockhart (London, 1926).

47 MGD to CG, 21 May 1887, G/G 30/12.

48 MGD to CG, 25 October 1896, MGD MS 46225, f. 280.

49 MGD to WEG, 28 August 1894, G/G 23/9; Gertrude Gladstone to WEG, 18 February 1897, G/G 22/8.

50 MGD to Rosebery, 5 August 1898, Rosebery MS 10015, ff. 124-5.

51 *Newnham Letter*, January 1926, 'Helen Gladstone: In Memoriam,' G/G 135/124.

52 HG to Henry Gladstone, 30 March and 30 August 1877, 5 July 1878, G/G 44/3; MGD to Henry Gladstone, 9 and 11 May 1878, G/G 43/2.

53 MGD to Henry Gladstone, 9 and 11 May 1878, G/G 43/2.

54 HG to MGD, 24 October 1880, 13 April 1885, MGD MS 46231, ff. 29, 67.

55 Correspondent to CG, 1 January 1886, G/G 52/2.

56 HG's memo to various relatives and friends, 12 July 1886, MGD MS 46231, ff. 76-8 and G/G 135/22; HG to Martin Holloway, 13 June 1886, G/G 135/22.

57 Nora Sidgwick to HG, 9 July 1886, G/G 135/22; MGD to CG, nd [c. 19 June 1886], MGD MS 46223, ff. 335-6.

58 HG to Henry Gladstone, 18 March 1886, G/G 44/4; HG's memo, 12 July 1886, MGD MS 46231, ff. 76-8 and G/G 135/22.

59 HG to Henry Gladstone, 11 August 1886, G/G 44/4.

60 HG to MGD, 11 July 1892, MGD MS 46231, f. 127.

61 MGD to Henry Gladstone, 12 June 1892, G/G 43/3.

62 HG to WEG, 2 November 1896, G/G 23/11; *Newnham Letter*, January 1926, 'Helen Gladstone: In Memoriam,' G/G 135/124.

63 HG to MGD, 8 March and 22 December 1897, MGD MS 46231, ff. 150-2, 155-7.

64 HG to Herbert Gladstone, 21 February 1901, G/G 52/2.

65 Masterman, *Diaries*, 492.

PETER T. MARSH

Tearing the Bonds: Chamberlain's Separation from the Gladstonian Liberals, 1885-6

A crisis that splits a political party naturally severs friendships and thus generates emotions with a motivating force of their own, independent of the public policy at issue. The relative weight of the divisive policy and personal estrangement in widening the split varies from crisis to crisis. In the crisis of 1885-6 over Irish Home Rule, the weight lay heavily on the personal side. The passions aroused by that crisis among politicians in Britain had little to do with Ireland and an extraordinary amount to do with loyalty among leaders, friends, and followers.

The subordinate importance of public policy in the Home Rule crisis has been abundantly underscored by A.B. Cooke and John Vincent in *The Governing Passion*.[1] But the preoccupation of Cooke and Vincent with political manoeuvre obscures the power of the passion that the title of their book suggests. That passion was plural, not singular. It included desire for two different sorts of power: power to govern, and the power to control a political party. And faced with the need to choose between the two, some of the contending leaders preferred the second. Another passion gripped many men at all levels even more strongly: the need, even the craving for loyalty between leaders and followers. Lord Salisbury made his demand for loyalty from leaders to followers the cornerstone of his statecraft.[2] Gladstone's ability to turn fairly drastic proposals for Irish self-government into the central issue of British politics, with the support of most of the Liberal party, rested largely upon the magic of his personal appeal rather than upon the merits of his proposals, which kindled little enthusiasm in Britain. But the lightning rod through whom the fiercest passions about loyalty and disloyalty passed was Joseph Chamberlain.

All of Chamberlain's relationships were highly charged. He drew family, friends, and followers to him with a consuming intensity. They were drawn by his 'vivid and resolute energy, fearless tenacity of will,'[3] startling candour in private and rousing fire in public, his generous loves and contemptuous hates. He in turn was drawn to the circles of people with whom he surrounded himself by a yearning for companionship, an appetite for ideas and information, a need for appreciation, admiration, and applause, and by a desire for power.

He encompassed his friends in an embrace that burned both ways. As John Morley later recalled, 'The friend ... was an innermost element in his own existence. To keep a friend, to stand by him, to put a good construction on whatever he said or did, came as naturally to him as traits of self-love come to men in general. This was, of course, bound up with expectations to match.'[4] In the final analysis what Chamberlain required of his friends was co-operative subordination. Though he valued vigorous, even hard-hitting conversation, he could not tolerate fundamental disagreement from those he loved. Those who accepted his terms surrendered their autonomy. Those who had known his love but refused to pay the ultimate price eventually pushed him away; but they could never do so completely, and frequently looked back at his candle, haunted by wistfulness or eaten up with anger. Chamberlain responded to defections from his intimate circle with agonized incomprehension. He was unable to understand the logic of his departing friend on the particular issue dividing them, and was also unable to discover how to accommodate close friendship to fundamental disagreement, yet was no more able than the departing friend to sever the bond completely.

The same pattern applied in attenuated form to the relations between Chamberlain and those followers who were not his close friends. He did not expect full agreement from them on all important principles. He recognized the existence of divergent concerns among the motley array of radicals. He brought bracing freshness to the task of working out policies to accommodate these differences, and he was wonderfully, indeed disconcertingly flexible in tactics. But in arranging accommodations he insisted on his own order of priorities; and once he had hammered out a programme to rally the troops, he wanted unity of action. Glorious in action himself as a captain of the radical host, he thought he had won its loyalty. He recognized bemusedly that a number of radicals preferred the often less forceful, looser style of leadership that Gladstone employed to embrace the wider divergencies within the Liberal party as a whole. But Chamberlain had no premonition about the resentment smouldering among the radicals, whose dearest priorities had been subordinated in the driving campaigns and quick marches upon which he had marshalled them over the past dozen years. When many of these radicals pulled away from him in the spring of 1886, he expected from them at least respect for his integrity in giving up office rather than support a policy of which he disapproved. But still too fascinated by Chamberlain simply to prefer another leader, the now Gladstonian radicals turned on him in anger. Outraged and unable to understand the speed with which erstwhile followers turned away, Chamberlain repaid their rank and file with cold contempt and their sergeants with venom.

It was feelings of this sort that tore Chamberlain and the Gladstonian Liberals asunder in 1886. Ireland was almost incidental to their separation – Ireland but not Gladstone. Gladstone catalyzed the angry separation, which in turn damaged him politically and personally, as it did everyone whom it involved.

The first and in some ways most decisive of the Liberal friendships to be ruptured over the Home Rule crisis was that between Chamberlain and John Morley. They had been close friends for more than a dozen years, since 1873 when together they had launched a radical assault upon the Liberal party from within. The bond between the two men had deepened personally in 1875, when Morley responded sensitively to Chamberlain after the death of his wife, Florence. Still, the relationship between the two men was essentially one for work. It was a well-matched partnership, based on attraction between complementary opposites. Morley, a philosophical heir of John Stuart Mill and a gifted writer, editor of the *Fortnightly Review* and then of the *Pall Mall Gazette*, was mesmerized by Chamberlain as a man of action. Chamberlain, without formal education beyond a good secondary school, craved the intellectual nourishment and careful argument that Morley offered him. For ten years the two men kept in close touch with each other, frequent meetings threaded together by a stream of letters.

There were within the friendship, however, sources of tension that rose towards the surface after Morley entered the House of Commons as member for Newcastle in 1883. Morley not only admired men of action: to some extent he wanted to be one himself, though without surrendering his 'spiritual power'[5] as a thinker. Throughout the first decade of his friendship with Chamberlain, Morley toyed ambivalently with the possibility of joining him in the Commons, a possibility to which Chamberlain responded with similar ambivalence. On balance Chamberlain welcomed the prospect, wanting nevertheless to keep Morley in an essentially subordinate role. Chamberlain envisaged Morley as his intellectual companion, a function to which Morley, if elected to Parliament, might usefully add service as the ears and emissary of Chamberlain on the back benches.

But Morley soon began to send up intermittent signals of a determination to be his own man. They came on a wide variety of subjects, domestic and foreign as well as Irish.[6] Cumulatively they indicated a potentially wide divergence between the two men. The line that Morley took on the government's treatment of Russia in the spring of 1885, resisting the truculent tendencies of some in the cabinet, including Chamberlain, suggested that Morley might prove to be the foremost radical supporter of Gladstone's usual desire for a pacific foreign policy. A similar reflex made Morley more hostile than Chamberlain to coercion of Ireland under any circumstances. Still more ominous for their partnership, Morley quietly welcomed the possibility of Ireland dominating the political agenda after the next election as a way of retarding the pace of domestic reform in England, which Chamberlain wished to accelerate. Morley accordingly began to place a much higher premium than he had done in previous years on maintenance of the unity of the Liberal party, including its moderate section with whom Chamberlain had reached a pitch of exasperation.

Viewed retrospectively from the standpoint of policy, the split between Morley and Chamberlain appears to have been inevitable. The latent personal strain between Chamberlain's assumption of dominance and Morley's ambition simply pushed emotional dynamite into the fissure. But *post hoc propter hoc* is the historian's besetting illusion. Aside from their high degree of personal compatibility, there was a good deal of room for political accommodation between the two men, as Morley was quite aware until the turn of the year. 'I cannot bring myself up to your [anti-nationalist] pitch about Ireland,' he wrote to Chamberlain in September 1885; but, he went on, 'I don't suppose that we differ an atom as to the next step to be taken, whatever it may be.'[7] Liberals of every stripe, radical as well as moderate, were struggling to reconcile a variety of conflicting policy objectives to which most of them in differing degrees adhered: preservation of individual enterprise together with greater sensitivity to social inequities; more generous accommodation of Ireland's distinctive needs and aspirations together with maintenance of the Union; respect for the individual components of the empire together with development of imperial strength. No one was to be more acutely aware than Chamberlain during the debates on the Home Rule Bill in 1886 that the issue splitting him from so many other radicals was not a matter of principle but rather a question of accommodating two principles to which they all adhered. What he pleaded for from Morley was quiet discussion of the practicalities of the situation. What Morley gave him instead was public declamation on Irish policy and private outpouring of personal feelings.

Chamberlain emerged from the general election of 1885 more impatient with the whigs and moderate Liberals than he had been since the heyday of his collaboration with Morley in the mid-1870s. For five years he had been frustrated by the constraints of service in Gladstone's cabinet, weighted down as it was with whigs, and by its lacklustre performance. Over the last few months, in the campaign leading up to the general election, he had exchanged brickbats with the whig leaders every bit as heavily as with the tories. He felt sure that the whigs' cold response to his proposals for land reform had cost the Liberals a number of county constituencies, and hence deprived them of an absolute majority in the new House of Commons. He wanted, therefore, to leave the minority Conservative ministry of Lord Salisbury in office, precariously propped up by the Irish Nationalists, who had co-operated with the Conservatives in the election. Such a situation would give the radicals time to come up with some policy to woo urban working-class constituencies, where they had not done well, and then to precipitate a crisis in the expectation that a Liberal ministry dominated by the radicals would emerge. Morley emerged from the election, however, with reverse priorities. He was disgusted primarily by the unprincipled 'imposture' of toryism.[8] He did not wish to pull his punches in that direction and hence deflate the spirit within the Liberal party in order to focus on its internal struggle.

The disagreement between the two men quickly became personal. Chamberlain challenged Morley's commitment to himself and the radical cause by questioning Gladstone's worth as leader of the Liberal party. He denounced the manifesto that Gladstone had issued at the beginning of the election campaign as good enough for the tories, but 'not nearly good enough for us.'[9] Morley responded with a scarcely veiled critique of his friend and his cause: 'I object to anything that looks like deliberate isolation on personal grounds from the rest of the party, at a moment when there is no great *practical* issue that I know of, on which Radicals take a line of their own.'[10] He went on to pay respectful attention to the party's loyalty to Gladstone, and then added to the discussion the subject of Ireland, on which he said he intended to take a line of his own.

Chamberlain caught the warnings. He increased his estimate of Gladstone's support within the party, and he tried to pursue the subject of Ireland with Morley.[11] But Morley only increased his distance. He delayed his reply to Chamberlain for several days, and then delivered it in public, violating the canons of friendship. Addressing his constituents at Newcastle, he indicated his willingness to support Gladstone if the leader should propose a separate parliament for Ireland. The excuse he gave to Chamberlain for speaking out, that 'it was necessary to my mental peace,'[12] was expressive less of political calculation than of personal unsettlement.

Chamberlain realized instantly, faster than his intellectual friend, that the speech at Newcastle marked a deep breach in their political comradeship. He told Morley so as calmly yet as firmly as he could manage.[13] His anger flashed only towards Gladstone. Chamberlain's assessment of the new state of the relationship between the two friends staggered Morley, who stumbled back and forth to find his footing. In replying to Chamberlain, he aligned himself with Gladstone on the subject of Ireland yet tried to resist the conclusion that this alignment involved the severance of his political connection with Chamberlain. The intensity of Morley's ambivalence towards his friend found vent in two passages. 'As you know,' he said, 'I have no sort of ambition to be an admiral of the fleet. But I'll be hanged if I'll be a powder monkey.' And he alluded to a loan that Chamberlain had made to him some years back to encourage his literary enterprise. 'When I read in the newspapers, your threatened advertisement that you will "no longer be responsible for my debts,"' Morley wrote, 'it will be time enough for me to consider.'[14]

'We can't help ourselves,' Chamberlain concluded. He recognized the violation of friendship implied by Morley's refusal to discuss the subject of Ireland in their private correspondence before he declared himself at Newcastle; and Chamberlain pointed out that, in his letters, Morley had dealt 'entirely with the personal aspect of the [Irish] question and [did] not answer my arguments, or tell me what scheme of Home Rule commends itself to your own mind.' Chamberlain would have welcomed a quiet discussion with Morley as they had so often had in happier days, canvassing the implications of the various options open to radicals on Irish policy and the tactical question of how to pursue the desired end. Now he accepted, indeed exaggerated the fact that the time for discussion of these subjects between the two men had passed. He abandoned the attempt. But Chamberlain was as blind to the reason for Morley's violation of their friendship as Morley was to the reality of what he was doing. Forgetting the douses of cold water that for years he had thrown on Morley's interest in entering Parliament, Chamberlain exclaimed, 'Have I not ... done everything in my power, directly & indirectly, to contribute to your well-deserved advance to political power and influence?'[15]

Morley accepted that claim. Displaying his classical learning, he described his debt to Chamberlain in terms that rendered an explanation for his own behaviour almost impossible. 'Tacitus says something about his "dignity" being started by one Emperor, increased by a second, and carried still further by a third. It is always a delight to me to think that "dignitas mea", whatever it may amount to, has been "inchoata, aucta, et longius pervecta", not by three men but by one, and that one yourself.'[16] Morley refused to recognize that he might be deserting one emperor for a rival, greater, and more congenial one. Not until Chamberlain abandoned his attempt to discuss the Irish question with him did Morley try even sketchily to respond on the subject.

Both men struggled at the beginning of the new year to maintain their private friendship. They tried 'snug' meals together, followed by evenings at the theatre.[17] They toyed with possible cabinet arrangements to preserve their collaboration in the event of a Liberal return to power.[18] But at the same time, with other friends, they spoke out against each other. Chamberlain gave angry notice of their estrangement to Henry Labouchere, an expression of wounded feelings at the expense of calculated manoeuvre, for Chamberlain knew that Labouchere was in touch with Gladstone, to whom indeed Labouchere promptly transmitted this news.[19]

Gladstone made deft use of the rift, with Morley's sometimes eager, sometimes hesitant co-operation. Morley took the initiative, offering to write editorials on Ireland along the lines of Gladstone's thinking for the quasi-official Liberal newspaper, the *Daily News*, if Gladstone would indicate to him where his mind was tending.[20] While writing the fourth editorial towards the end of January, after the fall of the Conservative ministry, Morley received a summons from Gladstone, who was trying to construct a cabinet. Gladstone asked Morley to be chief secretary for Ireland, thus rivetting Morley's attention on the subject of his disagreement with Chamberlain and reducing the vulnerability of the prospective Liberal government to radical attack in the event of Chamberlain's defection.

Morley wanted to accept the offer but hesitated to pay the final price in loyalty. To Gladstone's dismay, he asked for a couple of hours to consult Chamberlain. Still in Chamberlain's thrall, Morley wanted his blessing. Chamberlain too was about to join the ministry, though on strained terms, treading cautiously to protect himself against exactly the sort of Irish policy that the appointment of Morley would suggest. Chamberlain blanched at Morley's news, and while saying that of course Morley must accept, he left Morley in no doubt about the probable consequences to their political fortunes and friendship.[21] Morley went away more hesitant than he had come. But when he returned to Gladstone to express his doubts, the old man swept them aside and then laid them to rest by giving Morley the impression that he meant him to be 'a special ally.'[22]

Morley's switch of allegiance was not quite complete. For a few days he clung to the illusion that he could serve as a buffer between Gladstone and Chamberlain. Thereafter, for a month, he and Chamberlain communicated with each other like foreign powers, rarely and with studied correctness, aware of the near probability of open warfare.

Chamberlain precipitated the break at the cabinet on 12 March, when he forced Gladstone to begin to declare his hand on Ireland. Immediately afterward, Morley tried to persuade Gladstone to keep communications with Chamberlain open. But when Gladstone refused, Morley joined him in making plans for a final showdown with Chamberlain on 26 March, and for replacing him as president of the Local Government Board in the expected event of his resignation.[23] In the lapse of time between Chamberlain's resignation and Gladstone's presentation of his Home Rule Bill to the House of Commons, Morley served as mouthpiece for his new master to his old: 'Mr. Gladstone ... allows me to say ...'[24] Chamberlain in turn ransacked Morley's old speeches and writings for damaging passages to help Lord Randolph Churchill, the Conservative tribune, who was to follow Morley in the Commons debate.[25]

The change from mouthpiece to sword for his new master against his old came quickly. The point at issue was whether Ireland, if given a parliament of its own in Dublin, should also continue to send representatives to the House of Commons at Westminster. After some early ambivalence, Chamberlain had focused on Irish representation at Westminster as indispensable to the supremacy of the imperial Parliament, the unity of the Kingdom, and the maintenance of the empire. With corresponding tenacity Morley regarded the removal of the Irish from Westminster as indispensable to the government's scheme. His insistence on this point enabled Gladstone to present himself as willing to compromise in the interests of the party but unable to do so because that would precipitate further resignations from his cabinet. Morley and his former captain not only maximized the point at issue between them but also talked about the disagreement in loaded terms. Morley insisted that for the government to concede Chamberlain's demand would amount to 'go[ing] down on our knees' to him.[26] Chamberlain replied with his peerless talent for wounding offence. In a letter to Labouchere that was read out to the cabinet, Chamberlain repeated Morley's private comment of some months back that he did not want to be admiral of the Fleet but that he would not consent to be a powder monkey. Chamberlain drove the point in with venom, the more burning because it was true: 'He has now changed his ship and his captain, but he has to recognise that his position in the service is much the same as before.'[27]

The Home Rule crisis also divided Chamberlain politically from his only other close friend outside Birmingham, Sir Charles Dilke. Ultimately this friendship, unlike that with Morley, ended completely, but the connection between Chamberlain and Dilke wore out slowly over many years. The division between them over Home Rule did not go as deep as with Morley because Dilke's loyalty to Chamberlain had been brought to the fore in a strange way, but with overriding force, by Chamberlain's response to the personal trauma through which Dilke was still living.

Until the summer of 1885, the friendship between Chamberlain and Dilke was unique because there was no element of subordination in it. The two men were equally matched colleagues, partners in the active (as distinct from intellectual) leadership of the Liberal party's radical wing. Inevitably there was some rivalry in their relationship, an ingredient to which observers were alert, because only one of them could become prime minister; but the loyalty of the partnership was its most remarkable feature.

Then, in July of 1885, Dilke was plunged into one of the most scandalous, graphically detailed divorce cases of Victorian England. Because Chamberlain stood to gain as well as lose through the discredit of his colleague, and also had opportunity to affect the course that the parties to the divorce case took, his loyalty to Dilke over these months has since been impugned, as it was at the time. But that was not as Dilke saw it. Etched forever in his mind was the total support Chamberlain gave him at the blackest moment of his life, when the news of the scandal first broke, when the world backed away from him in embarrassment and he staggered in despair.

Preoccupied by his own crisis, Dilke was only mildly caught up in the wrenching of political friendships that began in December. He was, therefore, paradoxically, more aware of the lack of clearly defined differences on matters of Irish policy over which the various protagonists began to divide.[28] His heart stayed with Chamberlain. But as the debate developed, his mind moved with Morley, particularly on the question of Irish representation at Westminster. Until the end of April 1886, Dilke kept heart and mind together by pointing out to Chamberlain that, if only he could bring himself to vote for the principle of the Home Rule Bill, he could emerge as Gladstone's successor in the leadership of a Liberal party purged of whigs. Dilke held out this prospect for Chamberlain genuinely, out of realism as much as gratitude. The divorce scandal had destroyed the grounds for rivalry between them.

As Chamberlain, however, managed to sharpen the focus on Irish representation at Westminster, Dilke was forced to decide between what he believed to be the best interests of the nation and the party on the one hand and a bald assertion of his personal affection for his friend on the other[29] – and he would have to make and record that choice as an elected representative in the House of Commons. Dilke concluded that he had to make his political decision on public grounds. He reached it by himself, for a short while out of touch with his friend, but then he warned Chamberlain of what he was about to say. Stunned, Chamberlain refrained from writing back till late on 3 May, after Dilke would have announced his decision to his constituents, but before the morning newspapers could bring Chamberlain word of what Dilke had said. 'My pleasure in politics is gone,' Chamberlain wrote at midnight. 'The friends with whom I have worked so long are many of them separated from me ... You must do what your conscience tells you to be right ... But ... The present crisis is of course life and death to me.'[30] Next morning, after reading the papers, Chamberlain sent Dilke a short congratulatory note that ended, however, not with his usual 'Yours ever,' but with the cool formality of 'Yours sincerely.'[31]

Unable to bear the pain he had given his friend, Dilke broke through the reserve with which the two men conventionally expressed their emotions: 'I am driven distracted by your tone,' he wrote.[32] Dilke's ardour opened Chamberlain up: 'I feel bitterly the action of some of these men, like Morley, Illingworth, & many others, who have left my side at this time although many of them owe much to me ... With you it is different. We have been so closely connected that I cannot contemplate any severance ... I feel that there is no longer security for anything while Mr. Gladstone remains the foremost figure in politics. But, as between us two, let nothing come.'[33] 'Nothing,' Dilke replied, 'could ever come really between us, because it takes two to make a fight, & even if your mind were turned against me it would come back to me when you found as you would find that nothing could ever turn my mind against you.'[34] 'Let us,' Chamberlain concluded, 'agree to consider everything which is said or done for the next few weeks as a dream.'[35] There were to be moments of pain in the dream. When the members of Parliament trooped back into the chamber after voting on the Home Rule Bill early in June, the file of Gladstone's supporters was led by Dilke.[36]

Nothing could so sharply penetrate the austere reserve with which Chamberlain covered his deepest feelings as the desertion of close friends and followers. Yet his friends were not the source of his difficulty. Only one man, Gladstone, could have made Home Rule for Ireland the battle-cry of the party in such a way as to undercut Chamberlain's position within it. The defection of Chamberlain's friends was politically serious only because Gladstone beckoned them along an alternative path.

To begin with, Gladstone's challenge to Chamberlain was a matter of method rather than of deliberate antagonism. What Chamberlain wanted was open, mutually respectful discussion among the key Liberals, led but not dominated by Gladstone. Instead Gladstone wrapped himself in silence or ambiguity and ignored most of his colleagues. By keeping his distance, by immersing himself in works of political philosophy rather than in discussion or correspondence, by keeping his own counsel, Gladstone focused attention on the uniqueness of his leadership. In effect he demanded from his party unquestioning trust. Chamberlain did not want to challenge Gladstone's leadership, at least not yet; but the method of conduct that Gladstone chose to pursue made Chamberlain appear to be motivated simply by ambition. For the first three months of the crisis, the challenge of Gladstone to Chamberlain did not go beyond this difference in approach. Until the middle of March 1886, Gladstone oscillated between suspicion of Chamberlain's intentions and reluctance to dispense with him and thus drive him into opposition. But as soon as Chamberlain challenged Gladstone face to face on the Irish policy towards which the old man was moving, he spurned all attempts at genuine conciliation and treated Chamberlain with veiled but steady, deepening, personal and political hostility.

In contrast to the passion of his response to desertions among erstwhile allies and followers, Chamberlain responded to Gladstone's treatment of him with remarkable circumspection. It is, in fact, possible to discern in Chamberlain's behaviour towards his leader as they moved apart a model of the way in which Chamberlain hoped that his lieutenants and followers would handle incipient disagreement with himself. The prospect of a contest with Gladstone for the allegiance of the party gave Chamberlain pause, and he quickly raised his estimate of the Grand Old Man's grip.[37] Whenever Gladstone gave him opportunity, Chamberlain presented his arguments to his leader cogently – but got no response. Chamberlain longed for clear, pragmatic discussion before decisions were reached. Instead, except from Labouchere, he met with vague assertions of principle or silence. Noting insults in Gladstone's treatment of him but not sure what to make of them, worried by Gladstone's long stretches of silence yet drawing attention to ambiguities in his language which held open the possibility of co-operation, Chamberlain kept the peace until mid-March. Even then, for another two months, he tried half-heartedly to bridge the gulf that Gladstone and he were simultaneously creating between themselves. Only from the middle of May, sure now of Gladstone's cold antagonism, did Chamberlain fight to destroy.

Throughout the months of crisis, apart from the six weeks when they sat in the same cabinet, Gladstone held Chamberlain at arm's length. Most of what discussion there was between the two men passed through the mediation of Henry Labouchere. Gladstone kept even this mediation indirect: Labouchere conducted his correspondence on Gladstone's side through Gladstone's son, Herbert. But the old man closely monitored his son's responses.[38] He could, as Labouchere commented, 'give lessons to Machiavelli.'[39] He used Labouchere, whenever it seemed useful, as an intermediary with the Irish Nationalist leader Parnell as well as with Chamberlain. Labouchere was perfectly suited for the part. As MP for Northampton and publisher of the irreverent weekly *Truth*, he possessed impeccable social credentials, experience as a diplomat, and a raffish style of life and language that made him easy to disown.

He accepted and played the part of mediator with relish. Entertaining at his villa on the Thames or chain smoking in the lobby of the House of Commons, he revelled in his style and enjoyed the company of those who would reply in kind. Yet serious purpose underlay his irreverence. He had become a convinced advocate of thoroughgoing Home Rule, partly out of genuine respect for Ireland's nationality, but primarily in order to clear the way for resolutely radical reform in England. He feared that, until removed by Home Rule, the Irish question would enable England's conservatives, both whig and tory, to 'arrest democratic progress.'[40] Clearing the way would not, however, be enough. The radicals had to learn to act with the same self-assurance that had enabled the whigs to dominate the Liberal party for so long. And the man to teach the radicals was Chamberlain. Labouchere recognized early that the person most willing and best able to dispose of the question of Ireland by giving it internal autonomy was Gladstone. He wanted that to happen in such a way as to clear the path for Chamberlain's succession to the leadership of the Liberal party. Labouchere therefore transmitted the information he received from Gladstone's camp and from Chamberlain back and forth much more straightforwardly than his racy style suggested. In spite of repeated discouragements, his patience was inexhaustible because his immediate purpose was vital to his long-range hopes – inexhaustible until Chamberlain crushed his hopes by defeating Gladstone's Home Rule Bill.

At the outset of their correspondence over the crisis, which began early in December as soon as the results of the general election were in, Labouchere and Chamberlain took up positions from which, through many twists and turns, they never departed. 'Would it not be well,' Labouchere began, 'to use the GOM to settle this question & get it out of the way?'[41] to which Chamberlain replied, 'we must sit on his Irish proposals.'[42] Chamberlain had known for some weeks that Gladstone contemplated a generous accommodation of Irish nationalism, more generous than Chamberlain, from his knowledge of Birmingham, believed English working men would tolerate.[43] Hitherto he had raised the spirits of his electors in Birmingham and the radical host in Britain with the boldness (whether verbal or substantive) of his proposals. He still wanted to be resolute. But on this occasion he wanted resolute delay: delay in responding to the demands of the Irish until they learned to lower their expectations to a level acceptable to the English Liberal electorate.

The outcome of the general election, however, created an unstable situation in which deliberate delay would be hard to manage, particularly for the Liberals. By sweeping Ireland and throwing the Irish vote in England behind the Conservatives, Parnell and the Nationalists had prevented the Liberals from securing a majority in the new House of Commons. Yet while the Liberals had not won the election, the Conservative government had certainly lost it. With 280 seats, they fell 86 short of even the barest majority. Nor was Parnell in a commanding position: he led a contingent of precisely 86, enough to give Lord Salisbury's ministry only the most precarious renewal of its lease on life. The natural Liberal instinct would be to throw the tories out; but that could be done only in collaboration with Parnell. Though Parnell had not quite secured for himself the balance of power, he was in a position to entertain bids.

With the canny instincts of a Birmingham businessman, Chamberlain wanted to suspend the bidding until Parnell lowered his price. Suspension of the bidding would require the Liberal parliamentary party to tolerate the minority Conservative ministry for a while longer. That might be managed. After all, Parnell had so angered Liberals by throwing his weight against them in the general election that they were far from eager to co-operate with him. But suspension of the bidding also required the consent of the party leaders, pre-eminently Gladstone. As Labouchere cynically observed, 'At 76, a waiting policy may be a patriotic one, but it is one of personal effacement.'[44] Yet Gladstone too wanted delay, to encourage the incumbent Conservative government to seek a consensual settlement of the vexed relationship between England and Ireland with Liberal as well as Irish co-operation. Hence, although there was plenty of room for ultimate disagreement on Ireland between Gladstone and Chamberlain, there was also room for practical co-operation.

The dealings between the two men after the election, however, got off to an awkward start that underscored the challenge they posed to each other. A small cabal of radicals, including Dilke and Morley, met at the end of the elections under Chamberlain's roof in Birmingham. They reached only the vaguest of agreements, not enough to keep them together, as events would soon show; but the first hint about what they had decided, in a speech that Dilke gave back in London, aroused suspicion in Gladstone's home at Hawarden. Dilke suggested that the Conservative government should be left in office to struggle with the parliamentary dilemma created by its alliance with the Irish, while the radicals prepared for the next leap forward in the domestic policy of the country as a whole. This message was read at Hawarden as an attempt to begin a transfer of the leadership of the party from Gladstone, who was too old to be expected to remain in charge for a protracted stretch, to Chamberlain. Gladstone's son Herbert reacted to Dilke's speech by intimating to the national press (perhaps with Morley's approval)[45] that his father contemplated the creation of a separate legislature and executive in Dublin for Irish domestic affairs. Whatever else this leak to the press indicated, it drew all eyes back to Gladstone and demonstrated the breathtaking ease with which he could assert himself as the leader of his party and indeed the most powerful man in British politics.

News of the leak to the press reached Chamberlain just before he was to address his constituents in the Birmingham Town Hall. With the quick presence of mind that he could bring to bear when the stakes were high, he developed a line of argument in his speech[46] that wove together appreciation of Gladstone's primacy, the desire of the Liberal rank and file to vent their spleen on the tories, and his own wish to leave Parnell to find out what he could get from his current tory allies before turning back chastened to the Liberals. Chamberlain's speech came to Gladstone as a pleasant surprise. It lessened his doubts about Chamberlain's loyalty. It also kindled a hope of finding support from this unexpected quarter for the policy of temporizing silence that he wanted to observe until the Conservative government decided what it would do about Ireland. He wrote immediately to thank Chamberlain for his words and to secure his co-operation.

But though both men wanted to temporize, there was a critical difference in their sense of timing. Gladstone was waiting for the government to act. If it failed, he was ready to try his own hand: 'the hour glass,' he told Chamberlain, 'has begun to run for a definitive issue.'[47] Chamberlain was anxious for a longer delay, until Parnell learned to accept from the Liberals, and they readied the English electorate to accept, a settlement less generous than the Nationalists and more generous than the electorate were currently willing to tolerate. He expressed himself clearly to his chief: 'If there were a dissolution on this question, & the Liberal party or its leader were thought to be pledged to a separate Parliament in Dublin, it is my belief that we should sustain a tremendous defeat. The English working classes, for various reasons, are distinctly hostile to Home Rule carried to this extent, & I do not think it would be possible to convert them before a General Election.'[48]

Gladstone did not reply to this warning, nor was he anything like this candid with Chamberlain on the question at hand. But the old man was evasive with all of his interlocutors, and he urged Chamberlain to 'Be *very credulous* as to any statements about my views & opinions. Rest assured that I have done & said *nothing* which in any way points to negotiation or separate action.'[49]

Over the next month and more, despite persistent indication of the drift in Gladstone's thinking towards a separate parliament in Dublin, Chamberlain clung to this assurance and occasional others like it. While the 'vague generalities'[50] in which John Morley expressed his views about Ireland infuriated Chamberlain, he drew relief from the much more obscure pronouncements of their mutual leader. Each way Chamberlain looked, he foresaw disaster for the radicals: 'The question,' he told Labouchere, 'is whether it is better to be smashed with Mr G. & the Parnellites or without them.'[51] The only way out that he could discern lay in taking one step at a time, paying no more attention than absolutely necessary to the ultimate policy alternatives. Once Parliament convened in mid-January and everything seemed to point to the fall of the government of Lord Salisbury and his replacement as prime minister by Gladstone, Chamberlain contrived to bring about the transfer of power on a motion about English agricultural labourers that had nothing to do with Ireland.

Gladstone and Chamberlain sustained this ambiguity through the formula upon which they agreed to govern the new ministry's enquiry as to what should be done about Ireland. While Gladstone's concerns tended to point towards an ambitious scheme and Chamberlain clearly preferred a more restricted one, neither man ruled the other possibility out of consideration; and Gladstone assured Chamberlain that his entry into the ministry would not compromise his 'unlimited liberty' to debate and accept or reject whatever concrete scheme the cabinet brought under discussion.[52] The two men seemed able to accommodate each other, if not on policy, at any rate on the ground rules for arriving at a policy over the coming weeks or months.

But the personal relations between the two men remained disturbed. Though Gladstone occasionally expressed relief when he thought that Chamberlain was working with him, he found the company and co-operation of peers much more congenial. During December, when he had cut himself off from most of his former colleagues, he corresponded readily with Granville, Spencer, and Rosebery, all earls. He raised his eyebrows at the end of January when Chamberlain suggested himself for secretary of state for the colonies, but did not hesitate to install the much less experienced Lord Rosebery as secretary of state for foreign affairs. In conversation with the Queen, Gladstone accused Chamberlain of lacking straightforwardness, trustworthiness, and public spirit.[53] He galled Chamberlain by attempting to reduce the official salary of Jesse Collings, the trusty friend whom Chamberlain wanted as his second at the ministry to which Gladstone assigned him, the Local Government Board.

'Will Mr. G – at 76 – frankly lean on the Radicals for the last steps of his journey?' Chamberlain mused. 'His treatment of myself argues for the negative but,' he went on, 'that may be due to personal feeling. If so it will yield to the gentle pressure of circumstances.'[54] Once back in the harness of office, the two men got off to a gently promising start. Gladstone singled Chamberlain out, asking him to come and expound his ideas on Ireland. Their conversation went well from Chamberlain's point of view, and encouraged him to think that 'a closer inspection of the difficulties has brought Mr Gladstone nearer to me.'[55] Both men focused on the vexed subject of Irish land. Chamberlain hoped in this way to reduce the demand for Irish autonomy, while Gladstone hoped at least to postpone debate on that more divisive subject.

A month passed between this conversation and the first meeting of the full cabinet at which Ireland was discussed, and during that month something fateful went wrong. It had something to do with the bearing of Irish land on Irish government. The two questions were inseparable. The land scheme that Chamberlain sketched for Gladstone at the beginning of the month focused on relief for small farmers and would be administered by an authority in Ireland modestly designed to handle little more than this function. The much more costly land scheme that Gladstone circulated to the cabinet early in March was designed to buy out and hence ease the apprehensions of the great landowners. Everything about the scheme implied that its purpose was to pave the way for a generous accommodation of the Irish desire for political autonomy. Chamberlain may have read the contrast between the two schemes as proof that Gladstone's period of ambiguity had come to an end, that he had reached decisions hostile to the advice Chamberlain had repeatedly given him.

This reading may well have been right; but there was still room for doubt or at least for exploration of possible amendments to Gladstone's proposals. Instead of trying to carry out such an exploration in a conciliatory spirit, Chamberlain insisted that Gladstone reveal his full hand. For three months Chamberlain had clung to nothing more substantial from Gladstone than ambiguity, fearful of the trap door that the old man could spring under his feet at any moment. Though Gladstone had kept the door latched, he had deepened Chamberlain's anxiety by treating him slightingly on all but a couple of occasions. In preparing his Irish proposals at the beginning of March for submission to the cabinet, Gladstone extended his consultations beyond the two ministers, Spencer and Morley, who were responsible for Ireland, to include his trusted friend, Lord Granville, and even the irascible chancellor of the exchequer, Harcourt: but not Chamberlain. Though these consultations were kept secret, rumour was rife. When Chamberlain read the memorandum on Irish land that Gladstone circulated to the cabinet in preparation for its meeting on 13 March, his mood blackened.

Gladstone had scarcely opened the subject at the meeting when Chamberlain interrupted him. Chamberlain brushed aside the land proposals and pushed to the subject of Irish government that loomed behind them. After protesting against this disruption of the order of business and at the unfairness of a demand for his proposals on Irish government, which were as yet no more than sketchy, Gladstone admitted that he could see no valid alternative to a separate Irish legislature in Dublin. Having extracted that admission, Chamberlain enclosed himself for the rest of the meeting in steely silence.

While Chamberlain handled himself stiffly in this meeting, Gladstone tried to be reasonable and accommodating. When the cabinet next met, on 26 March, the two men switched roles. During the two-week interval Chamberlain had displayed uncertainty. To begin with, he tendered Gladstone his resignation, and then suspended it at the prime minister's request. More adept than anyone else at reading public opinion, Chamberlain could not find any guidance from that source now.[56] Though he still spoke with bravado and carried himself with brisk assurance, he entered the meeting of the cabinet on the 26th hoping that an accommodation could be worked out. His desire was evident to Rosebery and Morley.

But in the fortnight between the two meetings, while Chamberlain wondered about stepping back from the edge, Gladstone did nothing to hold him. By the 26th it was the prime minister who was cold and uncompromising. After some discussion around the cabinet table, Gladstone pushed a note over to one of his colleagues: 'There is no use in indefinitely prolonging talk.'[57] A month later he reflected: 'With men like most of my colleagues it is safe to go to an extreme of concession. But my experience in Chamberlain's case is that such concession is treated mainly as an acknowledgment of his superior greatness and wisdom, and as a fresh point of departure accordingly.'[58] Chamberlain immediately resubmitted his resignation, and Gladstone accepted it.

After nearly four months of uncertainty, Gladstone had decided to do without Chamberlain. For the next two and a half months, the contest waged under the heading of Home Rule for Ireland was essentially between these two men for the support, or at least understanding, of the radicals in and out of Parliament. The two men conducted their contest for the parliamentary radicals by manoeuvring over the terms of the Government of Ireland Bill, often through the mediation of Labouchere. The battle for the allegiance of the radicals in the country at large was waged in the two constituency organizations with which Chamberlain was most closely identified: the Birmingham Liberal Association and the National Liberal Federation.

In each case, Chamberlain had an uphill fight and paid a high price for modest success. First the National Liberal Federation and finally Labouchere reacted to his breach with Gladstone by impugning Chamberlain's motives and consigning him to the company of history's traitors. It took a lot of careful effort on his part to carry the Liberals of Birmingham with him; and though his victory there was complete, it was not accompanied with all of the old enthusiasm. In the House of

Commons Chamberlain won more support from whigs and moderate Liberals than from the genuine radicals.

Radical opinion moved promptly and powerfully towards Gladstone in the two weeks that passed between Chamberlain's resignation and Gladstone's presentation of the Home Rule Bill to the House of Commons. In the meantime, because Chamberlain felt unable to explain his action except with reference to the bill, he kept silent. The air filled with suspicion that his motive in resigning was ambition to drive out the Grand Old Man. The flow of letters of support that Chamberlain was accustomed to receive fell off to a trickle. He questioned the wisdom of his own course. The one thing that kept him sure that he had no other to follow was the blank refusal of Gladstone on 26 March to make any accommodating response to Chamberlain's criticism of his proposals.

Two days after Gladstone introduced his Government of Ireland Bill, Chamberlain stood up in the Commons, no longer on the Treasury bench but below the gangway, surrounded by suspicious radicals. He still commanded respect, and as he advanced to the table to deliver his speech, a bunch of spring violets in his lapel rather than the usual orchid, he was greeted with a hearty cheer. He had scarcely begun to speak when Gladstone attacked. Against the intentions of the Queen and the efforts of Chamberlain to ensure that he had broad permission to explain the grounds for his opposition to the government's Irish legislation, Gladstone leapt up at Chamberlain's first mention of the Land Bill to prevent him from going on. Both men knew that the Land Bill, to be introduced to the Commons in ten days' time, was the part of the government's Irish proposals most vulnerable to criticism from the 'left.' That bill would take an immense amount of revenue, which might otherwise be spent on English domestic reforms, in order to buy out the great owners of Irish land and thus reduce their hostility to Home Rule. Gladstone used his long experience of constitutional usage, and his authority as the person through whom communication between a resigning minister and the Queen had to pass, not only to limit Chamberlain's remarks to the Home Rule Bill now before the Commons, but even to prevent him from reading to the House the letter of explanation he had written to Gladstone for this very purpose in mid-March, when he first tendered his resignation.

Obviously thrown by Gladstone's prohibition, Chamberlain groped for a way to recast his speech and present his case. He managed to do so, in spite of Irish jeers, by talking about the Land Bill hypothetically. Then he turned, as he had originally intended, to the features of the Home Rule Bill that he found offensive, particularly to the removal from the House of Commons of representatives from Ireland though the island would remain subject to imperial taxation. Afterwards Chamberlain was exhilarated by his escape from the snare Gladstone had laid for him. But he was also more impressed than ever with 'the power of the G.O.M. over the minds of men.'[59]

The theatre of combat between the two men moved out of the House of Commons during the next month and into the country. Even before Gladstone presented his Land Bill to the Commons in mid-April, he recognized that Chamberlain's stand 'was paralysing the party outside Parliament.'[60] As Chamberlain approached his meeting with the Liberal Association in his own city on 21 April, he knew very well that the sound that went out from there would be heard by radical MPs everywhere who were oscillating in allegiance between the old leader and himself; and these MPs could bring to bear on Gladstone the one form of pressure likely to persuade him to accommodate Chamberlain.

The meeting of the Birmingham Liberal Association in the Town Hall mirrored the tensions among Liberals in the country at large. Francis Schnadhorst, the redoubtable organizer, hoped that the party would dispose of the problem of Ireland by granting it Home Rule in order to concentrate on England's domestic needs.[61] Though anxious to keep Gladstone and Chamberlain in tandem, he resented what he felt to be Chamberlain's inadequate appreciation of his political judgment as distinct from organizational acumen. J.T. Bunce, the equally redoubtable editor of the *Birmingham Daily Post*, shared Schnadhorst's anxiety to keep the two leaders together; but, like several of Chamberlain's other Birmingham lieutenants – Powell Williams, Jesse Collings, and R.W. Dale – Bunce was uneasy about the imperial implications of Gladstone's scheme for Home Rule.[62] Bunce had to fight hard within the executive council of the association to gain for Chamberlain an opportunity to present his case to the Liberals of the whole city and not just to his own constituents in Birmingham West.

More than on any occasion during the debates on Home Rule in the House of Commons, Chamberlain had to fight for survival when he addressed the Birmingham two thousand on 21 April. He began quickly with an assertion, upon which all could agree, of the cardinal importance that the subject of Ireland had assumed.[63] Then he grasped the central, strained issue of leadership. He attributed the dominance that the question of Home Rule had acquired so suddenly after a general election in which it had not bulked large, at any rate within Britain, solely to the initiative of Gladstone. He went on to say that the faults of the proposed legislation stemmed from lack of consultation with the cabinet and the party in the country. That general point made, Chamberlain plunged into the task of criticizing Gladstone's proposals. He did so much more vigorously than he had in the House of Commons. He could not hope in the Commons for overwhelming agreement. But that was precisely what he needed from his home base. He therefore sought to pulverize the local opposition with comprehensive, tough, at times contemptuous argument. To drive home his point that Ireland would not rest lastingly satisfied with the Dublin parliament that Gladstone offered, Chamberlain described the fetters and undemocratic divisions with which Gladstone proposed to burden the Dublin parliament, and then asked his audience how they would react to a similar scheme if applied to Birmingham: 'You would not pick it from the gutter.' Yet he took up a position of only conditional opposition to the Home Rule Bill. If, before pressing that bill to a second reading, the government modified it, especially by retaining Irish representation at Westminster, Chamberlain promised to give Gladstone 'whatever humble support I can; but if not, then my duty is clear, and at all hazards I will perform it.' He ended with a plea, in that case, for the same kind of sympathetic understanding that Gladstone had received on former occasions when he too had separated himself from governments on grounds of conscience. With only two votes to the contrary, the meeting passed a motion of unabated confidence in Chamberlain.

There was one last hurdle for him to surmount if the meeting was to conclude successfully. The Gladstonians at the meeting, led by Schnadhorst, wanted to postpone until a later date a vote on the next motion, which was to support the position that Chamberlain had taken up on Gladstone's proposals. No sooner was the motion for delay made than Chamberlain intervened to crush it. He did so with rough vehemence, for he needed an expression of Birmingham's unhesitating support: and he got his way.

He received from Birmingham more than support. Birmingham gave him its trust. It believed in him as he believed in himself. The leading Unitarian minister in the town, Henry Crosskey, wrote to him next day: 'Permit me to add my warm appreciation – & more than appreciation – of your sacrifice of such splendid opportunities of carrying out long cherished purposes as the Cabinet gave, to conscientious convictions. If all statesmen wd. subordinate the love of power to faithfulness to principle, it wd. be a happier day for our country.'[64] The Liberals of Birmingham still admired Gladstone personally, an admiration Chamberlain recognized and shared; but they believed as much in the commitment to high-minded public service of 'our Joe' as in that of the Grand Old Man.

The balance of trust in other constituency associations around the country weighed heavily towards Gladstone, though respect for Chamberlain and his arguments induced many of them to frame resolutions that combined cordial support for the principle of Home Rule with gentle pleas for modification in the government's proposals. Chamberlain appreciated the dimensions of the tide of opinion among the active constituency workers who shaped the resolutions of these associations: but he insisted, acutely as it turned out, that opinion among the rank and file was more evenly divided and that, when election day came, many of them would demonstrate their uneasiness by staying at home.[65]

Gladstone did not read the electoral auguries so acutely. He was led to exaggerate the tide of popular Liberal opinion towards him by the action that the National Liberal Federation took two weeks after the meeting of the Birmingham Association. Both organizations were Chamberlain's progeny; but while the lesser remained in his thrall, the greater had come to resent the assumption that he and his Birmingham henchmen should take the lead in framing its policy.[66] The leaders of the National Liberal Federation from other cities, from Leeds, Liverpool, Bradford, and Sheffield, received assistance in their rebellion from Schnadhorst, who was secretary to the national association. These men wanted to express their minds and the thinking of their cities directly to Gladstone, without Chamberlain's interposition. When Chamberlain loyalists placed on the agenda for the 5 May meeting of the federation a resolution on the subject of Ireland that adhered strictly to Chamberlain's line, James Kitson of Leeds, that year's president, took the unprecedented step of substituting for it an exclusively Gladstonian amendment. The depth of the feeling in the federation erupted at the meeting when Alfred Illingworth, one of the MPs for Bradford, speaking about Chamberlain's opposition to the government's Irish proposals, used the word 'traitor' and evoked 'loud and long-continued cheering.'[67] It was this sort of treatment of his character and motives, even more than the massive vote of the federation for the Gladstonian amendment, that galled Chamberlain.

After recessing for Easter, Parliament had reassembled shortly before the meeting of the federation. Its action thus influenced the judgment and temper of the two chief protagonists as they resumed their efforts to enlist radical support in the Commons. It was in the Commons that the climactic battle would be fought. The action of the National Liberal

Federation encouraged Gladstone to believe that, if he held off a vote by the Commons on the second reading of his Home Rule Bill for at least another month, pressure from constituency associations would push the Liberal half of the House of Commons, aside from Lord Hartington's whigs and a scattering of maverick radicals, into line. Together with the eighty-six Irish Nationalist MPs, that would be enough to carry the bill. What he needed to do for the moment was to respond to Chamberlain's criticisms of the bill with just enough reasonableness to keep the number of radical defectors down to a handful.

The conciliation might have to go far enough to oblige Chamberlain himself to abstain or even to vote for the second reading. Though there was no thought of bringing him back into the cabinet, at least until the current controversy had been resolved, the split among the radicals in Parliament might still have been surmounted. As Chamberlain stressed again and again, almost all of them now accepted, as he did, the principle of Home Rule. They divided only on the terms upon which Home Rule should be given to Ireland, particularly on whether and how Ireland should continue to be represented in the imperial House of Commons.

Chamberlain would have to sustain the radical defection assiduously in order to persuade Gladstone simply to keep him within the Liberal fold. The affront to Chamberlain's dignity was unmistakable; the slurs cast by men like Illingworth on his honour unendurable. To vindicate himself in the face of Gladstone's slights and Illingworth's aspersions, he had to be given obvious concessions on the terms of the bill, and he would feel driven to magnify and publicize what he gained. Between Chamberlain's wounded self-esteem and Gladstone's reinforced faith that Liberal opinion in the country was on his side, there was little chance for accommodation.

While the conduct of the National Liberal Federation had reduced the prospects for compromise, the drift of opinion within the parliamentary party heightened the need for it. Chamberlain had delivered his most cogent criticism of the government's Irish bills well away from Parliament in the Birmingham Town Hall, while Gladstone had concentrated his best efforts in the House of Commons. Yet, paradoxically, Gladstone drew his greatest strength from Liberal organizations out of doors while Chamberlain gathered strength within the Commons. By the beginning of May he was able to frighten the government with his tally of the number of Liberal MPs who could be expected to vote against the second reading of the Home Rule Bill as things then stood. More than half of the defectors were whigs or moderate Liberals following the leadership of Lord

Hartington. But a generous third, some though not all of them radicals, followed Chamberlain's lead. It was this third that held the balance. If they abstained or voted for the second reading of the bill, it would pass. If they voted no, it would fail. Debate on the second reading was scheduled to begin on Monday, 10 May, less than a week after the meeting of the National Liberal Federation.

The opening of debate on the second reading was preceded by a weekend of intense negotiations through Labouchere between Gladstone and Chamberlain, twisted on both sides.[68] The subject matter of the negotiations had narrowed since the introduction of the Home Rule Bill from whether Irish representation should continue at Westminster to the extent and frequency of that representation. It was not a question of principle but of negotiating power between Gladstone and Chamberlain, power derived from support. Each of the protagonists sought to heighten what he required of the other while displaying himself to nervous supporters as the more reasonable or potentially successful of the two. Chamberlain opened the weekend with a letter published by *The Times* in which he spelled out his demands.[69] His letter convinced Gladstone, fortified by Morley, that they could not hope to win his co-operation. Gladstone, in cabinet council, resorted to vague formulas of pacification designed to corner rather than conciliate Chamberlain. Apprehensive that they might succeed, Chamberlain made contingency plans for Hartington or the Conservatives to lay bare the inadequacy of any formula offered publicly by the government that fell short of his requirements. When the debate opened on Monday, Gladstone, more confident than most of his colleagues, offered his concessions in such vague language that Chamberlain and most of his sympathizers took it as proof of Gladstone's essential inflexibility. The last real hope for compromise faded.

Lesser hopes flared up and flickered over the next three weeks, until the end of May. After insisting that, from now on, any offers and responses between the government and himself should be delivered in public, Chamberlain drew Herbert Gladstone aside privately to ask whether the Home Rule Bill might be withdrawn for further discussion and revision if he first announced his willingness to accept the principle of an Irish parliament.[70] Herbert's father was not interested. But what stiffened Chamberlain's spine against further offers was not so much Gladstone's lack of interest in this particular one, as the contumely that Gladstone's followers piled on Chamberlain's head. 'I cannot struggle against the torrent of lies & slanders directed against my personal action,'

Chamberlain complained to Labouchere. 'I have been I believe more anxious for reconciliation than anyone of my followers or present allies. I have not to my knowledge said a single bitter word about Mr Gladstone or expressed either in private or in public anything but respect for him & belief in his absolute sincerity. Yet in spite of this the supporters of the Govt. are more bitter against me than against anyone else.'[71] Even as Chamberlain wrote this letter Sir Charles Dilke was presiding over a meeting of the London Liberal and Radical Council. Dilke tried to stem the tide of feeling against Chamberlain, but to no avail: speaker after speaker either ridiculed or denounced him. When Chamberlain read reports of the meeting in the next day's newspapers, he was stung by 'the brutality of some of the attacks. I am only human & I cannot stand the persistent malignity of interpretation of all my actions & motives ... I am "wounded in the house of my friends."'[72] Labouchere joined the attackers, for tactical reasons and so far without anger, but nonetheless cuttingly. 'My right hon. friend,' he told the House of Commons, is 'acting the part of a Conservative jackal ... [he] believe[s] that nothing is good which is not inaugurated by himself ... He had increased race prejudice and sectarian animosities' and hence deserved the epithet recently applied to Lord Randolph Churchill: 'he is half a traitor.'[73]

Amid this deepening chorus, Gladstone adhered to a pattern in his manoeuvring for support from Liberal MPs. Whenever he thought it prudent to offer concessions, he worded his offers vaguely until Chamberlain had rejected them. Then Gladstone clarified the offers to make Chamberlain look unreasonable. The last offer Gladstone made, at a meeting in the Foreign Office for all but the decidedly irreconcilable Liberal MPs, came close to succeeding in its intent of depriving Chamberlain of most of his support. Only an intervention by the Conservatives saved him from surrender or ignominious defeat. Taunted by Sir Michael Hicks Beach in the House of Commons, Gladstone denied that he envisaged an extensive reconstruction of the bill. This admission dashed the hopes that his speech at the Foreign Office had raised, and hence consolidated the support for Chamberlain.

At last sure of himself, Chamberlain broke the silence he had maintained for some time in the debate on the Home Rule Bill in the Commons. He delivered perhaps the most powerful speech he had ever given in the House. The most remarkable feature of the speech was the respect he paid to Gladstone: 'the British democracy,' he observed, 'has a passionate devotion to the Prime Minister – a devotion earned and deserved by 50 years of public service, and that sentiment is as honourable to him as it is to those who feel and express it.' The demand Chamberlain made with most feeling was for a measure of the same kind though not degree of respect for himself. Alluding to the line of argument that Labouchere had often made to him, Chamberlain said in closing: 'not a day passes in which I do not receive dozens or scores of letters urging and beseeching me for my own sake to vote for the Bill and to "dish the Whigs." Well, Sir, the temptation is no doubt a great one; but, after all, I am not base enough to serve my personal ambition by betraying my country; and I am convinced that when the heat of this discussion is passed and over, Liberals will not judge harshly those who have pursued what they honestly believed to be the path of duty, even although it may lead to the disruption of Party ties, and to the loss of influence and power which it is the legitimate ambition of every man to seek among his political friends and associates.'[74]

He continued to receive the trust he desired from Birmingham. Some of the finest men there responded to the mud that was being cast at him with the same uncomprehending dismay that he himself felt. 'How is it,' asked R.W. Dale, the Congregationalist leader, 'that Mr. Chamberlain is the object of so much bitterness? Lord Hartington and Mr. Bright are just as responsible as he is for throwing out the Bill ... He is loyally carrying out the principles on this question which he advocated at Warrington [during the general election] last year ... He may be mistaken, as other men have been; but he stands by the faith which he professes and has made the heaviest personal sacrifices in doing so.'[75] Powell Williams, one of Chamberlain's fellow MPs for Birmingham, gave him still sweeter support. Williams disagreed with Chamberlain's final decision to vote against the second reading, yet Williams intended to follow him: 'Partly because I value your friendship in a very special degree: and partly because, having supported you in the manly course you have taken, I will not be guilty, whatever may be my own opinion upon the particular point at issue, of the meanness of standing aloof from you in the critical moment.'[76] Henry Broadhurst, the trade union leader who sat for another of the Birmingham constituencies, was still a minor member and supporter of the government; but he parted from Chamberlain regretfully, suspecting that the treatment of Chamberlain by the ruling grandees of the party was actuated by class antagonism towards the pretensions of a man who had not come from the traditional elite.[77]

Gladstone's treatment of Chamberlain as the debate on the second reading came to its close stood in marked contrast to Chamberlain's treatment of Gladstone. The night before the Commons was scheduled to vote, Gladstone commented to Lord Rosebery: 'I think with great comfort of the fact that in all human probability all connection between Chamberlain and myself is over for ever.'[78] Next evening, concluding the debate, Gladstone devoted the most striking part of his speech to an indictment of Chamberlain:

My right hon. Friend says that a Dissolution has no terrors for him. I do not wonder at it. I do not see how a Dissolution can have any terrors for him. He has trimmed his vessel and he has touched his rudder in such a masterly way that in whichever direction the winds of Heaven may blow they must fill his sails ... I do not wonder that a Dissolution has no terrors for him, because he is prepared ... with such a series of expedients to meet all the possible contingencies of the case. Well, Sir, when I come to look at these practical alternatives and provisions, I find that they are visibly creations of the vivid imagination born of the hour and perishing with the hour, totally and absolutely unavailable for the solution of a great and difficult problem, the weight of which, and the urgency of which, my right hon. Friend himself in other days has seemed to feel.[79]

By all accounts, though a fine speech, Gladstone's concluding address did not sway a single waverer. Chamberlain more than held his own. The bill was rejected by a margin of thirty votes, more than had been expected.

When the vote was announced, the Irish contingent rose en masse to cheer the Grand Old Man. Then they turned on Chamberlain and shouted, 'Traitor! Judas!' In doing so, they set an example that many of the Gladstonians quickly followed. The evening after the vote, John Morley spoke to a Liberal club and directed his fire against Chamberlain's radical Unionists. Then, in a terrible twist of allusion, he applied the lines of Mark Antony on the assassination of Julius Caesar to the defeat of Gladstone:

> Look! In this place ran Cassius' dagger through;
> See what a rent the envious Casca made;
> Through this the well-beloved Brutus stabbed.

The phrase 'envious Casca' immediately stuck to Chamberlain – but wasn't Morley the 'well-beloved Brutus' who had stabbed his erstwhile Caesar? No one could have wounded Chamberlain more deeply.

Labouchere too felt betrayed by the master whom he would have loved to follow. His patient hope turned overnight into wild contempt. He looked upon Chamberlain 'much as the Apostles would have regarded

Judas if he had come swaggering into supper with an orchid in his
buttonhole and said that the Christian religion would not go on if his
"flower" were not adopted and himself recognised as its chief exponent.'[80]

Time would not heal these wounds. The angry estrangement between
erstwhile friends and followers wrecked an initially promising attempt
among Liberal leaders in 1887 to hammer out a common policy on
Ireland. These Round Table conferences broke down, not over Ireland,
but over Chamberlain's reaction to continuing attacks upon him by the
Gladstonians and over their reaction to his abrasive analysis of the lead
that Gladstone was giving to the party. Even when the new alignment
between Gladstonians and Unionists became a settled part of the political
landscape, the bitterness persisted. After the opening of the new century,
when Labouchere was an old man, Chamberlain saw him and, turning to
his companions, snarled, 'A bundle of old rags!'[81]

NOTES

1 A.B. Cooke and John Vincent, *The Governing Passion* (Brighton, 1974).
2 Peter T. Marsh, *The Discipline of Popular Government* (Hassocks, 1978).
3 Viscount Morley, *Recollections* (2 vols., New York, 1917), I, 147.
4 Ibid., 209.
5 D.A. Hamer, *John Morley* (Oxford, 1968), 77.
6 Michael Barker, *Gladstone and Radicalism* (New York, 1975), 4-5, and Hamer, *Morley*, 166-7.
7 Morley, *Recollections*, I, 204.
8 Morley to Chamberlain, 13 December 1885, Chamberlain Papers, University of Birmingham, JC5/54/663.
9 Chamberlain to Morley, 15 December 1885 (copy), Chamberlain Papers, JC5/54/665. All direct citations from letters by Joseph Chamberlain are by permission of the University of Birmingham.
10 Morley to Chamberlain, 16 December 1885, Chamberlain Papers, JC5/54/666.
11 Chamberlain to Morley, 21 December 1885 (copy), Chamberlain Papers, JC5/54/668.
12 Morley to Chamberlain, 24 December 1885, Chamberlain Papers, JC5/54/670.
13 Chamberlain to Morley, 24 December 1885 (copy), Chamberlain Papers, JC5/54/669.
14 Morley to Chamberlain, 28 December 1885, Chamberlain Papers, JC5/54/674.

15 Chamberlain to Morley, 29 December 1885 (copy), Chamberlain Papers, JC5/54/676.
16 Morley to Chamberlain, 1 January 1886, Chamberlain Papers, JC5/54/677.
17 Cooke and Vincent, *Governing Passion*, 321.
18 Ibid., 352.
19 Labouchere to Herbert Gladstone, 28 December 1885, and enclosure, Viscount Gladstone Papers, British Library, Add. MS 46015, ff. 125-8.
20 Hamer, *Morley*, 180.
21 Morley, *Recollections*, I, 214.
22 Cooke and Vincent, *Governing Passion*, 351.
23 Notes of 18, 22, and 23 March 1886, W.E. Gladstone Papers, British Library, Add. MS 44647, ff. 44-5 and 50-1.
24 Morley to Chamberlain, 7 April 1886, Chamberlain Papers, JC5/54/687.
25 Chamberlain to Churchill, 10 April 1886, Churchill Papers, Churchill College, Cambridge.
26 Quoted by Labouchere to Chamberlain, 1 May 1886, in Chamberlain, *A Political Memoir, 1880-92*, ed. C.H.D. Howard (London, 1953), 213.
27 Chamberlain to Labouchere, 2 May 1886 (copy), Chamberlain Papers, JC5/50/88.
28 Dilke to Chamberlain, 5 May 1886, Chamberlain Papers, JC5/24/175.
29 Ibid., and Dilke to Chamberlain, May Day 1886, Chamberlain Papers, JC5/24/177.
30 Chamberlain to Dilke, 3 May 1886, Dilke Papers, British Library.
31 Chamberlain to Dilke, 4 May 1886 (copy), Chamberlain Papers, JC5/24/486.
32 Dilke to Chamberlain, 5 May 1886, Chamberlain Papers, JC5/24/175.
33 Chamberlain to Dilke, 6 May 1886, Dilke Papers.
34 Dilke to Chamberlain, 6 May 1886, Chamberlain Papers, JC5/24/179.
35 Chamberlain to Dilke, 21 May 1886, Dilke Papers.
36 Louis Creswicke, *The Life of the Right Honourable Joseph Chamberlain* (4 vols., London, 1904-5), II, 100.
37 Chamberlain to Dilke, 19 December 1885, Dilke Papers, Add. MS 43887, ff. 216-17.
38 R.J. Hind, *Henry Labouchere and the Empire, 1880-1905* (London, 1972), 98 and 115.
39 Ibid., 119.
40 Ibid., 126.
41 Labouchere to Chamberlain, 5 December 1885, Chamberlain Papers, JC5/50/42.
42 Chamberlain to Labouchere, 7 December 1885 (copy), Chamberlain Papers, JC5/50/43.

43 Chamberlain to Labouchere, 11 December 1885 (copy), Chamberlain Papers, JC5/50/44; and to Dilke, 15 December 1885, Dilke Papers.

44 Labouchere to Chamberlain, 25 December 1885, Chamberlain Papers, JC5/50/54.

45 Hamer, *Morley*, 170.

46 *The Times*, 18 December 1885, 7.

47 Gladstone to Chamberlain, 18 December 1885, Chamberlain Papers, JC5/34/46.

48 Chamberlain to Gladstone, 19 December 1885, W.E. Gladstone Papers, Add. MS 44126.

49 Gladstone to Chamberlain, 18 December 1885, Chamberlain Papers, JC5/34/46.

50 Chamberlain to Labouchere, 26 December 1885 (copy), Chamberlain Papers, JC5/50/53.

51 Chamberlain to Labouchere, 3 January 1886 (copy), Chamberlain Papers, JC5/50/60.

52 Chamberlain, *Political Memoir*, 187-8.

53 Cooke and Vincent, *Governing Passion*, 357.

54 Chamberlain to R.B. Brett, 8 February 1886, Second Viscount Esher Papers, Churchill College, Cambridge, 5/4.

55 Chamberlain to Labouchere, 15 February 1886 (copy), Chamberlain Papers, JC5/50/68.

56 Cooke and Vincent, *Governing Passion*, 381.

57 W.E. Gladstone Papers, Add. MS 44647, f. 54.

58 J.L. Hammond, *Gladstone and the Irish Nation* (London, 1938), 495.

59 Cooke and Vincent, *Governing Passion*, 403.

60 Labouchere to Chamberlain, 17 April 1886, Chamberlain Papers, JC5/50/74.

61 Schnadhorst to Chamberlain, 13 February, and 15 and 21 April 1886, Chamberlain Papers, JC5/63/9, 15, and 16; and Schnadhorst to Labouchere, 4 April 1886, Viscount Gladstone Papers, Add. MS 46016, ff. 23-4.

62 H.R.G. Whates, *The Birmingham Post, 1857-1957* (Birmingham, 1957), 123.

63 *The Times*, 22 April 1886, 10.

64 22 April 1886, Chamberlain Papers, JC8/5/3/14.

65 Chamberlain to Dilke, 22 April 1886, Dilke Papers, Add. MS 49610, ff. 24-5; to Bunce, 30 April 1886 (copy), and to Labouchere, 30 April 1886 (copy), Chamberlain Papers, JC5/8/87 and 5/50/84.

66 Barker, *Gladstone and Radicalism*, 107-11.

67 Cooke and Vincent, *Governing Passion*, 413.

68 Ibid., 415-18.

69 *The Times*, 8 May 1886, 12.

70 Chamberlain to Labouchere, 11 May 1886 (copy), Chamberlain Papers, JC5/50/105; and Charles Mallet, *Herbert Gladstone* (London, 1932), 129-30.

71 Chamberlain to Labouchere, 17 May 1886 (copy), Chamberlain Papers, JC5/50/109.

72 Chamberlain to Dilke, 20 May 1886, Dilke Papers.

73 3 *Hansard*, 305: 1339-41 (18 May 1886).

74 Ibid., 698-700 (1 June 1886).

75 N. Murrell Marris, *The Right Honourable Joseph Chamberlain* (London, 1900), 260-1.

76 Williams to Chamberlain, 3 June 1886, Chamberlain Papers, JC5/72/6.

77 Henry Broadhurst, *Henry Broadhurst, M.P.* (London, 1901), 197.

78 Cooke and Vincent, *Governing Passion*, 431.

79 3 *Hansard*, 306: 1233-4 (7 June 1886).

80 Hesketh Pearson, *Labby* (London, 1936), 200.

81 Ibid., 281.

SUE BROWN

One Last Campaign from the GOM: Gladstone and the House of Lords in 1894

It was Asquith who later described Gladstone's call in 1894 for change in the relations between the two Houses of Parliament as 'the legacy which he left to his party.'[1] The description suggests dignity both in the selection and reception of the issue to which Gladstone devoted his final speech in the House of Commons and on which he would have liked to have pre-cipitated an early election. It may even conjure up the image of the Grand Old Man purposefully pointing his followers towards the Promised Land which age now prevented him from entering, with a party respectfully accepting the trust handed to them.

The reality was rather different. To his cabinet colleagues, Gladstone's resort to 'the question of the Lords' in February 1894 was both unexpected and unwanted. Indeed, the majority saw it as little more than a diversionary tactic aimed at covering over his fundamental disagree-ment with them on another issue. From their point of view, this broadening of the Gladstonian inheritance to take in a second 'heroic measure' to set alongside Home Rule was at best fortuitous, at worst gratuitous. Gladstone recognized and resented this assessment. Brooding in retirement on the peremptoriness with which his cabinet had dismissed his call for a dissolution against the Lords in the spring of 1894, he became more, not less, convinced that a great opportunity had been lost for advancing the issue with the Lords to a decisive stage. In retrospect, his initiative assumed a cogency which his colleagues had entirely failed to perceive at the time. Indeed, he described his grasp of what might have been achieved by the election campaign they had denied him as one of only four occasions in his career when he had exercised his one 'striking gift' of 'insight into the facts of particular eras, and their relations one to another, which generates in the mind a conviction that the materials exist for forming a public opinion, and for directing it to a particular end.'[2]

Who was right? Was the bid for a dissolution simply, as Gladstone's cabinet thought and as Professor Stansky has described it, an example of his 'uncanny skill in getting round an obstacle of his own creation'?[3] Or was he rather, in fixing on the issue of the Lords, 'characteristically rang[ing] ahead' in a necessary act of final leadership, as Professor Hamer has suggested?[4] And, whatever the origin of the 'legacy,' how clearly was it seen as such and what was its substance?

In one respect, Gladstone could hardly blame his colleagues for failing to appreciate the full importance of his initiative, since in first presenting it he went out of his way to underline its improvisatory character. That the inspiration was a sudden one is also suggested by the account of its origins left by Sir Algernon West, his private secretary at the time, who even claimed that he, rather than Gladstone, was the first to realize that by insisting on the Dudley amendment to the Employers' Liability Bill the Lords might have opened the way to an early dissolution.[5] Nor were the prospects for the initiative improved by the fact that at the time he launched it Gladstone was away from London and clearly somewhat out of touch with the progress of government business. On 13 January he had gone to Biarritz, ostensibly for reasons of health but, in reality, more as a way of distancing himself from his last and least favourite cabinet. Though the immediate cause of the breakdown in his relations with his colleagues was his opposition to the increase in the naval estimates that Spencer, the first lord of the Admiralty, was proposing, the disagreement on this issue was symptomatic of a wider disengagement from the affairs of his government and a lack of sympathy with most of his colleagues, particularly in the Commons.

The defeat of the Home Rule Bill in the Lords in September 1893 had left him with little to hold his continuing attention in politics. He did not follow the detail of the two main bills before the Commons in the special autumn session that was called to make up for the parliamentary time that had been lost on the Irish measure.[6] Nor did he exercise consistent direction over the activities of his government. The cabinet met infrequently and differences were rarely resolved there. Deafness and failing eyesight cut Gladstone off from his colleagues and increased his irritability, loquaciousness, and dictatorial manner of dealing with them. Above all, he was bored. There was no obvious way in which he could revive Home Rule in Parliament and no other great issues to excite his interest. He talked increasingly in the autumn of 1893 of early release from political life and sought without success for a way of bringing forward the dissolution that both he and the party managers agreed was to be made the occasion for his retirement.[7] Boredom made Gladstone unpredictable. It also fostered the growth of dissension between him and his colleagues.

The crisis over the navy estimates arose suddenly at the end of the year.[8] At first it appeared that Gladstone would reluctantly accept some increase and that accommodation with Spencer over the figures might be possible. But as discussion continued in the second half of December and the cabinet came round to the idea of higher spending, its chief moved in the opposite direction. His determination to resist became both firmer and more emotional. Initially, he had criticized the increase as extravagant and as a stimulus to 'militarism'; now he fell back on the argument that concession would damage his prestige.[9] At cabinet on 9 January an impasse was reached. Gladstone, however, refused either to give way or to resign, despite the fact that the government was under pressure to make an early announcement on the estimates. Instead, he announced that he would shortly be leaving for a holiday in Biarritz and that no cabinets were to be held in his absence.[10] These de Gaulle-like tactics failed. As Gladstone's stay in France lengthened, his colleagues, far from changing their minds on the estimates, began to accustom themselves to the possibility of his going. With some, manoeuvring for the succession and for place in a reconstructed administration intensified.[11]

Although in the autumn Gladstone had pleaded with West and Marjoribanks for early release from office, the cabinet's apparent willingness to dispense with him now bred a determination to go at a time of his, not their, choosing. The prospect of being forced out shocked him deeply, and it was not until 29 January that he appeared to accept that his refusal to give way on the estimates left him with no option but immediate retirement.[12] Almost nine years before his wife had written: 'Two things [Uncle William] is very strong about: that he should not go without a cry (he never yet has) or without old colleagues.'[13] Unless he wanted to make public the disagreement over the estimates, however, Gladstone now faced the prospect of going with neither cry nor colleagues, but having instead to base his resignation on no more than the 'rational, sufficient and ready to hand' pretext of the condition of his eyes and ears.[14]

The possibility of making an exit more satisfying to his temperament arose suddenly and, apparently, unexpectedly. The afternoon post on 30 January brought word not only of a forthcoming announcement in the *Pall Mall Gazette* of his imminent retirement, but also a report that the

House of Lords had insisted on reinserting the Dudley amendment into the Employers' Liability Bill despite its earlier rejection in the Commons by the unusually large majority of sixty-two. West gives a lively account in his diary of the inspiriting effect of the news on Gladstone. Both immediately agreed on the need to issue a denial of the *Pall Mall* announcement. Sir Algernon then had a cheering inspiration:

One thing occurred to me [he wrote], as bearing on the question, which was that rejection by the Lords of the Employers' Liability Bill might hasten the possibility of a dissolution. This seemed to make a great impression on him, and I rather emphasised it.

'Home Rule,' 'Fisheries,' 'Employers' Liability Bill,' and probably 'Parish Councils.'

I then said I would leave him for a bit to think it out ...

At dinner Mr. Gladstone was very cheerful, saying the whole position was now altered, and there was then no further allusion to the Navy Estimates.[15]

Even so, it was not until six days later that West's impromptu suggestion had fully matured in Gladstone's mind into the idea of an immediate dissolution on the Lords. Characteristically, it had by then assumed a comprehensiveness that was far beyond West's creativity. As if at a stroke, Gladstone appeared to have found a way out of all his varied difficulties. Resort to the issue of the Lords not only meant that he would be able to go out with 'a cry' but also provided a way round his problem with the estimates. If supply could be voted for a further month on the existing basis to cover the election period, a decision to increase provision for the navy could be deferred until after he had retired at the end of the election. A campaign fought on the two related issues of Home Rule and the House of Lords would also enable him, against all the odds, to fulfil his commitment to the Irish members to revive Home Rule in 1894. Above all, it would give him the opportunity to bow out from political life on a high note after further renewal of his moral and political energies in one last great campaign. The dominant theme of that campaign was already clear in his mind. It was the 'neat, compact sort of crime' committed by the Lords in wrecking the work of an entire session which would 'make the foundation of a charge against them.'[16]

Just as the apparent acceptance of his imminent retirement and news of its impending announcement in the *Pall Mall Gazette* had stimulated Gladstone into a last attempt at circumventing the inevitable, so it was the receipt of a letter from Edward Marjoribanks, the chief whip, on

4 February, delicately suggesting that he should couple his resignation from the premiership with retirement from the House of Commons, which seems to have triggered Gladstone into launching his new idea on his colleagues. He told West that

> the situation was now changed. It depended whether the House of Lords had completed its tale of iniquities: if so, he would obtain a provisional vote for Army and Navy first, and then ask the country to judge of him by the past – not the future – and to give a commission to the new Government to deal with the House of Lords ...
>
> Mr. Gladstone brilliant at déjeuner, being full of his new idea, saying he had strength enough, and physique enough for the fight with the Lords. But pointing to his eyes.[17]

Gladstone fleshed out his idea in letters to Marjoribanks, Morley, and Harcourt on this and the next day. To all of them he stressed the way in which the Lords' insistence on the Dudley amendment and subsequent reception of the Parish Councils Bill had opened up unexpected courses of action. To Morley, for instance, he wrote: 'the proceedings in the Lords appear to be raising a question altogether new and one perhaps capable of changing the situation ... You wrote on February 2 and this question does not seem to have come into your mind. Late in that day or perhaps on the following day it came into mine.' And in a postscript to a letter to Mundella defending his stand on the naval estimates he again went out of his way to underline the suddenness with which the political aspect had changed: 'The Lords may raise for us another not less urgent question crossing the scent. The unforeseen sometimes does much in politics.'[18]

Gladstone's description of the Lords' action as 'unforeseen,' however, was more indicative of how out of touch he was with the progress of government business through Parliament, than of the unexpectedness of the Lords' insistence on the Dudley amendment or of their comprehensive attack on the Parish Councils Bill when they first considered it at the beginning of February. The fact that the House of Commons was not sitting at the time inevitably focused public attention on the House of Lords in the first major test for nearly ten years of its attitude towards Liberal non-Irish legislation. Given the overwhelming Unionist predominance that had built up there since 1885, the modest revival in the prestige of the House as a result of its rejection of Home Rule, and the smallness of the government's majority in the Commons, there was little room for doubt that the Lords would mount some opposition to the Parish Councils

Bill if only to demonstrate the determination of the majority to be seen championing the sectional interests under threat from the measure. Nor was the Lords' insistence on maintaining their attack on the prohibition of 'contracting out' in the Employers' Liability Bill particularly unexpected. They had been encouraged in this by the dissent from the government line of a small number of Liberals in the Commons as well as by regional differences of view among the work force on the need to maintain 'contracted out' schemes which, as even the government admitted, offered fuller and more accessible compensation for industrial injuries than would be available under the act.[19] If anything, then, it was the very expectedness of the Lords' opposition that obliged Gladstone to try to present it as unexpected. He was on stronger ground, however, in not accepting its inevitability. While his colleagues tended to take the hostility of the House of Lords for granted, he refused to see it as a necessary fact of political life. His aim therefore was to revive their sense of shock and outrage at the obstructive conduct of the peers.

West was despatched to London to find out how serious the Lords' amendments to the Parish Councils Bill were and to test out the reactions of Gladstone's colleagues to the idea of an early dissolution. He was furnished with an additional argument in favour of the plan: this was that while Gladstone was prepared to stay on a little longer to lead the Liberals in a spring election, if the dissolution were delayed his services would no longer be available and the Liberals would have to fight the election without him.[20]

The speed with which Gladstone had developed his plan for an early election on the Lords was more than equalled by the haste with which his colleagues rejected it. Asquith, one of its strongest opponents, told West that there was still some way to go on the Employers' Liability Bill, while Kimberley, who had charge of the Parish Councils Bill in the Lords, explained, at customary length, 'how impossible it would be to throw it out and attack the Lords on its present aspect.'[21] As leader in the Lords, he also had the responsibility for summarizing his colleagues' reaction to Gladstone's initiative. He did so as politely as he felt able, telegraphing Gladstone that they were 'strongly and unanimously against proposal to dissolve.'[22] In private, both Harcourt and Morley were more trenchant: the one thought Gladstone's initiative 'simply insane,' the other 'that of all the extraordinary proposals recently made this was the most impossible and preposterous.'[23] Marjoribanks set out the objections more carefully: the party was not ready for an early election; the Lords had not gone far enough; the announcement on the estimates could not be put off till after the election; and the Liberals should not dissolve until they had either carried a Registration Bill or it had been thrown out by the Lords, since in the one case they might expect to gain a useful electoral advantage and, in the other, they would have a worthwhile cry against the Lords.[24]

These were all considerations that Gladstone later dismissed as 'secondary,' though at the time he admitted that there was some force in all but the second.[25] The real obstacle to acceptance of his proposal, he believed, lay rather 'in the disposition, and in the wants of disposition, prevailing among his immediate friends.'[26] They had made no concession to the authority that his position as leader should have given to his proposal, nor any allowance for the personal difficulties that had helped to shape it. Nor had they weighed the advantage of retaining his campaigning abilities in the fight with the Lords against the more tangible drawbacks listed by Marjoribanks.

Professor Stansky has suggested that it was the third of these – that an announcement on changes in the estimates could not be held over till after the election – that was crucial, since it 'eliminated' 'the major reason for dissolution.'[27] Gladstone's own recollections of the episode give a very different picture. Indeed, in a memorandum written in 1896, he even suggested that one of his reasons for delaying agreement on the estimates had been to allow the Lords sufficient time to show how far they meant to carry their opposition to the Liberals' domestic programme so that the government could 'then consider whether to raise a definitive issue with them.' Even if the contemporary record hardly bears out this explanation of his opposition to the increased estimates, it is fair to point out that Gladstone's isolation on that issue became less a reason for courting a second defeat in cabinet by raising the issue of the Lords, than a reason why the proposal for a dissolution was not properly considered by his colleagues. There is nothing to suggest that he would not have put forward the idea of a campaign against the Lords in the spring of 1894, whatever the state of his relations with the cabinet: the existence of the unresolved conflict on the estimates, however, left him too weak to pursue his initiative, while it gave others the excuse for not having to consider it on its merits. 'Had I not had cataract entailing early disability [he wrote]: had I not been eighty-three years old: had I not had vital controversy with my colleagues on the Estimates, such as to break up or dislocate our whole relations, I might have come to London and proved the question of dissolution.'[28] In fact, after his return to London on 10 February, he did not immediately give up the idea of a dissolution against the Lords, even though it could not release him from his problem over the estimates. So far as his colleagues were concerned, however, the idea had by then been decisively ruled out. As Rosebery later wrote, 'they [had] scarcely even considered it serious.'[29]

The brief episode of Gladstone's failure to get his colleagues' consent for 'one last great campaign' appeared to them, as it has largely appeared subsequently, as little more than a last, if desperate, example of his 'great if unconscious tenacity of office'[30] and of the way in which lack of time towards the end of his career produced a kind of political foreshortening, leading him into over-optimistic tactical miscalculation. Above all, it suggests an egotism verging on opportunism, for while an early election apparently offered a way for Gladstone to get round his own difficulties, both practical and temperamental, he would be doing so at the expense of his party. Immediate dissolution, which implied the loss both of Employers' Liability and Parish Councils bills, would send the Liberals to the polls on an old register with the party organization in poor shape and no significant achievements to offer the electorate. If they lost, however, Gladstone, unlike his colleagues, would not have to face the consequences, since, whatever the outcome, he intended to retire. Equally, however, if they won, his successors would be left to pursue an issue of his, not their, choosing, and one of particular difficulty. In offering himself only for the task of creating a sufficient Commons majority to tackle the Lords, he would be taking on much the easier part of the business. The problems of getting acceptance of any one plan of reform and of securing Royal Assent would fall to others.

Premature, ill-prepared, and even ill-informed Gladstone's initiative may have been, but it was neither as preposterous as his colleagues pretended nor as unpremeditated as he himself implied. Though the proposal might have proved less unpalatable if it had not contained a procedural device which relieved him of the necessity to give way on the estimates, and might have been less hastily dismissed if he had been able to introduce it in person, the speed with which the cabinet rejected it reflected the innate difficulty of dealing with the Lords, the practical drawbacks to an early election, the uncertainty of success in a campaign led by an octogenarian in poor health, and a feeling that Gladstone was putting his own interests above those of the party. Their response also revealed that characteristic of his colleagues which Professor Stansky has described as 'a curious passivity in the face of events, a less than passionate commitment to policies in which they professed to believe, a conviction that their decisions did not really matter.'[31] Half of them claimed to favour abolition of the House of Lords,[32] and all of them, when faced with engagements to speak at times when they had nothing particular to say, happily fell back on 'the maxim, "When in doubt slang the Lords." '[33] But confronted with the possibility of trying to deal with the Lords in earnest, they very readily assumed that the cup was not yet full or the time as ripe as it would become for action.

In this, they, like Gladstone, failed to take much account of the views of the party. There were signs of restiveness both in the National Liberal Federation and in the Commons throughout the 1892-5 Parliament at the caution with which the leadership were deploying the issue against the Lords. On the same day, for example, that Harcourt dismissed Gladstone's proposal as 'simply insane,'[34] Robert Hudson, the effective secretary of the federation, in conversation with Edward Hamilton, 'did not give an unfavourable account of electioneering prospects. The constituencies were, he admitted, in a very lethargic state last year: they never were and never would be enamoured of Home Rule; but there were signs now that they were waking up again. The chance of a conflict with the House of Lords was doing very inspiriting work.'[35] Nor did the cabinet appear to be aware of the fears of some Liberal Unionists about the consequences of an early dissolution on the Lords. A day before Gladstone had even proposed it, Henry James was writing to the Duke of Devonshire in some alarm about the growing expectation in the Liberal party of a March election: 'In the last two days all the Gladstonians I meet are triumphant – "Dissolution in March" they say, "Employers' Liability in the towns, and Parish Councils in the counties will do very well as cries for us." And so they will – it is a wretched affair.'[36] Clearly, if he had known of Gladstone's initiative, James would have found it a good deal less 'preposterous' than did Morley.

Nor, as Harcourt knew, was it entirely unpremeditated. The speed with which Gladstone was obliged to launch his proposal because of the unresolved disagreement on the estimates meant that he failed to do full justice to its strategic character. The idea of an election at the end of the session was thus presented not as the natural outcome of the general anti-Lords programme that he had laid down for his government in the immediate aftermath of the 1892 election, but as the result of unforeseen developments in Parliament. The omission was the more striking in view of the fact that, as long ago as July 1892, Gladstone had predicted an election against the Lords at the end of the 1893 session and set out an aggressive strategy for engineering it.

The plan developed out of his immediate recognition that the outcome of the election had left him with a majority that was quite inadequate for forcing Home Rule through the Lords and possibly so small that the Lords would feel able to frustrate the rest of the government's programme. His initial reaction was to abandon altogether the futile attempt to carry a Home Rule Bill and, instead, to present resolutions setting out the government's policy on Ireland. As far as the rest of the Liberals' enormous programme was concerned, he concluded that they would need to concentrate on those measures assumed to be beyond the reach of the Lords either because, like repeal of coercion in Ireland, they could be accomplished by administrative action, or, as with death duties and the taxation of ground rents, because of their financial content.[37] Under the stimulus of correspondence with Spencer and Harcourt, however, this essentially defensive strategy quickly assumed a more active character: by the end of July he was writing to Harcourt in a letter setting out the prospectus for his government:

I conceive that we have
1. To cast the balance fairly between Irish and British claims.
2. To anticipate mischief as most probable in the House of Lords.
3. To open on that House as many good *bouches à feu* as possible.
4. To frame our proposals with a view particularly to passing them through the Commons.
5. To study particularly with this view those subjects which can be very concisely handled in Bills.

He concluded his letter with a characteristic double negative designed to cover him against all eventualities: 'I see the not unlikelihood of another Dissolution before Session 1894: but after that even in my most sanguine moods I can only regard myself as a possible *amicus curiae*.'[38]

Although the idea of deliberately putting pressure on the Lords was possibly the most coherent, and certainly the most aggressive, line which a Liberal government with a small and unreliable majority could take, the clear outlines of the anti-Lords strategy soon became blurred. In part, this arose from the broadening of the government's legislative programme for its first session to include far more subjects than could be 'very concisely handled' and, in part, because the amount of parliamentary time consumed by Home Rule left little over, until the autumn session, for opening other '*bouches à feu*' on the Lords. Above all, however, the failure to pursue it really effectively was symptomatic of the lack of cohesion in Gladstone's last administration. Nonetheless, the prime minister did not wholly lose sight of it, and the prospect of conflict with the Lords engaged his attention sporadically throughout the autumn.

He persisted, for instance, in looking for an alternative to mere acquiescence in the Lords' rejection of Home Rule and floated the possibility of reintroducing his bill in the Upper House in 1894 as a way of keeping pressure on the peers and enabling them to 'repeat their offence' against Ireland.[39] It was an idea that he did not finally give up until the end of the year, despite the efforts of Asquith and Marjoribanks to dissuade him.[40] His approach to the autumn session was also rather different from that of his colleagues. While they were primarily concerned with making up for time lost on Home Rule by getting something on the statute book – the two main measures chosen for the session were selected not just because of their appeal to the urban and rural working classes but because they were considered relatively uncontroversial and thus likely to get through the Lords[41] – Gladstone's interest was more engaged by the prospect of building up the case against the Lords. Though he was only marginally involved in the framing of either measure, he kept an eye on the parliamentary progress of the first of the two to reach the Lords, and gave a lead in cabinet in the decision to 'Resist the Lords Amts. *simpliciter*' to the Employers' Liability Bill.[42]

Only when he became involved in the dispute over the estimates did he temporarily lose sight of the developing issue with the Lords. He rediscovered it at the end of January with a suddenness and apparent sense of surprise indicative of how completely the prospect of being 'put out'[43] of office had monopolized his attention during that month. It was this appearance of being taken unawares by a development that could not have seemed unexpected if he had remained in London and in touch with government business that both weakened the force of his proposal and failed to do justice to the length of time during which the idea of a dissolution against the Lords at the end of the government's first session had been maturing in his mind.

It continued to develop after his return to London as he became more, not less, convinced that the time had arrived for the Liberals to campaign against the Lords in earnest. In the three weeks of active political life remaining to him he concentrated almost exclusively on the attempt to advance the issue with the Lords. The results, however, were meagre.

On the Lords' further amendments to the Employers' Liability Bill, the disagreement between the two Houses had been narrowed down to the question of whether 'contracted out' schemes should be prohibited, as the government had proposed, or whether they could be sanctioned if they met certain conditions, as provided for in Lord Dudley's amendment. A middle course of allowing existing schemes to continue was favoured by a small group of Liberal MPs in the Commons and seen by the Duke of Devonshire as the obvious basis for settlement.[44] The government scrupulously avoided offering this and, on the bill's reappearance in the Commons on 12 February, proposed only the minimum concession necessary to keep it alive – a period of three years' grace for schemes already in operation. But they miscalculated. The compromise went too far for some and not far enough for others. It also failed to attract the Liberal Unionists. It was carried by a majority of only two, clearly not enough to recommend it as a basis for settlement with the Lords who, as expected, reinserted the full Dudley amendment. This left the government with no option but to drop the bill.

Although ministers had hoped to extract maximum propaganda value by moving dramatically that the Lords' amendments be 'laid aside,' the clerks ruled the motion out of order and the party summoned by 'a many-lined whip' in the expectation of a stirring attack on the Lords[45] heard instead a quite uncharacteristically inept speech from Gladstone proposing the 'discharge' of the Lords' amendments. He did not attack the Lords, and the superficiality of his knowledge of the bill and of the previous course of the debate on it was made manifestly clear.[46] The government thus lost the bill and failed to pin the blame for its loss as firmly on the Lords as they might have done.

Gladstone's main hope of provoking a crisis with the Lords, however, had always rested on the Parish Councils Bill. A much more complex measure that had become noticeably more radical during its long progress through the Commons, the councils bill opened a wide surface for attack. Although the Lords gave it an unopposed second reading on 25 January, in committee they ran riot, deluging the bill with amendments to restrict the operation of the newly created parish councils, retain the predominance of the propertied voter in local administration, limit the operation of compulsion in the acquisition of land for allotments, and restore church control in areas where it was threatened by the bill.

Gladstone was quite firm that there must be 'no paltering'[47] with these amendments and the government put up a resolute display when they were considered in the Commons on 15 February. Although they offered no concessions of significance, except on the appeals procedure against notice of compulsory hiring of land for allotments, the government nonetheless got support from Liberal Unionists in all divisions. Many of the Lords' amendments were negatived without a vote and the London

Poor Law clauses reinserted in full, despite the fact that the Lords' objections to them had been founded on the well-established ground that the Commons had given this part of the bill only the most cursory consideration.

On one particularly contentious issue, the composition of trusts for the administration of parochial charities, Gladstone intervened to forestall the adoption of a compromise acceptable to the House that would have narrowed the disagreement with the Lords. His defence of the Cobb clause, which provided that a majority of the trustees should be elected rather than appointed, was the more aggressive, given that it had originally been inserted as a result of radical pressure in the Commons and very reluctantly accepted by the government. But although the Lords had rejected it by an unusually large majority, and the Commons appeared willing to accept a suggestion that no more than half the trustees should be elected, Gladstone insisted on the reinsertion of the Cobb provision on the grounds that it had originally been approved by a majority of sixty-one in the Commons and there was thus no need to make any concession to the Lords.[48]

The Liberal Unionists were a critical factor in determining the fate of both the Employers' Liability and the Parish Councils bills. Chamberlain's determination to see the first killed overcame Devonshire's preference for compromise and helped to ensure that no accommodation was reached between the two Houses. Chamberlain was, however, alarmed at the comprehensiveness of the Lords' amendments to the second and the possibility that the government might throw up their bill and put the blame for its loss on the Unionist majority in the Lords.[49] At a party meeting held on 15 February there was general agreement on the need for compromise.[50] But while Liberal Unionist support reinforced the government's firm response in the Commons to the Lords' amendments, it also frustrated Gladstone's hopes of engineering a crisis on the bill. When the Lords met to reconsider it on 24 February the open split between Conservatives and Liberal Unionists forced a major climb-down by Salisbury, who withdrew his opposition to all those parts of the bill he had originally pledged himself to attack, except that concerning compensation to owners of compulsorily acquired land. Instead, he was only able to sustain amendments to two provisions, whose original character had been significantly altered under radical pressure in the Commons: the number of inhabitants in a parish required before a parish council could be set up and the composition of parochial charity trusts.

This retreat meant the end of any prospect of an early election against the Lords. On the day that the peers met to consider the bill, Gladstone finally made his long-deferred announcement to the cabinet that he would be retiring at the end of the session on grounds of ill-health.[51] Although it was now urgently necessary to wind the session up quickly and begin preparing for the new one, he was still reluctant to contemplate the concessions that might be necessary to get agreement on the bill. Harcourt 'found him breast-high to let out at the Lords, saying – "let us have no compromise; we must keep the raw and the grievance!"'[52] His cabinet, however, would not go along with this. Though he summarized their decision as one to 'resist' the Lords' amendments,[53] when debate resumed in the Commons, the front bench offered concessions on all but Salisbury's amendment on the population criterion.

Baulked of a dissolution against the Lords or a decisive conflict on the Parish Councils Bill, Gladstone had already turned to another possibility: the inclusion in the Speech from the Throne at the end of the session of some expression of regret at the lack of uniformity between the two Houses and a statement that something must be done to deal with it. From the start, the cabinet were unenthusiastic, and the proposal fell at its first hurdle when the Queen, as expected, objected.[54] Gladstone, by then on the point of retirement, was in no position to attempt persuasion.

Only one option remained, immune from the caution of colleagues or royal opposition: a valedictory statement in Parliament on the imminent need for change in the relations between the two Houses. Its occasion was the debate in the Commons on 1 March on the Lords' further amendments to the Parish Councils Bill, for, despite the general expectation that the Lords would be content with the concessions made by the government on 16 February, Salisbury insisted on the right of the Upper House to sustain its views. Though abandoned by the Liberal Unionists and supported by a much reduced Conservative majority, he again moved to raise the population limit and threw over the compromise on parochial charities that had first been mooted in the Lords and accepted by Balfour in the Commons.

Salisbury's aggression gave Gladstone an apt pretext for his criticism of the conduct of the Lords when he moved on 1 March for the acceptance under protest of their amendments. Inevitably, in what was his last House of Commons speech, Gladstone's indictment ranged beyond the immediate context. As in most of his speeches on the Lords, except those just before the 1892 election, he spoke with restraint and a lack of partisanship. He did not attack the peers for accepting from Conservative administrations what they refused Liberal governments. Instead, he criticized their conduct on four grounds, two of which were familiar and two of which he now developed more fully. The first two were the lack of that moderate leadership which, he had consistently maintained, was the only safeguard for the continued existence of an unreformed House of Lords, and the refusal of the Upper House to recognize the inevitable predominance over it of the elected House. The other two were the waste of parliamentary time resulting from the enforced loss of government bills carried with great effort through the Commons, and the growing frequency of the disagreements between the two Houses. Both of these latter points, but particularly the first, were matters of genuine and increased concern to Gladstone.

If the emphasis he now put on these difficulties was new, in another respect too he now went beyond anything he had previously said about the Lords. This concerned the way in which 'a solution' should be found to the 'tremendous contrariety and incessant conflict between the two Houses.' Since the House of Commons was a party to the quarrel with the Lords, he argued, it was not for it, but for the electorate, to resolve the conflict. Although the timing of an appeal to 'the authority of the nation' was for 'the Executive Government of the day ... alone' to decide, he now predicted that the acuteness of the problem was such that they would need to have recourse to an election 'at an early date.'[55]

Just as Gladstone's call for a dissolution against the Lords in 1894 was to appear more convincing in retrospect than at the time he made it, so his last speech in Parliament was subsequently to assume a central place in the Liberal canon despite the reservations with which it was initially received. Few then spotted its consciously valedictory character and the enhanced authority this gave to the retiring leader's assertion, which he had previously always avoided, that the time had finally arrived for the Liberals to seek fundamental change in the relations between the two Houses. Indeed, Henry Lucy wrote that its 'immediate effect ... was to discredit the supposition that resignation was imminent,'[56] while the *Daily Chronicle* commented that Gladstone must make up his mind on the question of the Lords and then either retire or say what he really thought.[57] And although some of those privy to Gladstone's decision to retire were moved by his 'call to the country to do battle against the tyranny of the House of Lords,'[58] others were less impressed. The normally sympathetic Edward Hamilton concluded that he had not 'been at his best'[59] and Rosebery 'deplored'[60] the speech. At the end of the debate, thirty-seven Liberals forced a division as a protest against the government's over-cautious approach to the Lords.

That Gladstone was bequeathing a political 'legacy' to his party was thus only dimly perceived at the time, partly because its content remained unclear. He had diagnosed what was wrong in the relations between the two Houses but stopped short of providing any specific cure. That this resulted from something more than an honourable decision on the part of an outgoing leader not to attempt to tie a divided party to any one method of Lords reform was clear from a long conversation he had with West the next day. Mr Gladstone, reported West,

> was sorry to differ with the Liberal Party in their wish to abolish the Lords. He objected to it because he thought it might bring the House of Commons in direct conflict with the Crown, and then he dreaded a second elected Chamber, which would be too strong.
>
> I did not tell him that the first reform should be expulsion of the Bishops, and he did not approve of my suggestion that the veto should be limited, as he then said the Lords would always exercise it in the way they do now.[61]

Public reticence had thus reflected private uncertainty. The reservations Gladstone expressed to West about all the most obvious ways of changing the relations between the two Houses were not, however, uncharacteristic. His disinclination to commit himself to any particular programme of Lords reform was fundamental to the restraint with which for most of his career he had handled the issue. As Edward Hamilton commented in 1884: 'The more Mr. G. contemplates the possibility [of reforming the House of Lords] the less he likes it. He does not see his way.'[62] Or again, earlier the same year: 'Mr. Gladstone regards the H. of Lords in much the same light as he regards the Established Church – that nobody would set up such institutions nowadays, but that it is quite a different thing to knock them down.'[63]

Indeed, it was not until the autumn of 1894, when Rosebery approached him for advice on the handling of the Lords issue, that Gladstone proved willing to plump for any specific course of reform, though even then he remained somewhat tentative: 'I have ... been reflecting [he wrote to Rosebery] on the big and embarrassing question of the House of Lords with the result that I am more and more inclinable to the plan which I think you rather seemed to favour: of letting the internal reforms at any rate for the present alone, and only taking effectual security for disabling them from arresting great reform on which the country has deliberately pronounced. And I do not think the *modus operandi* very difficult to decide on.'[64] This was as far as he was prepared to go – but though it pointed towards limitation of the Lords' veto it did not rule out joint conferences of the two Houses, with a limited attendance of peers, to settle disputes between them.[65]

Why was Gladstone so hesitant to commit himself to any one method of Lords reform and why, until the final weeks of his sixty-one years of political life, was he reluctant to signal to his party that the time had arrived for them to tackle the question of the Lords in earnest? The reasons for his caution go some way to explain his greater outspokenness at the end of his career.

In the first place, the whole notion of a reformed House of Lords ran counter to Gladstone's view of the role of the Upper House. He used House of Lords 'reform' in its strict sense as meaning improvement. But Gladstone saw no place in the British constitution for an 'improved' House of Lords, since to improve meant to strengthen and he thought of the Lords as essentially a weak institution which would, in time, wither away through its own inanition.[66] Beyond that, he was suspicious of all reform that had as its objective the elimination or weakening of the one element in the Lords which he regarded as a positive good – its institutionalization of the hereditary principle.[67] This apprehension, as he knew, cut him off from the mass of 'menders or enders' in his party, though he liked to think that they tolerated his views as 'the pardonable superstitions of an old man'[68] and in appropriate company, waxed eloquent on his predisposition to be 'an out-and-out inequalitarian.'[69]

Exposure to popular feeling against the Lords in 1884 had also left him wary about the extent to which expectations of political change resulting from House of Lords reform would ever be met. Forcible abolition was beyond both his own temperamental horizon and the realm of the practicable. Anything less, however, risked the creation of a legitimized and strengthened Second Chamber. 'Knocking the Lords' was easy; changing them much more difficult and the consequences unpredictable. Alteration in the composition of the Lords might remove the grievance over the source of its powers; limitation of its powers, however, would make it impossible to question the right of the House to exercise whatever more restricted powers then belonged to it. As he warned a Scottish ecclesiastical delegation in September 1884 on the question of reform of the Lords, 'One feels that the ventilation of an abstract opinion is one thing and giving practical effect to it another.'[70]

Ten years later, after a decade in which he had not entirely avoided the perils of which he had warned, he was, when on the point of retirement, freed from the responsibility of having to satisfy exaggerated expectations aroused by the expression of 'abstract opinions.' Nor was he obliged to choose any particular one of the various routes to an obstruction-free Liberal Parliament preferred by the different sections of his party. His conviction that the activism of the Lords had become an intolerable hurdle for Liberal governments could – and did – coexist with a continuing disinclination to consider ways of limiting it. The timing of his departure enabled him to avow openly the one without being obliged to throw over the other, and thereby removed one of the major constraints that had so far coloured his handling of the Lords issue. Thus what he offered the party was a campaign against the Lords, not a programme for reforming it.

In September 1881, when he believed that his retirement was imminent, he had written to Bright: 'It is I think one of the advantages of the last stages of public life that one may use it to say things which, though true and needful in themselves, could not properly be said by any man with twenty or even ten years of his career before him.'[71] The assertion, in his last House of Commons speech, of the need for an early election against the Lords was one of the best examples, and certainly the last, of his willingness to use the freedom which, he believed, the prospect of release from office gave him. It was not, however, either an irresponsible or an unpremeditated statement.

That Gladstone would choose to end his career by attacking the House of Lords had seemed likely for some time – and not only among die-hards appalled by his onslaughts on 'the classes.' In 1882 even the putting-down of a motion of censure against the Lords for its Committee of Inquiry into the operation of the second Irish Land Act was enough to start rumours in the Commons that Gladstone was about to retire.[72] There was then an appropriateness, even inevitability, about the choice of subject for his final parliamentary speech. In three out of four of the administrations he had headed, he had had to devote much of his energies to circumventing, mollifying, or rebuffing opposition from the Lords. In his last administration the Upper House had frustrated the major legislative ambition of the final phase of his political career. His conclusion that its activism was neither a temporary phenomenon nor one that the Liberals could continue to tolerate was both correct and authoritative, given his own experience of its effects and the general restraint with which he had reacted to it. In 1884, for example, he had behaved with deliberate and well-calculated forbearance in holding his party to the main task of carrying the Franchise Bill rather than dissipating its energies in a campaign to reform the Lords. But the issue thus postponed did not go away. In 1894 expectation of a major confrontation with the Lords was more intense than had been the case for a decade, and the scope for acting on it, however circumscribed, greater than it was to be for another fifteen years.

In retirement, Gladstone brooded on the 'lost opportunity.' Rosebery's failure to deploy the issue against the Lords effectively only confirmed Gladstone's view that in 1894 the chance of a decisive campaign against them had been thrown away. In a highly coloured memorandum he described it as 'one of the finest opportunities ever offered to statesmen' or 'an opportunity, so brilliant as could not have been hoped for.'[73]

Hurt feelings and the need for self-justification clearly contributed to the hyperbole of his retrospective accounts of his failure to secure a dissolution against the Lords. What they also suggest, however, in their vehemence and imaginative sweep, is that fact of which Rosebery quickly and painfully became aware, and which he used as an argument to soothe the Queen's apprehension about his own attempt to unite the Liberal party behind the single, overriding issue of Lords reform: 'The Government must bring in a resolution sooner or later to assert the predominance of the elected over the hereditary body. Then there will be a dissolution. If Mr. G. were at the head of the Govt. with his eloquence there might be a great majority for us. But as it is, I think we may be beaten or at any rate have at least only a small majority.'[74] In other words, a campaign against the Lords led by even an octogenarian Gladstone would have been qualitatively different both in substance and effect from anything his successor could mount. Whether the refusal of his colleagues to allow him such a campaign was quite such a disastrous loss to the party as he later claimed cannot, of course, be proven. Their defeatist and peremptory dismissal of his proposal for an early election was matched on his side by an exaggerated optimism about the outcome of a dissolution and an unwillingness to consider fully the practical objections to it. The fact that the election never took place and that the issue with the Lords was largely postponed for another fifteen years, however, has tended to lend credence to the view of Gladstone's cabinet critics that his motives in resorting to the idea of a campaign against the Lords were selfish, his calculations unrealistic, and his proposal implausible. Asquith's later assessment was more judicious: 'whether as a matter of tactics he or they were right is, and must always remain, a highly debateable question.'[75]

Clearly it was his instinct for extricating himself from apparently intractable problems that first drew Gladstone's attention at the end of January 1894 to the new possibilities opened up by resort to the question of the Lords. But one cannot dismiss his desire for one last great campaign as nothing more than an expedient response to immediate difficulties. Having begun to think his way into the new initiative, it quickly assumed in his thinking a cogency and predominance of its own, and far from smoothing over his disagreements with his colleagues it only intensified them. As so often, short-term necessity and longer-term strategy were soon closely linked. Just as his turning to Home Rule in 1885 in part from irritation at the immediate political prospect and from fear of losing control of his party does not materially detract from the courage and vision of that new departure, so the role played by personal exigencies in 1894 does not discredit his acute recognition of the immediate need for change in the relations between the two Houses. The obvious, if deceptive, egotism of his desire for a last campaign both relieved his colleagues of the need to consider it with real seriousness and obscured the merits of his proposal on its own account. As a result, he was obliged to bequeath to them not the half-accomplished task he had intended but a generalized legacy of Lords reform. Vaguely defined though it was, it took its place alongside Home Rule in a coherent inheritance of 'heroic measures' to which his immediate successors proved as unequal as they were, by and large, averse.

NOTES

1 Earl of Oxford and Asquith, *Fifty Years of Parliament* (2 vols., London, 1926), I, 212.
2 Gladstone Papers, British Library, Add. MS 44791, f. 51 (nd), printed in *The Prime Ministers' Papers: W.E. Gladstone, I: Autobiographica*, ed. John Brooke and Mary Sorensen (London, 1971), 136.
3 Peter Stansky, *Ambitions and Strategies: The Struggle for the Leadership of the Liberal Party in the 1890s* (Oxford, 1964), 37.
4 D.A. Hamer, *Liberal Politics in the Age of Gladstone and Rosebery* (Oxford, 1972), 192.
5 *Private Diaries of the Rt. Hon. Sir Algernon West*, ed. H.G. Hutchinson (London, 1922), 263-4 (Diary, 30 January 1894).
6 Edward Hamilton Papers, British Library, Add. MS 48661, ff. 128-9 (Diary, 16 November 1893), and *Private Diaries of Algernon West*, ed. Hutchinson, 215 (Diary, 4 November 1893).
7 *Private Diaries of Algernon West*, ed. Hutchinson, 213-14, 229, 233 (Diary, 27 October and 18 December 1893, and 4 January 1894).
8 For a detailed account see Stansky, *Ambitions and Strategies*, 19-35.

9 See, for example, Gladstone to A.J. Mundella, 5 February 1894 (copy), Gladstone Papers, Add. MS 44549, f. 183.

10 *Private Diaries of Algernon West*, ed. Hutchinson, 236-7 (Diary, 9 January 1894).

11 See Stansky, *Ambitions and Strategies*, 41-56.

12 *Private Diaries of Algernon West*, ed. Hutchinson, 261 (Diary, 29 January 1894).

13 Mrs Gladstone to Lady Frederick Cavendish, nd (but almost certainly written in the spring of 1885), Glynne-Gladstone MSS, St Deiniol's Library, Hawarden.

14 Memorandum headed 'Way Opened for Retirement,' dated 19 March 1894, Gladstone Papers, Add. MS 44790, f. 101 (printed in *Gladstone*, I: *Autobiographica*, ed. Brooke and Sorensen, 121).

15 *Private Diaries of Algernon West*, ed. Hutchinson, 263-4 (Diary, 30 January 1894).

16 Lord Morley, *Recollections* (2 vols., London, 1917), II, 7.

17 *Private Diaries of Algernon West*, ed. Hutchinson, 268 (Diary, 4 February 1894).

18 Gladstone to Marjoribanks, 4 February 1894, printed in ibid., 269-70. See also Gladstone to Morley, 5 February 1894 (copy), Gladstone Papers, Add. MS 44257, ff. 154-5; Gladstone to A.J. Mundella, 5 February 1894 (copy), Add. MS 44549, f. 183; and Gladstone to Harcourt, 5 February 1894, Harcourt Papers, Bodleian Library, Oxford.

19 See, for example, Asquith's speech introducing the bill's second reading on 20 February 1893, in 4 *Hansard* 8: 1948-60.

20 Gladstone to West, 4 February 1894 (copy), Harcourt Papers.

21 *Private Diaries of Algernon West*, ed. Hutchinson, 271 (Diary, 6 February 1894).

22 Kimberley to Gladstone, 7 February 1894, Gladstone Papers, Add. MS 44229, f. 213.

23 L.V. Harcourt Diary (copy), 497 and 499 (8 and 10 February 1894), Harcourt Papers.

24 Marjoribanks to West, 8 February 1894, printed in *Private Diaries of Algernon West*, ed. Hutchinson, 273.

25 'Crisis of 1894 as to the Lords and Dissolution,' dated 18 February 1897, Gladstone Papers, Add. MS 44791, ff. 55-6 (printed in *Gladstone*, I: *Autobiographica*, ed. Brooke and Sorensen, 113-15), and Lord Morley, *Recollections*, II, 7.

26 '1894 The Final Imbroglio,' dated 10 November 1896, Gladstone Papers, Add. MS 44791, f. 28 (printed in *Gladstone*, I: *Autobiographica*, ed. Brooke and Sorensen, 120).

27 Stansky, *Ambitions and Strategies*, 41.

28 '1894 The Final Imbroglio,' ff. 26-7 (printed in *Gladstone*, I: *Autobiographica*, ed. Brooke and Sorensen, 119-20).

29 Lord Rosebery, 'Mr. Gladstone's Last Cabinet,' *History Today*, 1 (December 1951), 36.

30 Ibid., 32.

31 Stansky, *Ambitions and Strategies*, xv.

32 Report of conversation with Harcourt, Edward Hamilton Papers, Add. MS 48665, f. 34 (Diary, 1 November 1894).

33 Campbell-Bannerman to Spencer, 7 February 1894, Spencer Papers, Althorp, Northamptonshire.

34 L.V. Harcourt Diary (copy), 497 (8 February 1894), Harcourt Papers.

35 Edward Hamilton Papers, Add. MS 48662, ff. 99-100 (Diary, 8 February 1894).

36 Henry James to the Duke of Devonshire, [3 February 1894], Chatsworth MS (uncatalogued).

37 Gladstone to Spencer, 13 July 1892 (copy), Gladstone Papers, Add. MS 44314, ff. 32-4, and Gladstone to Harcourt, 14 July 1892, Harcourt Papers.

38 Gladstone to Harcourt, 22 July 1892, Harcourt Papers.

39 Gladstone to Asquith, 7 October 1893 (copy), Gladstone Papers, Add. MS 44549, f. 139, and *Private Diaries of Algernon West*, ed. Hutchinson, 212 (Diary, 27 October 1893).

40 *Private Diaries of Algernon West*, ed. Hutchinson, 214 and 229 (Diary, 12 November and 18 December 1893).

41 Record of a conversation with Harcourt, Edward Hamilton Papers, Add. MS 48661, f. 102 (Diary, 26 October 1893).

42 Note of Cabinet, 14 December 1893, Gladstone Papers, Add. MS 44648, f. 138.

43 Alfred G. Gardiner, *The Life of Sir William Harcourt* (2 vols., London, 1923), II, 267.

44 Duke of Devonshire to Salisbury, 17 February 1894, Salisbury Papers, Christ Church, Oxford.

45 Edward Hamilton Papers, Add. MS 48662, ff. 125-6 (Diary, 21 February 1894).

46 4 *Hansard* 21: 851-8 (20 February 1894).

47 L.V. Harcourt Diary (copy), 504 (11 February 1894), Harcourt Papers.

48 4 *Hansard* 21: 764-9 (19 February 1894).

49 James L. Garvin, *Life of Joseph Chamberlain* (3 vols., London, 1932-4), II, 585-9.

50 *The Times*, 16 February 1894, 10.

51 Lord Morley, *Recollections*, II, 9.

52 L.V. Harcourt Diary (copy), 568 (24 February 1894), Harcourt Papers.

53 Gladstone Papers, Add. MS 44648, f. 164.

54 Gladstone to Ponsonby, 2 March 1894 (copy), Gladstone Papers, Add. MS 44680, ff. 128 and 180, and Add. MS 44549, f. 190; and L.V. Harcourt Diary (copy), 564 (23 February 1894), Harcourt Papers.

55 4 *Hansard* 21: 1151-2 (1 March 1894).

56 Henry W. Lucy, *A Diary of the Home Rule Parliament* (London, 1896), 311.

57 Quoted in *The Annual Register 1894*, 58.

58 Justin McCarthy to Mrs Praed, 2 March 1894, quoted in J. McCarthy, *Our Book of Memories: Letters of Justin McCarthy to Mrs. Campbell Praed* (London, 1912), 376.

59 Edward Hamilton Papers, Add. MS 48663, f. 4 (Diary, 1 March 1894).

60 *Private Diaries of Algernon West*, ed. Hutchinson, 288 (3 March 1894).

61 Ibid., 287 (Diary, 2 March 1894).

62 Edward Hamilton Papers, Add. MS 48638, f. 17 (Diary, 25 October 1884), printed in D.W.R. Bahlman, ed., *The Diary of Sir Edward Walter Hamilton* (Oxford, 1972), II, 717.

63 Edward Hamilton Papers, Add. MS 48636, f. 131 (Diary, 21 June 1884), printed in ibid., II, 641.

64 Gladstone to Rosebery, 24 November 1894, Rosebery Papers, National Library of Scotland, MS 10027, f. 178.

65 Dilke believed that Gladstone favoured a solution of this kind (Dilke Papers, British Library, Add. MS 43930, f. 201). On the whole it seems unlikely.

66 Edward Hamilton Papers, Add. MS 48655, f. 60 (Diary, 5 April 1891).

67 Shortened version of memorandum 'The Franchise Bill and the Present Situation,' dated 25 August 1884, Gladstone Papers, Add. MS 44768, f. 109.

68 Gladstone to the Queen, 6 March 1886, printed in *The Queen and Mr. Gladstone*, ed. Philip Guedalla (2 vols., London, 1933-4), II, 396.

69 Conversation with Ruskin in 1878, in *Some Hawarden Letters*, ed. L. March-Philipps and B. Christian (London, 1917), 37.

70 Speech notes, Gladstone Papers, Add. MS 44629, f. 39.

71 Gladstone to Bright, 29 September 1881 (copy), Gladstone Papers, Add. MS 44113, f. 158.

72 *The Times*, 28 February 1882, 10.

73 '1894 The Final Imbroglio,' f. 27 (printed in *Gladstone*, I: *Autobiographica*, ed. Brooke and Sorensen, 119-20).

74 Record of conversation with the Queen, 7 December 1894, Rosebery Papers, Box 108.

75 Earl of Oxford and Asquith, *Fifty Years of Parliament*, I, 212

K.A.P. SANDIFORD

Gladstone and Europe

No one can examine the vast body of private and public correspondence left by William Gladstone without recognizing that he regarded Europe as a compact family of nations with a common law and common interests. His 'European sense' has thus been rightly stressed by historians from Morley to Schreuder.[1]

Gladstone's devotion to Europe rested squarely on his conviction that European civilization represented an almost perfect synthesis of Christianity and Hellenism. All of his biographers have agreed that a reverence for Christian morality and Hellenic discipline provided the foundations of Gladstonian idealism. His European sense was constantly reinforced by his frequent visits to the continent, which gave him an unusual familiarity with its people and their aspirations. Of Europe and its people he certainly knew more than did most educated Englishmen, and he made a greater effort to learn several European languages. He became fluent in French, German, Greek, and Italian. He was thus able to carry on a wide-ranging correspondence with a variety of Europeans, as his voluminous manuscripts in the British Library so clearly show.

Gladstone was consequently less insular than his contemporaries in Victorian Britain. His correspondence with individuals like Döllinger, Lacaita, Müller, Panizzi, and Olga Novikoff permitted him to judge European problems in a less narrow fashion than Victorian chauvinists like Palmerston and Disraeli. He came to regard England as a prominent member of the European community with very serious responsibilities. Her obligations to Europe were moral and spiritual. With her vast material resources, it was England's mission to protect the weaker members of the European family and to provide cultural leadership on the continent. It was highly improper for England to pursue selfish policies in Europe for purely material objectives.

These Gladstonian doctrines are well known. They underlay all of his private and public statements on international politics. They are perhaps most articulately expressed in his great speech during the Don Pacifico debate, in his much publicized essay on 'England's Mission,' and in his celebrated Midlothian address before a huge audience at West Calder on 27 December 1879.[2] It was, in Gladstone's view, the Christian duty of England to set a good example to the rest of the world; to assist the weak against the strong; and to provide effective leadership within the Concert of Europe, without which the public law of that great continent would become unsafe.

It was indeed on the public law and the European concert that Gladstonian foreign policy came to rest. His Christian moralism persuaded him to sympathize with liberal movements, but his innate conservatism left him always with a reverence for authority and order. His approach to Europe, therefore, like his approach to everything else, was very complex and often ambivalent. His ambivalence in politics sprang directly from his peculiar sources of inspiration. He tried, throughout his career, to blend the teachings of Aquinas, Aristotle, Augustine, the Bible, Burke, Butler, Canning, Dante, Homer, and Plato. It was not always easy for him to reconcile such divergent philosophies. His respect for contemporaries like Aberdeen, Acton, Bright, Graham, Herbert, Mill, and Peel served only to complicate his politics even further. Thus Gladstone's treatment of Europe, like his treatment of most issues, was not always intelligible even to his colleagues in the cabinet.[3]

Nor should the evangelical influence of his father be underestimated. John Gladstone's role, like that of Peel, is especially evident in his son's approach to commercial and economic matters. Gladstone regarded material benefits as gifts from God to be highly treasured and constructively used. They were to be exploited, not for selfish gain, but in the interests of humanity in general. Such a philosophy led directly to an emphasis on strict economy, both private and national.[4] Linked with the Christian stress on the brotherhood of man under the fatherhood of God, it produced also a strong support for the principle of international free trade. Gladstone wanted all Europeans to husband their resources with great care while eliminating the trade barriers among themselves. Free trade and strict economy would reduce spending on armaments while removing fiscal obstacles that so often contributed to warfare.

Gladstone's belief in strict economy inspired a host of successful

budgets for which he has justly been acclaimed. It is, of course, the duty of
the chancellor of the exchequer to restrict public spending as much as
possible without endangering national security. But even Gladstone's
friends sometimes considered him too parsimonious. His fiscal achievements involved a serious reduction of Britain's military and naval
strength. His budgets not only frustrated his colleagues on several
occasions but also contributed to the gradual shift in the European
balance of power. Statesmen on the continent were very conscious of
Gladstonian economy, and it is therefore not accidental that British
foreign policy carried progressively less weight after the Crimean War.
While armaments were being improved on the continent, especially in
Prussia, Gladstone could boast that he, as the chancellor of the exchequer,
had reduced British spending from £73 million in 1859 to £66 million in
1866.[5] Gerald Graham is probably right in suggesting that such was the
superiority of the mid-Victorian navy that even Gladstone's economies
could not immediately destroy it.[6] Gladstonian finance, nevertheless, left
many British foreign secretaries quite seriously hamstrung after 1853.
The Gladstone Papers in the British Library reveal how often, and how
vigorously, Palmerston, Russell, and Somerset quarrelled with him over
economy and fortifications from 1859 to 1865.[7] Gladstone's resignation
from office in 1894 was occasioned by his refusal to sanction the increase
in the naval estimates proposed by his cabinet colleagues.[8]

The fact is that Gladstone looked too often upon Europe through the
eyes of the British chancellor of the exchequer. Intermingled with his
Christian moralism and respect for European law was a curious obsession
with balancing the budget. Financial considerations were no less important than moral ones. Indeed, he made no distinction between them.
Prodigal spending was a moral evil.[9] Hence his aversion to warfare and
empire, both of which tended to be far more costly than their results could
possibly be worth. Even though, as he told his wife, the Egyptian war was a
'great stroke for public order, liberty and justice,' Gladstone much
regretted that Arabi's follies were going to cost the British treasury almost
£5 million.[10] His criticism of Disraeli's acquisition of Cyprus was partly
based also on the premise that that island would cost large sums of British
money without any equivalent return.[11]

The close link, in Gladstone's mind, between economy, armaments,
warfare, and morality is best exemplified by his approach to the Crimean
War. His intention was to budget for the British war effort simply by
doubling direct taxation.[12] He strenuously objected, on moral grounds, to
the idea of borrowing to pay for warfare. Such loans, he argued, saddled

posterity unjustly with the responsibility of paying for the aggressions of their ancestors. The force of circumstance compelled Gladstone in 1855 to abandon his original proposals, but he never wavered from his basic philosophy. He remained firmly convinced that the expenses of warfare were meant to serve as a natural deterrent to militarism.[13]

Such a philosophy often led Gladstone into a posture of pacifism. Yet he could never have been mistaken for a Quaker. He deliberately refused to join the peace movement, rightly holding (throughout his career) that an inflexible commitment to a peaceful programme was most impolitic. He disagreed even with his friend Bright on this ground. There were, in his judgment, certain causes which required the use of force. Violence on the part of a lawless member of the community had to be curtailed by vigorous counter-measures. He could not therefore accept the Cobdenite gospel of non-intervention, or the Quaker demands for peace at any price.[14]

Gladstone was thus, as A.J.P. Taylor has pointed out, a most unusual kind of pacifist.[15] He regarded war as a legitimate instrument of diplomacy to be used for morally justifiable objects. It was Britain's moral duty, as an important member of the European concert, to frustrate the illegal and ambitious projects of the Tsar in 1854. Thus, as Gladstone always insisted, the Crimean War had been honourably fought by Britain for worthy causes. Britain had not engaged in hostilities simply to protect the road to India, or to defend Islam. She had fought to protect the public law of Europe.[16]

The constant vigour with which Gladstone defended the decision of the Aberdeen coalition to fight against Russia in the Crimea has tended to obscure the fact that his whole approach to that question in the 1850s was extremely complex. He wanted, initially, to stay clear of the Russo-Turkish quarrel. He took the view that, until the Turks obeyed British advice, they had no claim to British support. He thought it rather odd that some of his colleagues should wish to take up cudgels for the Muslims through fear of Russia. But once he had convinced himself that Russian aggressions in Romania constituted a violation of the public law of Europe, he gave his support to Palmerston's more belligerent proposals.[17]

As soon as he thought that the Russians had conceded the vital points for which Britain had ostensibly gone to war, Gladstone readjusted his stance. He denied that Britain had a right to promote selfish interests in the Crimea, and violently opposed the extension of the war after 1855. He denounced Palmerston for prolonging the conflict without due regard for human life and limb; and then he rejoiced when the Paris treaty was signed in 1856.[18]

Gladstone welcomed that treaty because he saw it as a triumph for the European concert. He was relieved to see that provisions were made to ensure against future oppression of Christians in the Ottoman empire, and that the Russians no longer had the exclusive right to interfere on their behalf. But he expressed some grave doubts also. He was dissatisfied, for example, with the prospect of guaranteeing the integrity and independence of a 'Mahomedan' state; with the treatment of the Danubian principalities, which ought to have been offered some degree of local autonomy; and with the Black Sea clauses, which he considered inapplicable in time of war.[19]

These are the kinds of Gladstonian reservations which make it impossible for historians to offer simplistic judgments about his attitude towards the Eastern question. He began by rejecting the idea of a British war in that region, either for British or Turkish objectives. He then supported the British decision to expel the Russians from Romania, but abandoned Palmerston for prosecuting that struggle beyond what he thought were its necessary limits. He praised the treaty which brought the war to an end, but he prophetically warned everybody of its imperfections.

Similarly complex was Gladstone's approach to the Italian question. He tried at first to induce the conservative rulers to forestall the forces of revolution in Italy by granting moderate reforms. Only very gradually and grudgingly did he move away from this position between 1850 and 1859. The refusal of the conservatives to follow his advice led Gladstone slowly into the anti-Austrian camp. He began to recommend the expulsion of Austria from Italy, but even during the Italian War of Liberation his main concern was European peace. He argued for British neutrality at the outbreak of war, proposed a North Italian kingdom that would work in close communication with Austria to preserve tranquillity, and did his utmost to keep alive the Anglo-French alliance which he thought more vital to European stability than Italian independence. It was only after the Italian kingdom had become a *fait accompli* that he gave full support to the idea of Italian unity.[20]

Gladstone's much vaunted Italian fervour has thus been exaggerated by contemporaries and posterity, but it is still true to say that he displayed more sympathy for the Italian patriots than for their Albanian, Armenian, Hungarian, Ionian, Polish, Serbian, and Syrian counterparts. This was partly due to his classical training and to his frequent visits to Italy after 1832, which brought him into increasingly closer contact with Italian liberals like Giacomo Lacaita and Antonio Panizzi. His belief in order and efficiency also caused him to rejoice when the new

Italy, under Piedmontese direction, behaved in an efficient and orderly manner.[21]

Gladstone's Italian policy, however, is better understood when placed within the wider context of his overall approach to Europe. In this connection, there are two vital factors which historians have generally tended to overlook. The first is his growing hatred of Austria, which became almost an obsession after the Crimean War. The second is his peculiar attachment to France, which he never really lost – even during periods of acute Francophobia in England after 1859.

Gladstone's approach to Austria was almost Palmerstonian. He accepted the Austro-Hungarian empire as an integral feature of the European system, with the potential to check Russian advances from the east or Napoleonic indiscretions from the west. He much feared, however, that the Austrian empire had been left too ungainly by the Treaty of Vienna. It was by no means an easy assignment to control such a mixture of Germans, Magyars, Czechs, Slovaks, Poles, Italians, and others. Gladstone felt that Austria would become a much more effective element in the European system by consolidating her forces north of the Alps and detaching herself from Italy. As he saw it, the major difficulty with the Austro-Italian connection was that the Austrians were culturally inferior to the Italians and could only maintain their authority by the use of brute force.[22]

By 1858 Gladstone had gradually reached the conclusion that Austrian policies at home and in Italy were detrimental to European stability. He became increasingly disturbed by the thought that superior might, abetted by the despotic powers on the continent, could bring about the oppression of a people whose state of civilization was more advanced than that of the conqueror. He grew more and more critical of Austria's behaviour (even in the Danubian principalities) and called upon his countrymen to abstain from supporting her claims in 1859. By this time, Gladstone had convinced himself that Austrian government had been a signal failure in Italy since 1815. By 1866 he was calling unequivocally for the amputation of Venetia from Austria and the completion of Italian unification. He now trusted that Britain would contemplate no assistance to Austria in the recovery of lost provinces that she had never governed effectively in the first place. He concluded that Austria was in fact being strengthened by the loss of diseased limbs.[23]

Gladstone's anti-Austrian prejudice lasted throughout his career. He consistently lamented Austria's conduct and ambitions in Bosnia and Herzegovina. He advised Disraeli's government, in 1878, to ignore the

Austrian claims in the Balkans. He was most distressed therefore to discover that Austria had profited so greatly and so undeservedly from the Treaty of Berlin.[24] It was this antipathy towards the Austrians which did much to strengthen Gladstone's sympathy for Italy.

Equally significant was his respect for France. Gladstone worked harder than anyone else in England to keep the western alliance alive after the seizure of Nice and Savoy by Napoleon III. He considered the Anglo-French alliance as the cornerstone of the European concert. He was thus willing to follow the French in their crusade on Italy's behalf. In 1860 he looked to the alliance as the means to frustrate the friends of Austria, who might otherwise be tempted to undo the work of Cavour and the Italian patriots. To counter the anti-French sentiments so freely expressed in the British journals and Parliament after the Treaty of Villafranca, he redoubled his efforts to conclude the Anglo-French commercial agreement, for which Cobden had striven so manfully. To the end of his days, Gladstone looked back on the commercial treaty of 1860 as a great diplomatic event that went far towards easing the tension between the western allies. He had to admit, in retrospect, that the strictly commercial results of this agreement were somewhat disappointing, but he sincerely believed that, without it, the two countries might well have drifted into war.[25]

Although Gladstone was anxious to co-operate with France to save Italy from Austria, he was concerned not only about the price of French chivalry but also about the French garrison in Rome. He feared that Napoleon III might disturb the European order by seeking too much compensation for his Italian services. He had also come to the conclusion that it was immoral for an alien power to sustain by force of arms the temporal authority of the Pope in central Italy. Hence his ambivalence in dealing with France throughout the 1860s. He accepted the seizure of Nice and Savoy with better grace than the majority of his countrymen, but he totally repudiated the French policy in Rome. As early as 1858, he had noted rather acidly that 'the liberalism of Pius IX was worth almost as much as the Christianity of Taeping and the Chinese rebels.'[26] It was inconsistent therefore for Napoleon III to assist in the expulsion of corrupt Austrian rulers from Italy while simultaneously propping up, in Rome, the papal régime, which was 'perhaps the worst, and certainly the most ridiculous' of all European governments.[27] By 1859 Gladstone was ready to recommend essential changes in the temporal role of the papacy. As he became increasingly sympathetic to the Italian national movement during the 1860s, he grew increasingly hostile to the Vatican. He wanted to unify Italy without destroying the Pope's spiritual authority, but he gradually came to view the papacy as an anti-social and anti-national force in that peninsula. Hence the virulence of his *Vatican Decrees*, published in 1874.[28]

To Gladstone's dismay, French troops remained in Rome until 1870. It was thus the Roman question which helped to complicate his attitude towards France. His approach to that country remained far from straightforward. On the one hand, he was willing to seek French help, in 1864, to protect Denmark from the aggressions of Austria and Prussia.[29] On the other, in 1863, when the French were most enthusiastic to support the Poles against Russia, Gladstone remained conspicuously indifferent. It is therefore very obvious that there were elements of pragmatism and flexibility in his treatment of France.

It was Queen Victoria perhaps who best understood the reasons for Gladstone's ambivalence with respect to France. As she astutely observed, Gladstone liked the French people and fully recognized the value of the Anglo-French compact as a vital aspect of the European system – but he never felt comfortable with a Bonaparte on the French throne.[30] Nor had Gladstone much cared for Louis Philippe. In the evening of his career, he reflected rather wistfully that the whole history of Europe would have been much different had France (rather than Belgium) been governed by King Leopold. He made the intriguing observation that France during the Second Empire was much like Rome under Augustus, except that Louis Napoleon lacked the wisdom of the great Octavian.[31] Mistrust of Napoleon III and respect for the French nation combined to produce considerable ambiguity in Gladstone's attitude towards France.

Even after Napoleon III was dead, however, some of these Gladstonian doubts persisted. He very much wanted to keep alive the Anglo-French understanding; but he failed to appreciate that nations, including his own, were not as idealistic as he was himself. Thus, for instance, he never quite understood the French manoeuvres in Egypt; and he was totally baffled by their seizure of Tunis. He was distressed by these French misdeeds not only because they endangered the European concert but because they also promoted the selfish aims of Bismarck.[32]

Gladstone, of course, never liked Bismarck, who stood for all those things which he himself abhorred. The Prussian statesman was a rabid patriot who consistently subordinated European to German interests. He defied the public law of Europe in his ruthless determination to construct a powerful Germany. He acquired Schleswig, Holstein, Lauenburg, Alsace, and Lorraine, attaching them arbitrarily to a German empire from which Austria was equally arbitrarily excluded. Bismarck accomplished all of these miracles in defiance of European opinion. Indeed, he openly despised all opinions and principles that could not be enforced by practical means. It was his avowed and deliberate separation of morals and ethics from politics and diplomacy that alarmed Gladstone most of all.[33]

Gladstone's hatred of Bismarck led him to oppose the settlement of 1871 with much violence. He was greatly offended by the notion that two French provinces, against their will, could be detached from their traditional roots and forcibly grafted onto a Germanic system. He did his utmost to prevent this tragedy – only to find himself practically isolated within his own country. The Queen, his own foreign secretary, and the majority of the cabinet could not be persuaded to abandon the policy of strict neutrality which Britain had announced at the beginning of the Franco-Prussian war.[34]

Gladstone thus viewed the new Germany, as he always did France, with what can only be described as mingled emotions. He did not approve of the manner in which that nation had been created, and he intensely disliked its creator. But he was not averse to the growth of a united Germany as a stabilizing element in Europe. He publicly expressed the view, during the Austro-Prussian crisis of 1866, that such a decisive civil war was a good thing for the Germans. It would finally put an end to the crippling rivalry between their two leaders and thus allow the German state to develop in greater harmony. As his dislike for Bismarck was outweighed by his animosity towards Austria, he could readily accept the new Germany as a nation which was unlikely to upset the old European traditions. He welcomed it as a conservative system, with the potential (like the new Italy) to contribute to the European family of nations in a very positive way.[35] Gladstone's main concern here, as elsewhere, was the question of order and efficiency. But his sincere and profound belief in the essential badness of Bismarck left him much puzzled by this German phenomenon. He never quite understood how it was possible for such a palpably corrupt tree, in defiance of Biblical law, to bring forth such good fruit.

Gladstone's preference for France was thus partly based on a total mistrust of Bismarck and a contempt for Austria. These were strange sentiments indeed in the breast of an avowed 'European.' In the long run they were to undermine the very Concert of Europe which he so desperately wished to preserve. His prejudices also forced him into a pro-Russian stance, much to the consternation of the bulk of his countrymen. His friendship for Russia, like his sympathy for France, marked him out as different from the majority of Victorians, who took the more traditional view that the French and the Russians were Britain's most dangerous rivals. Gladstone rejected that thesis precisely because he understood that it was based on commercial and material considerations. He himself could see no valid Christian reason why Britain should enjoy a monopoly of the world's commerce.

Gladstone was also drawn towards Russia because – as he had just reason to complain – she was the only reliable defender of the oppressed Christians in the Ottoman empire.[36] He had agreed that Britain should fight against Russia in 1854 because, in his judgment, the Tsar had unfortunately chosen to break the law. But he was very conscious of the paradox that Britain, a Christian nation, should be involved in a war against another Christian state to uphold the integrity of a despotic and non-Christian empire. He spent the rest of his life trying to explain how he could ever have given support to such a curious programme. But he wanted to end the Anglo-Russian war as soon as possible, and it was on that score that he parted company with Palmerston in 1855.

After the Crimean War, Gladstone regretted that Russia should have been forced to accept the notorious Black Sea clauses, and he was not unhappy to see them altogether rescinded by an international conference in 1871. He did object to the Tsar's unilateral repudiation of these clauses in the midst of the Franco-Prussian crisis, but he was still anxious to preserve amicable Anglo-Russian relations, particularly in view of Bismarck's aggressiveness.[37]

Throughout the 1870s Gladstone campaigned actively against the Russophobia which seemed to have possessed the majority of his countrymen. He warned them against encouraging Turkish misrule in the Balkans through their violent anti-Russianism.[38] These warnings fell on deaf ears, as Gladstone and his Russian friend, Mme Novikoff, had cause to lament.[39] During the Berlin negotiations, he made another plea for the just treatment of Russia's claims in the Balkans.[40] Indeed, as early as 1858, he had observed that Russian aggression in the Danubian principalities was but the symptom; conditions for which Turkey had been responsible were the real disease which caused the Crimean War.[41] He urged Disraeli in the late 1870s to focus more critically on the wrongs of Turkey and less on the ambitions of the Tsar.[42]

Gladstone's attitude towards Russia was actually no less complicated than his approach to the other Great Powers. He was quite clearly influenced by his friendship with Olga Novikoff, who was a fervent

Russian patriot. But he was also suspicious of the Tsar. He knew that the Russian ruler could not defend Christian interests in Turkey without exacting some kind of price. He was fearful of a repetition of Villafranca. Although he constantly derided the irrational British devotion to India, he was also alarmed enough about Russian manoeuvres in Afghanistan to assume an unusually belligerent pose during the Penjdeh crisis.[43]

On the whole, however, Gladstone saw the Anglo-Russian alliance as a potential bulwark of the European concert. It would check the ambitions of the two nations he most despised: Austria and Turkey. He very much regretted that Victorians like Disraeli could be so mesmerized by imperialistic chimeras as to support these autocratic powers that had no reasonable claim to British sympathies. He chose, of course, to ignore the fact that the Tsarist régime was no less autocratic than that of the Sultan. What impressed him here, as always, was efficiency and order. Whatever the nature of the Russian system, it was at least more stable than the Ottoman.

Gladstone, in fact, became increasingly disenchanted with Turkish rule. As early as 1853 he was disturbed by the prospect of going to war in the Near East to support a Sultan who had consistently disregarded British advice.[44] He lamented, in 1858, that such a ramshackle system should be artificially supported by the European concert.[45] By this time he had come to the conclusion that Turkish corruption was the source of all the mischief in that region. In short, Turkish government over the Danubian provinces was no better than Austrian rule south of the Alps.[46]

In 1863, as a member of Palmerston's cabinet, Gladstone had to make a temperate speech during a parliamentary debate on the Turkish dependencies. He suggested that it would be better for Britain to inculcate in the Turks a spirit of liberality and justice rather than to provoke them into rash measures that might precipitate the collapse of the Ottoman empire. Britain's best policy was to encourage humane treatment of the Christians in Turkey and to urge the Sultan to fulfil his engagements of 1856.[47] As an opposition member in 1867, he was able to take a firmer anti-Turkish stand when he blamed the misrule of the Sultan for the Serbian insurrection.[48]

By the 1870s Gladstone had become violently anti-Turkish. He drew attention to the fact that the Turks, with their inferior culture, had too long been permitted (with British encouragement) to oppress the superior Greeks.[49] He had made exactly the same point twenty years earlier with respect to the Austrians during the Italian crisis. It reflected his Graeco-Roman prejudices and training. He continued to criticize the

Sultan with increasing bitterness. Indeed, he once described the Turkish ruler as 'a bottomless pit of iniquity and fraud. He is not only a liar, but seems as though he might compete with Satan for the honour of being the father of it, and stand a fair chance of winning.'[50] It is impossible to read Gladstone's letters and speeches on the Eastern question and not be aware of his emotionalism. His contempt for the Sultan coloured his whole approach to the Balkan problem after 1856. He reached the conclusion that Turkey was hopelessly incorrigible, and that all hope of peace in southeastern Europe depended upon the removal of Turkish authority. He saw no reason why Britain should try to prolong Turkish power over an area which the Sultan had never been able to govern efficiently.[51] By 1877 Gladstone had become totally anti-Islamic. His devotion to Christian moralism came close to making him an outright bigot.

Just as Gladstone's support of Italian unity was based partly on the conclusion that Austrian government there had in effect become disruptive, so too did his support of Balkan autonomy rest upon the assumption that the Sultan was no less idiotic than all the other Turks. This kind of emotional approach is especially obvious in his Bulgarian pamphlets and speeches. His commitment to Hellenism and Christianity drove him further and further away from the Treaty of Paris. He blamed the Turks for undermining that settlement and he called upon the Concert of Europe to protect the Christians rather than to maintain the archaic Ottoman system.

This is not to say that Gladstone's approach to the Eastern question was perfectly straightforward. He did gradually conclude that Christians should not be misgoverned by Muslims, but this did not mean that he wanted to grant them immediate national independence. He was for a long time quite concerned about Greek competence to handle their own affairs, and it was partly for this reason that he had rejected the idea of a union between Greece and the Ionian Islands. He was more eager to find a stable government for the Greeks and Ionians than to grant them independence. It was only after the Greeks had demonstrated the capacity to govern themselves efficiently that Gladstone gradually became bolder in his demands for Hellenic rights.[52]

The same doubts and complications arise in his attitude towards Armenians, Bulgarians, and Romanians. His concern for order and tradition prevented him from supporting these national movements unreservedly. So too did his respect for European law and stability. In 1866, for example, he told Clarendon bluntly that Romanian independence was a matter of European convenience. He was not unwilling to promote the cause of Romanian liberty but he could do so only with the co-operation of the rest of Europe and in such a way as not to violate the Treaty of Paris.[53] As late as 12 July 1880 he was objecting to the unification of Bulgaria on the ground that it would provoke Austro-Russian hostilities and destroy the European concert.[54] In the 1890s, while still protesting vigorously against Turkish brutality, he appreciated how impractical it was for Britain, without European help, to assist the Armenians in a material sense.[55]

Gladstone's contempt for the Sultan inspired him to promote the Greek and Montenegrin causes with Palmerstonian zeal after the Berlin treaty of 1878. He also sympathized with the European subject races who had, in his view, suffered much at Turkey's hands. But he approached the whole question of liberal nationalism with a pragmatism that is often ignored by historians. He dealt with each case on its own merits and treated it in accordance with the exigencies of the moment. He made bold speeches and statements while in opposition, but adopted a more circumspect and conservative approach to national movements while he was in office. Almost invariably he subordinated liberal-nationalist issues to the requirements of European stability, and he clearly preferred to recommend constructive reforms rather than self-determination.[56]

Gladstone's conservatism in foreign affairs is most obviously reflected in his treatment of Polish and Hungarian nationalism. He was not prepared to do anything for the Magyars or the Poles. In these cases, there was no Sultan to denounce or Graeco-Roman legacy to defend. He had no faith in the ability of the Poles to govern themselves, and chose therefore to defend the Tsar, whose position in Poland (as he explained to the House of Commons) was most delicate. He preferred to support the Russo-Polish connection, which was already more than a century old, and to recommend moderate reforms rather than revolution.[57]

So strong was Gladstone's commitment to tradition that he was even prepared to perpetuate Turkish suzerainty over Egypt so long as the Sultan, odious as he was, could be induced to implement some constructive Egyptian reforms.[58] This Gladstonian emphasis on mild reform, and on order and efficiency, is evident also in Ireland, where he was most reluctant to abandon the Anglo-Irish connection, and thus spent the last thirty years of his life vainly trying to kill the Irish nationalist movement with kindness.

It seems fair to conclude therefore that the conservative element in Gladstone's foreign policy has been underestimated by most historians. He is still being described in general terms as liberal, moralistic, pacific, and European. His approach to Europe is too often summarized under abstractions such as public law, non-intervention, European concert, Christian idealism. These phrases cannot, of course, be avoided by the historian but they have to be used discreetly, for the facts do not fit such categories neatly enough. Gladstone's approach to Europe was complicated in the extreme. It was governed, in the first place, by a unique blend of Gladstonian logic and simple emotion. His own philosophical bases made it very difficult for him to arrive at political solutions in a straightforward manner. The basic foundations of his idealism were not always easy to reconcile. Hence the complexity of his thought and the flexibility of his politics. The result was a certain unpredictability that annoyed his own countrymen as well as Europeans. On the continent, Gladstone could promote war or peace, interference or abstention, tradition or change.

This kind of flexibility was partly the result of internal dilemmas which Gladstone had to resolve in his own fashion and in his own time. But it sprang also from the fact that Europe itself was in a constant state of flux. It must never be forgotten that Gladstone's public career coincided with the great period of European industrialization. The continent was changing at a dramatic pace and Gladstone was forced to adapt to these changes.

It cannot possibly be doubted that Gladstone made a deliberate effort to readjust to these European developments. There is a strong sense of dynamism about his evolving ideology. Even in his old age there is a suggestion of steady growth. The gradual evolution of Gladstonianism has been just as difficult for posterity to understand as for his contemporaries to accept. There was constant friction, in fact, between Gladstone and his ministerial colleagues. Cabinet disagreements remained a common denominator in all of the administrations with which he was associated. This ministerial discord was very clearly reflected in the irresolute and vacillating foreign policies pursued by Liberal governments after 1850.

Gladstone's misfortune lay in the fact that so few of his contemporaries shared his ideals.[59] Most Victorians, for instance, were anxious to promote British material interests wherever and however they could. His great faith in the Concert of Europe was shared neither by his own party nor by Europeans.[60] His lofty sense of England's mission was likewise rejected by the majority of Englishmen, who were caught up, after 1870, in the extraordinary wave of jingoistic imperialism. His obsession with Ireland and Egypt after 1880 also did serious damage to Britain's position on the continent. Gladstone failed to grasp this entirely, or to appreciate fully the fundamental relation between European politics and African strategies. These failings were most obvious to his younger colleagues, who often combined to thwart his idealistic approach. The result was that he could do little to alter policies that he had so vigorously denounced while in opposition. Moreover, the Queen increased Gladstone's difficulties by occasionally insisting on a more spirited (or Disraelian) programme.

It is useful to remember, therefore, that Gladstone's European policy was not always his own. Like Palmerston before him, he had to make concessions to his colleagues and to support in public programmes which he had privately disapproved. This goes far towards explaining the dichotomy between Gladstonian idealism and Gladstonian diplomacy in practice. His approach to Europe, nevertheless, was often characterized by a greater degree of pragmatism than either his colleagues or later historians have been willing to allow. Even so, in Gladstone's old age, Liberal divisions became so sharp that constructive approaches to European problems were hardly possible. His own peculiar brand of politics ceased to appeal either to the whigs or to the radicals. Reformers like Chamberlain had no patience with what they regarded as vague Gladstonian abstractions, and pragmatists like Goschen preferred policies to parables. On Ireland and the budget, Gladstone could eventually grasp the intricate details of a broad strategy, but on many other issues he was less imaginative or useful.

This defect placed Gladstone at a considerable disadvantage as a diplomatist, precisely because of the nature of diplomacy itself; it deals as much with concrete interests (land, trade, political advantages) as with principles (public law, justice, humanity). To subordinate the concrete to the abstract is a fatal blunder in this field, and it was doubly so in Gladstone's case since he was working among Europeans who were envious of British wealth and suspicious of Britain's motives. The bald fact is that, for all of Gladstone's rhetoric on the values of Christian morality and Hellenic discipline, Europeans could discern no essential difference between Liberal and Conservative policies during the Victorian age. This is not surprising. Gladstone betrayed the same anxiety over Belgium in 1868-70 that all British statesmen have done in modern times.[61] He rejected Disraeli's annexation of Cyprus, but failed to undo it after 1880.[62] He staunchly supported the building of the Suez Canal as a great international boon in 1858, objected to Disraeli's purchase of those famous shares in 1875,[63] and thereafter did nothing to put that matter right. Nor was there, in the European mind, any significant change in British imperial policies after 1880.

Gladstonian idealism found itself at a double discount during the last quarter of the nineteenth century. It did not appear, in the first place, to produce any remarkable changes in Britain's diplomatic or imperial strategies. Second, that period was too much dominated by the European obsession with material objects. Europeans had just discovered new techniques and new instruments – ironically with the aid of British capital and technology – and were much impressed with their own commercial and industrial prospects.[64] The great emphasis was no longer on ideology (if it ever had been), but on matter.

Politicians reflected this emphasis in their search for territorial expansion, financial profit, or simple diplomatic advantage. Bismarck, a far more clever politician than Gladstone, could freely refer to the use of blood and iron without any qualms of conscience. Like Palmerston and Disraeli, Bismarck understood that politics had to do with power; and, more clearly even than they, he recognized the relation between political power and material strength. His own remarkable successes after 1862 were based, not on the moral virtues of the Germans, but quite evidently on the industrial and military superiority of Prussia. These Bismarckian triumphs created an indelible impact on the contemporary European mind. The German message was more readily obvious than the Gladstonian.

The generation after 1860 is therefore not inaptly styled the Age of Bismarck. It was he who dictated the form and content of European diplomacy in Gladstone's time. International politics became dominated by industrial competition, militant nationalism, and a good deal of what sociologists would later describe as Social Darwinism. Whatever the connection between his public gospel and his actual policy, Gladstone had meanwhile established for himself an enormous reputation as the great Victorian crusader. But there was no place for a priest in this physical game of rugger that European diplomacy had become. Thus could Gladstone be consistently ridiculed by Bismarck, who revealed to all Europeans that his bite bore little relation to his bark. There was a distinct hint of Palmerstonianism in Gladstone's tendency to lecture to Europeans, but he lacked Palmerston's patriotic fire and pugnacity. In Europe, Gladstone came to be considered a professor and not a policeman.

NOTES

This paper has been made possible by a grant from the Research Board of the University of Manitoba. I must also thank my colleagues, Professors John Finlay and John Kendle, who offered very valuable suggestions.

1 Indeed, in his *Gladstone and the Irish Nation* (London, 1938), J.L. Hammond devoted a whole chapter to 'Gladstone's European Sense' (49-66). R.T. Shannon, in *Gladstone and the Bulgarian Agitation 1876* (London, 1963), saw this as an important element in persuading Gladstone to re-enter politics (4-7). C.J. Lowe, in *The Reluctant Imperialists: British Foreign Policy, 1878-1902* (London, 1967), saw his European approach as largely responsible for his failure in Egypt (I, 9-10). And D.M. Schreuder analyzed this feature of Gladstone's politics with much intelligence in his *Gladstone and Kruger* (London, 1969), 37-97.

2 3 *Hansard* 112: 543-90 (27 June 1850); Gladstone, 'England's Mission,' *Nineteenth Century* (September 1878), 560-84; *Midlothian Speeches 1879*, intro. M.R.D. Foot (Leicester, 1971), 114-29.

3 The ideological differences between Gladstone and his colleagues forced the Liberals to labour under an enormous handicap after 1868. This is much stressed by J. Bryce, *Studies in Contemporary Biography* (London, 1904), 452-60; M. Barker, *Gladstone and Radicalism: Reconstruction of Liberal Policy in Britain, 1885-94* (Hassocks, Sussex, 1975); D.A. Hamer, *Liberal Politics in the Age of Gladstone and Rosebery* (Oxford, 1972); and H.C.G. Matthew, *The Liberal Imperialists* (Oxford, 1973), 12-27.

4 Hammond, *Gladstone and the Irish Nation*, 72-3; Philip Magnus, *Gladstone: A Biography* (London, 1954), 112.

5 See John Morley, *The Life of William Ewart Gladstone* (3 vols., London, 1903), II, 42-51, especially 51, where he claims that Gladstone managed to reduce spending on military and naval estimates to £24 million by 1866; and Magnus, *Gladstone*, 143-52.

6 G.S. Graham, *The Politics of Naval Supremacy* (Cambridge, 1965), 56-60.

7 There are literally hundreds of letters in the Gladstone, Palmerston, and Russell papers dealing with the great ministerial quarrel over economy and armaments. De Grey, Herbert, and Somerset also played a prominent part in this controversy, which reached a peak during 1859-60 when there was a particularly violent British public reaction to the Treaty of Villafranca.

8 Magnus, *Gladstone*, 414-23; J.P. McIntosh, *The British Cabinet* (London, 1962), 303.

9 Hammond, *Gladstone and the Irish Nation*, 73.

10 *Gladstone to His Wife*, ed. A. Tilney Bassett (London, 1936), 239.

11 Gladstone, 'England's Mission,' 566-7; *Midlothian Speeches*, 126.

12 J.B. Conacher, *The Aberdeen Coalition, 1852-55* (Cambridge, 1968), 257.

13 O. Anderson, *A Liberal State at War: English Politics and Economics during the Crimean War* (London, 1967), 13-15, 195-7; Magnus, *Gladstone*, 115.

194 K.A.P. Sandiford

14 P. Brock, *Pacifism in Europe to 1914* (Princeton, 1972), 346-400; N.W. Summerton, 'Dissenting Attitudes to Foreign Relations, Peace and War, 1840-90,' *Journal of Ecclesiastical History*, 28 (April 1977), 151-74.
15 A.J.P. Taylor, *The Trouble Makers: Dissent over Foreign Policy, 1792-1939* (London, 1957), 67-94.
16 Conacher, *Aberdeen Coalition*, 257-64; P. Stansky, *Gladstone: A Progress in Politics* (Boston, 1979), 67.
17 Gladstone to Aberdeen, 18 and 21 October 1853, 2 December 1853, and 26 January 1854, Aberdeen Papers, British Library, Add. MS 43070, ff. 392-3, 399-402, 406-9; 43071, ff. 6-8; Conacher, *Aberdeen Coalition*, 194, 205-8, 243; Magnus, *Gladstone*, 114-15.
18 3 *Hansard* 138: 1036-75 (24 May 1855); 139: 1794-1825 (3 August 1855); 142: 92-109 (6 May 1856).
19 3 *Hansard* 142: 92-109 (6 May 1856).
20 D. Beales, *England and Italy, 1859-60* (London, 1961); S. Gopal, 'Gladstone and the Italian Question,' *History*, 41 (1956), 113-21; D. Schreuder, 'Gladstone and Italian Unification, 1848-70: The Making of a Liberal?' *English Historical Review*, 85 (July 1970), 475-501; Gladstone, 'The War in Italy,' *Quarterly Review*, 105 (April 1859), 527-64.
21 3 *Hansard* 184: 1241-2 (20 July 1866).
22 Gladstone, 'The War in Italy,' 537-53.
23 Ibid.; 3 *Hansard* 150: 44-66 (4 May 1858); 184: 1248-52 (20 July 1866).
24 Gladstone, 'Liberty in the East and West,' *Nineteenth Century* (June 1878), 1174; Gladstone, 'England's Mission,' 561.
25 3 *Hansard* 157: 309-26 (9 March 1860); 161: 1577-8 (7 March 1861); *Cambridge History of British Foreign Policy, 1783-1919*, ed. A.W. Ward and G.P. Gooch (3 vols., Cambridge, 1922-3), II, 486-7; Morley, *Life of Gladstone*, II, 22-3; Stansky, *Gladstone*, 82. To his wife, on 11 January 1860, Gladstone described the treaty as potentially a 'great European operation' (*Gladstone to His Wife*, ed. Tilney Bassett, 128).
26 Gladstone, 'Past and Present Administrations,' *Quarterly Review*, 104 (October 1858), 549.
27 Gladstone, 'The War in Italy,' 534.
28 Schreuder, 'Gladstone and Italian Unification,' 494-6.
29 Reminiscing in the 1890s, Gladstone gave the impression that he was certainly in favour of joint action on the part of England and France to check the Germans in January 1864; see Gladstone Papers, Add. MS 44791, ff. 128-30. This might not have been so clear to his colleagues at the time; see Morley, *Life of Gladstone*, II, 116-17; and K.A.P. Sandiford, *Great Britain and the Schleswig-Holstein Question, 1848-64* (Toronto, 1975), 86.

30 *The Letters of Queen Victoria, 1862-78*, ed. A.C. Benson and Viscount Esher (London, 1907), 2nd series, II, 55; T. Aronson, *Queen Victoria and the Bonapartes* (London, 1972), 132.

31 L.A. Tollemache, *Talks with Mr. Gladstone* (London, 1898), 79, 118.

32 A. Marsden, *British Diplomacy and Tunis, 1875-1902* (New York, 1971), 39, 67-73, 77; *The Political Correspondence of Mr. Gladstone and Lord Granville, 1876-86*, ed. A. Ramm (2 vols., Oxford, 1962), II, 380.

33 E. Eyck, *Gladstone* (London, 1938), 451; R.J. Sontag, *Germany and England: Background to Conflict, 1848-94* (New York, 1938; rpt 1964). See also D. Schreuder's excellent essay on Gladstone in *The Conscience of the Victorian State*, ed. P. Marsh (Syracuse, 1979), 97-8.

34 Morley, *Life of Gladstone*, II, 346-8; *The Foundations of British Foreign Policy, 1792-1902*, ed. H.W.V. Temperley and L.M. Penson (London, 1938), 323-7. This question is best treated by Schreuder in 'Gladstone as "Trouble-Maker": Liberal Foreign Policy and the German Annexation of Alsace-Lorraine, 1870-1,' *Journal of British Studies*, 17 (spring 1978), 106-34.

35 3 *Hansard* 184: 1247-52 (20 July 1866); W.E. Mosse, *The European Powers and the German Question, 1848-71* (Cambridge, 1958), 317.

36 3 *Hansard* 233: 416-36 (23 March 1877): Gladstone laments that 'of the little that has been done for the Christian subjects of Turkey by the Powers of Europe nearly all is due to Russia' (col. 427). See also Gladstone, 'The Hellenic Factor in the Eastern Problem,' *Contemporary Review* (December 1876), 25-7.

37 Morley, *Life of Gladstone*, II, 349-58; W.E. Mosse, 'Public Opinion and Foreign Policy: The British Public and the War Scare of November 1870,' *Historical Journal*, 6 (1963), 38-58.

38 3 *Hansard* 234: 402-39 (7 May 1877); Gladstone, 'The Hellenic Factor,' 26.

39 There is much interesting Gladstone-Novikoff correspondence in the Gladstone Papers, British Library, Add. MS 44268. See, especially, two letters from Gladstone to Mme Novikoff, dated 1 April 1878 and 16 November 1880, ff. 173-4, 233.

40 See, eg, his articles in 1878 in the *Nineteenth Century*.

41 Gladstone, 'Past and Present Administrations,' 554.

42 See, especially, Gladstone, 'The Peace to Come,' *Nineteenth Century* (February 1878), 209-11; and his parliamentary speeches on the Eastern question.

43 Magnus, *Gladstone*, 324-5.

44 Gladstone to Aberdeen, 2 December 1853, Aberdeen Papers, Add. MS 43070, ff. 406-9.

45 In Gladstone, 'Past and Present Administrations,' 554-60.

46 Ibid.

47 3 *Hansard* 171: 140-7 (29 May 1863).

48 Ibid. 185: 441-5 (15 February 1867).

49 In Gladstone, 'The Hellenic Factor,' 5-6.

50 Gladstone to Argyll, 26 October 1880, Gladstone Papers, Add. MS 44544, f. 83.

51 Although this point is made most unequivocally in 'Liberty in the East and the West,' 1173-4, and in his famous Bulgarian pamphlet, it is implicit in all of Gladstone's statements on Turkey after his moderate parliamentary speech on the Eastern question on 29 May 1863.

52 Morley, *Life of Gladstone*, I, 618-19; Magnus, *Gladstone*, 135-8; Gladstone to Mrs Gladstone, 2 January 1863, in *Gladstone to His Wife*, ed. Tilney Bassett, 143; M.M. Robson, 'Lord Clarendon and the Cretan Question, 1868-9,' *Historical Journal*, 3 (1960), 38-55; Gladstone to Argyll, 16 December 1862, Gladstone Papers, Add. MS 44533, ff. 64-5; Gladstone to Clarendon, 21 December 1868, ibid., 44133, f. 149; Gladstone, 'The Peace to Come,' 209-26.

53 Gladstone to Clarendon, 5 March 1866, Gladstone Papers, Add. MS 44133, f. 57; W.E. Mosse, *Rise and Fall of the Crimean System, 1855-71* (London, 1963), 137.

54 *Political Correspondence*, ed. Ramm, I, 145; P. Knaplund, *Gladstone's Foreign Policy* (London, 1935; rpt 1970), 149-50.

55 P. Marsh, 'Lord Salisbury and the Ottoman Massacres,' *Journal of British Studies*, 11 (May 1972), 63-83; R. Douglas, 'Britain and the Armenian Question, 1894-7,' *Historical Journal*, 19 (1976), 113-33.

56 K.A.P. Sandiford, 'W.E. Gladstone and Liberal-Nationalist Movements,' *Albion*, 13 (spring 1981), 27-42.

57 3 *Hansard* 172: 1093-1105 (20 July 1863).

58 Lowe, *Reluctant Imperialists*, I, 45; *Political Correspondence*, ed. Ramm, I, 448; T.J. Spinner, *George Joachim Goschen: The Transformation of a Victorian Liberal* (Cambridge, 1973), 90.

59 J. Roach, 'Liberalism and the Victorian Intelligentsia,' in *The Victorian Revolution: Government and Society in Victoria's Britain*, ed. P. Stansky (New York, 1973), 323-53.

60 C. Holbraad, *The Concert of Europe* (London, 1970).

61 R. Millman, *British Foreign Policy and the Coming of the Franco-Prussian War* (Oxford, 1965), 126, 129, 198-207; Mosse, *European Powers*, 313-14; *Foundations of British Foreign Policy*, ed. Temperley and Penson, 335-7.

62 W.F. Monypenny and G.E. Buckle, *Life of Benjamin Disraeli, Earl of Beaconsfield* (6 vols., London, 1910-20), VI, 301, 355.

63 Ibid., V, 407-9, 451; 3 *Hansard* 150: 1384-92 (1 June 1858).

64 *Britain Pre-Eminent: Studies in British World Influence in the Nineteenth Century*, ed. C.J. Bartlett (London, 1969), 7-50.

D.M. SCHREUDER

The Making of Mr Gladstone's Posthumous Career: The Role of Morley and Knaplund as 'Monumental Masons,' 1903-27

John Morley: 'You know the saying that nobody is worth much who has not been a bit of a radical in his youth, and a bit of a tory in his fuller age.'

Mr. Gladstone (laughing): 'Ah, I'm afraid that hits me rather hard. But for myself, I think I can truly put up all the change that has come into my politics into a sentence; I was brought up to distrust and dislike liberty, I learned to believe in it. That is the key to all my changes.' (Biarritz, Sunday, 27 December 1891)

Although my early years were in a party since Conservative, I am not aware of ever having given an anti-liberal vote on colonial affairs. (Gladstone to Sir Henry Parkes, 3 October 1889)[1]

It was John Morley who once wrote of Gladstone's *'curious* instinct for liberty.'[2] This intriguing comment provides a suitable beginning for an essay of historiographical review. I am here concerned with the formative influence that the pioneers of modern Gladstone scholarship have had on our later understanding of Gladstonian Liberalism, in both its domestic and international contexts. More than other writers, it was indeed John Morley and Paul Knaplund who particularly gave substance to that formative founding modern perception of Gladstonian statesmanship. Other writers were subsequently to modify this established and soon to be orthodox view: I think not least of J.L. Hammond in the interwar period, and of Philip Magnus in the 1950s.[3] But in so many ways they worked from a theme already surely struck by Morley and Knaplund. Over the last two decades or so, intensive work on the Victorian Liberal party, on aspects of high-Victorian government, and on a myriad of Victorian themes, has come to place that pioneer orthodoxy under distinctly critical focus.[4] A 'new Gladstone,' or new orthodoxy hardly exists, while the old portrait is at a certain discount. An interesting question for the moment is, therefore, how did the original orthodoxy emerge? I shall sketch an answer to that issue, working from the already valuable critical literature on the subject – not least that of M.R.D. Foot (1968-69), David Hamer (1978), A.O.J. Cockshut (1974), and Colin Matthew (1974-); as well as Derek Beales (1981) on Gladstone and biography, and R.M. Crawford on Knaplund's history (1967). But I shall *also* look to what Gladstone, Morley, and Knaplund said about themselves, in both their writings and in their more deliberately self-conscious fragments of autobiography. The making of a new orthodoxy of interpretation I leave to the burgeoning scholarly industry concerned with 'Mr Gladstone.'[5]

The beginnings of the old orthodoxy are at least as interesting as its recent revisions. John Morley had come to offer his interpretation of Gladstone's career and of Gladstonian Liberalism at that critical moment when history had just begun to take its measure of the GOM, and when Victorian liberalism was undergoing an acute sea-change in content – as younger post-Gladstonian liberals battled both to shape the 'New Liberalism' and to claim descent from the great tradition that ran back through Gladstone to an earlier age.[6] Knaplund came to the subject essentially after the Great War, at a time when the international aspect of liberalism was at a particularly vulnerable moment in European and American thought. Major changes were also taking place in the British settlement empire, as the metropole came to respond to that force which Richard Jebb had, in 1905, dubbed 'colonial nationalism' – an assertiveness of identity on behalf of the various dominions of white settlement.[7] Knaplund made it his task to address the problem of international security and the League of Nations, as well as the spasmodically emerging concept of the 'Commonwealth,' through the idiom and the ideals of Gladstonian Liberalism. The effect was largely reinforcement of Morley's general interpretation at that point where Knaplund felt a potential lacuna existed: 'and thus to supplement Morley's *Life of Gladstone*,' as he modestly wrote of his own work in 1927.[8]

In fine, if it was John Morley who really gave us the first intellectually coherent and persuasive treatment of Gladstonian politics – a treatment quite distinct from the commentary in pious hagiography that preceded Morley – then it could be argued that it was Paul Knaplund who attempted to cast Gladstonian external politics in the same large and heroic mould that had characterized Morley's domestic image. In both cases, complementary as they were, the ultimate overall effect was one of powerful historical conceptualizing, which also involved 'monumentalizing.' Morley and Knaplund gave us a vision of Gladstonian Liberalism that had developed naturally out of their own world views, their culture and context. The convincing portrait that emerged derived in part from a sensitive perception of the manner in which Gladstone had self-consciously come to interpret his own complex life and its religious aspirations. There was also persuasive artistry involved. Morley wrote extremely well: 'The modern scholar may be envious of the skill with which he effortlessly draws together a wide range of information to be found in the manuscript sources, or the deft touch with which he vividly recreates the atmosphere of some forgotten debate,' is the just opinion of the historian of the Aberdeen coalition.[9] And Knaplund also had considerable powers of concentrated and emotive expression.[10] The cumulative effect of their pioneering scholarship may indeed have been to create an interpretation of an heroic nature; the archetypal Christian liberal statesman redolent of myth walks their pages. But they are not makers of a cardboard saint. Gladstonian Liberalism is an attractive force of humanizing power in their hands.

Having made these essentially positive comments, the point of departure for this discussion remains the fact that Morley and Knaplund's 'Gladstonianism' is a very particular phenomenon. Max Beerbohm once depicted John Morley, in a deliciously irreverent cartoon of 1903, as the 'monumental mason' creating a saintly Gladstone, equipped with Irish harp – though the monumental bust was made to stand on a plinth that had carved into its base some of the more controversial Gladstonian 'achievements,' such as the death of Gordon at Khartoum, and the British defeat at Majuba Hill. The 'monumentalizing' aspect of Morley's labours may not have been on the scale suggested by Beerbohm, but it *is* there. 'Morley saw Gladstone's career as a whole, as one glorious achievement, as a lengthy saga of power being unshackled,' in the words of A.O.J. Cockshut's deeply perceptive assessment of Morley's book as a bio-graphical study. Moreover, this monumentalizing had a very particular characteristic in its ultimate, resulting portrayal: 'Morley's interpretation, in its simplest terms, is this. Gladstone was by nature a man of stupendous moral, intellectual and political gifts. These gifts were hampered in their exercise, and thwarted in their public usefulness, by inherited Tory opinions. Very gradually, this man of great gifts worked himself loose from his restrictions, discarding nothing of value that he had held, but developing all the time in the direction of liberty, liberty for himself in the use of his transcendent powers, and liberty for the people whom he led, in whose wisdom and trustworthiness Gladstone came more and more to believe. Thus, when Gladstone supports a cause of which Morley disapproves, like the retention in 1865 of the Anglican test for membership of Convocation at Oxford, it is always, in Morley's view, because he *had not developed far enough.*'[11]

This general perspective complements a view I have long pressed: that evolving Gladstonian Liberalism was as much atavistic and conservationist in its content as progressive and 'liberal.' But what now needs to be developed is the manner in which the 'monumental masons' were partly inspired, consciously or otherwise, by Gladstone himself. As Cockshut rightly suggests, Morley indeed portrays Mr Gladstone as one of the great 'liberators' of the nineteenth century; and Knaplund came to see in Gladstonian Liberalism a great force of moral emancipation for mankind. These historical views, though, all too well accorded with Gladstone's own view of his age. For as Derek Beales has so perceptively argued, Gladstone's political thought involved relating his actions to historical trends; with that history being to the GOM 'predominantly a history of emancipation – that is, of enabling man to do his work of emancipation, political, economical, social, moral, intellectual' (17 March 1894).[12] In the hands of Morley and Knaplund, Gladstonianism became a key agent in the legislative and diplomatic history of Victorian liberal progress, liberating individual consciences, social and political groups, local cultures, regional communities (not least Celtic), political nationalities and 'peoples struggling to be free'; even, as Colin Matthew has suggested,[13] liberating the great material forces in the economy, through the budget and free trade, as well as the intellectual and sentimental well-springs in Christian cultures. Individuals were to be 'liberated' from history itself in an age of progressive change, in which the possibilities for public moral direction, or of selfish mischief, were great. After early Gladstonian false starts in public life – idealism and moral sensibility wasted in the impractical argument for a tory confessional state[14] – the Morley-Knaplund view closely follows Gladstone himself, in seeing a progressive education in liberty, and its practical expression, as the key to the making of a great liberal. Morley subtly suggests how this happened, while connecting the mature 'liberal Gladstone' to the young idealist. Gladstone himself was deeply concerned to reconcile change and consistency in his politics: and his great biographer continued the complex justification by incorporating change within a chain of ethical preoccupations of enduring character. 'The middle of December 1882 marked his political jubilee,' as Morley summed up the epic journey of emancipation and development in Book viii of the celebrated *Life*:

It was now half a century since he had entered public life, and the youthful graduate from Oxford had grown to be the foremost man in his country. Yet these fifty courses of the sun and all the pageant of the world had in some ways made but little difference in him. In some ways, it seemed as if time had rolled over him in vain. He had learned many lessons. He had changed his party, his horizons were far wider, new social truths had made their way into his impressionable mind, he recognised new social forces. His aims for the church, that he loved as ardently as he gloried in a powerful and beneficent state, had undergone a revolution. Since 1866 he had come into contact with democracy at close quarters; the Bulgarian campaign and Midlothian lighting up his early faith in liberty, had inflamed him with new feeling for the voice of the people. As much as in the early time when he had prayed to be allowed to go into orders, he was moved by a dominating sense of the common claims and interests of mankind. 'The contagion of the world's slow stain' had not infected him; the lustre and the long continuity of his public performances still left all his innermost ideals constant and undimmed.'[15]

On this theme of both continuity and irrevocable change, Gladstone could not have done better himself. The consistency is there in the form of principles and ideals; the changes are placed in a pattern of liberal enlightenment; and the whole is given a personal imprint of integrity. Possessed of this attractive and, of course, distinctly 'inside view,' Morley is able to provide an explanation for the shape of Gladstonian politics that not only reconciles tactics and timing with enduring ideals, but also avoids crude interpretations of Gladstonian development in terms of sudden changes of mind, or potentially damaging opportunistic switches of position. Rather, we are given the portrayal of the steadily developing liberator of infinite potentiality. Thus '1886,' for example, finds Gladstone able to outflank Lord Salisbury and the Conservatives on Irish self-government, thanks to 'his vehement sympathy with the principle of nationality, the irresistible attraction for him of all the grand and eternal commonplaces of liberty and self-government,' forces for action happily described, in almost Gladstonian terms themselves, as 'the strong natural impulses of the liberal leader.'[16]

In Paul Knaplund's work on Gladstone's international politics, I find it interesting that he evokes the image of 'conversion' to assist in his exposition of the making of Gladstone as a liberal, a liberator, and a force of moral progress.[17] Concerned initially in his work with Gladstone's colonial policy, Knaplund felt able to narrow the compass of enquiry so as to fix, in a fairly precise way, the period in which Gladstone underwent this metamorphosis from tory to liberal. 'While a Tory, Gladstone seems to have been unmoved by the rumblings from beyond the sea, and he had then little faith in the utility of political concessions. In 1837 he denied that grievances existed in British North America and hoped the government would not give up just claims and weaken imperial ties "for the sake and on the ground of speculative organic changes." Three years later he gave a rather grudging support to the Canadian Union Act. Little, he thought, could be hoped from this measure. He took, on the whole, a gloomy view of the situation.'[18] But then came the Peelite experience, and the force of utilitarian and radical ideas about empire. Gladstone now edged towards liberalism, though 'while Secretary of State for Colonies, from December 1845 to June 1846, his mind was not fully made up on the question of colonial policy.'[19] Within the apparently critical period 1846-9, however, this liberal inclination was finally fixed. Indeed, '*by 1848* he had become fully convinced that local autonomy offered the only solution of Britain's intra-imperial problems.'[20] And again: 'By the end of the forties, Gladstone held very strongly that the new communities must be founded in freedom. He struck heavy blows at the current idea that they should be trained by slow degrees for self-government. This he called "miserable jargon" to be classed with "the spawn of most mischievous opinions with regard to our colonial policy generally." To apply nursery methods to Englishmen was folly. Thereby they would be trained, not for freedom, but for dependence.'[21]

In short, where Morley was to follow Gladstone in suggesting a complex, difficult transformation into liberalism, from misplaced and mistaken early toryism – 'a man's mind seldom moves forward towards light and freedom on a single line' – Knaplund was to stress an experience that involved a slightly more direct political road to Damascus, or at least an earlier irrevocable change to liberalism: '*Once converted* to the liberal view on this question, he [Gladstone] fought bravely in its behalf. To him, liberty was the birthright both of Englishmen beyond the sea and those who remained at home ... If reared in freedom, Gladstone believed the new communities would overcome the difficulties of the early critical years and later remain faithful to the mother country. In his opinion, the human ties of love and affection could be depended on for keeping the empire together. As a result in part of his work, Britain's imperial relationship gained that flexibility wherein lies its chief strength [in 1923].'[22]

Interestingly, when writing in the 1920s, Knaplund came to see the Gladstonian experience as part of a larger historical 'progress' in the form of the 'origin and history of the British Commonwealth of Nations,' embracing not merely 'evolution' in policy, but an 'evolutionary process' itself.[23] Thus the verification for Gladstonian liberal ideas on empire was seen to reside not merely in the Victorian 'liberal empire of settlement,' but in the very lessons of the *later* history of the commonwealth: 'these principles were put on record as formally accepted by the Imperial Conference of 1926.' And, more than that, 'when his work and achievements are studied and evaluated, it stands clearly revealed that William Ewart Gladstone must be reckoned among the great architects and builders of the British Commonwealth of Nations.'[24]

Gladstone himself, of course, had made it part of his own 'orthodoxy' of general, personal explanation that he had simply grown away from the illiberalism of his youth as he came to grasp the full implications of 'liberty' in his thought. He would even dare to criticize his beloved Oxford on this basis – 'Oxford had rather tended to hide from me the great fact that liberty is a great and precious gift of God' – though it was also Oxford that *'laid the foundations of my liberalism.'* Indeed, 'I declare that while in the arms of Oxford, I was possessed through and through with a single-minded and passionate love of truth ... so that, although I might be swathed in clouds of prejudice, there was something of an eye within, that might gradually pierce them.'[25] Gladstone also favoured the image of organic growth as permanent change. For example, 'the Reform Bill frightened me in 1831, and drove me off my *natural* and previous bias.'[26] But above all, with all the powerful capacity of that imaginative mind, Gladstone could ultimately come to cast his own career within the notion of an alignment with the great progressive forces of a liberal age. Most famously, over the franchise issue, he came to declare his attachment to liberalism as *the* historical force of the age. And an autobiographical note of July 1892 succinctly expressed this mystery as a 'great fact' – 'that liberty is a great and precious gift of God, and that human excellence cannot grow up in a nation without it.' Less well known is the interpretation given in his delightful *A Chapter of Autobiography* (1868), within the context of Irish Church policy, of his movement towards political liberalism. There he refers to the 'silent changes, which are advancing in the very bed and basis of modern society'; and speaks evocatively of living in an era when the nation was passing 'from a stationary into a progressive period,' when the 'movement of the public mind has been of a nature entirely transcending former experience.' The morally responsible statesman acted accordingly in the face of such ethically charged public opinion in a democratic Christian state:

If it is the office of law and of institutions to reflect the wants and wishes of the country (and its wishes must ever be a considerable element in its wants), then, as the nation passes from a stationary into a progressive period, it will justly require that the changes of its own condition and views should be represented in the professions and actions of its leading men. For they exist for its sake, not it for theirs. It remains indeed their business, now and ever, to take honour and duty for their guides, and not the mere demand or purpose of the passing hour: but honour and duty themselves require their loyal servant to take account of the state of facts in which he is to work, and, while ever labouring to elevate the standard of opinion and action around him, to remember that his business is not to construct, with self-chosen materials, an Utopia or a Republic of Plato, but to conduct the affairs of a living and working community of men, to have self-government recognised as in the last resort the moving spring of their political life, and of the institutions which are its outward vesture.[27]

Morley and Knaplund had therefore an impeccable Gladstonian source in developing their portrayal of the liberating statesman: no less than Gladstone himself. In their sympathetic portrayal of the great man, they absorbed his own highly persuasive autobiographical interpretation of his life and thought. And who could condemn them for succumbing to so powerful, coherent, and disarming an explanation: 'the basis of my liberalism is this. It is the lesson which I have been learning ever since I was young. I am a lover of liberty. And that liberty which I value for myself I value for every human being, in proportion to his means and opportunities. That is the basis on which I find it perfectly practicable to work in conjunction with a dislike to unreasoned change, and a profound reverence for everything ancient, provided that reverence is deserved. There are those who have been so happy that they have been born with a creed which they can usefully maintain to the last. For my own part, as I have been a learner all my life, a learner I must continue to be' (speech at Norwich, 16 May 1890).[28] In fine, Gladstone had developed his own personal 'inner history' of explanation against his critics. His pioneer expositors assisted in its transformation into public history.

What is the basis for revising their early histories, for recasting the work of the monumental masons? Indeed, for questioning the Gladstonian view about 'Gladstone-by-Gladstone'? Partly it is simply a question of detailed knowledge of Gladstonian politics within Victorian public life generally. Furthermore, behind the matter of micro-detail, there is the deeper issue of historical reinterpretation in a post-liberal age.[29] The challenge is to make an interpretation that is sympathetically perceptive in understanding Gladstone and his politics, while treating critically the evocative understanding he offered of himself. We can do well by looking first to Morley and Knaplund at work.

By the time Gladstone died in the early hours of Thursday, 19 May 1898 – which happened to be Ascension Day – he had come to judge his own life in most equivocal terms. He still felt himself to be the worst of sinners, finding the patterns of Providence in the complexities of society, state, and empire. And he saw his sixty years of political labour also leading to mixed results. There were achievements, to be sure, not least those associated with the creative first Liberal government of 1868-74. But there was also a list of 'Errors,' both of instance and general direction, to be drawn up. Being Gladstone, he appears to have drawn up several.[30] He could also contemplate the collection of small diary volumes and know, as only he knew, about the personal crises, strains, and lapses that had marked his private journey, his attempts to discipline self, and mortify the flesh, in a struggle for 'worldly piety.'[31]

Yet this is hardly how the great mass of Victorians at home and abroad had come to perceive 'Mr Gladstone.' Broadly, they associated him with the deepest verities of their culture. They largely agreed with Lord Salisbury's magnanimous valedictory estimation, that Gladstone would primarily be remembered as a great Christian statesman. They associated Gladstonian finance with much of the golden aura of mid-Victorian prosperity. Indeed, Gladstone could be taken to be a Victorian achievement in himself. The man of power was yet the man of peace; the man of outstanding intellect was yet the child in Christ; the man of international stature was profoundly English when confronted with, say, ultramontanism. For many of the devoutly faithful, in an age of evangelical revival, Gladstone held a central place in a kind of Protestant iconography of conscience-politics: he personified the moralizing of political culture, the gradual liberation of dissent from mere Anglican toleration to full emancipation. Perhaps, ultimately, this Anglican of Anglicans would assist nonconformity to capture the heights of the state and disestablish the English church. All was possibility in this mythology; and all was spiritual progress and liberation.

Of course, this cult of Gladstone, ably described by David Hamer, had its contemporary critics.[32] A long career of hopes unfulfilled among one-time ardent apostles had left pockets of disenchanted groups along the wayside of the great career. The more militant leaders of dissent, and even some of the more moderate shapers of dissenting opinion among the nonconformists, had, for example, come to suspect that Gladstone had drawn them into a consensus role in party liberalism and rewarded them with much less than they expected, especially in matters where it really counted – such as primary education and the universities. The evangelical heart still inhabited an Anglican constitution: and so Gladstone's ecclesiastical reforms gave an impression that they were defending the church as well as increasing liberty. The higher bourgeoisie and intelligentsia had always found him somewhat strained and artificial. The Christian pilgrim never quite seemed to match the master tactician, the orator of consummate casuistical skill, or the 'eager will,' redolent of ambition and determination for high executive office and residency in the corridors of power.

The moral gravitas of the Christian statesman was an enormous asset in an age of public earnestness, and this image was ideal for projection in the burgeoning popular press from the late 1850s. But, close up, the gravitas could seem all too like self-righteousness; the call to constant duty like self-projection; and the pious manner, together with a ready invocation of Divine Plan, like the rationalization of a self-willed individual of restless determination. Within the Liberal party ranks there was also the growing realization that the 'People's William' had a very particular view of democracy, radicalism, the relative position of issues in the development of a party programme, and the priorities of cabinet action. The Canningite tory in Gladstone was just as likely to surface in discussion as the apostle of popular liberalism. Increasingly, indeed, there emerged a generation of liberals, among whom Joseph Chamberlain would be a precursor, who felt that Gladstone-the-Liberal inhibited the development of a reform politics that focused on issues of material welfare. Was Gladstone's principled liberal reformism not perhaps essentially about reforming institutions, and facilitating the functions of a laissez-faire state? And were the election 'cries' of Irish church and, later, Irish Home Rule, not a brilliant means of centring liberalism on Mr Gladstone and his version of institutional reform, at the expense of other, more socially oriented political reform issues?[33]

Certainly, the contemporary critics of the 'Gladstone cult' have left a record that in many ways makes Gladstone actually seem more human than the view provided by the hagiographers – even if the individual that emerges is less omniscient, less heroic, less attractive, and, if it can be measured, 'less liberal.' Walter Bagehot's 1860 portrayal of Gladstone – written after close observation and a long interview – essentially depicts a political animal of the highest order, highly sensitive to opinion, tactics, and policy.[34] Salisbury's shrewdly cynical contemporary assessment concerning the source of Gladstone's interventions in domestic and foreign policy – when the opportune action became the opportunistic tactic – is equally not easily set aside, and is certainly not damaged by the claim of Gladstonian apologists that the great liberal launched his reforming initiatives and missions from a personal sense of moral 'righteousness and ripeness.'[35] The validity of these particular views is open to question: but they do, cumulatively, throw rather significant obstacles across the line of interpretation that takes as its guide the attractive but questionable autobiographic explanation of Gladstone moving steadily and irrevocably in his ideas from 'right' to 'left' on the political spectrum: from illiberalism to liberalism.

Not that the cult much felt the impact of these kinds of troublesome inner complexities. Gladstone out-of-doors and in the constituencies radiated a style and charisma through the oratory of gravitas, principle, and high-minded reform of civil rights: so much so that he came to exist, in image, as a public figure very different from the Peelite master cabinet politician. In this development Gladstone was hardly unique. In an earlier age of lesser communications, as Marcus Cunliffe has described, George Washington had indeed become a living monument even before death.[36] The same can be observed for Gladstone. By the 1870s there was the Gladstone who lived in the northern newspapers and dissenting tracts; the figure – quite literally – who appeared in countless stylized etchings and photogravure portraits in countless hallways and dining rooms; as well as the plethora of bits of Gladstoniana with the famous profile on tiles, Staffordshire mugs, bits of Wedgewood pottery, tea-caddies, and even engraved on miniature silver-plated axes to commemorate his suitably healthy and manly hobby, described by critics as the demolition of trees by axe in the lovely Flintshire countryside. For ardent parents there were also, of course, the great names to be taken up: by the late-Victorian period, a veritable small army of little boys must have reacted to the call of 'William Ewart.'

It was to this audience, naturally, that the many popular contemporary *Lives* of Gladstone were directed by piously determined biographers before the statesman's death in 1898. A good example, indeed a better than average example, is that by George Barnett Smith: it is literate; compressed with reliable factual data; gives a detailed record of the Gladstone career; and yet it describes a man just short of canonization. Writing in 1879, Smith concluded thus:

We have now reached the close of our survey of Mr. Gladstone's literary and political career. In both aspects the average reader seems to toil after him in vain, so great is his facility in resource, so extraordinary his power of seizing upon and comprehending the facts and bearings of our foreign and domestic policy, so copious and inexhaustible the eloquence with which he illustrates and enforces his views – whether those views relate to the immortal works of Homer, the scandals of the Neapolitan prisons, the questions raised by Ecce Homo, the details of the last budget, the principles which should pervade industrial art, the dogmas of the Romish Church, the duty of man in relation to education and religion, or the policy of the Beaconsfield Administration ... [Moreover, he] is preeminently a Christian statesman. The golden thread of Christian principle runs through all his utterances ... Mr. Gladstone has invariably 'worn his heart upon his sleeve,' and disposed for ever of the idea that tortuousness and subterfuge are necessary to the successful political leader ... Mr. Gladstone has demonstrated that simplicity of character, frankness and unreservedness of speech and moral sensibility are not incompatible with true political greatness.[37]

The situation facing the 'authorized biographer' on Gladstone's death was therefore rather considerable. The family, the public, the party, liberals at home and abroad – they all had high expectations of the *Life*. How were the several existing public 'Gladstones' to be reconciled? Would the full disclosure about Mr Gladstone's personal life really serve the public memory of the Anglican pilgrim? Above all, would it be possible to compress a complex and tortuous career of over sixty years into a coherent and persuasive image of the liberator? Indeed, could the powerful interpretation already put abroad of Gladstone by Gladstone be denied?

There was also the eminently practical question of who should be the biographer.[38] Who was equal to the task of comprehending the entirety of the Gladstone life and career? Was a scholarly polymath not needed to write the life of a public polymath?

Lord Acton's name was immediately canvassed, but he demurred. In fact, on the day of Gladstone's funeral, Acton had met with John Morley at Cambridge to discuss the question of the expected biography – Gladstone's closest intellectual guide discussing the beginnings of the 'posthumous career' with the political confidante closest to the GOM in his closing years. According to Owen Chadwick, Acton had Morley at the top of a short list, with G.O. Trevelyan and James Bryce after Morley.[39] Morley himself proposed Herbert Paul. Despite certain personal misgivings about Morley as an individual, Acton pressed his name strongly on the Gladstone family, arguing that Morley would handle the politics well, and that the 'lack of sympathy on the religious side' would not be too limiting a factor. The family seems to have found attraction in the idea of having Morley treat the politics in a big volume that eschewed the theology, and then having another author provide a personal sketch that sensitively portrayed the spiritual Gladstone.[40] By the end of the summer of 1898, Morley had been approached by the Gladstone heir, and by 6 September they had come to an agreement. The autumn found Morley already confronting not merely the massive archives Gladstone had left in the Octagon strong-room off the 'Temple of Peace' – his Hawarden study – but facing the critical question of how he was to portray Gladstone to an intensely interested family, party, and public.

Morley was to write a great Victorian biography. And he was to do so largely by making a work of art that reflected the skills, the predilections, and the preoccupations of the literary artist. In his *Recollections* he tells us how carefully he planned the book, its making and emphasis. 'Though the subject was inspiring, it was no occasion for high attempts in literary expression. The difficulty was of another kind. The first quality required was architectonic; it lay in distribution of periods and phases, the right scale for a thousand episodes, right proportions among wide and varied fields of incessant public policy and personal activity. To overmaster and compress the raw material, and to produce from it the lineaments of a singularly subtle and elastic mind, and the qualities of one of the most powerful and long-lived athletes that ever threw himself into the parliamentary arena – *hic labor, hoc opus!*'[41]

He lived up to this plan, revealing both stamina and an admirable conceptualizing control of his subject. Largely withdrawing from active political life, Morley immersed himself in another life: mastering the documents, reading the many Gladstone publications, consulting the parliamentary record and parliamentarians, but, above all, secluding himself to write his *Life* of Gladstone. Even if the final book was 'far larger than I expected or liked,' the 700,000 words and 1975 pages in three volumes, weighing over seven pounds, came from Macmillan, as he could justly boast, 'punctually as if by Act of Parliament' in October 1903.[42]

What had Morley made? The reviewers were delighted and the reading public expressed their pleasure in strong sales, even if the family was more guarded in response. The strengths of the *Life* of 1903 still stand, and they are threefold. First, Morley had comprehended the diversity and complexity of Gladstone's life. He had worked voraciously –

should one say 'manfully,' for a Victorian writer? – to master Gladstone's documentary deposit. To this he had added a great range of printed and oral sources. He had, moreover, made the sensible decision to include his own memories of the later Gladstone and their frequent private discussions – so we get 'memoir' too. Tollemache made a name for himself by collecting his 'talks with Mr. Gladstone' into a book. Morley merely included his own valuable oral testimony within the *Life*. Second, Morley was also – and this is more difficult to present or assess – a man of honesty and integrity, who wanted to tell the truth about his subject within certain limits of discretion, both personal and public. The *Life* surely involved hero-worship; but it was a positive view based on very close knowledge of Gladstone and of the Gladstone archive. Morley was a stylist, and as such quoted both selectively and economically from the rich evidence he had to hand, but he did not wilfully mislead the reader. His scholarship, in the quotation of documents, is cavalier by modern standards; where he does mislead, over words or phrases, it is in the venial sense of relying too heavily on researchers' transcripts or of unchecked galley proofs.[43] But, above all, his preoccupation was to render Mr Gladstone intelligible, in the round. What we lose in exactness we gain in what W.K. Hancock has elsewhere referred to as 'span and measure' in historical writing. Gladstone lives in this *Life* – and he does so in a manner that leaves no doubt as to his charisma, personal qualities, and 'presence.'[44]

Lastly, Morley is admirable in *trying* to connect Gladstone's religious sensibilities with the masterful cabinet politician. Morley was a free thinker,[45] deeply drawn to the issue of public ethics in the state.[46] He admired Mill because of this ethical goal in his thought, and he admired Gladstone as practical agent of that ethical vision for an industrial and liberal-democratic society. Gladstone was fundamentally a man of public action, of interventions in the life of the state, of restless energy, and of ambition; but one who also possessed the gift of great personal faith. Finding practical expressions for moral sensibility, and trying to relate Godly service to a realization of egotistical ambition, formed a core problem in Gladstone's personal and public life. His *Diaries* reveal, in their daily markings, this Gladstonian fascination – obsession perhaps? – in fulfilling himself through action and faith. Morley knew much of this: he certainly grasped the nub of the matter in portraying Gladstone as fundamentally a man of the state, whose 'interventions' and 'missions,' cabinet service and party leadership, were informed by a highly developed sense of conscience. State and church met in his being. Or in Morley's lucid and evocative analysis: 'Here we mark a signal trait. Not for two centuries, in the historic strife of Anglican and Puritan, had our island produced a ruler in whom the religious motive was paramount in the like degree. He was not only a political force but a moral force. He strove to use all the powers of his own genius and the powers of the state for moral purposes and religious. Nevertheless his mission in all its forms was action. He had none of that detachment, often found among superior minds, which we honour for its disinterestedness, even while we lament its impotence in result. The track in which he moved, the instruments which he employed, were the track and the instruments, the sword and the trowel, of political action; and what is called the Gladstonian era was distinctively a political era.'[47] Nicely, he adds below this analysis: 'churches also have their parties.'[48]

Morley's interpretation takes its strength, then, from that kind of shrewdly intelligent yet sensitive understanding of Gladstone in action. It also essays a compelling but highly personal view of Gladstone's ideological and party evolution as a public figure. And Morley honestly makes a point of saying this is so: 'That my book should be a biography without trace of bias no reader will expect. There is at least no bias against the truth ... I should be heartily sorry if there was no sign of partiality and no evidence of prepossession.'[49] In fact, there is a great deal of 'evidence of prepossession' – and it is here that we enter into serious debate with Morley.

We have been given our lead in this contention by Morley's own historian, who has emphasized the degree to which the *Life of Gladstone* was shaped by Morley's acute intellectual and political problems at the turn of the century. In David Hamer's telling words, 'Morley simply did not know how or why he should act in politics. Feeling, that is, conviction, about "rightness" and "wrongness" in regard to certain questions, remained, but not the ability or knowledge for translating it into action relevant to the particular circumstances and climate of opinion of this "new world" into which he had "survived." '[50] Accordingly, as his own biographer has argued, writing the life of Gladstone was both highly instructive for the 'lost' in the contemporary world that Morley sadly contemplated;[51] and also a way of stepping outside the controversies over the 'New Liberalism,' the 'New Imperialism,' and the impending problems of the new century.[52]

In addition, Morley's attraction to the biographical treatment of history – whether of actors or thinkers – reflected on his more general theory of society and democracy.[53] On this Peter Stansky has remarked sharply, yet not unfairly, that 'whatever his Radical position on certain issues,' such as education or Ireland, more generally 'he was an élitist who believed in a democracy that should dedicate itself to ratify the decisions of sage rulers from the middle and upper classes, rather than bothering to put forward leaders of its own from the multitude.'[54] The locomotive of history was to be very much dependent upon that elite at the controls; and, as a consequence, Morley-the-intellectual came to be absorbed with particular kinds of questions concerning the role of the individual in history. Two such are pertinent here, as Hamer reveals.[55] The first concerned the role of biography in performing an educative and edifying function in the culture. Here is the explanation for the otherwise unexpected dedication of the *Life*: 'To the electors of the Montrose Burghs I beg leave to inscribe this book in grateful recognition of the confidence and friendship with which they have honoured me.' The second and even more critical dimension to Morley's emphasis on the individual in history concerned his belief that it was the individual who provided the *lien* between politics as tactics and politics as ethical action.[56] It was the conscience of the individual of moral integrity that prevented 'compromise' – Morley's estimation of the key to practical progress in the state – from indeed becoming mere opportunism, or adventurous Bonapartism. As Morley explained it, in the key introductory passage to his now largely forgotten essay *On Compromise* (which he saw as following Mill's *On Liberty*): 'The interesting question in connection with compromise obviously turns upon the placing of the boundary that divides wise suspense in forming opinions, wise reserve in expressing them, and wise tardiness in trying to realise them, from unavowed disingenuousness and self-illusion, from voluntary dissimulation, and from indolence and pusillanimity.'[57] Gladstone was fascinating, and laudable, simply because that is exactly the point of action in the executive life of the state at which he operated. Gladstone was therefore not merely the best political hope of *On Liberty*; he became the copybook moral statesman of *On Compromise*. Absolutely fundamental consequences for historical interpretation followed.[58] In terms of Gladstone's complex character and personality, it was clearly not in Morley's interest to deploy all the protean evidence that he had surely read in the diaries of, for example, his subject's often bleak introspection and self-criticism; the struggles with will and flesh; the swithering, to use an appropriate Scottish term, of a man sometimes at war with his own soul, especially in middle age. Nor, indeed, was it in Morley's interest to portray a man of moral rigour who yet had a life private from his wife. Rather, 'Nobody ever had fewer secrets, nobody ever lived and wrought in fuller sunlight.'[59]

Furthermore, and equally important, Morley was preoccupied with explaining the life of a great liberator, not merely recording the achievements of a man of moral worth or political significance. It was liberalism that 'defined the age,' with all its transitions and changes: 'If we seek a word for significance of it all, it is not hard to find. Alike with those who adore and those who detest it, the dominating force in the living mind of Europe for a long generation after the overthrow of the French monarchy in 1830 has been that marked way of looking at things, feeling them, handling them, judging main actors in them, for which, with a hundred kaleidoscopic turns, the accepted name is *Liberalism*.'[60] And it was 'Liberalism' that subsumed all the great emancipating forces of the era: 'Respect for the dignity and worth of the individual is its root. It stands for pursuit of social good against class interest or dynastic interest. It stands for the subjection to human judgment of all claims of external authority ... In law-making it does not neglect the higher characteristics of human nature, it attends to them first. In executive administration, though judge, gaoler, and perhaps the hangman will be indispensable, still mercy is counted a wise supplement to terror ... Treitschke, the greatest of modern absolutists, lays it down that everything new that the nineteenth century has erected is the work of Liberalism.'[61] In Morley's terms, Gladstone was one of the great facilitators of progress. Gladstone's conservationist instinct − his reverence for institutions, for tradition, authority, and the social order of Victorian England − is hardly a central feature of Morley's Gladstonianism. In releasing himself from entering the central puzzle of Gladstonian politics − the role of atavism in ideas and sympathies − Morley revealed how closely he had absorbed Gladstone's own history of his progressive development as a quintessential liberal.

In fact, of course, atavism can be seen to have infused the whole mature phase of Gladstonian politics and thought. It should not surprise us. For although Gladstone broadened his conception of politics over the decades, he also drew from intellectual and moral sources that endured from beginning to end. His ultimate significance as a public figure lay in the fact that he encapsulated political forces of great potential change; but the social theory that accompanied this threatening potentiality was strikingly consistent for the tory or liberal Gladstone. The question indeed arises whether, party aside, the mature Gladstone fundamentally 'changed' the ideological underpinnings of his politics. The 'church and state' issue, so important to Gladstone, is singularly revealing on just this matter of interpreting his atavism.[62]

The beginnings of Gladstone's fascination with the Christianizing function of the church in the life of the state are well understood, and Morley was hardly unaware of it. In those first two major publications – *The State in Its Relation with the Church* and *Church Principles Considered in Their Results*, written and revised between 1838 and 1842 – Gladstone set out his early and high ideal of an Anglican confessional state, governed by an equally high-minded body of tory guardians. Peelite Conservatives saw Gladstone as priggishly unworldly, indeed simply unwise, in propagating such palpable chimerical doctrines for an increasingly industrial, and religiously plural, modern society. Gladstone himself was later to portray his early Anglican zealotry and bigotry as a venial error.[63] Morley now followed Gladstone, who had developed an intriguing thesis as to his 'extrication' (Gladstone's own significant term) out of, and away from, Puseyism, Oxford idealism, and landed toryism. In fact, in terms of ultimate aspirations and perspective, the mature Gladstone ever regretted that a confessional state had been made impossible by religious, denominational pluralism. To be sure, he made the best of social reality by accepting that the conscience of the state must reside outside the formal *established* church-state relationship. And, indeed, in his democratic politics he was ultimately to take conscience 'out-of-doors.' It was to reside, as he explained in the *Chapter of Autobiography*, in the heart of all respectable right-minded Christian voters in the 'political nation:' 'we are still a Christian people. Christianity has wrought itself into the public life of fifteen hundred years. Precious truths, and laws of relative right and the brotherhood of man, such as the wisdom of heathenism scarcely dreamed of and could never firmly grasp, the Gospel has made to be part of our common inheritance, common as the sunlight that warms us, and as the air we breathe. Sharp though our divisions in belief may be, they have not cut so deep as to prevent, or as perceptibly to impair, the recognition of these great outlines and fences of moral action.'[64] Yet of course Gladstone was still fascinated with the functions of the established church – in the larger sense of believers and seekers after the faith – within the state. Insofar as Gladstone was a true optimist, as Ian Bradley's recent study would argue, this rested rather more on an evangelical sense concerned with the 'leavening' of society by Christian tenets of belief than on simple views of material progress per se. Gladstone's answer to the gloomy Tennyson of *Locksley Hall Sixty Years After* was just such a statement of 'progress,' and one that depicted the Victorian achievement in terms of the spiritualizing of material advances.[65]

More specifically, the atavistic tendencies in Gladstone's religious sensibilities revealed an enduring High Anglican concern for dogma, the apostolic succession, ritual, and the authority of the episcopacy. Owen Chadwick and Colin Matthew have both indicated why a powerful sense of religious nationality kept Gladstone from travelling on the road to Rome with the apostasies of Hope-Scott and Newman.[66] We should also, therefore, note that the other side of Gladstone's Anglicanism and anti-Romanism was a loathing for moves to theological liberalism, which he saw as the thin end of the wedge of humanism. Gladstone was to attack the relativism and rationalism of *Robert Elsmere* (1888) for this very reason. Likewise, he increasingly feared Erastianism as endangering the dogma of the church; and he became as stirred as he did over the Gorham affair simply because he deeply suffered any diminution of the authority of the church as a church.[67] It might also be added that Gladstone rejected revisions of the great mysteries of church teachings to make them more reasonable. Like Newman, he preferred his religion full of myth and imagery, which allowed contemplation of mysteries in faith, not their 'explanation.' Gladstone's last serious intervention in theological debate was significantly to be focused on a call to a proper dogma of 'Hell.'

Several political consequences followed – if not from a dogma of retribution, then from the atavistic aspects of his Anglicanism. For a start, Gladstone's notion of 'freedom of conscience' actually lay in dogma and authority, just as did his view that individual liberty and freedom in the state best existed under law and authority vested in historic institutions – themselves dominated by that disinterested elite who met the criteria of aristocratic and landed-society values, Oxbridge, and the public service in the age of the Northcote-Trevelyan Report. In *State and Church* Gladstone had given the aristocracy a value as high as the clerisy in Coleridge's ideal moral order; so now his cabinets, and his advisory 'court' of followers and associates, were filled with competent whiggish aristocrats or 'manly' products of the upper bourgeoisie, such as his favoured chancellor of the exchequer, H.C.E. Childers. Whether Gladstone ever actually said that the English had 'a sneaking kindness for a lord' – the doubt is thanks to the sharp editorial eye of George Kitson Clark[68] – the broader truth is that Gladstone himself gave the aristocracy a very high place in his general social theory. He did not hide this fact. Indeed, he emphatically remarked, on a variety of occasions, that he was an out-and-out inegalitarian. He believed in 'the rule of the best,' as he put it, in an era when the aristocratical order was still, in so many ways, the ruling order.[69] Certainly, until they deserted him over Irish Home Rule, Gladstone had few doubts of the moral import and role of an aristocratical elite in English public life. Moreover, the 'People's William' was not the product of a commitment on Gladstone's part to any radicalizing of the constitution or its social base, but the result of his particular brand of conscience politics – the emphasis on civil rather than political rights, on the moral potential of mankind in a laissez-faire environment, rather than on the politics of welfare.[70]

The general point is also well made if Gladstone's relationship to nonconformity is seen in historical perspective.[71] Dissent formed one major social element of his mass constituency, something the Anglican Gladstone came to recognize as much as the liberal Gladstone: 'they are the backbone of the party,' as he frankly declared of nonconformity. It was tempting for Morley again to follow Gladstone, whose presumably 'natural' liberal instincts had at last led to an increasing rapprochement with organized dissent, and away from the blinkers of that early establishmentarian Anglicanism. Had not Gladstone declared, as early as 1851, in the debate over the Ecclesiastical Titles Bill, that 'we cannot change the profound and resistless tendencies of the age towards religious liberty'? And had he not used the argument again as part of his justification for disestablishing the Irish church?[72] One political result was the forging of a great force of emancipation; the Liberal party became the Gladstonian vehicle for connecting Peelites and nonconformists – not to mention whiggery – in the cause of conscience politics. Yet the danger inherent in emphasizing the liberationist aspect of Gladstone's connection with organized dissent is that, again, it fails to hold in suspension, within the overall interpretation, Gladstone's atavistic thought about the church and the role of nonconformity within the state.

In bald terms, it can be said that Gladstone indeed expressed an increasing sympathy towards dissenters; and that he was, correspondingly, increasingly impressed by the earnest, moral impact of nonconformity on English society and its values.[73] It is also true that he favoured the fullest extension of concepts of 'toleration' towards non-Anglicans in the state; and that his name came to be associated with much liberating legislation affecting the complex relationship of church, state, and nonconformity – not least in terms of church rates, or university tests for admission to Oxbridge. Yet these trends and postures in his politics need a very careful reading. Above all, it must be kept in mind that Gladstone was always a strong denominationalist, a fervent Anglican who believed the church to be playing a morally proper role in national service, not least by virtue of its being the denomination of the majority of Englishmen (though he here certainly excepted the Celtic cultures).

Thus, much as he sympathized with nonconformists, they were still dissenters from the Catholic tradition. Seen in this way, Gladstone's magnanimous and conciliatory attitude towards nonconformity became part and parcel of what was also a form of defensive Anglicanism.[74] 'Acts like these weaken the invading enemy,' he himself plainly remarked of the reforms in civil prerogatives as they affected dissenters in the 1860s.[75] After his noted private meetings with moderate leaders of nonconformity in the same decade, his journal can be found describing them as pleasant, but still dissenters, with 'teeth and claws not very terrible.'[76] And as Olive Anderson has expertly shown over church rates, Gladstone's tactic was in fact to try to defend the vestry in the one area where it might be defended, in the counties.[77] Over the issue of entry into the old universities, he recognized the overwhelming case for admitting nonconformists to degrees, but he hoped in making this concession to blunt their case for a controlling share of the historic educational institutions through convocation: this was to be kept pristinely Anglican. The 1870 school and religion issue, where Gladstone ultimately disappointed even more moderate dissent, in fact found him running true to form. He revealed his vital concern for denominational instruction, independent of state control, and for the survival of Anglicanism in the face of the rising tide of nonconformity.[78]

Gladstone's acceptance of a religious pluralism in English society surely emerged from a sense of Christian fellowship and evangelical sensibility. And that sense of community with dissent did indeed translate itself into emancipatory legislation. It could also be remarked, in party political terms, that Gladstone's personal constituency in the nation did indeed expand greatly in the 1860s to draw in much support from the 'world' of nonconformity. John Bright presumably had this in mind when he extravagantly described the Liberal party as 'the party of Christ.' Yet this image of Gladstonian Liberalism owed as much to aspirations pressed in the regional newspapers, including of course the active organs of dissenting towns, as it did to the oblique overtures made to mass nonconformity by Gladstone himself, in his innovative and important northern tours of the early and mid-1860s. He offered electors high moral probity in finance, dignity and status in national life, and a moralized version of English external policies. He was not offering dissent a pre-eminent role in the governance of the state, though that is what could have been construed by those wishing to find such an interpretation in the Gladstonian posture towards nonconformity. In their mutual misapprehension, Gladstonian Liberalism and English dissent served each other with signal success.[79]

The sense in which Gladstone claimed to have acted throughout as a liberal is fascinating because his mature thought on national affairs was infused with elements and concepts that reconciled 'beginnings' with 'present,' and that endured as dogmatic points of reference in a long career of intellectual and tactical development. It is an understanding of Gladstonian politics without the singular clarity of the progressive model that ultimately emerges in Morley's magnificent progression of episodic events. Gladstone certainly 'grew'; and, as he himself liked to stress, he had indeed been a 'learner' all his life. There was also a core to his social and ethical thought, on the state and its politics, that was as constant as his abiding attachment to the venerable, historic institutions of the state and church. Freedom and authority lived co-terminous within that social theory; and, ultimately, the Gladstonian view of power in a stratified, hierarchical social order came to rest in an ideal of 'balance,' in classes and interests, under the law. Much of his politics aimed at moving individuals in society to find fulfilment outside and beyond class interests; just as he increasingly portrayed party liberalism as a force that transcended class, in the sense of a national moral order of the earnest civic-minded individual.[80] He was also, increasingly, to argue that the evolving British constitutional arrangements were the best in the world, for they had managed to accomplish what he took to be a fundamental task in an age of acute transition, of knitting the forces of 'old' and 'new' in the emergence of the modern order. He appears to have applied the same notions to church as to state. He saw the established church as the corporate expression of laity, clergy, and episcopacy, bound together by historic, dogmatic authority. He supported the Anglican revival of convocation, just as he supported expansion of the franchise, as providing a broader social base for traditional authority.[81]

Such a perspective on Gladstonian politics and churchmanship is accordingly in some tension with that view of the naturally emerging liberator Gladstone himself so favoured. It also points in a direction somewhat different from perspectives that find an essential conservative hidden in the 'People's William.' Complex and complicating as it may be, I would argue for a view of Gladstonian politics as an expression of modes of thought and policy that drew their vitality and power from a compound of elements that actually lived in a state of 'generative tension,' to use Herbert Butterfield's evocative idiom from *Christianity and History*:[82] authority and liberty, elitism and democracy, constitutionalism and conscience politics, in constant interaction.

The litmus test with Gladstone was always his churchmanship.[83] And it is therefore not surprising that perhaps the most revealing exposition of the Gladstonian dilemma over 'party' has come within a study of *Politics and the Churches in Great Britain, 1832-68*, where G.I.T. Machin remarks that, by 1859, 'Gladstone had developed considerably in a liberal direction' over his eighteen Peelite years: though he also shrewdly adds that Gladstone's progress in domestic reform had by then taken him 'no further than progressive Conservatives, and that he was less liberal than some of these in certain respects. For example, over church rates he was less advanced than Lord Stanley.'[84] Once firmly anchored among the whigs and liberals, however, Gladstone did indeed show further signs of progress towards more advanced views.[85] Environment had its effect, and Gladstonian development moved along, in its own uniquely fitful if creative manner.

Such complexity of development and of tactics helps to explain Lord Acton's view on this matter. He knew Gladstone well and long; and he had come to an interpretation in which he had Gladstone moving towards the Actonite liberal position, by a distinctly spasmodic process of intellectual discovery and change.[86] In short, far from seeing Gladstone as he portrayed himself – as the 'natural liberal' – Acton saw Gladstone as a brilliant cabinet politician who was only slowly learning to place politics within a philosophically 'liberal' position. A similar view of Gladstonian development has been expressed by J.B. Conacher in his examination of politics in the Palmerston era, when he refers to the way in which Gladstone had actually backed into party liberalism.[87]

If this general interpretation is at all helpful in making sense of Gladstone's domestic politics, it should also guide us in examining his international and colonial politics. And here we come face to face with the influence that the writings of Paul Knaplund have had on the established view of Gladstone as statesman. Morley treated the overseas policy, of course; but it was Knaplund who provided the detailed examination that did so much to strengthen and amplify the view already sketched by Gladstone's biographer.[88]

Knaplund's work on Gladstone spans a much longer period than that of Morley – roughly forty years, in fact. Yet there is such a remarkable consistency in his overall perspective that his writings can be looked upon as a single, monumental scholarly achievement and edifice: almost a kind of Mount Rushmore in print. At the core of Knaplund's settled view was the notion, shared with Morley, of a creative and liberating force in Gladstonian thought and action: the concern for nationality and national movements of liberation; the energetic defence of human rights in public campaigns involving moral issues; and within the world of 'Greater Britain' – to deploy Sir Charles Dilke's phrase of 1868[89] – there was additionally the general liberation of the bonds of the British settlement empire. This last theme was particularly close to Knaplund's heart and he made much greater play than had Morley with the Gladstonian version of the Victorian view of the ancient Greek 'empire': a commonwealth of co-equal peoples and nations, held together by shared cultures and by the sentiment engendered in freedom.

Gladstone's resolution of the old antithesis between *libertas* and *imperium* clearly captivated Knaplund, and his writings find their greatest power where he deals with what he took to be a transformation of the settlement empire by a complex process involving the metropolitan and colonial societies, a process guided by the beacon of light of liberalism. Quite early on in Knaplund's writings we come upon the arresting idea that what is being depicted is much more than a new, acceptable, liberal concept of 'empire as colonialism.' Rather, pitching it much higher, Knaplund seeks to describe, in his redolent phrase, 'the making of nations' in the dominions of settlement.[90]

Just why Knaplund came to advance that view about the Gladstonian liberal impact on the empire, and why it occupied so central a place in his own thought as revealed by his historical scholarship, has yet to be established. In a very general sense, it could be said that he stands in linear intellectual descent from Morley (and Gladstone himself!). But this is an incomplete and somewhat unfair judgment on a scholar of great individual qualities. Knaplund himself makes plain, in the introduction to his major work on *Gladstone and Britain's Imperial Policy* (1927), that he was not content with Morley's working out of the theme; and in a number of forceful papers written in the interwar period, he argued for both a more detailed and yet a less confined view of the utility of Gladstonian liberal ideas taken to British external policies. This position Knaplund held tenaciously with what can almost be termed a heedless courage through-out the changing fortunes of the British empire-commonwealth, down to the very beginnings of de-colonization in the 1950s.[91] It is a case of awesome consistency and commitment that deserves closer inspection.

We know much about Morley. But who was Paul Knaplund?[92] While his name is rightly attached to major British historical writings concerning the empire, he was neither British nor even a citizen of the empire, nor indeed called 'Knaplund' as a child. Born a Scandinavian in 1885, the eleventh child of a far from affluent Norwegian fishing family, he grew up in the rural village of Bödo on the upper west coast. His family were named Johnson, and he only took up the name by which he is better known when he moved from his region of 'Knaplundoy' to the United States. He emigrated in the year of the Liberal triumph in England, 1906. We should also note that the America to which Paul Johnson went as an immigrant, with no English and even less capital, was a very particular social environment: he went to the mid-west, first living amidst a strong overseas Norwegian community, and remaining a proud mid-westerner all of his life. The Norwegian dimension of his character is thus more than mere exotic detail. It is, in addition, part of his own identity as Paul Knaplund of Wisconsin, USA.

From that childhood I would merely extract certain vital details to establish points of reference in his intellectual biography. In a charming autobiographical 'essay,' he himself gives valuable indicators of the connections between origins, character, and scholarship.[93] He came from a community possessed of a strong sense of family and of discipline, together with a powerful Christian puritan influence, acting through reformed Lutheranism, which flourished in the village. There was also a commitment to education as a means of 'getting on' in the world and as a valued possession in itself within a community alive to major world issues. Russian invasion was often canvassed; the British and American colonial wars in South Africa and the Pacific at the turn of the century were debated; Marxist ideas found discussion. Much the most important element, however, was religion in the guise of reformed Christianity. Piety, a reserved manner, moral gravitas, and a powerfully emotive concern for conscience were the hallmarks of Knaplundoy and of the Johnson family. Paul Knaplund was not a 'born again' Christian, but his abiding faith had about it the stamp of vital Christianity that marked British nonconformity; and we know, too, that the young man was in fact acquainted with the writings of C.H. Spurgeon and W.V. Moody, quite apart from observing other familiar public manifestations of popular conscience politics, through temperance campaigns and educational reform issues. The road from Bödo to Wisconsin, and then to Hawarden, was thus physically extended, indeed tortuous. But it was intellectually very much less extended.[94]

Knaplund the professor always admired the community of his beginnings because of what he described as its 'reliance on the validity of private [Christian] judgement,' together with a belief 'in the equality of men before God,' something he felt to 'be deeply ingrained in these quiet, independent folk.' He was indeed later, on one occasion, to yoke

Hawarden to Bödo. He set out his undoubted admiration of Gladstone by comparing an evening spent discussing the GOM with the Gladstone descendants to the memories of a grand old Scandinavian agriculturist. 'There [at Hawarden] a son and daughter of Gladstone had told [Knaplund] of events in the life of their famous father, that earnest, singularly gifted statesman who, from his position of power, had wrestled with the problems in government, society and religion. In many respects, the farmer and the statesman differed as widely as is humanly possible. But as they were both with "god's sigil" [sign] upon their brows, they were alike. Both were men of character, fortitude, integrity and the will to achieve. Both had walked humbly before God.'[95] Perhaps the best entry into Paul Knaplund's scholarship is to see him as one of Gladstone's 'nonconformist interests.'

It was Knaplund's early American experience that brought about the more technical connection with historical work and with scholarship on Gladstone. He was twenty-one when he went to the United States; and after a few agonizingly hard seasons on the farms of mid-western Scandinavian emigrant homesteaders, he entered a theological seminary. The next six years of his life were spent at Red Wing Seminary on the Wisconsin border north of Ostrander, where he had been engaged in farm work. By the eve of the Great War in 1914 Paul Knaplund had put discipline, work, and faith to good effect. He had acquired an education suitable for a high school teaching appointment – albeit part-time, in Decora, Iowa; he had become a naturalized American; and he had enrolled in the summer programme of the University of Wisconsin to upgrade his qualifications. Events moved quickly now to shape his future life. A further diet of hard earning, through part-time work – on farms and the railway, janitoring and teaching – and sheer application, brought him an MA, and then a PH D, at the University of Wisconsin, all in years that overlapped the First World War.[96]

Choice of subject came about in an intriguing manner that connected Bödo to British colonial history. Knaplund had enrolled in the European Studies Program and was assigned to A.P. Dennis, who taught British and empire history. In focusing his master's thesis on British policy in South Africa, Knaplund had drawn from childhood and family memory: Bödo 'had been much interested in the Boer War.' He had also 'recently read that the [Afrikaner] states conquered by the British during the war had been given self-government, and had combined with other South African colonies into a union.' He duly produced a good thesis, with a good liberal theme at its heart: the triumph of magnanimous imperial devolution in winning the loyalty of the former Boer adversaries through the grant of self-government; after the failure of Milner's high imperialism, Gladstonian Liberalism provided the beneficent parentage of this 'home rule' strategy to meet the challenge of local nationality.[97]

At thirty-one years of age Knaplund set out on his PH D. His topic was a development and amplification of certain dimensions of the master's thesis: 'Intra-Imperial Aspects of Britain's Defence Problems, 1870-1914.' Completed in June 1919 it acted, in a sense, as his war service. The theme was again redolent of a certain liberal idealism: how the granting of local self-government and local self-defence in the settlement dominions had proved to be a strength, and not a weakness, in the evolution of imperial defence. Knaplund regarded the dominion military contributions in the Great War as the ultimate vindication of an empire of liberal devolution in general; and more particularly, of the policy of self-reliance, within a 'family' of associative commitment, begun under Gladstone and Cardwell. Knaplund, it might be said, was much more impressed with the implementation of the principles of the noted Mills committee on defence than with the political divisions in the settlement colonies caused by the imperial call to arms in 1914 and the imperial declaration of war in the name of Britain and empire.[98]

I would notice four characteristics of this initial pioneer Knaplund scholarship that were to be important in giving direction to many of his later major publications. First, their almost contemporaneous quality is striking. The MA studied an event of 1910 in 1914; and the PH D traced a theme to within two years of its date of completion. Put simply, Knaplund's history was often to be deeply informed by events and ideas still at issue about him in British colonial history. Two later books on the commonwealth (1942 and 1956) revealed the sense in which history had immediate, moral meaning in Knaplund's hands. Second, there is a developing belief in the efficacy and moral value to be found in the growth of a liberal empire. Indeed, liberalism and devolution within the settlement empire were conceived of as a process with a strongly evolutionary inner dynamic. Knaplund's view had scant time for a less heroic reading that would point to the liberal empire as either (a) the result of party political dynamics that created changes in British constitutional history, and that were then taken to the Greater Britain beyond, or (b) a pragmatic, *ad hoc* solution to the centrifugal forces of the colonial periphery that had necessitated some adjustment in the character of the empire, in the face of nascent colonial nationalism. The degree to which liberal devolution aimed at consolidation of the settlement empire in

Gladstone's policies is also underplayed. Nor is there much canvassing of those dimensions of the Gladstonian colonial church policy that were intended to act as an influence on local culture, in terms of the values of the mother country; or, indeed, of the enduring Gladstonian faith in the survival of old-style elites in the governance of the colonies. Third, there is the fact of the increasingly central role given to Gladstone in this thesis of an evolving liberal empire. It is the Gladstonians who set up the right principles of free association, and it is they who offer a policy of principled, but practical idealism, to counter the nationalistic-imperial call that comes in the age of Palmerston and Disraeli. Crystal Palace was thus, for example, contrasted by Knaplund with Midlothian, little to the benefit of Disraeli and the tory view of empire. 'The true spirit of overseas Britain was appreciated more fully by Gladstone who, as a follower of Burke, insisted that "freedom and voluntaryism" should govern the relations between Britain and her colonies, and who proclaimed his firm belief that if given freedom, they would of their own volition, aid Britain generously in her times of trial. This faith was splendidly vindicated [in 1899, 1914 and 1939].'[99]

That passage was written when Paul Knaplund was seventy-seven years old, in the 1962 edition of the *New Cambridge Modern History*. It is extraordinarily close to the views he had advanced as a post-graduate of thirty-one, in 1916. A fourth point concerns the derivation of the two major studies that really established Knaplund's name as a scholar of the nineteenth-century empire. They apparently grew, with great natural-ness, out of his graduate work, his world-view, and his religious commitment. The work on James Stephen, and then on William Gladstone, was an historical extension, back in time as it were, of preoccupations and themes manifested in Knaplund's initial imperial researches at Wisconsin. He was looking to the historical and moral roots of a theory of empire as 'commonwealth of nations.' And he wasted little time while he pursued those origins. In 1921 (aged thirty-six) he had at last become an assistant professor at his *alma mater*. The years 1922-7 found him making research trips to England. He worked on two projects: British colonial policy in the age of Stephen and Gladstone; and, less well known, the collected speeches of Sir Edward Grey, whom he personally interviewed. The two projects had as their link, of course, the idiom of liberalism in politics. The first gave historical depth and perspective to Knaplund's fascination with the moral efficacy of liberal devolution in laying the basis of commonwealth; the second offered a more con-temporary explanation of liberal idealism in international relations, not least in connection with systems of collective security.[100] The work on

Grey was largely done in London, where Knaplund stayed at Connaught House, living with American and colonial post-graduates, and joining the 'South African Student Association.' The work on Gladstone involved journeying to Hawarden, where Knaplund was assisted by Tilney Bassett, the Gladstone archivist, and also by Mary Drew, Gladstone's daughter, who had expressed a concern that her father was yet to be fully appreciated. Knaplund was not inclined to challenge Mary Drew. He was acutely aware of the failing fortunes of liberalism in the debate over American isolationism in the aftermath of Versailles and the Wilson ascendancy; and cognizant, too, of the attack that was being ranged back at the Gladstonian influence on the making of the liberal idealist tradition in international politics. In general historical terms, there was also afoot in the 1920s a zestful debunking of things Victorian – Lytton Strachey's view worked a suitable nettle on lingering Victorian sensibilities. And beyond that, scholars such as C.A. Bodelsen and R.L. Schuyler were soon to characterize the mid-Victorian age as one of separatism, and a failing imperial will or posture.[101]

Knaplund set out to challenge these views. The first salvo in his attack came as early as December 1923 in an article about 'Gladstone's Views on British Colonial Policy.' The very opening paragraph signalled Knaplund's interest and underlying suppositions: 'William Ewart Gladstone's attitude towards the colonies ... has been misinterpreted ... This need not occasion surprise. The closing years of his long political career witnessed a decline in popularity of the idealistic liberalism of the mid-nineteenth century. To an age deeply influenced by the latter-day doctrine of force Gladstone's policies, based upon the principles of the earlier period, seemed weak and bordering on treason. People began to think "imperially," and in doing so struck at the men and measures which had laid a deep and broad basis for Britain's Commonwealth of Nations.'[202] Knaplund was indeed determined to confront, head-on, any notion that Gladstonian Liberalism had failed in a practical sense to fulfil its ideals. Moral efficacy was undoubted; far from endangering the empire, it had made a new style of empire possible: 'It was constructive statesmanship of the highest order to give up the old system and grant freedom to the new settlements in British North America, Australia and South Africa. Few steps have been so singularly justified by later events, or will prove of greater historical importance.'[103] This was a bold and assertive theme on which Paul Knaplund was to hang almost a lifetime's scholarship.

It was R.M. Crawford who once dubbed Paul Knaplund 'the least theoretical of historians.'[104] This may be true, in that there is little conscious extrapolation of theory. But it all depends on how we measure 'theory.' In fact, Knaplund worked from a very distinct paradigm of explanation: liberalism as a creative force of moral order in public affairs. This gives great coherence and force to his history. It also, as in the case of Morley, raises difficult questions of analytic explanation in its absorption of Gladstone's own interpretation of his political ideas and their worth.

Knaplund's treatment of Gladstone's colonial policy is an excellent expression of this general problem. In his determination, for example, to remove the stigma of separatism from the Gladstonian legacy overseas he stressed the importance of the liberal ideal taken to empire. But in making this proper correction of the 'anti-imperialists,' Knaplund introduced his own problem of interpretation. For what his view does not sufficiently stress is the 'imperial' or consolidating elements in Gladstone's view of the function of liberal colonial policy. In company with the new political economists of his time – men such as McCulloch, Nassau Senior, and J.S. Mill – Gladstone saw free trade as establishing its own linkages in a network of empire. Gladstone also placed much emphasis on the significance of types of 'systematic colonization,' offered not so much by Wakefield and Buller, as by James Fitzgerald and Cornewall Lewis: colonies founded by the 'correct' settlement society fragments would naturally remain British. In addition, colonial church policy, advocated by Bishops Selwyn and Gray, assisted in a like manner. It stressed the need for local autonomy and accepted voluntaryism; but it also presumed that, by working through such agencies as the Colonial Bishops' Fund, the overseas Anglican church would be putting forth its best energies along lines that worked for rather than against the unity of a Greater Britain. All of this does not gainsay the liberal ethos that suffused Gladstonian thought about changing imperial relations; but it does suggest a more pragmatic view about the rationale behind an acceptance of colonial devolution. It was a response to local context, but it was a response that involved as much a calculation of beneficial imperial results as an expression of an idealistic view of empire.[105]

More directly, the areas of emigration, responsible government, and colonial defence make the point even more explicitly. Again, there is indeed reform in the name of liberal tenets; but whether these changes were not aimed at conservation of empire, rather than its 'liberation,' is a moot issue. For example, Gladstone's support of systematic colonization was on very carefully chosen ground. When James Fitzgerald invited that support, in proposing a colonizing scheme not entirely dissimilar to the famed Canterbury Association, Gladstone replied in the positive, with well-developed caveats:

I should feel chiefly anxious for these two things – First, that the principle of freedom in the colonial institutions should be applied to the case of Vancouver's Island with the smallest possible amount of restraint or qualification. I wish very much to see it tried out how far the original and liberal application of this principle will go towards repairing the most palpable fault and weakness in modern colonisation, namely, the want or rarity of persons of superior cast who may form something of a natural aristocracy in an infant state.

Secondly, I hope that you will make your Company as far as possible a Company of landlords or landsellers, and as little as possible one of traders ... [and this] without disadvantage to such purchasers or tenants as the ordinary market will supply.[106]

In the crucial period when Gladstone was identified by Knaplund as having 'converted' to a liberal view on colonies, we find in a document such as this – of September 1848 – confirmation of the reforming, liberal tendency in Gladstonian thought, yet also some of the significant qualifications that relate to Gladstone's conservative social theory, now to be applied in the overseas settlement provinces of a Greater Britain.

Responsible government engaged the same complex and qualified status in Gladstonian thought. There is support for devolutionist policies along the lines, in rationale if not in rhetorical expression, of other Victorian politicians concerned about the changing relationship with settler societies; but there is, yet again, the range of Gladstonian qualifications that point in less liberating and more consolidating directions.[107] First, Gladstone ever wished to see a division of power in the colonial constitutions, with key matters reserved to the crown. Second, there is the classic Gladstonian interest in supporting, where possible, 'upper houses' in the new constitutional arrangements of self-governing colonies. Third, there was the ever-present Gladstonian concern about the very circumstances in which responsible government would be granted. He feared the effect of petty party politics in 'new societies' of little constitutional or cultural maturity; and he worried over race relations and frontier policy in fragile colonial polities such as Natal and New Zealand. In plain terms, within the liberal Gladstone there was also the imperial statesman, an eminent Victorian with eminently Victorian views about social hierarchy and the social dynamics for a burgeoning colonial world. Gladstone had the great political imagination to realize that England could not place its ethos on an overseas settlement society in the manner of 'a stamp in wax,' as he put it.[108] But he also had a strong tactical sense and a pragmatic concern for securing the stability of the world into which he was born, making liberalism as much a vehicle of conservation as of liberation.

Perhaps most striking of all, there is Gladstone's unhappy relationship with the history of colonial tariffs and 'preference.' As an evolving free trader, he could hardly be expected to be anything but hostile to tariffs levied anywhere. But in the case of the settlement colonies he was particularly fierce in his protests, for he had expected them to follow the British way as an integral part of 'Greater Britain.' Devolution in colonial authority also, of course, carried the risk that the colonies might not follow the Gladstonian prescription for 'happy Englands' abroad. And here came the rub, as settlement societies in Canada, New Zealand, and Australia all began to look to preferential tariffs as a means towards a more 'national' policy on trade and development. Gladstone gave this drift of events one of his famed black-eyed glares. Such developments, he argued, were a negation of his basic concept of a mutually responsible empire. And when that favourite colony of settlement, New Zealand, moved in the direction of tariffs, he was much shaken. Indeed, in reviewing the nature of the tariff policy proposed, Gladstone was led to ask the Colonial Office somewhat pointedly if this meant that Canterbury could, say, levy a duty on Nottinghamshire boots while setting a lower rate, a differential rate, for those from New South Wales. 'Yes, they could,' came the response – on which Gladstone pronounced the emphatic view that such developments were the antithesis of his idea of a liberal empire, and indeed brought the imperial connection to 'near ... reductio ad absurdum.'[109]

In fact, in this revealing instance, the task fell to staunch whigs in his cabinet to explain to the liberal Gladstone why the colonies had every right to take their much vaunted freedom and voluntary association at face value; and therefore why, given the reality of a devolved empire of authority, preferential policies would have to be stomached. As an architect of that policy, Gladstone was very grudging in accepting the opinion of his colonial and foreign secretaries. He argued that he did 'not see upon what foundation any duty of military and naval protection on our part is to rest, if the foreign relations of Colonies are to pass out of our hands into theirs.' The voice here is, of course, that of the mature Gladstone, at the height of his liberal ascendancy in the 1870s, and not that of the 'tory' of forty years before: and yet he could still question the degree to which the colonies could claim full freedom in an empire of imperial association and responsibility. 'Wd. Mr. Duffy' (premier of Victoria), as he once charged, 'be kind enough to give us a definition of the colonial relation, or to rights and duties, on the one side; and on the other, as he would have it. What will be the remaining duties of the colony towards the Mother State?'[110]

It is very pertinent to our concern here that Knaplund not only knew of the existence of this kind of evidence, but even printed part of it as an appendix to his 1927 book on Gladstone's imperial policy. Yet here we must notice the gloss he placed on such Gladstonian fulminations against colonial premiers who acted out the possibilities of liberal devolutionist policy: 'In the case of the Australian differential tariff controversy it may be said that [Gladstone] *temporarily deserted* his doctrine of voluntaryism.'[111] In fact, of course, the opposite is closer to reality: the issue is deeply revealing of a general and consistent attitude on Gladstone's part towards the meaning of a liberal empire of devolution with local 'responsible government.' The whole issue was also revealing about the connections between local autonomy and 'home rule' in all its variants.

Gladstone's aim, in all these forms of colonial constitutional adjustments and developments, was clearly not to precipitate but to avert another 1776. Equally, in moving to what he deemed an appropriately Athenian version of empire for an age committed to liberty and the liberal empire, he could yet place this within a Gladstonian framework of mutual responsibilities, between parent state and local overseas policy. This perspective could even find a domestic experience when we look to the principled issues involved in Irish Home Rule policy after 1886. What strikes the modern age in reading the Gladstonian proposal is not so much its liberationist tendencies, but rather the limited and qualified sense in which Dublin was to enjoy a degree of devolved local government.[112] We also notice the range of reserved powers held by Westminster under all the variants of 'Home Rule' put forward by Gladstone. Yet we should not be so surprised. In drafting the 1886 bill Gladstone had at hand the British North America Act of 1867; and what concerned him in that constitutional document was not the relationship between Britain and Canada, in which much latitude was in the process of evolving, but the carefully delineated relationship between Ottawa and the provincial capitals, between federal Parliament and local 'home ruling' assemblies.[113]

At the heart of Knaplund's powerful and persuasive portrayal of Gladstonian colonial policy there exists accordingly a constant and unresolved tension. In developing a thesis that draws its very breath and vitality from the Gladstonian idiom of creative liberal statesman, he ultimately undervalues the way in which Gladstone placed his concept of liberal devolution within a defined set of obligations, relations, and imperial structures. We can surely still share Knaplund's dilemma without subscribing to his solution, for it is difficult to capture the sense in which Gladstonian Liberalism was concerned here with both liberal reform (devolution, autonomy, freedom, voluntaryism) and imperial conservation (reserved powers, delineated responsibility, circumscribed status, and qualified home rule in colonial societies).[114]

Very much the same issues also arise, albeit in an even more complex manner, when Gladstone's position on national movements of liberation is even cursorily considered. I shall take only two examples, and briefly at that: but I think there is enough typicality in each case to establish the general interpretation. The starting point is clearly the ringing Gladstonian call to support 'peoples struggling to be free.' Yet Gladstone himself never said this principle had universal application at all times, or applied to all self-proclaimed national movements.[115] It is his apologists who are inclined to miss the kinds of complex qualifications that the working cabinet politician, premier, and conservationist placed on that posture.

Take for example the famed Gladstonian involvement with the Italian Risorgimento.[116] What is interesting here is not any natural link between Gladstone and the national movement, but rather his very gradual and critical approach to supporting a full-blooded drive to oust the Austrians. Gladstone had not stood out against '1848' in Europe for nothing. Thus, when he came to give his full and whole-hearted support to the Risorgimento, he did so in the conviction that he acted as a friend of both freedom and the authority of a proper moral order. In particular, he did so believing that such flagrant abuses of civil rights as he found in the gaols of Naples betokened a real collapse of true moral authority in the state; believing also in Cavour, and the distinctly respectable middle-class Piedmontese leadership that he offered to the new nation; and perhaps even believing that Cavour required that support in the face of the possibility that the Risorgimento might become the absolutely triumphant vehicle of Garibaldi, who offered a somewhat different perception of European national movements and their legacy. While Gladstone can therefore rightly enjoy the name of 'Italy' on the monument of his achievement, it should be remembered that the service he provided stemmed from a belief that he was supporting an ethical order of ultimate stability, authority, and freedom under law denied by the rule of the House of Habsburg. Cavour represented the moral order of responsible government, of mixed interests, and social hierarchy. Here was a classic expression of that dualistic character of Gladstonian Liberalism, of change and conservation – as the *Letters to Lord Aberdeen* have declared ever since Gladstone published these controversial pamphlets in the early 1850s as statements of principle and practice, of liberation and authority, of nationality, civil rights, and a new moral order for Italy.[117]

At the point where foreign and imperial policy intersect, there is an interesting example that can be canvassed for a later period, and involving a different set of national forces, this time within the British Empire. In 1881 the Gladstone government revoked the British annexation of the Transvaal, undertaken by the Disraeli government in a surge of frontier advance, through belligerent federalism, in April 1877.[118] Following Morley, there is an inclination to see the Pretoria convention of August 1881 as a vindication of the Gladstonian concern for nationality, itself brought to life by the revolt of the Transvaal Boers against the earlier British tory-imperial annexations. This is to mix consequence with practice. In fact, the record now shows that, despite Gladstone's emotive pledge to the Boers in the Midlothian campaign – where they were bracketed with other 'peoples' who had been subjected to belligerent Beaconsfieldism[119] – his initial disposition on coming to power was to consider the possibility of trying to meet the problems of troubled South Africa by a revived attempt to implement the previously denounced federalist strategy.[120] And the Transvaal Boers were to find their home within such local autonomy as a federal structure would allow: the British North America Act on the highveld. The Transvaal Boers, however, read the British policy as being a cruel disappointment, and so took appropriate violent action.[121] They revolted, with some immediate success, culminating in the British defeat at Majuba Hill in February 1881. Finally, Gladstone asserted himself: he would not avenge Majuba, despite howls in the popular press to do so. Instead, a negotiated retrocession of the Transvaal would take place in Pretoria, leading to Boer 'independence.'[122] Even then, however, two things should be observed. First, Gladstone acted not only because he was concerned to meet the demands of the republican burghers in triumphant revolt towards retrieving their independence, but also from concern at facing a pan-Afrikaner revolt that threatened to draw in the sympathetic Cape Dutch as 'political cousins' to the Boer of the interior. Not to have made peace in 1881 would have been to have risked South Africa itself within the empire.[123] Second, it is worth examining closely the document that returned the Transvaal Afrikaners to their independence.[124] The Pretoria Convention was still hedged with qualifications concerning the external policy of the Boer state. It was, in truth, to be 'home rule' within locked doors. South Africa was strategically too important to follow the principle of national self-determination in an unqualified manner. Gladstonian Liberalism always contained that kind of hard realism: reform yet conservation.[125]

In his recent inaugural lecture at Cambridge (20 November 1980), Professor Derek Beales spoke to the theme of 'History and Biography.' He argued the case for biography as illuminating the more general aspects of an era; and he reflected thoughtfully on how an exceptional individual, such as Gladstone, can assist the historian in perceiving the past, for Gladstone 'self-consciously related his actions to what he discerned as the tendencies of history' over a public career of more than sixty years. In that sense, Gladstone acted as a 'contemporary historian' (my phrase), for he indeed had, in Derek Beales' words, 'a Braudelian feel for trends.' Here was both a precious and a dangerous deposit for the later historian: 'Modern scholars have adopted, perhaps unconsciously, many of his interpretations of his own age.'[126]

Exactly. Yet we can apply this notion even more directly to the pioneer interpretations of Gladstone and Gladstonianism. It was of the essence of Gladstone's thought to relate ideas to practice and to attempt to place 'practice' within a pattern of what he deemed to be 'natural progress.' Just as he pondered the Doctrine of Providence in relation to events of this world, so too he constantly cast and recast his understandings of the public developments of the state in response to the processes of change that were transforming not merely the material, but also the moral sensibilities of mankind. Even more personally, in his ember years, as the Gladstone Papers now reveal, he privately reflected on what he considered to be the essence of his political talent, and he couched this gift or talent within the Doctrine of Providence: 'I am by no means sure, upon a calm review, that Providence has endowed me with anything which can be called a striking gift. But if there be such a thing entrusted to me, it has been shown, at certain political junctures, in what may be termed appreciation of the general situation, and its result. To make good the idea, this must not be considered as the simple acceptance of public opinion, founded upon the discernment that it has risen to a certain height needful for a given work, like a tide. It is [rather] an insight into the facts of particular eras, and their relations one to another, which generates in the mind a conviction that the materials exist for forming a public opinion, and for directing it to a particular end.'[127] In addition, well before old age, Gladstone had already in fact begun this reflective activity and, in many ways, unhistorical practice, of reinterpreting the immediate past in the light of his own sociological deductions. A brilliant synthesizer of concepts and ideas, Gladstone made a history of his time by looking to pattern and sequence within which his powerful imagination could arrange the past in highly interpretative relief forms. This activity perhaps reached its creative height in his evocative *A Chapter of Auto-biography* (November 1868); but it extended, of course, to numerous autobiographical fragments and conversations thereafter. He was busy with the past, reflecting on individuals and events, until close to death in 1898.

It is because Gladstone offered so much to future biographers and historians – both through his massive private papers carefully docketed, and also through his public pronouncements (13,000 columns of *Hansard*, twelve volumes of speeches, and several hundred publications), let alone his eight volumes of collected essays (*Gleanings*, 1879, and *Later Gleanings*, 1897) – that he is paradoxically so difficult to interpret in his own times, and in time itself. The great challenge to Gladstone scholars is to analyze his actions beyond his own interpretative frames of reference. For the historian of the Victorian state and empire, the critical issue to confront is Gladstone's overriding conceptualization of his age as essentially one of progressive liberation: it was that time when the nation passed 'from a stationary into a progressive period'; politics now reflected not the habits of old elites, but rather the conduct of 'the affairs of a living and working community of men, who have self-government recognised as in the last resort the moving spring of their political life, and of the institutions which are its outward vesture.'[128]

This essentially creative and dynamic view of politics placed emphasis on change, on reform, on liberty and liberation. It subtly subsumed the role of reform as a means of conserving and consolidating inherited values, institutions, and social structures. It had small place for the functioning of atavistic ideas or inclinations. And yet when the ultimate rationale for many major Gladstonian reform policies are examined within their contemporary context, it is this preservationist aspect that stands out quite as strongly as the elements that point to change. Reflecting on his father's politics, from the vantage point of the later 1920s, Herbert Gladstone interestingly came to a similar conclusion about the essence of the famed 'interventions' and 'missions.' 'Mr. Gladstone's principle,' he wrote perceptively in *After Thirty Years*, 'was to uphold all institutions, tenets, practices, dogmas, whether social, political or religious, established by the work and views of the best and greatest authorities of the past, until weakness or error were demonstrated. On that principle he acted in great things and small through life.'[129] As a brilliantly imaginative, remedial conservationist, Gladstone also constantly worked to reinterpret authority (and dogma) in the light of social changes. At no point did he move to a revolutionary perspective on change and reform that set society or community free of the past. Rather, in Herbert Gladstone's idiom concerning his father's thought, 'Mr. Gladstone was [ever] active in his citadel, maintaining its structure, abandoning faulty outworks, constructing new ones.'[130]

Gladstonian Liberalism was, in the last resort, a force for stability and order in an age of acute destabilizing transition. And Gladstone himself was at pains to defend change, timely reform, adjustments, and major initiatives very much along the lines of balancing an older order in the face of the dynamics of an industrializing Europe. 'Miserable indeed,' as he remarked as early as 1851, 'would be the prospect of the coming times, if we believed that authority and freedom were simply conflicting and contradictory elements in the constitution of a community, so that whatever is given to one must be deducted from the other.'[131] He was ultimately to argue, in the case of the Italian national revolution, that its effect would be 'conservative of the general peace' of Europe. Placing 'law and order on a solid foundation' often meant 'quiet and unostentatious reform ... lest the strength of offended and indignant humanity should rise up as a giant.'[132] The idiom could be domesticated: the genius of English constitutional arrangements lay in their capacity to absorb change while yet protecting the fundamentals of English public values and order.

Not that Gladstone saw this reconciliation of change and tradition as being a quietist form of social control. In this balance of social rights and social structure within the Victorian state, there lay the real possibility of individual liberation. 'Regularity, combination and order ... have of themselves a marvellous virtue,' he argued in the context of his churchmanship, but in words that could just as well apply to the first principles of his statesmanship. They 'subordinate the individual to the mass, they enlarge by healthy exercise the better and nobler parts of our nature ... make a man more a creature of habits, and less of mere impulse; they weaken the relative influence of the present, by strengthening his hold upon the future and the past, and their hold upon him.'[133]

Indeed, just as he protested that in his churchmanship he was neither tractarian nor evangelical, so in his politics he was fundamentally a man of the middle ground, drawn to the reconciliation of contending forces, classes, and regions – though strong things had sometimes had to be done in the name of a moral order. 'That noise of rushing steam when it escapes, alarms the timid: but it is a sign that we are safe. The concession of reasonable privileges anticipates the growth of furious appetite.' The just society, and the morally sensible community, were one and the same with the nation-state that had found a harmony between change and tradition, between society-at-large and its elite governance 'by the best.'[134]

Here was his version of the liberal democratic state. It was indeed 'liberal' in turning its back on the old autocratic order of European politics. 'I am deeply convinced that ... all systems whether religious or political, which rest on a principle of absolutism, must of necessity be not indeed tyrannical, but feeble and ineffective systems.' It was also 'democratic' within Gladstone's atavistic social theory: 'methodically to enlist the members of a community, with due regard to their several capacities, in the performance of its public duties, is to make that community powerful and healthful, to give a firm seat to its rulers, and to engender a warm and intelligent devotion in those beneath their sway.'[135] It becomes commonplace therefore to detect this concern for stability, for conservation, for peacemaking, extending in Gladstone's thought to a concern for external policy as well. He saw Great Britain as acting the role of moral exemplar in international affairs – the friend not merely of freedom but of a just regulation of international politics, through collective action in the Concert of Powers. Such a commitment entailed support for international law and the resolution of conflict through international arbitration. Selective and pragmatic intervention abroad was to be contemplated when it was deemed morally imperative – most famously over Italy and Belgium – the justification here being not the defence of English interests, but the abuse of power by illegitimate régimes that brought authority into disrepute by offending against human rights or by denying legitimate national-cultural aspirations. The aim throughout was to secure a moral commonwealth of peace among nation-states, and certainly not to act as irredentist agitator within international politics. In principle, Gladstonian Liberalism was commit-ted unequivocally to supporting 'peoples struggling to be free.' In practice, each such national movement, with its revolutionary potential, was to be examined most carefully in terms of its character and consequences. And here Gladstone's social theory ensured that he placed a highly critical eye on the resulting 'order' within a national community, as also between nation-states.

Libertas and *imperium* could also find reconciliation within Gladstonian thought and policy because here, too, the principles were derivative of the conservationist in the great liberal. The non-settlement empire of

Victoria's subjects in India, the West Indies, Africa, and the tropics of southeast Asia was perceived as being a great moral test and trust in guardianship, inherited from history, and now involving great moral responsibilities for future development. The settlement empire of colonial immigrant polities abroad involved more complex issues, where a commitment to freedom and self-government found its qualification in concerns over the maturity of the colonial society in conducting its domestic affairs; the character of its economic and constitutional status; and Gladstone's own personal presumptions about the British character of these local, colonial variants of the parent culture, in which local autonomy was taken to be reconcilable with imperial connection. In this concern for such a 'division of powers' in the colonial constitution – later itself applied to reforming the Anglo-Irish relationship through the famed 'Home Rule' initiative – Gladstonian policy revealed its concern with reforming consolidation as a means to secure a morally efficacious and defensible imperial system.

We are all conservative in certain respects.[136] Gladstone's statecraft is fascinating simply because it was such a complex compound of atavism and reforming energies, of aristocratic sympathies and radical potentialities, of conserving instincts and creatively dramatic new departures in domestic and international politics, of declared highly principled aims and highly tactical actions. The complexity that was Gladstone can be glimpsed in occasional Victorian vignettes, such as the striking passage in Lionel Tollemache's *Talks with Mr. Gladstone*:

January 13th, 1896. – Mr. and Mrs. Gladstone and Mrs. Drew dined with us.
He remarked on our being in the same rooms as before.

т. – You see I have strong Conservative instincts.
g. – So have I. In all matters of custom and tradition, even the Tories look upon me as the chief Conservative that is.
т. – Two years ago a Conservative м.р. spoke of you as the strongest Conservative influence in Parliament. This being so, I wondered why, in the interests of Conservatism, he did not join your party.

Mr. Gladstone smiled and seemed pleased.
I note, in passing, that my Conservative friend probably regarded Mr. Gladstone as the best controller and moderator of the political changes which have become inevitable; insomuch that the English Government under his guidance might be compared to the Athenian Government under the guidance of Pericles: 'it was nominally a democracy, but in reality the supremacy of the first citizen.'[137]

Such contemporary commentary is deeply valuable. For indeed, the simple and autobiographical construction that Gladstone primarily offered of his career – his emerging out of illiberalism under the hammer of freedom – will no longer stand scrutiny in the light of these complexities. And, indeed, it becomes necessary to part company with that attractive early view as established by our pioneer 'monumental masons' – working not least from sketches both conceptual and autobiographical drawn by Gladstone himself – that stressed the consistent evolution of a liberal out of the young 'Verkrampt' tory fanatic. An alternative, over-arching unity of explanation has yet, of course, to be made. But when that is attempted, students of Gladstonian Liberalism will find that Paul Knaplund has laid a scholarly basis for reinterpreting the complex linkages between domestic liberalism and external policy. And they will also discover that it was John Morley who so shrewdly grasped that Mr Gladstone's attachment to liberalism was indeed complex, epic in expression, and yet also 'curious.'

NOTES

1 John Morley, *The Life of William Ewart Gladstone* (3 vols., London, 1903), III, 474. Gladstone to Henry Parkes, 3 October 1889, Parkes Papers, Mitchell Library, Sydney, New South Wales, ML MS A30.

2 Morley, *Gladstone*, III, 144.

3 J.L. Hammond, *Gladstone and the Irish Nation* (London, 1938); Philip Magnus, *Gladstone* (London, 1954).

4 See, for example, the range of Gladstone research summarized in *The Gladstone Diaries*, ed. M.R.D. Foot and H.C.G. Matthew (Oxford, 1968-); Ian Bradley, *The Optimists: Themes and Personalities in Victorian Liberalism* (London, 1980); David Hamer, 'Gladstone: The Making of a Political Myth,' *Victorian Studies*, 22 (autumn 1978), 29-50; and D.M. Schreuder, 'Gladstone and the Conscience of the State,' in *The Conscience of the Victorian State*, ed. P.T. Marsh (Syracuse, 1979), 73-134.

5 In making this historiographical essay I am deeply indebted to M.R.D. Foot, 'Morley's Gladstone: A Reappraisal,' *Bulletin of the John Rylands Library*, 51 (1968-9), 368-80; A.O.J. Cockshut, *Truth to Life: The Art of Biography in the Nineteenth Century* (London, 1974), ch. 10; David Hamer, *John Morley: Liberal Intellectual in Politics* (Oxford, 1968); H.C.G. Matthew's introductions to *The Gladstone Diaries*, III-IV (Oxford, 1974), and V-VI (Oxford, 1978); and Derek Beales, *History and Biography*, an inaugural lecture, 20 November 1980 (Cambridge, 1981). I have also benefited from private communication with Dr Matthew and with Professor Foot. The

first volume of Professor R.T. Shannon's important two-volume study, *Gladstone* (London, 1982), was published after I had completed this paper.

6 See, for example, Michael Freeden, *The New Liberalism: An Ideology of Social Reform* (Oxford, 1978); Peter Clarke, *Liberals and Social Democrats* (Cambridge, 1978); K.O. Morgan, *The Age of Lloyd George* (London, 1971), esp. 17-38.

7 Richard Jebb, *Studies in Colonial Nationalism* (London, 1905), is the pioneer. See also the excellent analysis in Ronald Hyam, *Britain's Imperial Century* (London, 1976); Bernard Porter, *The Lion's Share* (London, 1975); and A.F. Madden, 'Changing Attitudes and Widening Responsibilities, 1895-1914,' in *The Cambridge History of the British Empire*, ed. E.A. Benians, Sir James Butler, C.E. Carrington, III (Cambridge, 1959), 339-405.

8 Paul Knaplund's major work in this context is *Gladstone and Britain's Imperial Policy* (London, 1927), and *Gladstone's Foreign Policy* (London, 1935). The reference here is to *Gladstone and Britain's Imperial Policy*, 5.

9 J.B. Conacher, *The Aberdeen Coalition* (Cambridge, 1968), 42n.

10 R.M. Crawford's commentary is in *Paul Knaplund*, a volume of tribute published by the State Historical Society of Wisconsin (Madison, 1967), 12-21.

11 Cockshut, *Truth to Life*, 187.

12 Morley, *Gladstone*, III, 535.

13 H.C.G. Matthew, 'Disraeli, Gladstone and the Politics of the Mid-Victorian Budget,' *Historical Journal*, 22 (1979), 615-43.

14 Schreuder, 'Gladstone and the Conscience of the State.'

15 Morley, *Gladstone*, III, 88.

16 Ibid., 260.

17 Knaplund, 'Gladstone's Views on British Colonial Policy,' *Canadian Historical Review*, 4 (December 1923), esp. 304.

18 Ibid., 306-7.

19 Ibid., 307.

20 Knaplund, *Gladstone and Britain's Imperial Policy*, 15.

21 Knaplund, 'Gladstone's Views on British Colonial Policy,' 310.

22 Ibid., 304.

23 Knaplund, *Gladstoné and Britain's Imperial Policy*, 9.

24 Ibid., 164.

25 Morley, *Gladstone*, I, 84-5.

26 Ibid., 70.

27 Gladstone, *Gleanings of Past Years* (7 vols., London, 1879), VII, 101-2.

28 *The Times*, 17 May 1890, 14.

29 *The Gladstone Diaries*, now eight volumes to 1874, provides a basis for that

micro-evaluation, together with the mass of Gladstone Papers now open to scholars.

30 See *The Prime Ministers' Papers: W.E. Gladstone*, I: *Autobiographica*, ed. John Brooke and Mary Sorensen (London, 1971), 246-51.
31 See Schreuder, 'Gladstone and the Conscience of the State,' 84-5; and Alec Vidler, *Essays in Liberality* (London, 1957), chap. 5.
32 See Hamer, 'Gladstone: The Making of a Political Myth.'
33 Ably summarized in R.T. Shannon, *The Crisis of Imperialism, 1865-1915* (London, 1976); on Gladstonian politics, see pt 1.
34 Walter Bagehot's article was written for the *National Review*, 11 (July 1860), 219-43.
35 Salisbury's analysis first appeared in the *Quarterly Review*, 120 (July 1866), 259-82.
36 Marcus Cunliffe, *Washington: Man and Monument* (New York, 1958), chap. 1.
37 G. Barnett Smith, *Gladstone* (London, 1879), 569-72.
38 See Foot, 'Morley's Gladstone'; and Owen Chadwick, *Acton and Gladstone: The Creighton Lecture in History 1975* (London, 1976).
39 Chadwick, *Acton and Gladstone*, 56.
40 Foot, 'Morley's Gladstone,' 369.
41 John Morley, *Recollections* (2 vols., London, 1917), II, 91-2.
42 Ibid., 92. I owe the figures cited to Foot, 'Morley's Gladstone.'
43 Foot, 'Morley's Gladstone,' 373.
44 Cockshut, *Truth to Life*, 175-92, is good on capturing its quality as biography.
45 Morley, *Gladstone*, I, 3.
46 See Morley, *Recollections*, II, 90ff; Hamer, *Morley*; and Cockshut, *Truth to Life*, 177ff.
47 Morley, *Gladstone*, I, 2-3.
48 Ibid., 3.
49 Ibid., 5.
50 Hamer, *Morley*, 333, is very valuable here, and I am greatly indebted to his exposition of Morley's thought.
51 Ibid., 332.
52 Ibid., 336.
53 Ibid., 40-50, for an excellent outline of Morley's ideas and their evolution.
54 *John Morley: Nineteenth Century Essays*, ed. Peter Stansky (Chicago, 1970), xiv-xv.
55 Hamer, *Morley*, 39-48.
56 Ibid., 45-6; see also F.W. Hirst, *Early Life and Letters of John Morley* (London, 1927).

57 John Morley, *On Compromise* (London, 1886), 4.

58 See Cockshut, *Truth to Life*, 188.

59 Morley, *Gladstone*, I, 6; and *The Times*, 19 January 1904, on 'the whole man.' See also Hamer, *Morley*, 44-5.

60 Morley, *Recollections*, I, 20.

61 Ibid., 21.

62 Alec Vidler, *The Orb and the Cross* (London, 1945), is an excellent pioneer study of Gladstone and 'State and Church.' Since I wrote this paper, Perry Butler has published his splendid study, *Gladstone: Church, State, and Tractarianism* (Oxford, 1982).

63 Printed in *The Prime Ministers' Papers: W.E. Gladstone*, I: *Autobiographica*, ed. Brooke and Sorensen, 246-50.

64 Gladstone, *Gleanings of Past Years*, VII, 150.

65 Bradley, *The Optimists*; Gladstone's response to Tennyson and to *Locksley Hall Sixty Years After* is in the *Nineteenth Century*, 21 (January 1887), 1-18.

66 See Chadwick, *Acton and Gladstone*, esp. 18–19, 56; and Matthew on Gladstone's 'religious nationality' in *Diaries*, III, xxvi-xxviii.

67 *Correspondence on Church and Religion of William Ewart Gladstone*, ed. D.C. Lathbury (2 vols., London, 1910), I, 85-118.

68 G.M. Young, *Portrait of an Age: Victorian England* (1936), ed. G. Kitson Clark (London, 1977), 315n.

69 See an expansion of these ideas in D. Schreuder, 'Gladstone and Italian Unification: The Making of a Liberal?' *English Historical Review*, 85 (July, 1970), esp. 498-500.

70 Robert Kelley, 'Midlothian: A Study in Politics and Ideas,' *Victorian Studies*, 4 (December 1960), 119-40.

71 See N.J. Richards, 'British Nonconformity and the Liberal Party, 1868-1906,' *Journal of Religious History*, 9 (1977), esp. 388-99.

72 Gladstone, *Gleanings*, VII, 127.

73 See Stephen Koss, *Nonconformity in Modern British Politics* (London, 1975).

74 G.I.T. Machin, 'Gladstone and Nonconformity in the 1860s: The Formation of an Alliance,' *Historical Journal*, 17 (1974), 347-64.

75 Ibid., 352; and Schreuder, 'Gladstone and the Conscience of the State,' 111.

76 *The Gladstone Diaries*, ed. H.C.G. Matthew (Oxford, 1978), VI, 413.

77 Olive Anderson, 'Gladstone's Abolition of Compulsory Church Rates: A Minor Political Myth and Its Historiographical Career,' *Journal of Ecclesiastical History*, 25 (1974), esp. 186ff.

78 See Schreuder, 'Gladstone and the Conscience of the State,' esp. 110ff.

79 Machin, 'Gladstone and Nonconformity in the 1860s'; and J.R. Vincent, *Pollbooks: How Victorians Voted* (Cambridge, 1967), 45.

80 Bradley, *The Optimists*, esp. chap. 6.
81 F.B. Smith, *The Passing of the Second Reform Bill* (Cambridge, 1966).
82 Herbert Butterfield, *Christianity and History* (London, 1949).
83 G.I.T. Machin, *Politics and the Churches in Great Britain, 1832-68* (Oxford, 1977), is an excellent guide to that 'churchmanship' in action.
84 Ibid., 297.
85 Ibid., 298.
86 See Chadwick, *Acton and Gladstone*, 18.
87 J.B. Conacher, 'Party Politics in the Age of Palmerston,' in *Entering an Age of Crisis*, ed. P. Appleman, W.A. Madden, M. Wolff (Indiana, 1959), 168-70.
88 Gerald Graham has provided a sympathetic and brief introduction to Knaplund's corpus of work in 'Paul Knaplund: Historian of the British Empire,' in the tribute to Knaplund published by the State Historical Society of Wisconsin, 22-30. A full bibliography of Knaplund's writings is included at the end of that volume.
89 Sir Charles Dilke, *Greater Britain* (London, 1868).
90 See Knaplund, *Gladstone and Britain's Imperial Policy*, 164.
91 See Knaplund, 'Great Britain and the British Empire,' in Vol. XI of *The New Cambridge Modern History*, ed. F.H. Hinsley (Cambridge, 1962), 383-410.
92 Paul Knaplund's charming autobiographical volume, entitled *Moorings Old and New: Entries in an Immigrant's Log* (Madison, 1963), makes fascinating reading and will clearly be very valuable for a biographer. I am here concerned essentially with his writings as an historian.
93 Knapland, *Moorings*, pt 1.
94 Ibid.
95 Ibid.
96 Ibid.; aspects of the PhD were published as 'Intra-Imperial Aspects of Britain's Defence Question,' *Canadian Historical Review*, 3 (June 1922), 120-42.
97 Knaplund, *Moorings*, pt 1.
98 Ibid.
99 Knaplund, 'Great Britain and the British Empire,' 407.
100 Knaplund, *Moorings*, pt 2, 240ff.
101 See R. Hyam and G. Martin, *Reappraisals in British Imperial History* (London, 1975).
102 Knaplund, 'Gladstone's Views on British Colonial Policy,' 304.
103 Ibid.
104 Crawford, *Knaplund*, 13.
105 See Matthew's introduction to Vols. III-IV of *The Gladstone Diaries* for a discussion of Gladstone's colonial church policy and emerging free-trade ideas. See also H.C.G. Matthew, 'Disraeli, Gladstone and the

Politics of the Mid-Victorian Budget,' *Historical Journal*, 22 (1979), 615-43.

106 Gladstone to J.E. Fitzgerald, 20 September 1848, Alexander Turnbull Library, Wellington, New Zealand (Manuscript Collection).

107 See 'Memorandum on Colonies,' Gladstone Papers, Add. MS 44738, f. 234.

108 See Gladstone's speech, 'Our Colonies,' 12 November 1855, an address to the Chester Mechanics' Institute, for his most sanguine and synthetic liberal statement on the settlement empire. Printed in full in Knaplund, *Gladstone and Britain's Imperial Policy*, 185-227.

109 Quoted in ibid., 107.

110 Ibid., 113 and 247-9.

111 Ibid., 138.

112 D.M. Schreuder, 'Locality and Metropolis in the British Empire: A Note on Some Connections between the British North America Act (1867) and Gladstone's First Irish "Home Rule" Bill (1886),' in *Studies in Local History: Essays in Honour of W.A. Maxwell*, ed. T.R.H. Davenport et al. (Cape Town, 1975), 48-58.

113 See Nicholas Mansergh, *The Commonwealth Experience* (London, 1969), esp. 23-4.

114 C.F. Goodfellow, *Great Britain and South African Confederation, 1870-81* (Oxford, 1966); D.M. Schreuder, *Gladstone and Kruger: Liberal Government and Colonial 'Home Rule,' 1880-86* (London, 1969).

115 D.M. Schreuder, 'Gladstone as "Troublemaker": Liberal Foreign Policy and the German Annexation of Alsace-Lorraine,' *Journal of British Studies*, 17 (spring 1978), 106-35.

116 Derek Beales, *Britain and Italy, 1859-60* (London, 1961); Schreuder, 'Gladstone and Italian Unification.'

117 Gladstone's 'Letters to Lord Aberdeen' are reprinted in his *Gleanings*, IV, 1-69. See also conclusion in Schreuder, 'Gladstone and Italian Unification,' 496-501.

118 C.W. de Kiewiet, *The Imperial Factor* (London, 1937); and D.M. Schreuder, *The Scramble for Southern Africa, 1877-95: The Politics of Partition Reappraised* (Cambridge, 1980), chap. 1.

119 There is a modern edition of Gladstone's *Midlothian Speeches*, ed. M.R.D. Foot (Leicester, 1971).

120 Goodfellow, *Great Britain and South African Confederation*.

121 Schreuder, *Scramble for Southern Africa*, 84-8.

122 Ronald Robinson and J.A. Gallagher, with Alice Denny, *Africa and the Victorians: The Official Mind of Imperialism* (London, 1961), chap. 3.

123 See Schreuder, *Gladstone and Kruger*, on the Cape Dutch.

124 The Conventions are printed in full in ibid., Appendices.

125 Shannon, *Crisis of Imperialism*, 69ff; Robinson and Gallagher, *Africa and the Victorians*, on the imperial politics of liberalism.

126 Beales, *History and Biography*, which I found deeply valuable.

127 *The Prime Ministers' Papers: W.E. Gladstone*, I: *Autobiographica*, 136.

128 Gladstone, *Gleanings*, VII, 101-2.

129 Herbert Gladstone, *After Thirty Years* (London, 1928), 80.

130 Ibid., 81.

131 Gladstone, *Gleanings*, VI, 15; the passage occurs in his paper 'On the Functions of Laymen in the Church' (1851).

132 Gladstone, *Gleanings*, IV, 136-7.

133 Ibid., VI, 16.

134 Magnus, *Gladstone*, 257.

135 Gladstone, *Gleanings*, VI, 17. See also Herbert Gladstone on his father's 'individualism' and its rejection of collectivism, in *After Thirty Years*, 88-9: 'Mr. Gladstone from his earliest days was an individualist. To ask why he did not sooner grasp some of the tenets of collectivism is about as reasonable as to ask why Cuvier did not discover the theory of evolution, or why Tynod remained ignorant of wireless transmission ... Mr. Gladstone was no visionary, no theorist, but a man of action, who saw things as they were ... His outlook was national and international, not for a class, whether employers or employed, but for all.'

136 I owe the idiom to Michael Oakeshott.

137 Lionel A. Tollemache, *Talks with Mr. Gladstone* (New York, 1898), 149.

TREVOR LLOYD

Comment

The essays in this book are intended as a tribute to two men who – in their different spheres and their different levels of achievement – can be called Victorians. That word of many meanings certainly implies loyalty to some old-fashioned virtues like duty, hard work, a decent reticence, and a belief in a Higher Power capable of bringing about steady improvement if human beings will respond as they should. Differences there are, but those who have read about Gladstone or known Jim Conacher will recognize the pattern.

Although Gladstone has receded from view as a figure to whose memory a direct political appeal can be launched, there has been sustained interest in him over the years among historians and the general reading public. Perhaps interest declined in the decades just after his death, and Disraeli came to be considered a more interesting and more up-to-date personality. For scholars a revival of interest began with the opening of Add. MSS 44,000 – the 700 volumes of Gladstone Papers in the British Museum. A life designed for the general reader by G.T. Garratt, Tilney Bassett's account of the Gladstone Papers, and the publication in 1938 of J.L. Hammond's commanding *Gladstone and the Irish Nation* meant that by the time of the Second World War Gladstone had been restored to the footing of equality with Disraeli that would have been taken for granted sixty or seventy years earlier.[1] Since then scholars have conducted a struggle by proxy between the two men which, while obviously not marked by any of the personal hostility, does show the same vigour and tenacity as their great debate. Disraeli has been the subject of the best of the biographies completed in recent decades, though Lord Blake does conclude it with a striking tribute to Gladstone.[2] Popular lives of Disraeli by Roth and by Pearson came out in the 1950s; Magnus's

Gladstone was somewhat more ambitious but not totally successful.[3] A good deal has been published about Disraeli's early life that could not be included in Monypenny and Buckle for reasons of propriety. Less entertaining than much that has been published on Disraeli but of considerable scholarly value is Ramm's edition of the Gladstone-Granville letters.[4] Half-a-dozen other volumes will be discussed later on because their direct relevance to issues addressed in this volume makes it appropriate to examine them in close relation to the essays that parallel or extend their contribution.

Coming to work still in progress, Gladstone's *Diaries* are neatly balanced by Disraeli's *Letters*.[5] Even while this volume of essays was being prepared, Shannon has moved back from the Bulgarian agitation to publish the first half of a new life of Gladstone, and two further volumes of *Diaries* have been published.[6] In a sense all of this weight of publication about Gladstone goes back to Morley; perhaps the connection is more obvious with J.L. Hammond than with some other writers, but it is certainly true that Morley's *Life* has for decades held a place of preeminence both as a scholarly biography and as a work of political instruction intended to mobilize opinion in the direction taken by the later Gladstone (and by his biographer).[7] In some areas of political activity it has helped the winning side on to victory: Gladstone's ideas about liberal attitudes to questions of nationalism and foreign policy have flourished and become the normal language of politics in this century. Sometimes the language is used in circumstances that underline the wrong-headedness of twentieth-century writers who accuse the Victorians of hypocrisy; vice pays virtue the tribute of talking about foreign policy in the Gladstonian framework of self-determination, the rights of small nations, and the need to try to avoid war. In many instances, however, this language is employed with conviction.

Gladstonian finance and domestic policy, which at one time commanded at least as much support as his views on foreign policy, no longer enjoy such respect. In some countries the idea of a balanced budget is seen as a piece of impossible fundamentalism; Gladstone's hope that the national debt could be paid off is not on any finance minister's programme; government intervention is seen as the necessary condition for prosperity. The right to vote has been diffused at least as widely as Gladstone would have thought proper; only a very serious (or a transitory) disqualification can keep anyone outside the pale of the constitution, and Gladstonian measures like the Ballot Act and the limitation of election spending have helped make politics more democratic. Whether these changes have made elections much more like the disinterested weighing by the electorate of appeals to the heart and the head that Gladstone hoped to see is another question; even his own denunciation of Beaconsfieldism in 1880 owed some of its success to the bad economic conditions of the time, and Gladstone did his best to convince voters that the government had made bad conditions worse. Since then the world has gone through a phase of believing that governments can make economic conditions better, and has found that this belief is not always justified in practice. Returning to Gladstonian limits on the activity of the state is, probably fortunately, outside the bounds of possibility, but perhaps it is easier now than it has been for some time to understand why a humane man of great administrative capacity would want to restrain the power of the state. Whatever the overall benefits brought by government intervention, enough mistakes have been made to lend support to at least part of the case against it. Probably we have more difficulty in understanding Gladstone's ideas about liberty because the boundaries of liberty have in some ways been so far expanded, but this is a question that arises naturally later on, when discussing what the authors in this book have to say about Gladstone.

Their scholarly contribution comes in the shape of four pairs of essays on important topics: the impact of his religious beliefs and activities on the early stages of Gladstone's political life; his view of the role of women and the family in social and political life; the last two occasions on which Gladstone tried to use his gift for building up and marshalling opinion for dealing with a political issue that had not yet come to the fore; and the question of revising generally held views about Gladstone. As these issues are central to an understanding of Gladstone they have naturally received a good deal of attention lately, and the best way to look at these essays is to review the position of Gladstone studies to see what these essays do to advance our knowledge.

Gladstone's religious beliefs and their effect on his political development have very recently been examined by Perry Butler, who refers to the religious history of the first fifty years of his life, but concentrates on the vital issues of the 1830s and 1840s. He is mainly concerned with strictly religious questions and pays much less attention to political principles, except when they flow directly from those questions, than either of the first two writers in this book.[8] Butler and Helmstadter differ fairly significantly in their views about the origins of the two main books that Gladstone wrote in the period. Both of them start from the careful preparation that Gladstone undertook by reading and reflection in the

1830s for writing a substantial book about the position of the church in the world. Butler believes that *Church Principles* (1840) was the book that Gladstone had had in his mind, and that *State and Church* (1838) was simply a controversial work provoked by the lectures about national churches that Chalmers had given earlier in the year.[9] This is a view that has often been taken of *State and Church* by writers who, before the publication of Gladstone's *Diaries*, had no way of knowing how seriously Gladstone had prepared himself for the work of writing it. Certainly *State and Church* was the book that received attention, and Helmstadter's demonstration of its firm foundations in Gladstone's reading about political and religious thought in the 1830s makes that attention seem fully deserved. Perhaps because he is so much less directly interested in the political aspects of Gladstone's thought, Butler does not see the extent to which *State and Church* followed from the study of a range of questions that politicians were bound to think about. Helmstadter sees Chalmers' lectures as simply a natural stimulus to publication which might have occurred at any time in the late 1830s, and he studies the book that they provoked as the full expression of Gladstone's feeling on the subject, while *Church Principles* is left on one side as a book about questions of less importance. This treatment certainly accords with the way that *Church Principles* has been ignored by writers then and later with a unanimity that would have been more striking if they had had reason to believe that it was the full and matured work of the man who had aroused so much interest two years earlier. If we take *State and Church* as the major work, and *Church Principles* as a subordinate volume, the response is easier to understand.

While Butler sees *State and Church* as the less deeply prepared book, he is of course fully aware that it has to be examined with care, and his slightly Macaulayesque analysis is used as the starting point of a subtle reinterpretation of Gladstone's career that shows just how many questions Gladstone had to settle in his mind when he faced the Maynooth issue and how much more freely he felt able to act in politics afterwards. However, Gladstone never became a 'march of mind' liberal and it may be worth considering whether the 'march of mind' account of *State and Church* given by Macaulay covers the case.[10] The book said a number of things that the stern unbending tories wanted to hear, and they assumed that such things could be said only from their point of view. By 1847 some of them could see that Gladstone was following a policy that Christopher Wordsworth described as 'accommodation and compromise.'[11] These complaints and the feelings of some tories of the Inglis school that they did not want Gladstone as their representative at Oxford were perfectly natural, but their disappointment could very well have been the result of an initial failure to understand *State and Church*. Everybody from Macaulay onwards has noticed that there are sections in favour of religious toleration in the book. Macaulay said that these sections simply recognized the political limits to the strength of the church and that they could easily be outflanked by anyone, such as Hurrell Froude, who wanted the church to be 'vastly more bigoted.' A present-day comparison shows the problem raised by these sections of the book: several modern states are committed to the same principles as *State and Church*, in the sense that they say political power ought to be confined to people who hold the right opinions (which usually means belonging to the single party that monopolizes power), but they concede that other people who are not able to join the ruling party ought to be tolerated. In practice, these assurances of toleration have been betrayed often enough to show exactly what Macaulay was afraid of. But the fact that some states betray their principles does not mean that the principles themselves are untenable, and the stern unbending tories and even Macaulay himself might have considered the possibility that the youthful Gladstone meant what he said when he expressed support for toleration.

Helmstadter's exploration of this possibility rests on a powerful argument drawn from Gladstone's devotion to Aristotle. Butler follows the majority view about Gladstone, referring to his attention to Aristotle but implicitly accepting the assumption in Macaulay's attack on Gladstone that Gladstone was a Platonist. All the noblest arguments for censorship and repression are Platonist; Aristotle had no doubts that some states are better than others but, at least by comparison with Plato, he believed we ought to make the best we could of every existing state. Helmstadter makes it clear that, at the time of writing *State and Church*, Gladstone thought the Church of Ireland could make progress in converting the Irish nation to Anglicanism, which he undoubtedly thought would be a great improvement on a largely Catholic Ireland (and a seriously committed Anglican could hardly see it in any other way). By the time of the crisis over the Maynooth grant, however, he had become convinced that social order in Ireland was in danger. A Platonist might possibly have gone on opposing all concessions to other churches; the Aristotelian Gladstone whom Helmstadter presents was more ready to accept the facts of the situation. Because he had no difficulty about the desirability of toleration he could accept the Maynooth grant once he felt it was necessary for the stability of society, and he could move easily enough to accepting and implementing the great majority of nineteenth-century steps towards removing religious disabilities without undergoing much of the painful conflict of principle that the older interpretations of Gladstone always implied. Tolerating Bradlaugh without sharing any of his religious views was much easier for an Aristotelian than for a Platonist.

The question was kept alive much longer than would otherwise have been the case by the political developments outlined in Conacher's 'Mr. Gladstone Seeks a Seat,' which ended when he became a member for Oxford University.[12] His period there was so marked by successive struggles on issues that involved the place of religion in politics that Butler might have been expected to pay more attention to the divisions on church issues to be found among Gladstone's constituents, who made up a large part of the section of the Church of England that took theology seriously. The division between 'Catholic' and 'Protestant' High Churchmen that Kenyon makes in his paper may be too rough-and-ready a line for strictly theological debate, but lines of political divisions always have to be drawn in a fairly rough-and-ready way. It is always slightly surprising for a political historian to find that Newman wrote in his *Apologia* about the qualities needed for the leader of a party – a party, that is, in the struggles that dominated and embittered his last decade in the Church of England – but his language reflected the facts of the situation and Kenyon's division of the mid-century High Churchmen looks convincing.[13] Gladstone was temperamentally unsuited to belong to the 'high and dry' section; they really were stern and unbending and were perfectly ready to stand motionless in opposition to all change. Gladstone did share their dislike for the Erastian ideas into which politicians are apt to slip; if one has to deal with the civil service and the diplomatic service, there is a slight danger of coming to think of the church as some sort of theological service. Gladstone's aversion to having the church treated in this way was as keen as that of the 'high and dry' section. *State and Church* opposed Erastianism and could be seen as doing so from the 'high and dry' point of view. But Gladstone was willing to resist Erastianism by changing the status of the church and came closer to advocating disestablishment as the proper response to the 1850 Gorham Judgment than any one would have expected. This naturally led him into the company of anti-Erastians who wanted to resist state intervention by appealing to the idea of the Catholic church. The representatives of the 'No Popery' school among the 'Protestant' High Churchmen were horrified, and expected to see Gladstone follow Newman and Manning into the Roman Catholic church. This was never within the realm of possibility, but the Protestants' concern can be understood. Gladstone's allies among the High Churchmen came from the section that was likely to join the Roman Catholic church. The Anglo-Catholics found Gladstone a man they could trust on general grounds, and accordingly forgave him votes on issues like Jewish emancipation, where they felt he was conceding too much to liberalism and the march of mind. Butler's description of Gladstone emerging from the Maynooth struggle and from the 'parting of friends' as a liberal Catholic has a wealth of meaning in it, but Kenyon's line of approach provides more illumination of specific future events. The most striking example of this is the way that it helps explain the Bulgarian agitation: Gladstone's cause attracted a degree of High Church support that must be immensely puzzling to anyone who thinks of the High Church in terms of Sir Robert Inglis and the stern unbending tories, but is immediately explicable to anyone who sees that Catholic High Churchmen were bound to try to apply the idea that the Church of England was a Catholic church to British politics.

Gladstone's religious views naturally had a great influence on his ideas about the family, which were strongly held, subtle, and likely to be over-simplified by his supporters. His resistance to divorce legislation – perhaps surprising in one whose family background was in some ways deeply Scottish – followed from his Christian principles. Most men at the time accepted the idea that a wife's adultery was intolerable because it meant that husbands could not be certain of the paternity of their heirs. Gladstone's resistance to divorce may now look old-fashioned, but his insistence that adultery was a sin and as wicked in men as in women meant that he placed the sexes upon a footing of equality at the point where their separate spheres intersected. He obviously believed in the idea of separate spheres, and he also believed in the family as an indestructible unit. Belief in the indestructibility of the family reinforced his opposition to divorce, and made it natural for him to think that within the family there should be only one vote, and that vote cast by a man standing at the head of the household. The franchise reforms completed in 1885 made the household into the dominant element in politics, and while this change was being discussed Gladstone made his final contribution to the debate on votes for women. Robson shows how far from certain it is that this was decisive, but it did run the risk of making him look like a villain who had been a tepid supporter of votes for women until it was actually time to do something to help them. Undoubtedly his opposition to votes for women was always expressed in terms that went no further than he thought the occasion required. Sir Henry James, a really determined opponent of votes for women, thought Gladstone's restrained opposition to the proposal in 1871 amounted to 'trimming' on the issue; and Gladstone certainly thought a party leader was entitled to take a little longer than most people to make up his mind on some issues, because he had to commit loyal party members as well.[14]

The complaints of the suffragists involved more than a simple failure to see how his ideas about the household and about women's position in it would affect his views on the vote. It is of course an indication of the extraordinarily high – even artificially high – standard of consistency claimed by Gladstone and expected of him that his 1871 speech was resurrected thirteen years later and examined in detail by people who would have been rightly shocked at any idea that 'when a woman says "No" she means "Yes"' but thought this was the way Gladstone behaved. How well would other nineteenth-century (to say nothing of more modern) politicians stand such a test? Robson's article makes a good case for saying that he survived the test at least as well as could be expected, though she also makes it clear why women objected to the tactical approach that Gladstone followed. Whether this was prudent of them is another matter. Perhaps the best that the suffragists could hope for was that he would not press his views upon his party quickly and would allow women as much time as possible to build up support among other members of the party before the weight of Gladstone's influence was put into the scales against them. Until 1884 supporters of votes for women could plausibly argue that the leaders of the party had an open mind on the subject, and that they would undoubtedly be swayed by seeing a considerable body of advocates of change within the party. They may even have had some success; Gladstone's arguments against including women in the Third Reform Bill may or may not have been decisive, but they were certainly not expressed in a way that openly tried to lay them down as principles to last for all time.

Jalland's paper suggests that, if he had been able to express his personal feelings without any regard for party sentiment, Gladstone would have liked to lay them down as permanent principles. The arguments on the suffrage issue that were based on the nature of the family have been better understood since the publication of Harrison's book on the opponents of votes for women, and the treatment of Gladstone's daughters shows how well the Gladstones fitted into the dominant pattern of Victorian family life.[15] Gladstone himself had been brought up in a family in which the position of women was honoured, but was treated as something completely cut off from the outside world of politics and business.

Checkland's *The Gladstones* is essentially a biography of Sir John Gladstone, and the exclusively domestic role he assigned to women is made perfectly clear.[16] People taking part in the current debate about 'the decline of the industrial spirit' in Britain will see some significance in the way that a distinguished historian treats the biography of a great merchant of the early years of the industrial revolution mainly as a prelude to the life of his son the great statesman, and it may be just as significant that this was Sir John's own assessment of the relative importance of their two roles. Within the family his sister Anne had a considerable influence on William; for questions of public life Sir John's opinion was decisive until the 1840s. He had always dominated the scene in his family, and several of his children were overwhelmed by his dynamic force. Any comment about the way William ran his own family must be qualified by the thought that he was a less totally dominant figure than his father had been.

Life in William's family has already been looked at in Joyce Marlow's *Mr. and Mrs. Gladstone* and in Georgina Battiscombe's *Mrs. Gladstone*.[17] In the ordinary way of things a popular writer, who has to rely on the sale of her books to earn a living, can expect to find that scholars have laid the foundation on which to build. Marlow and Battiscombe had to do a good deal of their own research as well as write entertaining books for the general market, and almost inevitably were not able to cover as much of the ground as scholars would have wished. The history of the family – and in particular, the role of women in keeping the family going – has not been covered at all thoroughly by scholars, and the general writers have had little to work on. Jalland's essay will do a bit to start putting this right. It starts with the basic assumption of Gladstone family life: running a household that was large by any standards outside those of the upper class needed two ladies of the house. Part of the problem was that, as Battiscombe showed, Mrs Gladstone was not a good organizer. Undoubtedly she helped Gladstone to continue his career longer than would otherwise have been the case – probably longer than was good for his colleagues or his party – but by the later years she had to have help. Gladstone's marriage was obviously happy, and he allowed his children what probably seemed to him a good deal of freedom. Nevertheless, the natural assumption was that the family unit took precedence over the hopes and ambitions of unmarried daughters and, as Jalland points out, the marriages of the sons as well as the daughters were delayed even beyond the age indicated by Victorian prudence and restraint. Life in the Gladstone family had advantages as well as disadvantages and most of its members fairly clearly gained more from their famous father than they lost, but Helen and Mary must have found the weight of gain and loss rather finely balanced. Mary emerges from Jalland's account as someone who gained a lot, whatever the losses; she could hardly have had her opportunities on the fringes of politics without the advantage of being related to the prime minister. All of the Gladstone family used their position in as responsible a way as possible and, even if Mrs Gladstone was occasionally a little vague, none of them caused the sort of embarrassment that Margot Asquith sometimes caused her husband.

Of the three daughters, Helen had gone furthest in the direction that women were to follow in the future. She had started in the outside world a little later than would now be usual, and she may have been helped in some very general sense by the fact that her father was the prime minister, but she soon reached a position at Cambridge (with prospects in London) that gave her quite an important part to play in the higher education of women. Such a post would look very unimportant from the perspective of 10 Downing Street, but it is hard to imagine any post open to a woman, other than that of a wife and mother, that Mr and Mrs Gladstone would have thought a better way for a daughter to spend her time than in helping her mother run the family household. Helen's position inevitably looks particularly unattractive; Mary had been in charge of the household when her parents were still in remarkably good health for their age and when her father was in office, whereas Helen had to take over when her parents' age was beginning to tell. She had the less interesting as well as less strenuous work of life in opposition to care for, though it must be added that she showed so little interest in party politics that this may not have meant much to her. The history of the two daughters shows how fixed and firm Gladstone's idea of family duty was in the last decades of the century, and how much of an effort it would have been for him to take the step towards equality and away from the purely domestic role of women involved in supporting votes for women. (It also throws some light on the position of the Liberal party in the last years of Gladstone's leadership when he had become something of a upas-tree, blighting all the vegetation around him.)

In the last eight or nine years of his political life the Liberals became irrevocably committed to Home Rule for Ireland and allowed Gladstone to let it dominate all the party proposals that were laying the foundations of 'the New Liberalism.'[18] At the very end Gladstone became convinced that an attack on the Lords was the obvious next step, an opinion to which his successor in the Liberal leadership, Lord Rosebery, became converted

after only a few months' experience. The two essays on this closing period
of Gladstone's career deal with an area in which historians have in the last
few years been adopting a less and less respectful attitude towards
politicians. In the past politicians were assumed to be primarily engaged
in advancing altruistic principles such as the good of the country, the
rights of the oppressed, or the stability of society. For fifteen or twenty
years a new group, working at first at Cambridge (of whom Cowling,
Cooke and Vincent, Jones, and Foster can be taken as the leading
members), have been putting forward the view that politicians should be
seen as concerned primarily with obtaining power.[19] They may believe
sincerely in the views they advocate or they may not, but this is of distinctly
secondary importance: they will do anything that will be accepted by other
politicians in the course of their struggle for power, including putting
their principles into practice if that seems advantageous.

Anyone who wants to see how radical an interpretation this is need only
look at Conacher's *The Aberdeen Coalition*.[20] The new school makes
something of a point of its readiness to consult all the accessible private
papers, but this is not really such a novelty. The depth of documentation
of *The Aberdeen Coalition* is not noticeably less than that of the Cambridge
authors, and the real difference is that Conacher's book rests on the
earlier assumption of good faith on the part of politicians, though it
acknowledges that some leaders (whigs, for the most part, and never
Peelites) fall short of the ideal. Cowling and his followers would say that
politicians have no business to have such ideals unless they devote a great
deal of care to making sure that they secure the power to carry them out.
The two strictly political essays in this book show some signs of the
influence of the Cambridge school. Brown is rather more willing to accept
the traditional assumptions: if Gladstone's 1894 proposal for an attack on
the House of Lords was to be taken simply as a motive to stay in office a
little longer it would then have to be analyzed in terms of the ministers
who would willingly have rallied to the new policy, those who would have
reckoned that it was not safe to oppose it, and those who would have felt
that it showed the importance of completing the process of pushing him
out that had begun with the naval estimates. In the event his colleagues'
complete absence of any enthusiasm for the idea meant that it had no
practical use for Gladstone as a way of staying in office. The importance of
Gladstone's initiative lay in the chance it gave his party to hold power if the
cabinet had united behind a policy that, as Brown indicates, was anything
but well thought out. At least until 1886 Home Rule was a phrase that
covered a wide range of meanings but, after he had committed himself

and his party to it, Gladstone spent a good deal of energy working out what it meant. The issue of the House of Lords was brought forward with so little intellectual preparation that it does give some support to the idea that policies are weapons in the struggle for power, to be snatched up first and polished afterwards. Brown's final view of Gladstone, which sees the issue as one that recapitulated so many ministerial struggles against the Lords, is certainly kinder and may explain Gladstone's seizing on an issue that did little for him personally but did point to the road the Liberal party found it necessary to travel in the future.

The question of the Lords in 1894 affected the position of only one man; Home Rule had affected the prospects of every politician of the first rank. Herbert Gladstone's ingenuous account of how he brought his father's conversion before the public is one of the statements that goes furthest to confirm the Cooke and Vincent view of politics, as we can assume that no politician is ever going to say straightforwardly 'I took this step in order to hold on to power.' Herbert Gladstone in *After Thirty Years* did say that he felt Chamberlain was using the issue of disestablishment to undermine his father's position, and that he decided to rally his father's supporters by bringing the issue of Home Rule into the open.[21] One can imagine W.E. Gladstone reflecting that – as Lloyd George put it many years later – the activities of Herbert Gladstone were a living proof of the liberal principle that political competence does not descend by hereditary succession. Still, while the Hawarden Kite was launched because of a miscalculation and a failure to understand that Hartington was much more dangerous than Chamberlain to Gladstone's position, it was admittedly intended to secure power.

Marsh's essay takes the general idea of the struggle for power and, by adding a new dimension to the analysis offered in *The Governing Passion*, presents it in a form that implies a much less sceptical idea of political activity. Even if a policy proposal is designed to secure power, whether within a government or within a political party, it will have this effect only if it is an idea that has some disinterested supporters. If it has no supporters it will not be an effective weapon to enable a politician to control his followers. Marsh shows Chamberlain struggling to keep on good terms with the leading Liberals, Morley, Dilke, and Gladstone, and then fighting to hold on to his followers when challenged by an idea that, whether adopted for the purpose or not, would have pushed him back to a subordinate position in the Liberal party if it became generally accepted. Chamberlain's resistance to it of course led to his departure from the Liberals; the interesting question is to see how he managed to escape from one of the striking political developments of the late 1880s, as Home Rule changed the framework of politics in a way that gave the two opposed party leaders, Gladstone and Salisbury, a firmer grip on their followers than leaders had had at any time in the previous thirty or forty years. Marsh shows how the political friendships that Chamberlain had built up during the previous dozen years did not survive the conflict over Ireland while, in contrast, Birmingham stood behind him so resolutely that he could change parties and still stick to enough of his former policies to mean that nobody could mistake him for a docile follower of the Unionist leadership.

Hitherto, the analyses of politicians' manoeuvrings in terms of the efforts of a dozen or so men at the top to gain or retain power have covered only rather short periods of time: Cowling, in his *Impact of Labour* and in his *Impact of Hitler*,[22] studies four years at a time, and that seems to be as much as anyone can manage: supporters of this sort of analysis would say that the intricate detail required would lead to books of impossible length if they dealt with a longer span of years, and deprecators of this approach would say that its practitioners tend to relegate shifts in public opinion to the background as something that politicians have to accept as fixed circumstances as they go about their daily business, an attitude that becomes quite impossible if one tries to write about the politics of a decade. But biographers can use the findings of this detailed analysis: in Feuchtwanger's recent life of Gladstone the treatment of the years studied in Vincent's *The Governing Passion* is more subtle than what goes before and after, because of the new material to be drawn upon.[23] But Feuchtwanger did not really set out to create a new picture of Gladstone even to the limited extent that Magnus did thirty years ago. Magnus's *Gladstone* presented a new, and sometimes endearing, account of Gladstone's family life, but in public affairs it followed Morley's account of Gladstone's long evolution in pursuit of liberty. Feuchtwanger has done much the same thing, using the old framework and incorporating new material in it, and then presenting the refurbished picture in as readily comprehensible a form for present-day readers as he can. Stansky's study is even more directly concerned to make Gladstone accessible rather than to provide new insights. The book is arranged around sensibly chosen themes, drawn from the traditional interpretation, and presents Gladstone in an easily digestible form.[24] The question of course is whether these various recensions of Morley have not exhausted the usefulness of an approach that is now eighty years old.

The last two essays in this book ask whether an entirely new picture is needed and argue that it is. Since they were written, the first volume of Shannon's new Life has appeared; and of course the steady appearance of successive volumes of Gladstone's *Diaries* strengthens the case for saying that new material demands a new analysis. It seems inconceivable that such an immense bulk of material could emerge without leaving its readers feeling that they have met a totally new Gladstone, and yet it turns out to be relatively difficult to define the difference that it is all going to make. Everyone knew that he was deeply religious, even though this was something on which it was not thought proper for Morley to dwell when writing his *Life*, and the *Diaries* underline the fact. Everyone knew that he was extraordinarily energetic and made full use of every moment of the day, and now the *Diaries* amply document this fact. Occasionally it looks as if the reviewers who lingered over the passages about self-flagellation and about prostitutes were doing so not out of any prurient interest but simply because it is the greatest novelty about the first sixty years of his life that has come to light. Readers might have hoped for explanations of what a supremely competent minister does with his time, to set against R.H.S. Crossman's *Diaries*, or for evocations of the social scene like Channon's, or even for revealing comments on his own shortcomings as penetrating as those of Harold Nicolson, but the sad fact is that writing a diary that is entertaining to read is one of those things that twentieth-century politicians do better than their nineteenth-century counterparts. Gladstone's memoranda, published by the Historical Manuscripts Commission, in which he looked back over his life and his political record, do provide a retrospective assessment as interesting and as convincing as any autobiography, but the *Diaries* do not come up to the nineteenth-century standards of the diaries kept (admittedly for much shorter periods) by Balfour, Carlingford, Chamberlain, and Stanley.[25] It is true that present-day historians still hold their breath in case there is a clearly dated entry 'Today decided to commit myself and my party to Home Rule,' which could answer a number of questions about 1885, but what has so far appeared has not transformed what historians write.

Shannon's first volume, covering the life of Gladstone up to 1865, raises the question that is suggested in the last two essays of original scholarship in this volume: Is a new way of looking at Gladstone now essential? Clearly Shannon believes that it is, and is determined to shake himself free of Morley. The new Life, written in a Guedallaesque style that fits its general approach very well, shows a considerable willingness to turn the conventions of Victorian biography inside out: Victorian biographers, who were normally members of the family or close friends of the departed statesman, set up impossibly high standards, and then set out to show that their subjects had lived up to these standards, an undertaking that sometimes stretched their sense of truthfulness to the limit and usually anaesthetized their sense of humour. Shannon is perfectly happy, for debating purposes, to retain these high standards and then to demonstrate that Gladstone did not always live up to them. What emerges is a picture of Gladstone always wrestling with his conscience and always winning, so that he does not have to become a clergyman, he does not have to stick to the strict (or Macaulayesque) version of the principles laid down in *State and Church*, he is able to take office under Palmerston in 1859 and generally make his way forward. It is fair to say that there is no suggestion that any of this involved hypocrisy. Shannon knows enough about the evidence, and about the way the human mind can work, to see that Gladstone was only responding in a reasonably conventional way to two formidable forces, the need to save his soul and the desire to achieve eminence in this world, that pressed on him more or less all his life. But Shannon judges Gladstone by rather higher standards than are applied to the other politicians of the period, and inevitably Gladstone does emerge looking rather ridiculous as a result. This way of handling the problem has the disadvantage that it does not always provide a substantial foundation for explaining the way that events developed. In 1859 the key point was that Palmerston wanted Gladstone in his government, and Shannon's account does not make the former's inclination at all easy to understand. It is clear enough that Palmerston did not want Gladstone out of any personal sympathy or friendship, and this makes it all the more necessary to demonstrate the dominance over the House of Commons that Gladstone had built up well before he began the appeals to the people that were the basis of his later power. But this is left out, or perhaps is too much taken for granted, and the result is that, while Shannon's Gladstone is rather more convincing than Morley's paragon in personal terms, he is much less explicable on the political side. The difficulty with demythologizing political leaders is that it is much easier to show their weaknesses than their strengths. Traill wrote that he 'never listened to him [Gladstone] even for a few minutes without ceasing to marvel at his influence over men,'[26] and Shannon does not adequately establish that influence as a fact that his readers understand and accept. Demythologizing without explaining the substance behind the myth is something that may be repaired when he comes to write about Gladstone the old chieftain, but the same weakness can be seen to a slight extent in the essays by Sandiford and Schreuder.

Both essays measure Gladstone by very high standards, not only standards of his own day but also more recent standards that show his continued relevance. Sandiford starts by reminding readers of a point touched on by Hammond but not mentioned by many other writers: Gladstone was a European in a sense that most Victorians were not. He read several European languages, travelled fairly widely in western Europe, and had friends on the continent in whose public problems he was deeply interested. No doubt Acton was more of a European, but in this sense Disraeli, Palmerston, and Salisbury were not Europeans, though of course they were quite as interested as Gladstone in European diplomacy.

The generation after 1860 is in diplomacy the age of Bismarck, and it is natural for Sandiford to judge Gladstone according to the standards of that age. It is not so certain that Gladstone was to blame for a decline in Britain's international standing that may have been at least as much the result of changes in the bases of power; the British statesman who emerged least successfully from a conflict with Bismarck was not Gladstone but Palmerston. Gladstone did not like the new facts of power, but he did his best to avoid running into unnecessary trouble over them. In the extremely puzzling diplomacy of expansion in Africa in the early 1880s he did what he could to keep on good terms with his European neighbours. Anyone who looks at French policy in Egypt in 1881 and 1882 will see that this could be very difficult. Britain could have kept in step with France only by entrusting policy to the noble Duke of York who marched his troops to the top of the hill and then marched them down again. Two generations of imperialists blamed Gladstone for not responding in a forceful way when Bismarck launched his brief drive for colonial expansion; recent diplomatic historians have argued that Bismarck was doing this in order to pick a quarrel with Gladstone, and have sometimes done so in terms that suggest that Gladstone ought to have let him have his quarrel.

A writer more cynical or more idealistic than Sandiford might have examined the possibility that the concept of the Concert of Europe really did fit the needs of Britain and of Europe more closely than the policy of Bismarck. Europe might have been happier if Gladstone's aspirations had turned into reality, though of course the case for Gladstonianism does owe a good deal of its strength to the fact that Bismarckianism is blamed for two destructive wars that might have taken place even in a world less committed to the politics of power. Even if the policy of the Concert of Europe was the best policy for everyone in the late nineteenth century, it could be argued that following the policy at a time when the rest of Europe was behaving differently was not necessarily the second-best policy that Britain could have followed. Still, the realistic Salisbury did confess, a dozen years later, that the pro-Turkish policy that Gladstone attacked in Midlothian might have been a matter of backing the wrong horse. Sympathy for nationalism sometimes led Gladstone to ignore the realities of power, but that is not quite the same as saying that it led him to ignore British interests. Over the generations world opinion has moved in a Gladstonian direction – it could even be said that it has gone too far in that direction. Sandiford would no doubt be right to argue that in practice some questions in the modern world can be settled only by blood and iron, and that world opinion has been too uncritical in its acceptance of the principles of the West Calder speech, but Gladstone's impact upon that world opinion may repay some attention in a long-term assessment of his role in diplomacy.

A general reappraisal of Gladstone's political impact is much more explicitly called for in Schreuder's very wide-ranging and stimulating article, which ends the strictly scholarly part of the book. As he says, Morley and (in a smaller area) Knaplund have imposed their picture of Gladstone upon two or three generations of readers.[27] They were men of their own time and, at least to some extent, men of Gladstone's time. Morley's dominant idea of a steady progress towards liberty is so compelling and fits so many aspects of the case that it is impossible to ignore. By now, ideas of liberty have changed so much that reconsideration is almost certainly needed, though it does not follow that Schreuder's demonstration that changes in language are needed is a proof that changes in substance are also required. Morley and Gladstone were exchanging their ideas about liberty just a little before A.V. Dicey explained the political development of Victorian England in terms of the growth of liberty followed by the growth of socialism, and yet the period seen by Gladstone and Dicey as one of increased liberty was the period of intolerable restraint and hypocrisy that Wells and D.H. Lawrence and Lytton Strachey stood ready to attack. Since that attack words like 'liberty' have been used in a much more absolute sense, and part of a re-examination of Gladstone might well take the form of seeing what restraints upon absolute liberty he thought would meet the situation. Restraints he clearly did expect. He once wrote to Manning: 'by this I mean liberty in the English sense, liberty under rule, and the whole question is what rule is admissible or desirable,' and there is no reason to think that he ever came to desire liberty in what he would have seen as the continental sense.[28] In 1884 he said that liberalism stood for trust in the people qualified by prudence, and his party did not disagree with this phrase. Vincent showed in *The Formation of the Liberal Party* that Gladstone hoped restraint would take the form of accepting the leadership of active and disinterested members of the traditional whig ruling class.[29] Even the events of 1886 did not induce Gladstone to see liberty in a different way. He was undoubtedly a reformer of the school that saw that 'much would have to change if the country was to stay the same,' and there is no reason to think that Morley saw things differently. A life of Gladstone that paid proper attention to his efforts to preserve what could be salvaged would be a sharp contrast to Morley's. But there is a risk that the author of such a book might be tempted to seize Arthur Balfour's comment that 'Gladstone is a tremendous old Tory,' without remembering that Balfour prefaced his remark with the judicious qualification 'except in essentials.'

Knaplund took the preservationist approach to reform for granted quite as much as any other author. He chose the British Commonwealth as his subject at a time when it seemed to be functioning as a model for all international organizations. Characterized by a readiness to think the best of other members and by a conviction that the sovereignty of each member need not inhibit the search for common policies, the commonwealth sought to follow a peaceful course of diplomacy while being prepared to fight if this turned out to be absolutely necessary. Such an approach may now seem ridiculously optimistic, but it was very much the mood in which the United Nations was launched at the end of the Second World War. Knaplund thought he was explaining the development of an institution that held out great hope for the future, and might not have found it easy to accept the idea that the subsequent dissolution of the commonwealth has been an unmixed blessing. But in explaining the institution as he saw it before him, he was simply doing his job as a historian, and there is no obvious reason to think that he was wrong in believing that the commonwealth of 1920-50 was to quite a considerable extent the product of Gladstonian principles.

Whether Gladstone would have expected this early twentieth-century commonwealth to survive is rather a different question. At one stage Gladstone and the Liberals of the 1860s were seen as people who positively wanted to dissolve the British Empire, and their attitude to New Zealand lent some support to this view. Knaplund argued that they wanted to keep the empire together as far as possible, and showed the consequences of their attitude. Schreuder writes as if it can be taken for granted that Gladstone never contemplated the dissolution of the empire, and on this constructs a picture of Gladstone as a politician concerned to 'question the degree to which the colonies could claim full freedom.'[30] But all that Gladstone had said was that he did 'not see upon what foundation any duty of military and naval protection on our part is to rest, if the foreign relations of colonies are to pass out of our hands into theirs.' This presents a simple dilemma: either the empire-commonwealth was to be a unit, however loosely integrated, in which there was a united defence and foreign policy, or it was not. On the whole Gladstone preferred the former arrangement, but he was certainly not going to resist any desire on the colonies' part for control of their own foreign policy – he was only going to say that in that case they would have to have defence policies of their own to protect them from the results of that desire. 'What,' Mr Gladstone might have asked, 'is the alternative that is proposed to this policy? Is it not that the British government should give what I believe is called a blank cheque to any vagary, nay, to any error, in the policy of our self-governing colonies?'

The oddity of the commonwealth that Knaplund described was that for a generation the circle seemed to have been squared. On a basis of isolationism, British sentiment, and a readiness to fight German expansionism, the commonwealth allowed its members freedom of action in foreign policy and still held together as a coherent political unit. But that feat of diplomacy could hardly survive the march of colonial freedom and the inclusion in the commonwealth of new nations with local concerns that meant very little to the other members of the commonwealth. The history of the commonwealth in the last thirty years shows that Gladstone was quite right to think that it could not survive without some institutional unity of the sort Schreuder discusses in his paper.

Gladstone's wisdom in this argument is still open to question. What is less open to question is the great range of his views and the complexity of the interplay between his views and his temperament. Morley may have seemed for some decades to have provided a definitive portrait of Gladstone; perhaps a new portrait of Gladstone can improve on it, but the real change in opinion about Gladstone is that people have come to see the difficulty of pinning him down. It was of course a vast over-simplification for Strachey to ask: 'Did his very essence lie in the confusion of incompatibles?' (And of course Strachey drew back from his over-simplification.)[31] Gladstone undoubtedly abides our questioning, but it seems unlikely that we shall get any answer more unambiguous than he gave in his lifetime. The essays in this book may not have settled points in perpetuity, but they do testify to the liveliness of Gladstone studies and to the industry and intelligence of those now working in the field.

NOTES

1 G.T. Garratt, *The Two Mr. Gladstones* (London, 1936); A. Tilney Bassett, *The Gladstone Papers* (London, 1930) – Bassett had previously edited *Gladstone's Speeches* (London, 1916); J.L. Hammond, *Gladstone and the Irish Nation* (London, 1938). W.E. Williams, *The Rise of Gladstone to the Leadership of the Liberal Party, 1859 to 1868* (Cambridge, 1934), and Erich Eyck, *Gladstone* (London, 1938), also indicate the rise in interest after the 1920s.

2 R. Blake, *Disraeli* (London, 1966); the reference to Gladstone is at 765.

3 Cecil Roth, *Benjamin Disraeli* (New York, 1952); Hesketh Pearson, *Dizzy* (London, 1951); Philip Magnus, *Gladstone* (London, 1954).

4 B.R. Jerman, *The Young Disraeli* (Princeton and London, 1960); W.F. Monypenny and G.E. Buckle, *The Life of Benjamin Disraeli, Earl of Beaconsfield* (6 vols., London, 1910-20); *The Political Correspondence of Mr. Gladstone and Lord Granville, 1868-1876*, ed. A. Ramm (2 vols., London, 1952), and *The Political Correspondence ... 1876-1886*, ed. A. Ramm (2 vols., Oxford, 1962).

5 *Benjamin Disraeli Letters, 1815-1837*, ed. J.A.W. Gunn, John Matthews, Donald M. Schurman, and M.G. Wiebe (2 vols., Toronto, 1982).

6 R.T. Shannon, *Gladstone and the Bulgarian Agitation, 1876* (London, 1963); R.T. Shannon, *Gladstone, 1809-1865* (London, 1982); vols. 7 and 8 of *The Gladstone Diaries*, ed. M.R.D. Foot and H.C.G. Matthew (London and Oxford, 1968-), appeared in 1982.

7 John Morley, *The Life of William Ewart Gladstone* (3 vols., London, 1903).

8 Perry Butler, *Gladstone: Church, State and Tractarianism* (Oxford, 1982).

9 W.E. Gladstone, *The State in Its Relations with the Church* (London, 1838), and *Church Principles Considered in Their Results* (London, 1840).

10 Butler, *Gladstone*, 151.

11 See above, 52.

12 J.B. Conacher, 'Mr. Gladstone Seeks a Seat,' Canadian Historical Association, *Report* (1962).

13 J.H. Newman, *Apologia pro Vita Sua* (London, 1864; rpt 1964), 38-9 and 170-1.

14 G.R. Askwith, *Lord James of Hereford* (London, 1930), 37.

15 Brian Harrison, *Separate Spheres* (London, 1978).

16 S.G. Checkland, *The Gladstones* (Cambridge, 1971).

17 Joyce Marlow, *Mr. and Mrs. Gladstone* (London, 1977); Georgina Battiscombe, *Mrs. Gladstone* (London, 1956).

18 Michael Barker, *Gladstone and Radicalism* (Hassocks, 1975), makes the Gladstonian Liberals sound so radical that it is hard to understand why they achieved so little between 1892 and 1895.

19 M. Cowling, *1867: Disraeli, Gladstone and Revolution* (London, 1967); A.B. Cooke and J. Vincent, *The Governing Passion* (Brighton, 1974); A. Jones, *The Politics of Reform, 1884* (Cambridge, 1972); R.F. Foster, *Lord Randolph Churchill: A Political Life* (Oxford, 1981).

20 J.B. Conacher, *The Aberdeen Coalition, 1852-1855* (Cambridge, 1968).

21 Herbert Gladstone, *After Thirty Years* (London, 1928), 307-10.

22 M. Cowling, *The Impact of Labour* (Cambridge, 1971), and *The Impact of Hitler* (London, 1975).

23 E.J. Feuchtwanger, *Gladstone* (London, 1975).

24 P. Stansky, *Gladstone: A Progress in Politics* (New York, 1979). R.H.S. Crossman, *The Diaries of a Cabinet Minister* (3 vols., London, 1975-7); Henry Channon, *'Chips'* (London, 1967); H. Nicolson, *Diaries and Letters* (3 vols., London, 1966-8).

25 *The Prime Ministers' Papers: W.E. Gladstone* (London, 1971, 1972); A.J. Balfour, *Chapters of Autobiography* (London, 1930); *Lord Carlingford's Journal*, ed. A.B. Cooke and J. Vincent (Oxford, 1971); *Joseph Chamberlain: A Political Memoir*, ed. C.H.D. Howard (London, 1953); *Disraeli, Derby and the Conservative Party: The Political Journals of Lord Stanley, 1849-1869*, ed. J. Vincent (Hassocks, 1978).

26 H.D. Traill, *The New Lucian* (London, 1884), 305-6.

27 Morley, *Gladstone*; P. Knaplund, *Gladstone and Britain's Imperial Policy* (London, 1927).

28 Butler, *Gladstone*, 226.

29 J. Vincent, *The Formation of the Liberal Party, 1857-1868* (London, 1966), 22-3 and 212-13.

30 See above, 228.

31 L. Strachey, *Eminent Victorians* (London, 1918; rpt 1948), 280.

Compiled by N. MERRILL DISTAD

James Blennerhasset Conacher: Publications, 1947-84

BOOKS

The Aberdeen Coalition, 1852-1855: A Study in Mid-Nineteenth-Century Party Politics.
Cambridge: Cambridge University Press, 1968. Pp. xiv, 607
The Peelites and the Party System, 1846-52. Newton Abbot: David and Charles,
1972. Pp. 246
Waterloo to the Common Market, Borzoi History of England, Vol. 5: *1815 to the Present.*
New York: Knopf, 1975. Pp. xvi, 368

EDITED BOOKS

François Du Creux, *History of Canada, or New France.* Trans. P.J. Robinson. 2
vols. Toronto: Champlain Society [vols. xxx and xxxi], 1951-2. Pp. xxviii, 775
*The Emergence of British Parliamentary Democracy in the Nineteenth Century: The
Passing of the Reform Acts of 1832, 1867, and 1884-1885.* Major Issues in History
series. New York: Wiley, 1970. Pp. xiv, 182

ARTICLES

'The Battle for Agira, July 24-8, 1943: An Episode in Canadian Military
History.' CHR 30:1 (March 1949), 1-21
'The Reformation in England: A Reconsideration of Henry VIII's Break with
Rome.' Canadian Catholic Historical Association, *Report*, 1955, 39-57
'The British Party System between the Reform Acts of 1832 and 1867.' Canadian
Historical Association, *Report*, 1955, 69-78
'Peel and the Peelites, 1846-50.' EHR 73:288 (July 1958), 431-52
'A Visit to the Gladstones in 1894.' VS 2:2 (December 1958), 155-60

'Party Politics in the Age of Palmerston.' In *1859: Entering an Age of Crisis*, ed.
Appleman, Madden, and Wolff. Bloomington: Indiana University Press,
1959, 163-80
'The Politics of the Papal Aggression Crisis, 1850-1851.' Canadian Catholic
Historical Association, *Report*, 1959, 13-27
'Mr Gladstone Seeks a Seat.' Canadian Historical Association, *Report*, 1961,
55-67
'Lessons in Twisting the Lion's Tail: Two Sidelights of the Crimean War.' In
Policy by Other Means: Essays in Honour of C.P. Stacey, ed. M. Cross and R.
Bothwell. Toronto: Clarke, Irwin, 1972, 77-94
'Graduate Studies in History in Canada: The Growth of Doctoral Programmes.'
[Presidential address,] Canadian Historical Association, *Report*, 1975, 1-15

ENCYCLOPEDIA ARTICLES

'Canada and the British Empire and Commonwealth.' *Encyclopedia Americana*
(1952), v, 476v-8a [revised as 'Canada, Britain, and the Commonwealth,' 1958
ed., and reprinted again in 1963]
'Fourth Earl of Aberdeen (1784-1860).' *Collier's Encyclopedia* (1978), I, 19-20
[unaltered reprint from earlier editions]

REVIEWS

M. Shulman, *Defeat in the West*; P. Simmonds, *Maple Leaf Up, Maple Leaf Down:
The Story of the Canadians in the Second World War*; D. Malone, *Missing from the
Record*; S. Galloway, *'55 Axis': With the Royal Canadian Regiment, 1939-1945*. CHR
28:3 (September 1947), 318-20
J.M. McAvity, *Lord Strathcona's Horse (Royal Canadians)*. CHR 29:2 (June 1948),
201-2
G.L. Cassidy, *War-Path: The Story of the Algonquin Regiment, 1939-45*; *The
Regimental History of the Governor General's Foot Guards*; W.T. Steven, *In This
Sign*. CHR 30:3 (September 1949), 283-5
J.E. Neale, *The Elizabethan House of Commons*. CHR 31:1 (March 1950), 71-3
E.C. Wright, *The Saint John River*. CHR 31:2 (June 1950), 200-1
C.E. Carrington, *The British Overseas: Exploits of a Nation of Shopkeepers*. UTQ 21:1
(October 1951), 99-101
A.L. Rowse, *The England of Elizabeth: The Structure of Society*. CHR, 32:2 (June
1952), 161-3
S. Maccoby, *The English Radical Tradition, 1763-1914*; R.L. Schuyler and H.
Ausubel, eds., *The Making of English History*; G.D.H. Cole and A.W. Filson,

eds., *British Working Class Movements: Selected Documents, 1789-1875*. CHR
33:2 (June 1952), 184-5

A.B. Erickson, *The Public Career of Sir James Graham*. CHR 34:1 (March 1953),
73-4

J.D. Mackie, *The Earlier Tudors, 1485-1558*. CHR 34:2 (June 1953), 185-6

'Some Recent Books in British History': J. Chamberlain, *A Political Memoir,
1880-92*; S.E. Finer, *The Life and Times of Sir Edwin Chadwick*; C.H. Firth, *Oliver
Cromwell and the Rule of the Puritans in England* [Oxford World Classics ed.];
N. Gash, *Politics in the Age of Peel*; K.H.D. Haley, *William of Orange and the
English Opposition, 1672-4*; A.L. Kennedy, *Salisbury, 1830-1903: Portrait of a
Statesman*; S. Maccoby, *English Radicalism, 1886-1914*; L.B. Namier, *Monarchy
and the Party System*; J.E. Neale, *Elizabeth I and Her Parliaments, 1559-1581*;
H. Nicolson, *George V: His Life and Reign*; L.B. Smith, *Tudor Prelates and Politics,
1536-1558*; H.R. Trevor-Roper, *The Gentry, 1540-1640*; G.M. Young,
Stanley Baldwin. CHR 34:4 (December 1953), 339-52

S.E. Morison, *Sicily-Salerno-Anzio: History of United States Naval Operations in
World War II*, Volume 9. CAJ 9:1 (January 1955), 113-16

'Some Recent Books on English History': I. Bulmer-Thomas, *The Party System
in Great Britain*; D. Cecil, *Lord M.*; R. Jenkins, *Mr Balfour's Poodle*; P. Magnus,
Gladstone: A Biography; M. St J. Packe, *The Life of John Stuart Mill*; H. Pelling,
The Origins of the Labour Party; W.B. Pemberton, *Lord Palmerston*; P.A.
Reynolds, *British Foreign Policy in the Inter-War Years*. CHR 36:1 (March 1955),
45-53

R.T. McKenzie, *British Political Parties*. IJ 10:4 (autumn 1955), 292-4

C. Read, *Mr Secretary Cecil and Queen Elizabeth*. CHR 36:4 (December 1955),
362-3

G.R. Elton, *England under the Tudors*; C. Morris, *The Tudors*; A.L. Rowse, *The
Elizabethan Age: The Expansion of Elizabethan England*. CHR 37:3 (September
1956), 280-2

'Some Recent Books in British History': P.W.S. Andrews and E. Brunner, *The
Life of Lord Nuffield*; A.W. Baldwin, *My Father: The True Story*; R. Blake, *The
Unknown Prime Minister: The Life and Times of Andrew Bonar Law*; T. Driberg,
Beaverbrook: A Study in Power and Frustration; L.B. Namier, *Personalities and
Powers*; J.H. Plumb, ed., *Studies in Social History: A Tribute to G.M. Trevelyan*;
J.H. Stewart Reid, *The Origins of the British Labour Party*; J.E. Wrench, *Geof-
frey Dawson and Our Times*. CHR 37:4 (December 1956), 356-64

W.S. Churchill, *A History of the English Speaking Peoples*. IJ 12:1 (winter 1956-7),
57-9 and 14:1 (winter 1958-9), 61-2

C.F. Comfort, *Artist at War*. CHR 38:1 (March 1957), 65-6

C.L. Mowat, *Britain between the Wars, 1918-40*. IJ 13:1 (winter 1957-8), 80-1

C.C. O'Brien, *Parnell and His Party, 1880-90.* CF 37:444 (January 1958), 234-5

L.B. Namier, *The Structure of Politics at the Accession of George III*, 2nd ed. CF 37:445 (February 1958), 259

H.R. Trevor-Roper, *Historical Essays.* CF 37:445 (February 1958), 262

H. Butterfield, *George III and the Historians.* CF 38:450 (July 1958), 93-4

E.M. Butler, ed., *A Regency Visitor: The English Tour of Prince Pückler-Muskau Described in His Letters, 1826-28.* CF 38:451 (August 1958), 116

G.D. Ramsay, *English Overseas Trade during the Centuries of Emergence.* CHR 39:3 (September 1958), 260 [unsigned]

D. Read, *Peterloo: The 'Massacre' and Its Background*; R.J. White, *From Waterloo to Peterloo.* CHR 39:4 (December 1958), 348-9

R. Bassett, *1931: Political Crisis.* CHR 40:3 (September 1959), 249-50

F. Eyck, *The Prince Consort: A Political Biography.* CF 39:464 (September 1959), 141

S.D. Bailey, *British Parliamentary Democracy.* CHR 40:4 (December 1959), 351 [unsigned]

G.R. Crosby, *Disarmament and Peace in British Politics, 1914-19.* CHR 40:4 (December 1959), 353 [unsigned]

J.W. Wheeler-Bennett, *King George VI: His Life and Reign.* CHR 41:1 (March 1960), 65-6

A.B. Erickson, *Edward T. Cardwell: Peelite.* CHR 41:2 (June 1960), 169-70

F.C. Mather, *Public Order in the Age of the Chartists.* AHR 66:1 (October 1960), 141-3

W.B. Pope, ed., *Diary of Benjamin Robert Hayden*, Volumes 1 and 2. CHR 41:4 (December 1960), 362 [unsigned]

J. Pope-Hennessy, *Queen Mary, 1867-1953.* CHR 41:4 (December 1960), 355-7

A. Wood, *Nineteenth Century Britain.* CHR 41:4 (December 1960), 362-3 [unsigned]

F.S.L. Lyons, *The Fall of Parnell, 1890-91.* QQ 67:4 (winter 1960), 694-5

Earl Lloyd George of Dwyfor, *Lloyd George.* CF 40:481 (February 1961), 258

S. Runciman, *The White Rajahs: A History of Sarawak from 1841 to 1946.* CF 41:487 (August 1961), 118-19

W. Ashworth, *An Economic History of England, 1870-1939*; H. Pelling, *Modern Britain, 1885-1955*; A.J. Youngson, *The British Economy, 1920-1957.* CHR 42:3 (September 1961), 246-9

R.B. McDowell, *British Conservatism, 1832-1914.* CHR 42:3 (September 1961), 253-4 [unsigned]

N. Gash, *Mr Secretary Peel: The Life of Sir Robert Peel to 1830.* CHR 43:1 (March 1962), 59-61

D. Beales, *England and Italy, 1859-60.* CHR 43:2 (June 1962), 165-6

F.K. Brown, *Fathers of the Victorians: The Age of Wilberforce. Catholic Historical Review* 48:3 (October 1962), 428-9

Lord Strang, *Britain in World Affairs.* IJ 17:4 (autumn 1962), 452-3

H. Dalton, *High Tide and After: Memoirs, 1945-60.* IJ 18:1 (winter 1962-3), 123-4

D. Southgate, *The Passing of the Whigs, 1832-1886.* VS 6:3 (March 1963), 289-90

I. Jennings, *Party Politics.* I: *Appeal to the People.* II: *The Growth of Parties.* III: *The Stuff of Politics.* CHR 44:2 (June 1963), 176-9

J.W. Wheeler-Bennett, *John Anderson, Viscount Waverley.* IJ 18:3 (summer 1963), 385-6

L. Broad, *Winston Churchill.* IJ 19:3 (summer 1964), 409-10

V. Cowles, *The Kaiser.* CF 44:524 (September 1964), 139

P. Magnus, *King Edward the Seventh.* CHR 46:1 (March 1965), 71-2

His Grace, the Seventh Duke of Wellington, ed., *Wellington and His Friends.* AHR 71:2 (January 1966), 565-6

V.B. Carter, *Winston Churchill as I Knew Him.* CF 45:541 (February 1966), 261-2

W.L. Burn, *The Age of Equipoise: A Study of the Mid-Victorian Generation.* CHR, 47:1 (March 1966), 78-9

A.J.P. Taylor, *English History, 1914-1945. Review of Politics* 28:2 (April 1966), 261-3

N. Gash, *Reaction and Reconstruction in English Politics, 1832-52.* AHR 72:1 (October 1966), 191

Viscount Chilston, *W.H. Smith.* CF 46:550 (November 1966), 192

D.C. Gordon, *The Dominion Partnership in Imperial Defense, 1870-1914.* JMH 38:4 (December 1966), 441-2

C.J. Bartlett, *Castlereagh.* IJ 22:4 (autumn 1967), 687-8

R. Blake, *Disraeli.* CHR 48:3 (September 1967), 288-9

J. Vincent, *The Formation of the Liberal Party, 1857-1869.* CJEPS 33 (1967), 480-1

W.L. Arnstein, *The Bradlaugh Case.* CJH 3:2 (September 1968), 114-15

M. Cowling, *1867: Disraeli, Gladstone, and Revoluton*; F.B. Smith, *The Making of the Second Reform Bill.* CHR 49:3 (September 1968), 305-6

A. Mitchell, *The Whigs in Opposition, 1815-1830.* AHR 74:1 (October 1968), 171-2

M.R.D. Foot, ed., *The Gladstone Diaries.* I: *1825-1832.* II: *1833-1839.* CHR 51:2 (June 1970), 209-11

K. Middlemas and J. Barnes, *Baldwin: A Biography.* IJ 26:4 (autumn 1971), 453-5

K. Bourne, *The Foreign Policy of Victorian England, 1830-1902.* JMH 44:1 (March 1972), 118-19

R. Blake, *The Conservative Party from Peel to Churchill.* AHR 77:2 (April 1972), 518-19

J. Ridley, *Lord Palmerston*. JMH 44:3 (September 1972), 422-4

J. Prest, *Lord John Russell*. JMH 46:1 (March 1974), 139-41

J. Brook and M. Sorensen, eds., *The Prime Ministers' Papers: W.E. Gladstone*. II: *Autobiographical Memoranda, 1832-45*. AHR 80:3 (June 1975), 642-3

H.V. Emy, *Liberals, Radicals, and Social Politics, 1892-1914*; A.K. Russell, *Liberal Landslide: The General Election of 1906*. JMH 47:4 (December 1975), 731-3

J. Prest, *Politics in the Age of Cobden*. EHR 94:370 (January 1979), 214

G.I.T. Machin, *Politics and the Churches in Great Britain, 1832-1868*. JMH 51:2 (June 1979), 344-6

P.M. Long, *A Bibliography of Gladstone Publications at St Deiniol's Library*. Victorian Periodicals Review 12:2 (summer 1979), 92

D.A. Hamer, *The Politics of Electoral Pressure: A Study in the History of Victorian Reform Agitations*; O. MacDonagh, *Early Victorian Government, 1830-70*. VS 22:2 (winter 1979), 219-22

K. Robbins, *John Bright*. AHR 85:1 (February 1980), 126-7

G.H.L. Lemay, *The Victorian Constitution: Conventions, Usages, and Contingencies*. VS 24:3 (spring 1981), 376-8

W. Thomas, *The Philosophic Radicals: Nine Studies in Theory and Practice, 1817-41*. Albion 14:4 (winter 1982), 313-15

E.M. Spiers, *Radical General: Sir George De Lacy Evans, 1787-1870*. AHR 89:4 (October 1984), 1071-2

ABBREVIATIONS OF JOURNAL TITLES

AHR   *American Historical Review*
CAJ   *Canadian Army Journal*
CF   *Canadian Forum*
CHR   *Canadian Historical Review*
CJEPS   *Canadian Journal of Economics and Political Science*
CJH   *Canadian Journal of History*
EHR   *English Historical Review*
IJ   *International Journal* (Quarterly of the Canadian Institute of International Affairs)
JMH   *Journal of Modern History*
QQ   *Queen's Quarterly*
UTQ   *University of Toronto Quarterly*
VS   *Victorian Studies*

While this list omits anonymous contributions, such as those written while Professor Conacher was attached to the Historical Section of the Canadian

Army, or edited while he served as joint-editor of the *Canadian Historical Review* (1949-56) and as general editor of the Champlain Society (1951-62), it does include some unsigned reviews to the authorship of which he has confessed. It has not been possible to trace all of Professor Conacher's many reviews, but the list offered here is very nearly complete. Too late to be included in this list is Professor Conacher's book *War and Peace, 1855-1856: The Palmerston Administration and the Crimean War*, which is to be published soon.

Contributors

SUE BROWN is agricultural attaché at the British Embassy in Washington, DC.

J.M.S. CARELESS is a University Professor at the University of Toronto.

N. MERRILL DISTAD is history and mediaeval studies bibliographer in the University of Toronto Library.

RICHARD J. HELMSTADTER is an associate professor in the Department of History, University of Toronto.

PATRICIA JALLAND is a senior lecturer in history, Western Australian Institute of Technology.

JOHN KENYON is an associate professor in the Department of History, University of Toronto, Scarborough Campus.

BRUCE L. KINZER is an assistant professor in the Department of History, University of North Carolina at Wilmington.

TREVOR LLOYD is a professor in the Department of History, University of Toronto.

PETER T. MARSH is a professor in the Department of History, Syracuse University.

ANN P. ROBSON is an associate professor in the Department of History, University of Toronto.

K.A.P. SANDIFORD is a professor in the Department of History, University of Manitoba.

D.M. SCHREUDER is a professor in the Department of History, University of Sydney.

Index

Augustus 184

Australia 225, 228, 229

Austria: WEG on state in 50; and Italian question 181, 230; WEG's approach to 182–3, 185, 187, 188; exclusion of from German empire 185; and Bulgarian question 189

authority: Bishop Butler's hierarchy of moral 23; WEG's view of dissent and principle of 27–8; WEG's view of liberty and 28, 215, 218; Morley on liberalism and claims of external 213; and WEG's notion of freedom of conscience 215; WEG's support of in Italy 230, 231; WEG worked to reinterpret 234; WEG on freedom and 234

Bacon, Francis 12, 15

Bagehot, Walter 206

Balfour, A.J. 103, 104, 111, 167, 257, 261

Balfour, Alice 111, 112

Balkans 183, 186, 187, 188

ballot 70, 74, 80, 245–6

baptismal regeneration 18, 26

Bassett, A. Tilney 225, 244

Battiscombe, Georgina 252

Bauer, Carol 91

Beach, Sir Michael Hicks 147

Beaconsfieldism 231, 246

Beales, Derek 198, 232

Becker, Lydia: assesses parliamentary campaign for women's suffrage 71; on WEG and women's suffrage 72, 77, 78, 80, 83, 84–5; denunciation of WEG by 73; misplaced optimism of 77–8; and myth of WEG's betrayal 86–7, 89, 91, 92; on

defeat of Woodall's amendment 88. *See also Women's Suffrage Journal*

Beerbohm, Max 199

Belgium 184, 191, 235

Bentham, Jeremy 12, 21

Berlin, Treaty of (1878) 183, 186, 189

Biarritz 155, 156, 197

Bible 17, 25, 66, 178

bigamy 67

biography, Beales on value of 232

Birmingham 131, 135, 136, 143, 148

Birmingham Daily Post 142

Birmingham Liberal Association 140, 142–3, 144

Biscoe, Robert 9

bishops 53–4, 169

Bismarck, Otto von 184–5, 186, 192, 259

Blackburn, Helen 88–90

Black Sea clauses 181, 186

Blake, Lord 244

Board of Trade 11, 55

Bodelsen, C.A. 225

Bödo (Norway) 221, 222

Boers, 231–2. *See also* Cape Dutch

Boer War 221, 222

Bonapartism 212

Bosnia 182

Bouverie, E.P. 72, 77, 78

Bowyer, Sir George 69

Bradford 144

Bradlaugh, Charles 8, 29, 249

Bradley, Ian 214

Braudel, Fernand 232

Bright, Jacob, and women's suffrage 69–79, 86–7, 91

Bright, John 148, 171, 178, 180, 217

British Commonwealth: emerging concept of 198; Knaplund on WEG and development of 202–3,

Estcourt, T.G. Bucknell 51
Eton 20, 101
Euclid 28
Europe: WEG's grand tour through
   47; Lord Aberdeen and revolutionary wars in 54; WEG's devotion
   to 177; WEG's knowledge of 177;
   WEG's perception of 177–92,
   230, 234, 235; Bismarck's defiance of public law of 184–5; and
   emergence of new Germany
   185; suspicions of Britain in 191;
   Bismarck's impact on 192; WEG's
   image in 192; WEG on Balkan Christians and powers of 195; Morley
   on liberalism and mind of 213;
   Sandiford's treatment of WEG and
   259–60. See also Concert of Europe
evangelicalism: WEG and 7, 18, 26, 47,
   178, 205, 234; Northcote's view
   of 55

family: and state 11, 21, 49; WEG on
   English state and idea of 50;
   WEG's attitude towards institution of
   250, 251, 252–3
Fawcett, Millicent 64, 65, 66, 90
Feuchtwanger, E.J. 5, 107, 256
finance, Gladstonian 178–9, 200, 217,
   245–6
Finchley 104
First World War 198, 222, 223
Fitzgerald, James 226
Fitzgerald, Lady O. 94
Flintshire 207
Foot, M.R.D. 198
Foreign Office 147
Fortnightly Review 125
Foster, R.F. 254
France: Burke on revolutionaries in

20; WEG on state in 50; WEG's
   stay in 156; WEG and British alliance
   with 181; WEG's approach to
   182, 183–4, 186; WEG and Prussia's
   war with 185; and German action
   in 1864 194; Egyptian policy of 259
franchise, WEG and grounds for excluding people from 69. *See also*
   Reform bills, women's suffrage
Franco-Prussian War 185
free trade 6, 178, 200, 226, 228
Froude, Richard Hurrell 45, 46, 248

Garibaldi, Giuseppe 230
Garratt, G.T. 244
Gathorne-Hardy, Gathorne 59
George, David Lloyd 255
Germany 182, 184–5, 262. *See also*
   Austria, Prussia
Gladstone, Agnes 98, 101–2, 102, 111
Gladstone, Anne 99, 252
Gladstone, Catherine (née Glynne):
   president of Women's Liberal
   Federation 95; and WEG's political
   career 97, 100–1, 106; attention
   given to by historians 98; inept
   household organizer 100–1,
   105–6, 252; prevents daughter
   Agnes from training as nurse
   102; treatment of daughters by
   102; and daughter Mary 102,
   103, 105–6, 108, 111–12, 113; on
   Rosebery and Mary Gladstone
   107; Mary Gladstone on 114, 118;
   visits Newnham 115; and daughter Helen's filial responsibilities
   116, 117, 253; Helen Gladstone
   on 117; as beneficiary of Gladstone
   family enterprise 119; on WEG's
   retirement 156; mentioned 85, 236

13; Burke on 17; Coleridge on
18; WEG's conception of corporate
personality of 18, 20–1; question
of personality of 19–21; WEG asserts
responsibility of to establish true
church 24–5; WEG's model for ideal
30–1; WEG recognizes limitations
on power of 31; WEG's changing
ideas about church and 43; mediaeval and modern conceptions of
49–50; secularization of English
50; Morley portrays WEG as man of
210; WEG's persistent concern
for function of church in life of
213–14; core of WEG's thought
on 218; WEG's version of liberal democratic 235; Gladstonian limits
on activity of 246
State and Church, WEG's: preparation
for writing of 3; writing of 4;
contemporary response to 4–5,
12–13, 49; historians' response to
5–8; WEG's adherence to principles
of 8, 35; influence of Oxford on
content of 8–9; Aristotle's influence
on 9–11; method of 14–16;
broad range of reading reflected in
17–24; treatment of establishment
of Church of England in 25–7;
case against Romanism in 28–9;
and problem of Ireland 31–3;
and Maynooth grant 32–4; central assertion of 43; orthodox High
Church views expressed in 47;
and ideal of Anglican confessional
state 214; value attached to aristocracy in 215; differences between
P. Butler and Helmstadter respecting 247–9; Shannon's treatment of 258

Stead, W.T. 109
Stephen, James 224
Strachey, Lytton 225, 260, 262
Strachey, Ray 90
Stuart, James 110
suffragists. *See* women's suffrage
movement
Syrians 181

Tacitus 129
Talbot, Mrs 101, 121
Talbot, Lavinia 105, 109
Talbots 102, 109, 121
Tariffs 228–9
Taylor, A.J.P. 180
Taylor, Helen 63, 92
Teignmouth, Lord 4
Tennyson, Alfred 214
Tennyson, Hallam 110
Terence 15
The Times 4, 52, 146
Thucydides 15
toleration, religious: justification of in
WEG's *State and Church* 14, 29–30,
248–9; WEG's record on 29, 216;
Graham's commitment to 53;
WEG on 56, 57
Tollemache, Lionel 210, 236
Tomlinson, W.E.M. 84
tories: 'stern and unbending' 5, 48,
58, 247, 250; WEG on 1884 Re-
form Bill and 84; and 1884 wom-
en's suffrage amendment 85, 88,
92. *See also* Conservative party
Tractarians: WEG and 7, 18, 26, 234;
Sidney Herbert on 54; Peel with-
holds church preferment from 53.
See also Anglo-Catholics, High
Churchmen
Tracts for the Times 47